PENGUIN CLASSICS

LETTERS FROM AN AMERICAN FARMER AND SKETCHES OF EIGHTEENTH-CENTURY AMERICA

Michel-Guillaume Saint-Jean de Crèvecoeur was born at Caen, France, on January 31, 1735, into an ancient but unaffluent branch of the Norman gentry. He received a sound classical education in Latin, rhetoric, mathematics, and theology from the Jesuits at the College de Mont. In 1755 Crèvecoeur sailed for New France and a cadetship in the French colonial army. He distinguished himself as an artillery officer during the French and Indian War and fought under Montcalm at the siege of Quebec. After the war, Crèvecoeur emigrated to the English colony of New York, changing his name to J. Hector St. John. In 1769 he was married to Mehetable Tippett, a member of a prosperous Tory family, and settled at Pine Hill, a 250-acre farm in Orange County, New York. The Edenic years at Pine Hill were shattered by the American Revolution, when Crèvecoeur—suspected by his Patriot neighbors of harboring monarchist sympathies—was persecuted, unjustly imprisoned, and forced to flee the colonies. The publication of his *Letters from an American Farmer* in 1781 was an instant success in Europe, and Crèvecoeur—lionized in the Parisian *salons* as well as in the court of Versailles—was awarded a consulship to the newly formed American republic. As consul, Crèvecoeur served as a political and cultural liaison between France and the United States; helped to organize and promote trade across the Atlantic; and corresponded with many of the greatest figures of the Enlightenment, including Franklin, Jefferson, and Madison. He died in Sarcelles, France, on November 12, 1813.

Albert E. Stone is Professor of English and Chairman of the American Studies Program at the University of Iowa. He is the author of *The Innocent Eye: Childhood in Mark Twain's Imagination* and the editor of *The American Autobiography: A Collection of Critical Essays* and *Twentieth-Century Interpretations of James's* The Ambassadors.

LETTERS FROM
AN AMERICAN FARMER

and

SKETCHES OF
EIGHTEENTH-CENTURY
AMERICA

by

J. Hector St. John de Crèvecoeur

**Edited with an Introduction by
Albert E. Stone**

PENGUIN BOOKS

PENGUIN BOOKS
Published by the Penguin Group
Penguin Books USA Inc.,
375 Hudson Street, New York, New York 10014, U.S.A.
Penguin Books Ltd, 27 Wrights Lane, London W8 5TZ, England
Penguin Books Australia Ltd, Ringwood, Victoria, Australia
Penguin Books Canada Ltd, 10 Alcorn Avenue,
Toronto, Ontario, Canada M4V 3B2
Penguin Books (N.Z.) Ltd, 182–190 Wairau Road, Auckland 10, New Zealand

Penguin Books Ltd, Registered Offices:
Harmondsworth, Middlesex, England

Letters from an American Farmer first published 1782
Sketches of Eighteenth-Century America first published
by Yale University Press 1925
Published in The Penguin American Library 1981
Reprinted 1983
Reprinted in Penguin Classics 1986.

18   17   16   15   14   13   12   11   10   9

Introduction copyright © Viking Penguin Inc., 1963, 1981
All rights reserved

LIBRARY OF CONGRESS CATALOGING IN PUBLICATION DATA
St. John de Crèvecoeur, J. Hector, 1735–1813.
Letters from an American farmer.
(Penguin Classics)
Bibliography: p.
Includes index.
1. United States—Social life and customs—
Revolution, 1775–1783.   2. United States—
Description and travel—To 1783.   3. Nantucket (Mass.)
—Social life and customs.   4. St. John de Crèvecoeur,
J. Hector, 1735–1813.   I. Stone, Albert E.
II. St. John de Crèvecoeur, J. Hector, 1735–1813.
Sketches of eighteenth-century America.   1981.
III. Title.   IV. Series.
E163.S73   1981   973.3   81-12076
ISBN 0 14 03.9006 5   AACR2

Printed in the United States of America

Contents

Introduction

American literature, as the voice of our national consciousness, begins in 1782 with the first publication in England of *Letters from an American Farmer*. Literature, that is, considered as arrangements of affective images embodied in the traditional forms of poetry, fiction, and drama, and expressing the spirit of place. Before 1782, a good many histories, travel accounts, psalmbooks, sermons, elegies, memoirs, and autobiographies (spiritual and otherwise) had been written in the colonies. Certain of these works—Benjamin Franklin's *Autobiography* is a notable and obvious example—could scarcely have been composed elsewhere or by members of another society. Just as Franklin is the first representative American, of the national period at least, his book seems also to bear unmistakably the stamp of this locale; it is an *American* artifact. Yet, as D. H. Lawrence has reminded us, Crèvecoeur deserves recognition as a literary Founding Father, too. "Franklin is the real *practical* prototype of the American," he observed in *Studies in Classic American Literature*. "Crèvecoeur is the emotional. To the European, the American is first and foremost a dollar-fiend. We tend to forget the emotional heritage of Hector St. John de Crèvecoeur."

7

If Americans long neglected this heritage, it was Europeans like Lawrence who kept it alive. This has been true almost from the beginning. In the half century after 1782, *Letters from an American Farmer* enjoyed only a moderate fame in the United States but in Europe went into edition after edition, appearing successively in London, Dublin, Belfast, Leipzig, Leyden, Paris, and Maastricht. Translated into French, Dutch, and German, it provided two generations of Europeans with their chief impressions of the American colonies. The book was, of course, tailormade for the Romantic imagination. Followers of Coleridge and Rousseau embraced it enthusiastically; physiocrat and pantisocratist alike were affected by a book offering the verifiable account (as they felt) of a transatlantic utopia under the wigwams. But with the advent of a more rationalistic age Crèvecoeur went into eclipse. By the 1830's and 1840's, Americans, though in the heyday of their Romantic period, were in no mood to appreciate Crèvecoeur's cosmopolitan and Anglophilic biases, and Europeans adopted newer and sharper images of America. The detached cultural analysis of de Tocqueville and the jaundiced social critiques of Mrs. Trollope and Dickens made the *Letters* sound old-fashioned and naïve. The eclipse lasted until the turn of the twentieth century, when Americans recovered their colonial past along with its architecture, the paintings of John Singleton Copley (another Anglophile), and the writings of Jefferson. Since then, three or four generations of Americans—that of Moses Colt Tyler, the late nineteenth-century literary historian, Vernon Parrington, the intellectual historian of the 1920s, and our own—have read Crèvecoeur with increasing interest and respect. Each finds something fresh and relevant in the book. Recent events teach both the American-ness and the European-ness of our culture; today, both Frederick Jackson Turner's frontier hypothesis and Oscar Handlin's histories of immigration are read with respect. Post–World War II generations, trained by the New Criticism and American Studies to respect the text *and* its cultural determinants, recognize Crèvecoeur's specifically literary qualities as earlier readers did not always do. Moreover, the opposing forces animating his life and thought—reason and emotion, nature and Nature, the real and the ideal, Enlightenment and Romanticism, Europe and the New World, civilization and the wilderness, aristocracy and democracy, revolution and social order—speak forcibly to modern readers schooled to consider complexity, tension, and ambiguity the proper marks of modern literary art. The present age, whose spokesman on these matters had been Marius Bewley, reads *Letters from an American Farmer* as a powerful document at once literary, freshly contemporary, and characteristically American.

"What, then, is the American, this new man?" Crèvecoeur was the first to ask. A necessary way to understand *Letters* and *Sketches* as the partly autobiographical replies to his own question is to twist it around and inquire: "What is this new man, the American writer?"

He is, first of all, a man of aliases and disguises—James, the American farmer of Pennsylvania. The reader speedily suspects that character and creator are two separate individuals. It helps to be aware of their very different histories. Though James speaks of a family farm inherited from his father, the actual author of the *Letters* was, like many colonists in the eighteenth century, an immigrant. But the twenty-four-year-old adventurer who arrived in New York in 1759 was no common European peasant or artisan. Michel-Guillaume-Jean de Crèvecoeur was born at Caen on January 31, 1735, into an ancient but unaffluent branch of the Norman gentry. By no means an untutored countryman, he received a sound classical schooling from the Jesuits at the College du Mont, in Latin, rhetoric, mathematics, and theology (against which, in good deistic fashion, he soon rebelled). In 1754 he paid an extended visit to distant British relatives at Salisbury, where he met and became engaged to a merchant's daughter. She died before the marriage could take place. From these years dates the admiration for England and English culture that animates his books.

Some time in the following year, 1755, the young man embarked for New France and a cadetship in a French regiment in the St. Lawrence Valley. For four years the "lover of peace" was a soldier. Apparently he became a good one, too, so proficient at engineering and mapmaking as to be commended in a report to Louis XV himself. Promoted to lieutenant upon the outbreak of the French and Indian War, the young officer took part in the assault on Fort William Henry at Lake George in 1757. On September 13, 1759, he received an honorable wound at the epochal battle in which Montcalm lost Canada for France on the Plains of Abraham. At that point Crèvecoeur's military star began to fade. He got into some obscure difficulty while convalescing and in the fall of 1759 surrendered his commission in return for the sum of 240 pounds. Thus supplied with freedom and a stake, he made his way southward into the British colonies, changing his name en route to J. Hector St. John (for reasons easy to understand). He landed at New York on December 16, 1759. Although he presumably did not wander down Canal Street with puffy rolls under his arms, young Mr. St. John faced his American future with much the same independent spirit that Benjamin Franklin had displayed in similar circumstances thirty-six years before.

The ex-cartographer found ready employment in the bustling colonies. "I never was but a simple surveyor of lands, a cultivator of my own grounds, or a wanderer through the forests of this country," he explained later to the Duke de la Rochefoucauld, but this résumé, like many of Crèvecoeur's autobiographical remarks, is only roughly correct. It omits the military career in Canada and confuses the chronology of occupations. Actually, the wandering through the forests preceded the farming and was, in fact, the somewhat less romantic job of traveling salesman. The new American, who became a naturalized subject of King George and an official resident of New York in 1765, journeyed with his instruments or his order book up and down the colonies from Nova Scotia and Vermont in the north to Virginia in the south. He may even have visited Bermuda and Jamaica. "Perhaps no other man before the Revolution," wrote Parrington, "was so intimately acquainted with the French and English colonies as a whole, with their near background of frontier and the great wilderness beyond, as this French American." During the spring and summer of 1767 he encountered "the great wilderness" when he joined a surveying and exploring party that went over the Appalachians and down the Ohio River to St. Louis, up the Mississippi to the Great Lakes at the present-day site of Chicago, and returned to New York via Fort Dearborn, Fort Niagara, the Mohawk Valley (where he visited the Oneida Indians), and Albany. In 1769 the wandering temporarily ceased, however, for in that year he was married to Mehetable Tippet, member of a prosperous and prominent Tory family of Westchester. On December 12, he purchased for 350 pounds a handsome piece of land in Orange County, four miles southeast of Goshen, which he named Pine Hill. The "farmer in Pennsylvania" who wrote the *Letters* and *Sketches* was thus, in fact, a New Yorker. At the age of thirty-four the ex–soldier-surveyor-salesman settled down to become a farmer and, as it turned out, a man of letters.

The succeeding seven years of Crèvecoeur's life were the happiest he was ever to experience. With all the fervor of a later Mark Twain looking back on his Hannibal boyhood, the American Farmer celebrated in after years the idyll (and the underlying fragility) of Pine Hill. Except for a trip to the upper Susquehanna River in 1774, he remained pretty close to his hearth, devoting himself to the soil and his growing family. Three children were born at Pine Hill, and their father's steady, loving husbandry gradually created a prosperous and peaceful homestead. Children and livestock, buildings, fields, meadows, and woodlands waxed and were molded by hard work into a harmonious agrarian whole. The celebration and elegy of this temporary Eden is found in the early chapters of both the *Letters* and *Sketches*. There was, as well, enough social and intellectual life to grace a farmer's leisure and redeem his drudgery. Neighbors like Cadwallader Colden, the Tippet relatives across the Hudson in Yonkers, and friends in New York like William Seton and Jean Pierre Têtard provided a circle of cultivated acquaintances. During long winter evenings he had time to read the gazettes, books like the Abbé Raynal's *Philosophical History of the Indies,* and, at the instigation of Seton, to begin writing down his own impressions of agrarian life. "Sweet and pleasant is the memory of farmer's days" he later inscribed on a gift that reminded him of Pine Hill.

The dream was abruptly destroyed in 1776 by the trauma of civil war. For two years, the master of Pine Hill, whose peaceful but generally pro-Tory sentiments were known, rode out the mounting antagonism and suspicions of his patriot neighbors. From another quarter he faced the threat of Indian raids. Crèvecoeur sought to avoid taking

sides, but as this became manifestly impossible he made
plans to escape to France. He had for some time anticipated the necessity of returning to his native country in
order to take legal steps to ensure that his children might
inherit the family estate. (His wife was a Protestant and
their marriage had been performed by Têtard, a Huguenot
pastor, so the union was irregular by French law.) Late
in 1778 he left Pine Hill and his family in the care of
friends and slipped into New York. There he encountered
persecution from the opposing side. An anonymous letter
brought him under the suspicion of the British garrison;
he was thrown into prison, and the trunkful of papers (including the manuscript of these two books) was confis-
cated. Seton and others soon secured his release, but
Crèvecoeur's health was seriously, perhaps permanently,
impaired. Living for a time on the charity of friends or by
occasional surveying jobs, separated from wife and children (for whose safety he entertained the liveliest fears),
the once happy farmer suffered in 1779 what we would
today call a nervous breakdown. The anxieties of this
troubled time suffuse the later letters—some of which may
have been written in New York—and are vividly drama-
tized in the later sketches. At last, in September 1780, he
and his trunk were allowed to board a ship that sailed
through the French blockade to Ireland. Landing finally
in England, he proceeded to London. There, in May 1781,
Crèvecoeur sold the manuscript of *Letters from an American Farmer* to the firm of Davies and Davis (Samuel John-
son's famous publishers) for thirty guineas. The book
appeared in London the following year, by which time its
author had escaped safely to France.

After recuperating at Caen, Crèvecoeur went to Paris,
where his personal charm, exotic history, and the spreading fame of his timely book won him speedy acceptance
into a brilliant circle of intellectuals that included Turgot,
Buffon, Franklin, and had as its queen bee Rousseau's
former mistress, the charming old Countess d'Houdetot.
He soon began work on an expanded (and extensively
altered) version of the *Letters* in French, a language he
had to relearn. That book was published, after some cen-
sorship difficulties, in 1784. At the suggestion of the Minister of the Marine, he wrote a comprehensive report for
the government on the American colonies, just becoming

an independent nation. As reward, his name was placed at the head of the list of consular appointees; given his choice of posts, he naturally selected New York. Thus in September 1783 he arrived a second time in the New World, this time as the official representative of Louis XVI. But he did not much regard his return as a triumph. "If I had but 200 pounds income, I would return to cultivating my land and my friends," he confided to de la Rochefoucauld, "and he who wanted it could become the consul."

The news of his family which greeted the returnee was indeed grim; Pine Hill had been burned to the ground in an Indian raid, his wife was dead, his children had disappeared. Almost by chance, he learned that a Bostonian, Gustavus Fellowes, had taken custody of the children. The new consul traveled to Boston, where he was reunited with his family and learned the curious story of their rescue. Fellowes, a complete stranger to Crèvecoeur, had undertaken the difficult journey to Orange County in the dead of winter. This he had done at the earnest urging of five fellow townsmen, all seamen who in 1781 had been cast ashore on the French coast and had been succored by a kindhearted Franco-American named Hector St. John de Crèvecoeur. This bit of poetic justice is of a piece with the pattern of the writer's topsy-turvy life, which at several points takes on the shape of fable.

In spite of family misfortune and death, his own ill-health and fears of failure, Crèvecoeur's career as consul in New York was a success in at least three realms. In the commercial sphere, he helped to establish a packet line that operated, somewhat irregularly, between Lorient and New York for ten years. The consul also officially encouraged the importation into the United States of such civilizing essentials as French wine, silk, gloves, pianos, brandy, and human hair.

In the twin causes so close to his heart—horticulture and literature—his labors were even more wide-ranging. He wrote newspaper articles on practical agriculture under the pen name "Agricola." He encouraged the use of the potato in France and of alfalfa in America. He helped to found a botanical garden in New Haven, for which he was given the freedom of that city, and another in New Jersey. He distributed French medical journals to American doctors, seeds to Harvard College, and copies of Washington's speeches to the French newspapers. Information furnished by Crèvecoeur formed the basis for the article in the monumental *Encyclopédie methodique* on the new United States of America. For these and other services he was elected to the Société royale d'agriculture and the American Philosophical Society. "There is nobody," wrote William Short, Jefferson's private secretary, "who understands more perfectly the interests of the two countries, as they relate to each other, and none more zealous to promote them mutually."

Yet Crèvecoeur never considered himself a successful diplomat. "I am continually conscious of my inexperience," he confessed to de la Rochefoucauld. When his health worsened in 1790, he requested medical leave and returned to Paris, never to see America again. While the French Revolution ran its bloody course, he again sought to avoid entanglement. This time he was more successful. Allowed to resign in 1792 from the diplomatic service, he retired, characteristically, to the countryside. Apart from stays at Hamburg and Munich, the remainder of his life was passed chiefly in provincial obscurity. From 1794 to 1800 he worked on his *Voyage dans la Haute Pensylvanie et dans l'État de New York,* which was published in 1801, the same year as Chateaubriand's *Atala.* Much other material remained unpublished at his death in 1813.

Crèvecoeur's was an intense, exotic, cosmopolitan life, whose basic pattern Thomas Philbrick aptly describes as "the quest for tranquillity and order in a world filled with violence and chaos." The literary products of that experience were but three books. Two of these have remained largely unread, but the third, *Letters from an American Farmer,* is an American classic.

What makes this work American? Nothing that is unique to Crèvecoeur but rather several qualities that in the test of time have turned out to be characteristic of numerous later writers in this country. Here, as elsewhere, cultural or national identity exists more in pattern than in idiosyncrasy.

The first distinctive mark might be called the posture of the provincial as he presents American life. It is a voice deliberately but deceptively self-mocking, a manner slyly satiric of the European reader before whom the untutored colonial pretends to prostrate himself. The American Farmer strikes this pose in the Introductory Letter, whose point of view is perfectly expressed in this passage:

My wife (and I never do anything without consulting her) laughs and tells me that you cannot be in earnest. "What!" says she: "James, would'st thee pretend to send epistles to a great European man who hath lived abundance of time in that big house called Cambridge, where, they say, that worldly learning is so abundant that people gets it only by breathing the air of the place? Would'st not thee be ashamed to write unto a man who has never in his life done a single day's work, no, not even felled a tree; who hath expended the Lord knows how many years in studying stars, geometry, stones, and flies and in reading folio books? Who hath travelled, as he told us, to the city of Rome itself! Only think of a London man going to Rome! Where is it that these English folks won't go? One who hath seen the factory of brimstone at 'Suvius and town of Pompeii underground! Would'st thou pretend to letter it with a person who hath been to Paris, to the Alps, to Petersburg, and who hath seen so many fine things up and down the old countries; who hath come over the great sea unto us and hath journeyed from our New Hampshire in the East to our Charles Town in the South; who hath visited all our great cities, knows most of our famous lawyers and cunning folks; who hath conversed with very many king's men, governors, and counsellors, and yet pitches upon thee for his correspondent, as thee calls it? Surely he means to jeer thee! I am sure he does; he cannot be in a real fair earnest.

The character who delivers this delightful barrage of innocent innuendo is the Farmer's wife, whom D. H. Lawrence derisively calls the Amiable Spouse. She has a sharper wit than Lawrence allows; in addition to Infant Son, her remoter American offspring are Mark Twain and Will Rogers. Her vernacular speech—right down to the final, authentic "real"—is a hallmark of the American comic tradition, which subsequently produced the Connecticut Yankee and other innocent spoofers of Europe like Henrietta Stackpole, the tart-tongued reporter in James's *The Portrait of a Lady*.

Another quality connecting Crèvecoeur to later literature is, quite simply, the provincial writer's choice of subject matter. His canvas is the American scene, its landscapes, peoples, institutions, values, and problems. Though there are omissions, we note at once how comprehensive his picture is of life in the new land. The sense of delight, novelty, discovery—the attitude of wonder that Wayne Franklin, in *Discoverers, Explorers, Settlers,* finds in so many early books of travel—is an engaging and revealing aspect of the America imaged in the *Letters,* as also in the early *Sketches.* Yet the panorama is not inclusive but selective. The amateur author has troubles with scale (most readers would say the Nantucket chapters are too long) and his narrative structure is loose. Still, the overall plan is plain: to typify the three chief American regions by describing life on his own farm, on Nantucket and the Vineyard, and in Charles Town. Each district has its distinctive mode of life, its own ecology—seafaring in New England, subsistence agriculture in the Middle Colonies, slavery in the South. Crèvecoeur's basic outlook is, of course, agrarian; cities are mentioned but usually ignored. This answers both to the historical facts (only a small proportion of Americans in 1770 dwelt in towns) and to the ideal bucolic argument of the author. Many other American writers have done likewise: accepting the America of common experience as their proper province, they have actually shaped that real world to private patterns and values. From *Walden* on, this has often meant turning away from urban life.

Underlying Crèvecoeur's panoramic report on the New World is a set of questions preoccupying the imaginations of Crèvecoeur's European readers. The colonial writer (whose unformed mind resembles in this respect the Lockean *tabula rasa* mentioned by the minister in the first letter) looks to the other side of the Atlantic for intellectual formulations by which his own experience can be ordered and hence understood. The Old World's queries about the meaning of the New might be itemized thus: Is Nature in America beautiful *and* beneficent? Are Indians really nature's nobility? Is the American democrat (essentially a European peasant settled now on his own land) actually a new man? What does the American Revolution signify? Though the passing of Romanticism rendered the first two questions largely meaningless, the latter two retained their relevance well into the present century. (Indeed, if the Revolution is an early paradigm of American violence, that relevance still remains.) None of these questions is merely a European query about a strange, fascinating country across the ocean; all are also Americans' queries about themselves. For Americans in Crèvecoeur's day and long after were by origin and outlook Europeans in the process of being changed by a new physical and social environment into a different people. Nothing has been more characteristic of the new society than its citizens' habit of interrogating themselves, of worrying endlessly about their own identity. One place where this tradition starts is in *Letters from an American Farmer*.

Answering Europe's questions proved no easy matter for Crèvecoeur. Romantic stereotypes about the natural world and its admirable animals and natives existed in his European-trained mind. When these preconceptions coincided with American experience, they spawned some of the most charming scenes of his two books, such as the plowing or the visit of the redmen to the cabin guarded by Andrew the Hebridean. But the "sweet relaxation" to be found in contemplating the benignities of man and nature was usually short-lived. Later experience taught a different lesson about America than did Jean Jacques Rousseau or the Abbé Raynal. The wasps foraging for flies on the very eyelids of the children later, with the king-birds, proved more fierce and vindictive than kind; fire and brimstone were finally needed to get in the hay. The Indians who dealt so playfully with the Scots immigrant behaved very differently when war was declared. Crèvecoeur is simply whistling in the dark when he observes of the Indians:

> Yet they have not, they will not take up the hatchet against a people who have done them no harm. The passions necessary to urge these people to war cannot be roused; they cannot feel the stings of vengeance, the thirst of which alone can compel them

to shed blood: far superior in their motives of action
to the Europeans who, for sixpence per day, may be
engaged to shed that of any people on earth.

Even Crèvecoeur's treasured physiocratic belief that "men
are like plants" who cannot fail to bring forth good fruit
when put into the soil of the new country withers under
the test of time. "The Man of Sorrows" testifies to a so-
berer conclusion: "Men are the same in all ages and in all
countries. A few prejudices and customs excepted, the
same passions lurk in our hearts at all times." Only Crèvecoeur's Quaker-like aversion to violence, which made him
distrust the American Revolution from the beginning and
blinded him to any benefits it might produce, never changed.

This conflict between belief and experience provides the
drama and the emotional tension that every reader feels
building in the later chapters of both books. It is a tension
the author does not or cannot resolve. Only with respect
to the cruelties of 'war—the insistent burden of the last
Sketches—is he wholly decided, but here no claims have
been advanced for the theoretical value of revolution. Elsewhere, dream and reality coincide uneasily in his consciousness, producing feelings so contradictory as to para-
lyze effective thought and action. With the genuine artist's
honesty he mirrors this dilemma. As a result, the *Letters*
and *Sketches* present not simply the vision of an American
paradise but also the desperate struggle to hold on to that
vision in the face of discord. Thus, *Letters* exhibits many
of the qualities identified by Richard Chase in *The American Novel and Its Tradition* as characteristic of our finest
fiction: idyll or melodrama as modes, the borderland as
the locale where actual and imaginary worlds can mingle,
alienation and disorder as themes, and, at the end, not development and resolution but persistence of those polari-
ties discovered in American experience. Readers who
recall only the early chapters may recoil from thus linking
Crèvecoeur's books to *The Scarlet Letter, The Prairie,* or
Moby-Dick, but "Distresses of a Frontier Man" and the
Sketches provide convincing evidence that these two works
are prototypical American romances. The *Letters* fits this
pattern especially well, I think, because of Crèvecoeur's
use of James as an innocent mouthpiece. This narrative
device sets up the kind of ironic interplay between naïve

actor and knowing narrator that, as David Minter has shown in *The Interpreted Design,* is characteristic of many American novels and autobiographies.

That it *is* fable and not essentially history, travelogue, or autobiography seems clear, not only from the details of the author's own life already recited but also by contrast with other works on the America of the Revolutionary era. Several such books come at once to mind as parallel pieces to *Letters from an American Farmer* in one respect or another: Franklin's *Autobiography* (1791), John Woolman's *Journal* (1774), William Bartram's *Travels* (1791), and Moreau de Saint-Méry's *American Journey 1793–1798.* Like Franklin, Crèvecoeur offers paradigmatic personal experiences for the edification of his readers. Like Woolman (whose writings he may have known), Crèvecoeur was a peace-loving Quaker, in spirit if not in fact. Like William Bartram, whose father is the subject of Letter XI (wherein his name is spelled Bertram), Crèvecoeur bridges the Enlightenment and Romanticism in his appreciation of nature. And Crèvecoeur was twice in a similar position as Moreau de Saint-Méry—that of a Frenchman giving firsthand impressions of American life.

To illustrate some of the ways in which Crèvecoeur's literary art comprehends and often exceeds the imaginative scope of these contemporaries, we might look at Crèvecoeur's description of the king-birds on James's farm:

Thus divided by two interested motives, I have long resisted the desire I had to kill them until last year, when I thought they increased too much, and my indulgence had been carried too far; it was at the time of swarming, when they all came and fixed themselves on the neighboring trees, from whence they catched those that returned loaded from the fields. This made me resolve to kill as many as I could, and I was just ready to fire when a bunch of bees as big as my fist issued from one of the hives, rushed on one of the birds, and probably stung him, for he instantly screamed and flew, not as before, in an irregular manner, but in a direct line. He was followed by the same bold phalanx, at a considerable distance, which unfortunately, becoming too sure of victory, quitted their military array and disbanded themselves. By this inconsiderate step, they lost all that aggregrate of force which had made the bird fly off. Perceiving their disorder, he immediately returned and snapped as many as he wanted; nay, he had even the impudence to alight on the very twig from which the bees had drove him. I killed him and immediately opened his craw, from which I took 171 bees; I laid them all on a blanket in the sun, and to my great surprise, 54 returned to life, licked themselves clean, and joyfully went back to the hive, where they probably informed their companions of such an adventure and escape as I believe had never happened before to American bees!

Tension, contrast, and conflict are common underlying issues in each of these authors' account of their American experience. Though Crèvecoeur's account of the bird and bees lacks the explicit aesthetic statement of Bartram, it touches on the practical, didactic, moral, and cultural concerns of the other writers. It does so, however, by treating language in a distinctly different manner. Crèvecoeur's characteristic utterance is through metaphor and fable; it is parable moving in the direction of myth.

One notices, first of all, the anecdote's deliberately factual tone, lulling the unwary reader into accepting everything at face value.* The number of devoured bees is carefully specified, likewise the number that miraculously escaped. Only by the last sentence do we begin to suspect that the author has been pulling our leg—or James's. In fact, a typical American tall tale has been unloaded. Yet, as in all humor, the "stretcher," as Mark Twain would call it, has a serious message. Behind the bees' behavior lies the same social truth that informs the parable of Andrew the Hebridean: freedom begins in solidarity and

---

* An interesting parallel, in subject and tone, to Crèvecoeur's episode is a story Franklin tells in a letter of April 15, 1773, to Barbeu Dubourg. The doctor informs his correspondent of three American flies trapped in a bottle of Madeira in Virginia and brought back to life—two of them, anyway—by exposure to the London sun. See *Benjamin Franklin's Autobiographical Writings,* edited by Carl Van Doren (New York: Viking Press, 1945), pp. 289–90. (I am grateful to Mr. Thomas Powers of New York City for bringing this to my attention, though I do not agree with him that both writers meant to be taken literally.)

cooperation but aims at liberating the individual from the group. The trouble here is that individualism results in death for a great many bees. The political overtones are obvious. D. H. Lawrence called this story "a parable of the American resurrection." But if Europe is the *king-bird*, the American bees—those "little democrats," in Lawrence's words—have effected a dubious escape from rapacious tyranny. Finally, the episode echoes the Jonah myth. Here man, perceiving nature as both predatory and beneficent, intervenes like God in the natural order, plays the dual role of judge and midwife, and helps to tip the balance, making nature in this case more kind than cruel. All of these possible interpretations coexist in the matrix of Crèvecoeur's prose, which, though superficially less "literary" than, say, Bartram's, has a meaningful complexity beneath its ingenuous surface.

Many other scenes in the *Letters* and *Sketches* also exhibit a protomythic imagination at work. Probably the most famous is that of the Negro slave in the cage, described in Letter IX. As Marius Bewley has convincingly demonstrated in *The Eccentric Design*, this scene is very close to being a symbolist statement. Crèvecoeur's command of complex language is here delicate and sure. Opening deceptively like a kindhearted eighteenth-century naturalist's diary, with phrases like "leisurely travelling along," "the day was perfectly calm and sultry," "a sudden shower," he springs the chilling scene all at once upon the unsuspecting reader. In the midst of a realistic description, a Christian eucharistic idiom is deftly introduced to heighten the horror as the insects hover about the caged slave, "eager to feed on his mangled flesh and to drink his blood." The Farmer's characteristic paralysis of will is again revealed. Finally, the episode ends with a masterful parody of the language of Enlightenment legalism: "the laws of self-preservation rendered such executions necessary," "supported the doctrine of slavery with arguments generally made use of," "with the repetition of which I shall not trouble you at present." Perhaps the nicest touch of all is the last word, "Adieu." Nowhere else does Crèvecoeur achieve such control of his medium or convey so clearly the almost tragic character of his American Farmer. Here, quite simply, is an archetypal image in American literature. When we realize that the author probably never

had such an experience at all, or indeed knew much about
the realities of slavery except from Raynal's book or from
his friend Têtard, we are even more convinced that Crèvecoeur was by predilection an embryonic novelist.

Certainly *Letters from an American Farmer* has been
one embryo from which, figuratively speaking, a succession
of significant American works has developed. The fictional
characters Crèvecoeur drew have had many avatars.
James, the American Farmer, is the precursor of the sen-
sitive, naïve individual alienated eventually from the community and longing, like Natty Bumppo or Huck Finn, to
head for the western territories. The self-made man in
both his disguises—Andrew the Hebridean and his callous
cousin of the *Sketches*—anticipates Cooper's rapacious
Yankees, Horatio Alger's heroes, Faulkner's Thomas Sut-
pen, and, by implication, the whole tribe of gray-suited
opportunists peopling the fictional Madison Avenue of
the 1950's and 1960's. The slave in the cage has spiritual
offspring in the books of Melville, Stephen Crane, Faulkner, Richard Wright, and Ellison, as have the poor
Quakers and Tories of the *Sketches;* all are victims of an
ongoing "American Revolution," which in the name of
liberty sometimes learns how to lynch. With respect to
subject matter, too, Crèvecoeur has to a remarkable extent
laid the ground plan for later literature. Out of the Nantucket chapters we may see emerging *Moby-Dick* and
Poe's *Narrative of Arthur Gordon Pym*. The scenes of
rural life suggest themes developed by Whittier, Thoreau,
and Frost. "What is an American?" sets the stage and re-
hearses the lines for a cultural dialogue that has never
ceased. Jefferson, de Tocqueville, Bryce, Turner, and
modern writers like Harold Laski, David Potter, Henry
Nash Smith, and John Kenneth Galbraith are lineal descendants of Crèvecoeur the cultural critic; their works
on American culture and character owe much to *Letters
from an American Farmer*. From the perspective of time
one can only agree with H. C. Rice, who wisely remarked
a generation ago that "one of the merits of Crèvecoeur is
to have seen, at a moment when most of his fellow Americans had neither the time nor inclination for literature, the
artistic possibilities in certain truly American themes which
later became matter for accomplished works of art."

* * *

If *Letters* does, in fact, establish Crèvecoeur as the literary pathfinder I and others claim him to be ("the first in our literature to find this dramatic voice in an imaginative work of power," A. W. Plumstead has called him), what are we to make of its far less well-known sequel? In a sense, *Sketches of Eighteenth-Century America* is not Crèvecoeur's creation at all. The title was affixed by three twentieth-century scholars (Henri L. Bourdin, Ralph H. Gabriel, and Stanley T. Williams) to a collection of a dozen essays omitted either by design, necessity, or accident from both the English and French versions of *Letters*. They were discovered in 1923 in Normandy by Bourdin. Upon their publication by Yale University Press, John B. Moore hailed *Sketches* as a remarkable literary find, one that, in his opinion, reordered all judgments about eighteenth-century American prose: "They constitute in general not only the most effective and imaginative work in either of Crèvecoeur's English books," he wrote in 1927, "but also the most effective work of the imagination that we possess written in America by an American during that century." He heaped particular praise on "Landscapes," the last and longest of the Revolutionary sketches. This powerful closet drama in six scenes reveals Crèvecoeur's acute sympathy for the neutral colonists caught in the crossfire between brutal, fanatical Patriots and all-but-defenseless back-country Loyalists. Even more vividly and explicitly than "Distresses of a Frontier Man," "Landscapes" and the other political sketches show how deep ran Crèvecoeur's feelings for England and the Crown; they also exhibit a capacity for satire (unseen because inappropriate or embarrassing in the *Letters*), which is by turns bitterly ironic, comic, and pathetic.

While later readers have not uniformly echoed Moore's enthusiasm—which at one point leads him to prefer "Landscapes" over every early American play, including Royal Tyler's *The Contrast*—he was the first seriously to compare and connect *Sketches* to the *Letters*. Thomas Philbrick has more recently offered a fuller and quite different evaluation. "*Sketches of Eighteenth-Century America* remains a non-book," he wrote in 1970, "an anthology of heterogeneous pieces that lacks a controlling form, a co-

herent point of view, and a unifying theme." He notes,
however, some important similarities between Crèvecoeur's
two English works: the epistolary strategy, the thematic
contrast between the early bucolic sketches and later
scenes of social conflict, and a specific (and ironic) parallel
between "Reflections on the Manners of the Americans"
and the earlier story in *Letters* of Andrew the Hebridean.

One Revolutionary sketch Philbrick singles out is "The
Wyoming Massacre." This is the only purely historical
narrative Crèvecoeur wrote in English. Though Philbrick
compares it favorably to Cooper and Parkman, he does not
emphasize one aspect of this vivid account of a Tory-led
Indian attack on the Pennsylvania frontier: that "The
Wyoming Massacre" is only half of the original sketch
Crèvecoeur wrote. For some unexplained reason, Bourdin,
Williams, and Gabriel divided in two a much longer account of a journey to the Susquehanna Valley. They published the first half as "Crèvecoeur on the Susquehanna"
in the *Yale Review,* but then chose not to include it in
Sketches. Many who are familiar with both pieces consider this a mistake. Plumstead, for one, calls the entire
essay "one of Crèvecoeur's finest," adding, "It is a great
misfortune that readers have been denied the opportunity
to read the piece entire, for if one places 'The Wyoming
Massacre' of *Sketches* after the end of the *Yale Review*
'Susquehanna', where it belongs (there is no break or suggestion of a break in the Bourdin typescript), one has a
mini-*Letters.* A beautiful wilderness and a happy pioneer
people are invaded by revolutionaries, killed and burned
by Indians and whites." In this Penguin edition, Crèvecoeur's entire essay is reassembled for the first time.
Though its inclusion in *Sketches* may not alter Gabriel's
assertion that "Crèvecoeur was not a historian; he was a
chronicler of unrelated episodes," nevertheless it will, I
believe, show more clearly how his imagination responded
to the historical sequence of events that saw the birth of
an American nation. Again and again, he reacted emotion-
ally to this movement—first, in the whole work *Letters
from an American Farmer* and later in briefer pieces like
"Susquehanna," "The Wyoming Massacre," and the unpublished "An Happy Family Disunited by the Spirit of
Civil War." He did so not simply to record his own and
his neighbors' suffering but, at a deeper level, to articulate

the ideological ambivalences that Myra Jehlen identifies by calling Crèvecoeur a "monarcho-anarchist." On the one hand, this Franco-American aristocrat felt a profound attraction to the British Crown. On the other, his vision of an American agrarian utopia rested upon the virtual absence or abdication of that imperial power; this utopia could only be imagined by pretending that the Townshend Acts had never occurred. This dreamy situation is never subjected to rational analysis or defense. Rather, the *Sketches,* like its predecessor, is the emotional history of one caught in contradiction. Conspicuously missing from both books is any discussion of events, issues, or political ideologies that could explain why colonists like Franklin or Jefferson, for example, might opt for independence while others might remain Loyalists. Thus, Crèvecoeur's Revolutionary writings, valuable as they are in providing fresh evidence of the feelings and attitudes of the inarticulate masses, document our first civil conflict only at the lower social and intellectual registers.

Nonetheless, *Sketches of Eighteenth-Century America* should not be dismissed simply as new source material for retrospective colonial opinion polls by social or psycho-historians. Although Philbrick is probably correct in emphasizing the book's wobbly form and tone and lack of thematic coherence, many of these leftover essays possess individual interest and freshness that go far toward explaining Moore's enthusiastic praise of half a century ago. Certain of them, in fact, retain an astonishing power to move modern readers by instructing us in some unpleasant truths about the birth pangs of our Republic. Crèvecoeur the satirist is an authentic expression of the United States of America's first man of letters. His career's prophetic significance consists both in myth-making and in saying nay to official values and hallowed ideologies, in speaking for minorities and outsiders. In the two centuries since the publication of *Letters from an American Farmer,* these have continued to be vital functions of the literary artist in America.

—Albert E. Stone

Suggestions for Further Reading

Biography
Mitchell, Julia Post. *St. Jean de Crèvecoeur*. New York: Columbia University Press, 1916.

Bibliography
Cutting, Rose Marie. *John and William Bartram, William Byrd II, and St. John de Crèvecoeur: A Reference Guide*. Boston: G. K. Hall, 1976.
Rice, Howard C. "The American Farmer's Letters, With a Checklist of the Different Editions." *The Colophon* Pt. XVIII, 1933.

Criticism
Beidler, Philip. "Franklin and Crèvecoeur's 'Literary' Americans." *Early American Literature* 13 (Spring 1978), 50–63.
Bewley, Marius. *The Eccentric Design*. New York: Columbia University Press, 1959, 102–106.
Cunliffe, Marcus. "St. John de Crèvecoeur Revisited," *Journal of American Studies* 2 (August 1975), 129–44.
Jehlen, Myra. "J. Hector St. Crèvecoeur: A Monarcho-Anarchist in Revolutionary America." *American Quarterly* 31 (Summer 1979), 204–22.
Lawrence, D. H. *The Symbolic Meaning: The Uncollected Versions of Studies in Classic American Literature*. Edited by A. Arnold. Arundel, England: Centaur Press, 1962, 53–70.

Marx, Leo. *The Machine in the Garden: Technology and the Pastoral Ideal in America.* New York: Oxford University Press, 1968, 107–16.

Mohr, James C. "Calculated Disillusionment; Crèvecoeur's *Letters* Reconsidered," *South Atlantic Quarterly* 69 (Summer 1970), 354–63.

Moore, John B. "The Rehabilitation of Crèvecoeur." *Sewanee Review* 35 (April 1927), 216–30.

Philbrick, Thomas. *St. John de Crèvecoeur.* New York: Twayne Publishers, 1970.

Plumstead, A. W. "Hector St. John de Crèvecoeur." In *American Literature 1764–1789, The Revolutionary Years,* edited by E. Emerson. Madison: University of Wisconsin Press, 1977, 213–31.

Rucker, Mary E. "Crèvecoeur's *Letters* and Enlightenment Doctrine," *Early American Literature* 13 (Fall 1978), 193–212.

A Note on the Text

This edition of *Letters from an American Farmer* is based on the London edition of 1783, published by Davies and Davis, which incorporated corrections made by the author to the original 1782 edition. Punctuation and spelling have been modernized.

The text of *Sketches of Eighteenth-Century America* follows, with one significant addition, that of the Yale University Press edition of 1925, edited by Henri L. Bourdin, Ralph H. Gabriel, and Stanley T. Williams. This first publication of *Sketches* was prefaced by the following "Note on the Text":

In preparing this text for publication, the editors have not attempted to reproduce exactly the manuscript of Crèvecoeur. Such a procedure would have meant a book of some historical and philological interest, but one encumbered with endless annotations and explanations. Crèvecoeur was a man of action; he wrote in the intervals of a busy life. He was an acute thinker, but no scholar. A poor speller, he was likewise careless of punctuation and syntax. He yielded without consistency to French idioms and English phrases—echoes of his early life—as well as to dialect pronunciations which he heard about him in America. Thus some parts of this manuscript, if repeated *verbatim,* would be, because of idiosyncrasies of spelling, punctuation, and grammar, nearly unintelligible and occasionally absurd.

The aim of the editor has been, therefore, to make the manuscript readable and, at the same time, to retain scrupulously Crèvecoeur's meaning—even, except in a few instances, his own phraseology and mannerisms of speech. For these letters, like those already published, have a distinct flavour. Crèvecoeur is certainly unlike any other eighteenth-century writer: a gifted Frenchman, educated for a time in England, living in and writing of pioneer America. That these letters, when printed, should express this indefinable quality is one object of the present book. Everything possible, consistent with clarity, has been done to preserve this tone; one may be confident that it will survive the changes made in punctuation and spelling. Punctuation, indeed, hardly exists in the manuscript. The changes, moreover, made by the editors are not comparable in extent or importance with those wrought in the first published papers by Thomas Davies and Lockyer Davis, his eighteenth-century English revisers.

The spelling has, then, as a whole, been modernized. Often Crèvecoeur's orthography is that of his age, as in such words as *compleat* and *antient.* Sometimes, however, he alters these forms. His vagaries are numerous. He can misuse *lie* and *lay;* he can repeat *bleating,* apparently phonetically, as *blaiting;* he frankly employs French words (or versions of them) instead of their English equivalents (*volupty, agricole, colon, carriere*); he can reduce Latin derivatives to, for example, *simetry* and *indgredients;* and he can talk of *gueeres* or of *woolfs* and *sckuncks.* These are a very few; a list of his grotesque spellings would reach far into the hundreds. Such have been corrected and have been put into modern form. (Occasionally an obsolete or archaic word has been retained, in its proper spelling, if the meaning is clear, to avoid the use of synonyms.) Any addition to the text or change in meaning or in the arrangement of words (other than prepositions, pronouns, articles, etc.) has been indicated by brackets. The capitalization has been normalized, the letters have been repunctuated, always with careful consideration of Crèvecoeur's emphasis and arrangement of ideas. In his grammar, his awkward constructions and unusual locutions have been permitted to stand when the meaning is clear; but hopelessly bad grammar has been corrected, and many minor changes have been made to prevent obscurity and absurdity. Such have been imperative in the use of prepositions, conjunctions, adverbs, past participles, agreement of subjects and verbs, and, particularly, in the case of Crèvecoeur's bewilderment before English pronouns. His continual confusion of the demonstratives *this* and *that* and of the relatives *who* and *which* suggests the nature of his difficulties with English grammar. After all, Crèvecoeur was bred in a foreign tongue.

The editors are sensible that these manuscripts may ultimately be subjected to intensive philological study as interest increases in the development of the English language in America. It has seemed best at this time to present these sketches for their literary rather than their philological interest.

H.L.B.
R.H.G.
S.T.W.

The sole alteration in the 1925 text occurs in Chapter VIII. Originally entitled "The Wyoming Massacre," this chapter, in Bourdin's typescript of the manuscript, consisted of a much longer sketch. The first half was published separately as "Crèvecoeur on the Susquehanna," in *Yale Review*, Vol. 14 (1925), pp. 552–84. The two halves are here reunited for the first time under a new title supplied by the present editor: "On the Susquehanna; The Wyoming Massacre."

Grateful acknowledgment is hereby made to Yale University Press and the *Yale Review* for permission to reprint this material. A similar expression of thanks is due New American Library for permitting the editor to adapt his Foreword to the 1963 Signet Classic edition of *Letters from an American Farmer* and *Sketches of Eighteenth-*

Century America. That introduction has been revised and
enlarged with a view to incorporating some of the insights
of recent Crèvecoeur scholarship, which has signally enlarged our understanding of this literary pioneer.

Letters from an American Farmer

Advertisements

TO THE FIRST EDITION, 1782

The following letters are the genuine production of the American farmer whose name they bear. They were privately written to gratify the curiosity of a friend and are made public because they contain much authentic information little known on this side of the Atlantic: they cannot therefore fail of being highly interesting to the people of England at a time when everybody's attention is directed toward the affairs of America.

That these letters are the actual result of a private correspondence may fairly be inferred (exclusive of other evidence) from the style and manner in which they are conceived; for though plain and familiar, and sometimes animated, they are by no means exempt from such inaccuracies as must unavoidably occur in the rapid effusions of a confessedly inexperienced writer.

Our farmer had long been an eye witness of the transactions which have deformed the face of America; he is one of those who dreaded and has severely felt the desolating consequences of a rupture between the parent state and her colonies, for he has been driven from a situation the enjoyment of which the reader will find pathetically described in the early letters of this volume. The unhappy contest is at length, however, drawing toward a period, and it is now only left us to hope that the obvious interests and mutual wants of both countries may in due time, and in spite of all obstacles, happily reunite them.

Should our farmer's letters be found to afford matter of useful entertainment to an intelligent and candid public, a second volume, equally interesting with those now published, may soon be expected.

To the Second Edition, 1783

Since the publication of this volume, we hear that Mr. St. John has accepted a public employment at New York. It is therefore, perhaps, doubtful whether he will soon be at leisure to revise his papers and give the world a second collection of the American Farmer's Letters.

Abbé Raynal, F.R.S.

Behold, sir, an humble American planter, a simple cultivator of the earth, addressing you from the farther side
of the Atlantic and presuming to fix your name at the
head of his trifling lucubrations. I wish they were worthy
of so great an honour. Yet why should not I be permitted
to disclose those sentiments which I have so often felt
from my heart? A few years since, I met accidentally with
your *Political and Philosophical History* and perused it
with infinite pleasure. For the first time in my life I reflected on the relative state of nations; I traced the extended ramifications of a commerce which ought to unite
but now convulses the world; I admired that universal benevolence, that diffusive good will, which is not confined to the narrow limits of your own country, but, on the
contrary, extends to the whole human race. As an elo-
quent and powerful advocate, you have pleaded the cause
of humanity in espousing that of the poor Africans. You
viewed these provinces of North America in their true
light: as the asylum of freedom, as the cradle of future
nations and the refuge of distressed Europeans. Why, then,
should I refrain from loving and respecting a man whose
writings I so much admire? These two sentiments are
inseparable, at least in my breast. I conceived your

genius to be present at the head of my study; under its invisible but powerful guidance, I prosecuted my small labours; and now, permit me to sanctify them under the auspices of your name. Let the sincerity of the motives which urge me prevent you from thinking that this well-meant address contains aught but the purest tribute of reverence and affection. There is, no doubt, a secret communion among good men throughout the world, a mental affinity connecting them by a similitude of sentiments: then, why, though an American, should not I be permitted to share in that extensive intellectual consanguinity? Yes, I do: and though the name of a man who possesses neither titles nor places, who never rose above the humble rank of a farmer, may appear insignificant, yet, as the sentiments I have expressed are also the echo of those of my countrymen, on their behalf, as well as on my own, give me leave to subscribe myself, sir,

Your very sincere admirer,

J. HECTOR ST. JOHN.

CARLISLE, IN PENNSYLVANIA.

LETTER I

Who would have thought that because I received you with hospitality and kindness, you should imagine me capable of writing with propriety and perspicuity? Your gratitude misleads your judgement. The knowledge which I acquired from your conversation has amply repaid me for your five weeks' entertainment. I gave you nothing more than what common hospitality dictated; but could any other guest have instructed me as you did? You conducted me, on the map, from one European country to another; told me many extraordinary things of our famed mother country, of which I knew very little, of its internal navigation, agriculture, arts, manufactures, and trade; you guided me through an extensive maze, and I abundantly profited by the journey; the contrast therefore proves the debt of gratitude to be on my side. The treatment you received at my house proceeded from the warmth of my heart and from the corresponding sensibility of my wife; what you now desire must flow from a very limited power of mind; the task requires recollection and a variety of talents which I do not possess. It is true I can describe our American modes of farming, our manners, and peculiar customs with some degree of propriety because I have ever attentively studied them; but my knowledge extends no farther.

And is this local and unadorned information sufficient to answer all your expectations and to satisfy your curiosity? I am surprised that in the course of your American travels you should not have found out persons more enlightened and better educated than I am; your predilection excites my wonder much more than my vanity, my share of the latter being confined merely to the neatness of my rural operations.

My father left me a few musty books, which *his* father brought from England with him; but what help can I draw from a library consisting mostly of Scotch divinity, the *Navigation of Sir Francis Drake,* the *History of Queen Elizabeth,* and a few miscellaneous volumes? Our minister often comes to see me, though he lives upwards of twenty miles distant. I have shown him your letter, asked his advice, and solicited his assistance; he tells me that he hath no time to spare, for that like the rest of us, he must till his farm and is moreover to study what he is to say on the Sabbath. My wife (and I never do anything without consulting her) laughs and tells me that you cannot be in earnest. "What!" says she; "James, would'st thee pretend to send epistles to a great European man who hath lived abundance of time in that big house called Cambridge, where, they say, that worldly learning is so abundant that people get it only by breathing the air of the place? Would'st not thee be ashamed to write unto a man who has never in his life done a single day's work, no, not even felled a tree; who hath expended the Lord knows how many years in studying stars, geometry, stones, and flies and in reading folio books? Who hath travelled, as he told us, to the city of Rome itself! Only think of a London man going to Rome! Where is it that these English folks won't go? One who hath seen the factory of brimstone at 'Suvius and town of Pompeii underground! Would'st thou pretend to letter it with a person who hath been to Paris, to the Alps, to Petersburg, and who hath seen so many fine things up and down the old countries; who hath come over the great sea unto us and hath journeyed from our New Hampshire in the East to our Charles Town in the South; who hath visited all our great cities, knows most of our famous lawyers and cunning folks; who hath conversed with very many king's men, governors, and counsellors, and yet pitches upon thee for

his correspondent, as thee calls it? Surely he means to
jeer thee! I am sure he does; he cannot be in a real fair
earnest. James, thee must read this letter over again, paragraph by paragraph, and warily observe whether thee
canst perceive some words of jesting, something that hath
more than one meaning; and now I think on it, husband,
I wish thee would'st let me see his letter; though I am but
a woman, as thee mayest say, yet I understand the pur-
port of words in good measure, for when I was a girl,
Father sent us to the very best master in the precinct."
She then read it herself very attentively; our minister was
present, we listened to and weighed every syllable; we
all unanimously concluded that you must have been in
a sober earnest intention, as my wife calls it, and your
request appeared to be candid and sincere. Then again,
on recollecting the difference between your sphere of life
and mine, a new fit of astonishment seized us all!

Our minister took the letter from my wife and read
it to himself; he made us observe the two last phrases,
and we weighed the contents to the best of our abilities.
The conclusion we all drew made me resolve at last to
write. You say you want nothing of me but what lies
within the reach of my experience and knowledge; this
I understand very well; the difficulty is, how to collect,
digest, and arrange what I know? Next, you assert that
writing letters is nothing more than talking on paper,
which, I must confess, appeared to me quite a new thought.
"Well, then," observed our minister, "neighbour James, as
you can talk well, I am sure you must write tolerably well
also; imagine, then, that Mr. F. B. is still here and simply
write down what you would say to him. Suppose the questions he will put to you in his future letters to be asked
by his viva-voce, as we used to call it at the college; then
let your answers be conceived and expressed exactly in
the same language as if he was present. This is all that he
requires from you, and I am sure the task is not difficult.
He is your friend; who would be ashamed to write to such
a person? Although he is a man of learning and taste, yet
I am sure he will read your letters with pleasure; if they
be not elegant, they will smell of the woods and be a little
wild; I know your turn, they will contain some matters
which he never knew before. Some people are so fond
of novelty that they will overlook many errors of language

for the sake of information. We are all apt to love and admire exotics, though they may be often inferior to what we possess; and that is the reason I imagine why so many persons are continually going to visit Italy. That country is the daily resort of modern travellers."

JAMES: I should like to know what is there to be seen so goodly and profitable that so many should wish to visit no other country?

MINISTER: I do not very well know. I fancy their object is to trace the vestiges of a once-flourishing people now extinct. There they amuse themselves in viewing the ruins of temples and other buildings which have very little affinity with those of the present age and must therefore impart a knowledge which appears useless and trifling. I have often wondered that no skilful botanists or learned men should come over here; methinks there would be much more real satisfaction in observing among us the humble rudiments and embryos of societies spreading everywhere, the recent foundation of our towns, and the settlements of so many rural districts. I am sure that the rapidity of their growth would be more pleasing to behold than the ruins of old towers, useless aqueducts, or impending battlements.

JAMES: What you say, minister, seems very true; do go on; I always love to hear you talk.

MINISTER: Do not you think, neighbour James, that the mind of a good and enlightened Englishman would be more improved in remarking throughout these provinces the causes which render so many people happy? In delineating the unnoticed means by which we daily increase the extent of our settlements? How we convert huge forests into pleasing fields and exhibit through these thirteen provinces so singular a display of easy subsistence and political felicity?

In Italy, all the objects of contemplation, all the reveries of the traveller, must have a reference to ancient generations and to very distant periods, clouded with the mist of ages. Here, on the contrary, everything is modern, peaceful, and benign. Here we have had no war to desolate our fields; our religion does not oppress the cultivators; we are strangers to those feudal institutions which have enslaved so many. Here Nature opens her broad lap to receive the perpetual accession of newcomers and to supply them with food. I am sure I cannot be called a partial American when I say that the spectacle afforded by these pleasing scenes must be more entertaining and more philosophical than that which arises from beholding the musty ruins of Rome. Here everything would inspire the reflecting traveller with the most philanthropic ideas; his imagination, instead of submitting to the painful and useless retrospect of revolutions, desolations, and plagues, would, on the contrary, wisely spring forward to the anticipated fields of future cultivation and improvement, to the future extent of those generations which are to replenish and embellish this boundless continent. There the half-ruined amphitheatres and the putrid fevers of the Campania must fill the mind with the most melancholy reflections whilst he is seeking for the origin and the intention of those structures with which he is surrounded and for the cause of so great a decay. Here he might contemplate the very beginnings and outlines of human society, which can be traced nowhere now but in this part of the world. The rest of the earth, I am told, is in some places too full, in others half depopulated. Misguided religion, tyranny, and absurd laws everywhere depress and afflict mankind. Here we have in some measure regained the ancient dignity of our species: our laws are simple and just; we are a race of cultivators; our cultivation is unrestrained; and therefore everything is prosperous and flourishing. For my part, I had rather admire the ample barn of one of our opulent farmers, who himself felled the first tree in his plantation and was the first founder of his settlement, than study the dimensions of the temple of Ceres. I had rather record the progressive steps of this industrious farmer throughout all the stages of his labours and other operations than examine how modern Italian convents can be supported without doing anything but singing and praying.

However confined the field of speculation might be here, the time of English travellers would not be wholly lost. The new and unexpected aspect of our extensive settlements, of our fine rivers; that great field of action everywhere visible; that ease, that peace with which so many people live together, would greatly interest the observer: for whatever difficulties there might happen in the object of their researches, that hospitality which prevails from one end of the continent to the other would in all parts facilitate their excursions. As it is from the surface of the ground which we till that we have gathered the wealth we possess, the surface of that ground is therefore the only thing that has hitherto been known. It will require the industry of subsequent ages, the energy of future generations, ere mankind here will have leisure and abilities to penetrate deep and in the bowels of this continent search for the subterranean riches it no doubt contains. Neighbour James, we want much the assistance of men of leisure and knowledge; we want eminent chemists to inform our iron masters, to teach us how to make and prepare most of the colours we use. Here we have none equal to this task. If any useful discoveries are therefore made among us, they are the effects of chance, or else arise from that restless industry which is the principal characteristic of these colonies.

JAMES: Oh! Could I express myself as you do, my friend, I should not balance a single instant; I should rather be anxious to commence a correspondence which would do me credit.

MINISTER: You can write full as well as you need, and would improve very fast. Trust to my prophecy, your letters at least will have the merit of coming from the edge of the great wilderness, three hundred miles from the sea and three thousand miles over that sea; this will be no detriment to them, take my word for it. You intend one of your children for the gown; who knows but Mr. F. B. may give you some assistance when the lad comes to have concerns with the bishop. It is good for American farmers to have friends even in England. What he requires of you is but simple—what we speak out among ourselves we call conversation, and a letter is only conversation put down in black and white.

JAMES: You quite persuade me—if he laughs at my awkwardness, surely he will be pleased with my ready compliance. On my part, it will be well meant, be the execution what it may. I will write enough, and so let him have the trouble of sifting the good from the bad, the useful from the trifling; let him select what he may want and reject what may not answer his purpose. After all, it is but treating Mr. F. B. now that he is in London, as I treated him when he was in America under this roof; that

is with the best things I had, given with a good intention
and the best manner I was able.

"Very different, James, very different indeed," said my
wife; "I like not thy comparison; our small house and cellar, our orchard and garden, afforded what he wanted; one
half of his time Mr. F. B., poor man, lived upon nothing
but fruit-pies, or peaches and milk. Now, these things
were such as God had given us; myself and wench did the
rest; we were not the creators of these victuals, we only
cooked them as well and as neat as we could. The first
thing, James, is to know what sort of materials thee hast
within thy own self, and then whether thee canst dish
them up." "Well, well, wife, thee art wrong for once; if I
was filled with worldly vanity, thy rebuke would be timely,
but thee knowest that I have but little of that. How shall
I know what I am capable of till I try? Hadst thee never
employed thyself in thy father's house to learn and to
practise the many branches of housekeeping that thy
parents were famous for, thee would'st have made but
a sorry wife for an American farmer; thee never should'st
have been mine. I married thee not for what thee hadst,
but for what thee knewest; dost not thee observe what
Mr. F. B. says beside; he tells me that the art of writing
is just like unto every other art of man, that it is acquired
by habit and by perseverance." "That is singularly true,"
said our minister; "he that shall write a letter every day
of the week will on Saturday perceive the sixth flowing
from his pen much more readily than the first. I observed when I first entered into the ministry and began to
preach the word, I felt perplexed and dry, my mind was
like unto a parched soil, which produced nothing, not
even weeds. By the blessing of heaven and my perseverance in study I grew richer in thoughts, phrases, and
words; I felt copious, and now I can abundantly preach
from any text that occurs to my mind. So will it be with
you, neighbour James; begin therefore without delay; and
Mr. F. B.'s letters may be of great service to you: he will,
no doubt, inform you of many things: correspondence
consists in reciprocal letters. Leave off your diffidence,
and I will do my best to help you whenever I have any
leisure." "Well then, I am resolved," I said, "to follow
your counsel; my letters shall not be sent, nor will I receive any, without reading them to you and my wife;

women are curious, they love to know their husband's secrets; it will not be the first thing which I have submitted to your joint opinions. Whenever you come to dine with us, these shall be the last dish on the table." "Nor will they be the most unpalatable," answered the good man. "Nature has given you a tolerable share of sense, and that is one of her best gifts, let me tell you. She has given you, besides, some perspicuity which qualifies you to distinguish interesting objects; a warmth of imagination which enables you to think with quickness; you often extract useful reflections from objects which present none to my mind; you have a tender and a well-meaning heart; you love description, and your pencil, assure yourself, is not a bad one for the pencil of a farmer; it seems to be held without any labour; your mind is what we called at Yale college a *tabula rasa*, where spontaneous and strong impressions are delineated with facility. Ah, neighbour! Had you received but half the education of Mr. F. B., you had been a worthy correspondent indeed. But perhaps you will be a more entertaining one dressed in your simple American garb than if you were clad in all the gowns of Cambridge. You will appear to him something like one of our wild American plants, irregularly luxuriant in its various branches, which an European scholar may probably think ill-placed and useless. If our soil is not remarkable as yet for the excellence of its fruits, this exuberance is, however, a strong proof of fertility, which wants nothing but the progressive knowledge acquired by time to amend and to correct. It is easier to retrench than it is to add; I do not mean to flatter you, neighbour James; adulation would ill become my character; you may therefore believe what your pastor says. Were I in Europe, I should be tired with perpetually seeing espaliers, plashed hedges, and trees dwarfed into pygmies. Do let Mr. F. B. see on paper a few American wild-cherry trees, such as Nature forms them here in all her unconfined vigour, in all the amplitude of their extended limbs and spreading ramifications—let him see that we are possessed with strong vegetative embryos. After all, why should not a farmer be allowed to make use of his mental faculties as well as others; because a man works, is he not to think, and if he thinks usefully, why should not he in his leisure hours set down his thoughts? I have composed many a good sermon as I followed my plough. The eyes not being then engaged on any particular object leaves the mind free for the introduction of many useful ideas. It is not in the noisy shop of a blacksmith or of a carpenter that these studious moments can be enjoyed; it is as we silently till the ground and muse along the odoriferous furrows of our lowlands, uninterrupted either by stones or stumps; it is there that the salubrious effluvia of the earth animate our spirits and serve to inspire us; every other avocation of our farms are severe labours compared to this pleasing occupation: of all the tasks which mine imposes upon me, ploughing is the most agreeable because I can think as I work; my mind is at leisure; my labour flows from instinct, as well as that of my horses; there is no kind of difference between us in our different shares of that operation; one of them keeps the furrow, the other avoids it; at the end of my field, they turn either to the right or left as they are bid, whilst I thoughtlessly hold and guide the plough to which they are harnessed. Do therefore, neighbour, begin this correspondence, and persevere; difficulties will vanish in proportion as you draw near them; you'll be surprised at yourself by and by; when you come to look back, you'll say as I often said to myself, 'Had I been diffident, I had never proceeded thus far.' Would you painfully till your stony upland and neglect the fine rich bottom which lies before your door? Had you never tried, you had never learned how to mend and make your ploughs. It will be no small pleasure to your children to tell hereafter that their father was not only one of the most industrious farmers in the country, but one of the best writers. When you have once begun, do as when you begin breaking up your summer fallow; you never consider what remains to be done, you view only what you have ploughed. Therefore, neighbour James, take my advice; it will go well with you; I am sure it will." "And do you really think so, sir? Your counsel, which I have long followed, weighs much with me; I verily believe that I must write to Mr. F. B. by the first vessel." "If thee persistest in being such a foolhardy man," said my wife, "for God's sake let it be kept a profound secret among us; if it were once known abroad that thee writest to a great and rich man over at London, there would be no end of the talk of the peo-

ple: some would vow that thee art going to turn an
author; others would pretend to foresee some great alter-
ations in the welfare of thy family; some would say this;
some would say that. Who would wish to become the
subject of public talk? Weigh this matter well before thee
beginnest, James; consider that a great deal of thy time
and of thy reputation is at stake as I may say. Wert thee
to write as well as friend Edmund, whose speeches I often
see in our papers, it would be the very selfsame thing; thee
would'st be equally accused of idleness and vain notions
not befitting thy condition. Our colonel would be often
coming here to know what it is that thee canst write so
much about. Some would imagine that thee wantest to
become either an assemblyman or a magistrate, which
God forbid, and that thee art telling the king's men abundance of things. Instead of being well looked upon as
now, and living in peace with all the world, our neighbours
would be making strange surmises; I had rather be as we
are, neither better nor worse than the rest of our country folks. Thee knowest what I mean, though I should be
sorry to deprive thee of any honest recreation. Therefore,
as I have said before, let it be as great a secret as if it
was some heinous crime; the minister, I am sure, will
not divulge it; as for my part, though I am a woman, yet
I know what it is to be a wife. I would not have thee,
James, pass for what the world calleth a writer; no, not
for a peck of gold, as the saying is. Thy father before
thee was a plain-dealing, honest man, punctual in all things;
he was one of *yea* and *nay,* of few words; all he minded
was his farm and his work. I wonder from whence thee
hast got this love of the pen? Had he spent his time in
sending epistles to and fro, he never would have left thee
this goodly plantation, free from debt. All I say is in good
meaning; great people over sea may write to our towns-
folks because they have nothing else to do. These Englishmen are strange people; because they can live upon
what they call bank notes, without working, they think
that all the world can do the same. This goodly country
never would have been tilled and cleared with these
notes. I am sure when Mr. F. B. was here, he saw thee
sweat and take abundance of pains; he often told me how
the Americans worked a great deal harder than the home
Englishmen; for there, he told us, that they have no

trees to cut down, no fences to make, no Negroes to buy
and to clothe. And now I think on it, when wilt thee send
him those trees he bespoke? But if they have no trees
to cut down, they have gold in abundance, they say; for
they rake it and scrape it from all parts far and near.
I have often heard my grandfather tell how they live there
by writing. By writing they send this cargo unto us, that
to the West, and the other to the East Indies. But, James,
thee knowest that it is not by writing that we shall pay
the blacksmith, the minister, the weaver, the tailor, and
the English shop. But as thee art an early man, follow
thine own inclinations; thee wantest some rest, I am sure,
and why should'st thee not employ it as it may seem meet
unto thee. However, let it be a great secret; how would'st
thee bear to be called at our country meetings the man
of the pen? If this scheme of thine was once known,
travellers as they go along would point out to our house,
saying, 'Here liveth the scribbling farmer.' Better hear
them as usual observe, 'Here liveth the warm substantial
family that never begrudgeth a meal of victuals or a mess
of oats to any one that steps in. Look how fat and well
clad their Negroes are.' "

Thus, sir, have I given you an unaffected and candid
detail of the conversation which determined me to accept
of your invitation. I thought it necessary thus to begin
and to let you into these primary secrets, to the end that
you may not hereafter reproach me with any degree of
presumption. You'll plainly see the motives which have induced me to begin, the fears which I have entertained, and
the principles on which my diffidence hath been founded.
I have now nothing to do but to prosecute my task. Remember, you are to give me my subjects, and on no other
shall I write, lest you should blame me for an injudicious
choice. However incorrect my style, however inexpert
my methods, however trifling my observations may hereafter appear to you, assure yourself they will all be the
genuine dictates of my mind, and I hope will prove acceptable on that account. Remember that you have laid
the foundation of this correspondence; you well know that
I am neither a philosopher, politician, divine, or naturalist,
but a simple farmer. I flatter myself, therefore, that you'll
receive my letters as conceived, not according to scientific
rules to which I am a perfect stranger, but agreeable to

the spontaneous impressions which each subject may inspire. This is the only line I am able to follow, the line which Nature has herself traced for me; this was the covenant which I made with you and with which you seemed to be well pleased. Had you wanted the style of the learned, the reflections of the patriot, the discussions of the politician, the curious observations of the naturalist, the pleasing garb of the man of taste, surely you would have applied to some of those men of letters with which our cities abound. But since, on the contrary, and for what reason I know not, you wish to correspond with a cultivator of the earth, with a simple citizen, you must receive my letters for better or worse.

LETTER II

ON THE SITUATION, FEELINGS, AND PLEASURES OF AN AMERICAN FARMER

As you are the first enlightened European I had ever the pleasure of being acquainted with, you will not be surprised that I should, according to your earnest desire and my promise, appear anxious of preserving your friendship and correspondence. By your accounts, I observe a material difference subsists between your husbandry, modes, and customs and ours; everything is local; could we enjoy the advantages of the English farmer, we should be much happier, indeed, but this wish, like many others, implies a contradiction; and could the English farmer have some of those privileges we possess, they would be the first of their class in the world. Good and evil, I see, are to be found in all societies, and it is in vain to seek for any spot where those ingredients are not mixed. I therefore rest satisfied and thank God that my lot is to be an American farmer instead of a Russian boor or an Hungarian peasant. I thank you kindly for the idea, however dreadful, which you have given me of their lot and condition; your observations have confirmed me in the justness of my ideas, and I am happier now than I thought myself before. It is strange that misery, when viewed in others, should become to us a sort of real good, though I am far from rejoicing to hear that there are in the world men so thoroughly wretched; they are no doubt as harmless, industrious, and willing to work as we are. Hard is their fate to be thus condemned to a slavery worse than that of our Negroes. Yet when young, I entertained some thoughts of selling my farm. I thought it afforded but a dull repetition of the same labours and pleasures. I thought the former tedious and heavy, the latter few and insipid; but when I came to consider myself as divested of my farm, I then found the world so wide, and every place so full, that I began to fear lest there would be no room for me. My farm, my house, my barn, presented to my imagination objects from which I adduced quite new ideas; they were more forcible than before. Why should not I find myself happy, said I, where my father was before? He left me no good books, it is true; he gave me no other education than the art of reading and writing; but he left me a good farm and his experience; he left me free from debts, and no kind of difficulties to struggle with. I married, and this perfectly reconciled me to my situation; my wife rendered my house all at once cheerful and pleasing; it no longer appeared gloomy and solitary as before; when I went to work in my fields, I worked with more alacrity and sprightliness; I felt that I did not work for myself alone, and this encouraged me much. My wife would often come with her knitting in her hand and sit under the shady tree, praising the straightness of my furrows and the docility of my horses; this swelled my heart and made everything light and pleasant, and I regretted that I had not married before.

I felt myself happy in my new situation, and where is that station which can confer a more substantial system of felicity than that of an American farmer possessing freedom of action, freedom of thoughts, ruled by a mode of government which requires but little from us? I owe nothing but a peppercorn to my country, a small tribute to my king, with loyalty and due respect; I know no other landlord than the lord of all land, to whom I owe the most sincere gratitude. My father left me three hundred and seventy-one acres of land, forty-seven of which are good timothy meadow; an excellent orchard; a good house; and a substantial barn. It is my duty to think

how happy I am that he lived to build and to pay for all these improvements; what are the labours which I have to undergo, what are my fatigues, when compared to his, who had everything to do, from the first tree he felled to the finishing of his house? Every year I kill from 1,500 to 2,000 weight of pork, 1,200 of beef, half a dozen of good wethers in harvest; of fowls my wife has always a great stock; what can I wish more? My Negroes are tolerably faithful and healthy; by a long series of industry and honest dealings, my father left behind him the name of a good man; I have but to tread his paths to be happy and a good man like him. I know enough of the law to regulate my little concerns with propriety, nor do I dread its power; these are the grand outlines of my situation, but as I can feel much more than I am able to express, I hardly know how to proceed.

When my first son was born, the whole train of my ideas was suddenly altered; never was there a charm that acted so quickly and powerfully; I ceased to ramble in imagination through the wide world; my excursions since have not exceeded the bounds of my farm, and all my principal pleasures are now centred within its scanty limits; but at the same time, there is not an operation belonging to it in which I do not find some food for useful reflections. This is the reason, I suppose, that when you were here, you used, in your refined style, to denominate me the farmer of feelings; how rude must those feelings be in him who daily holds the axe or the plough, how much more refined on the contrary those of the European, whose mind is improved by education, example, books, and by every acquired advantage! Those feelings, however, I will delineate as well as I can, agreeably to your earnest request.

When I contemplate my wife, by my fireside, while she either spins, knits, darns, or suckles our child, I cannot describe the various emotions of love, of gratitude, of conscious pride, which thrill in my heart and often overflow in involuntary tears. I feel the necessity, the sweet pleasure, of acting my part, the part of an husband and father, with an attention and propriety which may entitle me to my good fortune. It is true these pleasing images vanish with the smoke of my pipe, but though they disappear from my mind, the impression they have made on my heart is indelible. When I play with the infant, my warm imagination runs forward and eagerly anticipates his future temper and constitution. I would willingly open the book of fate and know in which page his destiny is delineated. Alas! Where is the father who in those moments of paternal ecstasy can delineate one half of the thoughts which dilate his heart? I am sure I cannot; then again, I fear for the health of those who are become so dear to me, and in their sicknesses I severely pay for the joys I experienced while they were well. Whenever I go abroad, it is always involuntary. I never return home without feeling some pleasing emotion, which I often suppress as useless and foolish. The instant I enter on my own land, the bright idea of property, of exclusive right, of independence, exalt my mind. Precious soil, I say to myself, by what singular custom of law is it that thou wast made to constitute the riches of the freeholder? What should we American farmers be without the distinct possession of that soil? It feeds, it clothes us; from it we draw even a great exuberancy, our best meat, our richest drink; the very honey of our bees comes from this privileged spot. No wonder we should thus cherish its possession; no wonder that so many Europeans who have never been able to say that such portion of land was theirs cross the Atlantic to realize that happiness. This formerly rude soil has been converted by my father into a pleasant farm, and in return, it has established all our rights; on it is founded our rank, our freedom, our power as citizens, our importance as inhabitants of such a district. These images, I must confess, I always behold with pleasure and extend them as far as my imagination can reach; for this is what may be called the true and the only philosophy of an American farmer.

Pray do not laugh in thus seeing an artless countryman tracing himself through the simple modifications of his life; remember that you have required it; therefore, with candour, though with diffidence, I endeavour to follow the thread of my feelings, but I cannot tell you all. Often when I plough my low ground, I place my little boy on a chair which screws to the beam of the plough—its motion and that of the horses please him; he is perfectly happy and begins to chat. As I lean over the handle, various are the thoughts which crowd into my mind. I am now doing for him, I say, what my father formerly did for me; may God enable him to live that he may perform the same operations for the same purposes when I am worn out and old! I relieve his mother of some trouble while I have him with me; the odoriferous furrow exhilarates his spirits and seems to do the child a great deal of good, for he looks more blooming since I have adopted that practice; can more pleasure, more dignity, be added to that primary occupation? The father thus ploughing with his child, and to feed his family, is inferior only to the emperor of China ploughing as an example to his kingdom. In the evening, when I return home through my low grounds, I am astonished at the myriads of insects which I perceive dancing in the beams of the setting sun. I was before scarcely acquainted with their existence; they are so small that it is difficult to distinguish them; they are carefully improving this short evening space, not daring to expose themselves to the blaze of our meridian sun. I never see an egg brought on my table but I feel penetrated with the wonderful change it would have undergone but for my gluttony; it might have been a gentle, useful hen leading her chicken with a care and vigilance which speaks shame to many women. A cock perhaps, arrayed with the most majestic plumes, tender to its mate, bold, courageous, endowed with an astonishing instinct, with thoughts, with memory, and every distinguishing characteristic of the reason of man. I never see my trees drop their leaves and their fruit in the autumn, and bud again in the spring, without wonder; the sagacity of those animals which have long been the tenants of my farm astonish me; some of them seem to surpass even men in memory and sagacity. I could tell you singular instances of that kind. What, then, is this instinct which we so debase, and of which we are taught to entertain so diminutive an idea? My bees, above any other tenants of my farm, attract my attention and respect; I am astonished to see that nothing exists but what has its enemy; one species pursues and lives upon the other: unfortunately, our king-birds are the destroyers of those industrious insects, but on the other hand, these birds preserve our fields from the depredation of crows, which they pursue on the wing with great vigilance and astonishing dexterity.

Thus divided by two interested motives, I have long resisted the desire I had to kill them until last year, when I thought they increased too much, and my indulgence had been carried too far; it was at the time of swarming, when they all came and fixed themselves on the neighbouring trees whence they caught those that returned loaded from the fields. This made me resolve to kill as many as I could, and was just ready to fire when a bunch of bees as big as my fist issued from one of the hives, rushed on one of these birds, and probably stung him, for he instantly screamed and flew, not as before, in an irregular manner, but in a direct line. He was followed by the same bold phalanx, at a considerable distance, which unfortunately, becoming too sure of victory, quitted their military array and disbanded themselves. By this inconsiderate step, they lost all that aggregate of force which had made the bird fly off. Perceiving their disorder, he immediately returned and snapped as many as he wanted; nay, he had even the impudence to alight on the very twig from which the bees had driven him. I killed him and immediately opened his craw, from which I took 171 bees; I laid them all on a blanket in the sun, and to my great surprise, 54 returned to life, licked themselves clean, and joyfully went back to the hive, where they probably informed their companions of such an adventure and escape as I believe had never happened before to American bees! I draw a great fund of pleasure from the quails which inhabit my farm; they abundantly repay me, by their various notes and peculiar tameness, for the inviolable hospitality I constantly show them in the winter. Instead of perfidiously taking advantage of their great and affecting distress when nature offers nothing but a barren universal bed of snow, when irresistible necessity forces them to my barn doors, I permit them to feed unmolested; and it is not the least agreeable spectacle which that dreary season presents, when I see those beautiful birds, tamed by hunger, intermingling with all my cattle and sheep, seeking in security for the poor, scanty grain which but for them would be useless and lost. Often in the angles of the fences where the motion

of the wind prevents the snow from settling, I carry
them both chaff and grain, the one to feed them, the
other to prevent their tender feet from freezing fast to
the earth as I have frequently observed them to do.

I do not know an instance in which the singular barbarity of man is so strongly delineated as in the catching
and murthering those harmless birds, at that cruel season
of the year. Mr. ——, one of the most famous and extraordinary farmers that has ever done honour to the
province of Connecticut, by his timely and humane assistance in a hard winter, saved this species from being
entirely destroyed. They perished all over the country;
none of their delightful whistlings were heard the next
spring but upon this gentleman's farm; and to his humanity we owe the continuation of their music. When the
severities of that season have dispirited all my cattle, no
farmer ever attends them with more pleasure than I do;
it is one of those duties which is sweetened with the most
rational satisfaction. I amuse myself in beholding their
different tempers, actions, and the various effects of their
instinct now powerfully impelled by the force of hunger. I
trace their various inclinations and the different effects of
their passions, which are exactly the same as among
men; the law is to us precisely what I am in my barn-
yard, a bridle and check to prevent the strong and greedy
from oppressing the timid and weak. Conscious of superiority, they always strive to encroach on their neighbours; unsatisfied with their portion, they eagerly swallow
it in order to have an opportunity of taking what is given
to others, except they are prevented. Some I chide; others, unmindful of my admonitions, receive some blows.
Could victuals thus be given to men without the assistance of any language, I am sure they would not behave
better to one another, nor more philosophically than
my cattle do.

The same spirit prevails in the stable; but there I have
to do with more generous animals, there my well-known
voice has immediate influence and soon restores peace
and tranquillity. Thus, by superior knowledge I govern
all my cattle, as wise men are obliged to govern fools
and the ignorant. A variety of other thoughts crowd on
my mind at that peculiar instant, but they all vanish by
the time I return home. If in a cold night I swiftly travel

in my sledge, carried along at the rate of twelve miles an hour, many are the reflections excited by surrounding circumstances. I ask myself what sort of an agent is that which we call frost? Our minister compares it to needles, the points of which enter our pores. What is become of the heat of the summer; in what part of the world is it that the N. W.* keeps these grand magazines of nitre? When I see in the morning a river over which I can travel, that in the evening before was liquid, I am astonished indeed! What is become of those millions of insects which played in our summer fields and in our evening meadows; they were so puny and so delicate, the period of their existence was so short, that one cannot help wondering how they could learn, in that short space, the sublime art to hide themselves and their offspring in so perfect a manner as to baffle the rigour of the season and preserve that precious embryo of life, that small portion of ethereal heat, which if once destroyed would destroy the species! Whence that irresistible propensity to sleep so common in all those who are severely attacked by the frost? Dreary as this season appears, yet it has, like all others, its miracles; it presents to man a variety of problems which he can never resolve; among the rest, we have here a set of small birds which never appear until the snow falls; contrary to all others, they dwell and appear to delight in that element.

It is my bees, however, which afford me the most pleasing and extensive themes; let me look at them when I will, their government, their industry, their quarrels, their passions, always present me with something new; for which reason, when weary with labour, my common place of rest is under my locust-trees, close by my bee-house. By their movements I can predict the weather and can tell the day of their swarming; but the most difficult point is, when on the wing, to know whether they want to go to the woods or not. If they have previously pitched in some hollow trees, it is not the allurements of salt and water, of fennel, hickory leaves, etc., nor the finest box, that can induce them to stay; they will prefer those rude, rough habitations to the best polished mahogany hive. When that is the case with mine, I seldom thwart their inclinations; it is in freedom that they work;

* Presumably New World—Ed.

were I to confine them, they would dwindle away and quit their labour. In such excursions, we only part for a while; I am generally sure to find them again the following fall. This elopement of theirs only adds to my recreations; I know how to deceive even their superlative instinct; nor do I fear losing them, though eighteen miles from my house and lodged in the most lofty trees in the most impervious of our forests. I once took you along with me in one of these rambles, and yet you insist on my repeating the detail of our operations; it brings back into my mind many of the useful and entertaining reflections with which you so happily beguiled our tedious hours.

After I have done sowing, by way of recreation I prepare for a week's jaunt in the woods, not to hunt either the deer or the bears, as my neighbours do, but to catch the more harmless bees. I cannot boast that this chase is so noble or so famous among men, but I find it less fatiguing, and full as profitable; and the last consideration is the only one that moves me. I take with me my dog, as a companion, for he is useless as to this game; my gun, for no man you know ought to enter the woods without one; my blanket; some provisions; some wax; vermilion; honey; and a small pocket compass. With these implements, I proceed to such woods as are at a considerable distance from any settlements. I carefully examine whether they abound with large trees; if so, I make a small fire on some flat stones in a convenient place; on the fire I put some wax; close by this fire, on another stone, I drop honey in distinct drops, which I surround with small quantities of vermilion, laid on the stone; and then I retire carefully to watch whether any bees appear. If there are any in that neighbourhood, I rest assured that the smell of the burnt wax will unavoidably attract them; they will soon find out the honey, for they are fond of preying on that which is not their own; and in their approach they will necessarily tinge themselves with some particles of vermilion, which will adhere long to their bodies. I next fix my compass, to find out their course, which they keep invariably straight when they are returning home loaded. By the assistance of my watch, I observe how long those are returning which are marked with vermilion. Thus possessed of the course, and in some measure of the distance, which I can easily guess at, I follow the first, and seldom

hunting bees

fail of coming to the tree where those republics are lodged. I then mark it; and thus, with patience, I have found out sometimes eleven swarms in a season; and it is inconceivable what a quantity of honey these trees will sometimes afford. It entirely depends on the size of the hollow, as the bees never rest nor swarm till it is all replenished; for like men, it is only the want of room that induces them to quit the maternal hive. Next I proceed to some of the nearest settlements, where I procure proper assistance to cut down the trees, get all my prey secured, and then return home with my prize. The first bees I ever procured were thus found in the woods, by mere accident; for at that time I had no kind of skill in this method of tracing them. The body of the tree being perfectly sound, they had lodged themselves in the hollow of one of its principal limbs, which I carefully sawed off and with a great deal of labour and industry brought it home, where I fixed it up in the same position in which I found it growing. This was in April; I had five swarms that year, and they have been ever since very prosperous. This business generally takes up a week of my time every fall, and to me it is a week of solitary ease and relaxation.

The seed is by that time committed to the ground; there is nothing very material to do at home, and this additional quantity of honey enables me to be more generous to my home bees, and my wife to make a due quantity of mead. The reason, sir, that you found mine better than that of others is that she puts two gallons of brandy in each barrel, which ripens it and takes off that sweet, luscious taste, which it is apt to retain a long time. If we find anywhere in the woods (no matter on whose land) what is called a bee-tree, we must mark it; in the fall of the year when we propose to cut it down, our duty is to inform the proprietor of the land, who is entitled to half the contents; if this is not complied with, we are exposed to an action of trespass, as well as he who should go and cut down a bee-tree which he had neither found out nor marked.

We have twice a year the pleasure of catching pigeons, whose numbers are sometimes so astonishing as to obscure the sun in their flight. Where is it that they hatch? For such multitudes must require an immense quantity

of food. I fancy they breed toward the plains of Ohio
and those about Lake Michigan, which abound in wild
oats, though I have never killed any that had that grain
in their craws. In one of them, last year, I found some
undigested rice. Now, the nearest rice fields from where
I live must be at least 560 miles; and either their diges-
tion must be suspended while they are flying, or else they
must fly with the celerity of the wind. We catch them
with a net extended on the ground, to which they are
allured by what we call tame wild pigeons, made blind
and fastened to a long string: his short flights and his repeated calls never fail to bring them down. The greatest
number I ever caught was fourteen dozen, though much
larger quantities have often been trapped. I have frequently seen them at the market so cheap that for a
penny you might have as many as you could carry away;
and yet, from the extreme cheapness you must not conclude that they are but an ordinary food; on the contrary,
I think they are excellent. Every farmer has a tame wild
pigeon in a cage at his door all the year round, in order
to be ready whenever the season comes for catching
them.

The pleasure I receive from the warblings of the birds
in the spring is superior to my poor description, as the
continual succession of their tuneful notes is forever
new to me. I generally rise from bed about that indistinct
interval, which, properly speaking, is neither night nor
day; for this is the moment of the most universal vocal
choir. Who can listen unmoved to the sweet love tales
of our robins, told from tree to tree? Or to the shrill cat-
birds? The sublime accents of the thrush from on high
always retard my steps that I may listen to the delicious
music. The variegated appearances of the dewdrops as
they hang to the different objects must present even to a
clownish imagination the most voluptuous ideas. The astonishing art which all birds display in the construction of
their nests, ill-provided as we may suppose them with
proper tools, their neatness, their convenience, always
make me ashamed of the slovenliness of our houses; their
love to their dame, their incessant careful attention, and
the peculiar songs they address to her while she tediously
incubates their eggs, remind me of my duty could I ever
forget it. Their affection to their helpless little ones is a

lively precept; and in short, the whole economy of what we proudly call the brute creation is admirable in every circumstance; and vain man, though adorned with the additional gift of reason, might learn from the perfection of instinct how to regulate the follies and how to temper the errors which this second gift often makes him commit. This is a subject on which I have often bestowed the most serious thoughts; I have often blushed within myself, and been greatly astonished, when I have compared the unerring path they all follow, all just, all proper, all wise, up to the necessary degree of perfection, with the coarse, the imperfect systems of men, not merely as governors and kings, but as masters, as husbands, as fathers, as citizens. But this is a sanctuary in which an ignorant farmer must not presume to enter.

If ever man was permitted to receive and enjoy some blessings that might alleviate the many sorrows to which he is exposed, it is certainly in the country, when he attentively considers those ravishing scenes with which he is everywhere surrounded. This is the only time of the year in which I am avaricious of every moment; I therefore lose none that can add to this simple and inoffensive happiness. I roam early throughout all my fields; not the least operation do I perform which is not accompanied with the most pleasing observations; were I to extend them as far as I have carried them, I should become tedious; you would think me guilty of affectation, and perhaps I should represent many things as pleasurable from which you might not perhaps receive the least agreeable emotions. But, believe me, what I write is all true and real.

Some time ago, as I sat smoking a contemplative pipe in my piazza, I saw with amazement a remarkable instance of selfishness displayed in a very small bird, which I had hitherto respected for its inoffensiveness. Three nests were placed almost contiguous to each other in my piazza: that of a swallow was affixed in the corner next to the house; that of a phoebe in the other; a wren possessed a little box which I had made on purpose and hung between. Be not surprised at their tameness; all my family had long been taught to respect them as well as myself. The wren had shown before signs of dislike to the box which I had given it, but I knew not on what ac-

count; at last it resolved, small as it was, to drive the
swallow from its own habitation, and to my very great
surprise it succeeded. Impudence often gets the better of
modesty, and this exploit was no sooner performed than
it removed every material to its own box with the most
admirable dexterity; the signs of triumph appeared very
visible: it fluttered its wings with uncommon velocity, an
universal joy was perceivable in all its movements. Where
did this little bird learn that spirit of injustice? It was
not endowed with what we term reason! Here, then, is a
proof that both those gifts border very near on one another, for we see the perfection of the one mixing with
the errors of the other! The peaceable swallow, like the
passive Quaker, meekly sat at a small distance and never
offered the least resistance; but no sooner was the plunder carried away than the injured bird went to work
with unabated ardour, and in a few days the depredations were repaired. To prevent, however, a repetition of
the same violence, I removed the wren's box to another
part of the house.

In the middle of my parlour, I have, you may
remember, a curious republic of industrious hornets;
their nest hangs to the ceiling by the same twig on which
it was so admirably built and contrived in the woods. Its
removal did not displease them, for they find in my house
plenty of food; and I have left a hole open in one of the
panes of the window, which answers all their purposes.
By this kind usage they are become quite harmless; they
live on the flies, which are very troublesome to us throughout the summer; they are constantly busy in catching
them, even on the eyelids of my children. It is surprising
how quickly they smear them with a sort of glue, lest
they might escape; and when thus prepared, they carry
them to their nests as food for their young ones. These
globular nests are most ingeniously divided into many
stories, all provided with cells and proper communications. The materials with which this fabric is built they
procure from the cottony furze, with which our oak rails
are covered; this substance, tempered with glue, produces
a sort of pasteboard which is very strong and resists all
the inclemencies of the weather. By their assistance, I
am but little troubled with flies. All my family are so accustomed to their strong buzzing that no one takes any

notice of them; and though they are fierce and vindictive, yet kindness and hospitality has made them useful and harmless.

We have a great variety of wasps; most of them build their nests in mud, which they fix against the shingles of our roofs as nigh the pitch as they can. These aggregates represent nothing, at first view, but coarse and irregular lumps; but if you break them, you will observe that the inside of them contains a great number of oblong cells, in which they deposit their eggs and in which they bury themselves in the fall of the year. Thus immured, they securely pass through the severity of that season, and on the return of the sun, are enabled to perforate their cells and to open themselves a passage from these recesses into the sunshine. The yellow wasps, which build underground, in our meadows, are much more to be dreaded, for when the mower unwittingly passes his scythe over their holes, they immediately sally forth with a fury and velocity superior even to the strength of man. They make the boldest fly, and the only remedy is to lie down and cover our heads with hay, for it is only at the head they aim their blows; nor is there any possibility of finishing that part of the work until, by means of fire and brimstone, they are all silenced. But though I have been obliged to execute this dreadful sentence in my own defence, I have often thought it a great pity, for the sake of a little hay, to lay waste so ingenious a subterranean town, furnished with every conveniency and built with a most surprising mechanism.

I never should have done were I to recount the many objects which involuntarily strike my imagination in the midst of my work and spontaneously afforded me the most pleasing relief. These may appear insignificant trifles to a person who has travelled through Europe and America and is acquainted with books and with many sciences; but such simple objects of contemplation suffice me, who have no time to bestow on more extensive observations. Happily, these require no study; they are obvious, they gild the moments I dedicate to them, and enliven the severe labours which I perform. At home, my happiness springs from very different objects; the gradual unfolding of my children's reason, the study of their dawning tempers, attract all my paternal attention. I have to contrive little

punishments for their little faults, small encouragements for their good actions, and a variety of other expedients dictated by various occasions. But these are themes unworthy your perusal, and which ought not to be carried beyond the walls of my house, being domestic mysteries adapted only to the locality of the small sanctuary wherein my family resides. Sometimes I delight in inventing and executing machines which simplify my wife's labour. I have been tolerably successful that way; and these, sir, are the narrow circles within which I constantly revolve; and what can I wish for beyond them? I bless God for all the good He has given me; I envy no man's prosperity, and with no other portion of happiness than that I may live to teach the same philosophy to my children and give each of them a farm, show them how to cultivate it, and be like their father, good, substantial, independent American farmers—an appellation which will be the most fortunate one a man of my class can possess so long as our civil government continues to shed blessings on our husbandry. Adieu.

LETTER III

WHAT IS AN AMERICAN?

I wish I could be acquainted with the feelings and thoughts which must agitate the heart and present themselves to the mind of an enlightened Englishman when he first lands on this continent. He must greatly rejoice that he lived at a time to see this fair country discovered and settled; he must necessarily feel a share of national pride when he views the chain of settlements which embellish these extended shores. When he says to himself, "This is the work of my countrymen, who, when convulsed by factions, afflicted by a variety of miseries and wants, restless and impatient, took refuge here. They brought along with them their national genius, to which they principally owe what liberty they enjoy and what substance they possess." Here he sees the industry of his native country displayed in a new manner and traces in their works the embryos of all the arts, sciences, and ingenuity which flourish in Europe. Here he beholds fair cities, substantial villages, extensive fields, an immense country filled with decent houses, good roads, orchards, meadows, and bridges where an hundred years ago all was wild, woody, and uncultivated! What a train of pleasing ideas this fair spectacle must suggest; it is a prospect which must inspire a good citizen with the most heart-felt

66

pleasure. The difficulty consists in the manner of viewing
so extensive a scene. He is arrived on a new continent;
a modern society offers itself to his contemplation, different from what he had hitherto seen. It is not composed, as
in Europe, of great lords who possess everything and of a
herd of people who have nothing. Here are no aristo-
cratical families, no courts, no kings, no bishops, no
ecclesiastical dominion, no invisible power giving to a few
a very visible one, no great manufactures employing
thousands, no great refinements of luxury. The rich and
the poor are not so far removed from each other as they
are in Europe. Some few towns excepted, we are all tillers
of the earth, from Nova Scotia to West Florida. We are
a people of cultivators scattered over an immense territory, communicating with each other by means of good
roads and navigable rivers, united by the silken bands
of mild government, all respecting the laws without dreading their power, because they are equitable. We are all
animated with the spirit of an industry which is unfet-
tered and unrestrained, because each person works for
himself. If he travels through our rural districts, he views
not the hostile castle and the haughty mansion, contrasted
with the clay-built hut and miserable cabin, where cattle
and men help to keep each other warm and dwell in
meanness, smoke, and indigence. A pleasing uniformity of
decent competence appears throughout our habitations.
The meanest of our log-houses is a dry and comfortable
habitation. Lawyer or merchant are the fairest titles our
towns afford; that of a farmer is the only appellation
of the rural inhabitants of our country. It must take some
time ere he can reconcile himself to our dictionary, which
is but short in words of dignity and names of honour.
There, on a Sunday, he sees a congregation of respectable
farmers and their wives, all clad in neat homespun, well
mounted, or riding in their own humble waggons. There
is not among them an esquire, saving the unlettered
magistrate. There he sees a parson as simple as his flock,
a farmer who does not riot on the labour of others. We
have no princes for whom we toil, starve, and bleed;
we are the most perfect society now existing in the world.
Here man is free as he ought to be, nor is this pleasing equality so transitory as many others are. Many ages
will not see the shores of our great lakes replenished with

inland nations, nor the unknown bounds of North America entirely peopled. Who can tell how far it extends? Who can tell the millions of men whom it will feed and contain? For no European foot has as yet travelled half the extent of this mighty continent!

The next wish of this traveller will be to know whence came all these people. They are a mixture of English, Scotch, Irish, French, Dutch, Germans, and Swedes. From this promiscuous breed, that race now called Americans have arisen. The eastern provinces must indeed be excepted as being the unmixed descendants of Englishmen. I have heard many wish that they had been more intermixed also; for my part, I am no wisher and think it much better as it has happened. They exhibit a most conspicuous figure in this great and variegated picture; they too enter for a great share in the pleasing perspective displayed in these thirteen provinces. I know it is fashionable to reflect on them, but I respect them for what they have done; for the accuracy and wisdom with which they have settled their territory; for the decency of their manners; for their early love of letters; their ancient college, the first in this hemisphere; for their industry, which to me who am but a farmer is the criterion of everything. There never was a people, situated as they are, who with so ungrateful a soil have done more in so short a time. Do you think that the monarchical ingredients which are more prevalent in other governments have purged them from all foul stains? Their histories assert the contrary.

In this great American asylum, the poor of Europe have by some means met together, and in consequence of various causes; to what purpose should they ask one another what countrymen they are? Alas, two thirds of them had no country. Can a wretch who wanders about, who works and starves, whose life is a continual scene of sore affliction or pinching penury—can that man call England or any other kingdom his country? A country that had no bread for him, whose fields procured him no harvest, who met with nothing but the frowns of the rich, the severity of the laws, with jails and punishments, who owned not a single foot of the extensive surface of this planet? No! Urged by a variety of motives, here they came. Everything has tended to regenerate them:

new laws, a new mode of living, a new social system; here they are become men: in Europe they were as so many useless plants, wanting vegetative mould and refreshing showers; they withered, and were mowed down by want, hunger, and war; but now, by the power of transplantation, like all other plants they have taken root and flourished! Formerly they were not numbered in any civil lists of their country, except in those of the poor; here they rank as citizens. By what invisible power hath this surprising metamorphosis been performed? By that of the laws and that of their industry. The laws, the indulgent laws, protect them as they arrive, stamping on them the symbol of adoption; they receive ample rewards for their labours; these accumulated rewards procure them lands; those lands confer on them the title of freemen, and to that title every benefit is affixed which men can possibly require. This is the great operation daily performed by our laws. Whence proceed these laws? From our government. Whence that government? It is derived from the original genius and strong desire of the people ratified and confirmed by the crown. This is the great chain which links us all, this is the picture which every province exhibits, Nova Scotia excepted. There the crown has done all; either there were no people who had genius or it was not much attended to; the consequence is that the province is very thinly inhabited indeed; the power of the crown in conjunction with the musketos has prevented men from settling there. Yet some parts of it flourished once, and it contained a mild, harmless set of people. But for the fault of a few leaders, the whole was banished. The greatest political error the crown ever committed in America was to cut off men from a country which wanted nothing but men!

What attachment can a poor European emigrant have for a country where he had nothing? The knowledge of the language, the love of a few kindred as poor as himself, were the only cords that tied him; his country is now that which gives him his land, bread, protection, and consequence; *Ubi panis ibi patria* is the motto of all emigrants. What, then, is the American, this new man? He is either an European or the descendant of an European; hence that strange mixture of blood, which you will find in no other country. I could point out to you a family whose grandfather was an Englishman, whose wife was Dutch, whose son married a French woman, and whose present four sons have now four wives of different nations. *He* is an American, who, leaving behind him all his ancient prejudices and manners, receives new ones from the new mode of life he has embraced, the new government he obeys, and the new rank he holds. He becomes an American by being received in the broad lap of our great Alma Mater. Here individuals of all nations are melted into a new race of men, whose labours and posterity will one day cause great changes in the world. Americans are the western pilgrims who are carrying along with them that great mass of arts, sciences, vigour, and industry which began long since in the East; they will finish the great circle. The Americans were once scattered all over Europe; here they are incorporated into one of the finest systems of population which has ever appeared, and which will hereafter become distinct by the power of the different climates they inhabit. The American ought therefore to love this country much better than that wherein either he or his forefathers were born. Here the rewards of his industry follow with equal steps the progress of his labour; his labour is founded on the basis of nature, self-interest; can it want a stronger allurement? Wives and children, who before in vain demanded of him a morsel of bread, now, fat and frolicsome, gladly help their father to clear those fields whence exuberant crops are to arise to feed and to clothe them all, without any part being claimed, either by a despotic prince, a rich abbot, or a mighty lord. Here religion demands but little of him: a small voluntary salary to the minister and gratitude to God; can he refuse these? The American is a new man, who acts upon new principles; he must therefore entertain new ideas and form new opinions. From involuntary idleness, servile dependence, penury, and useless labour, he has passed to toils of a very different nature, rewarded by ample subsistence. This is an American.

British America is divided into many provinces, forming a large association scattered along a coast of 1,500 miles extent and about 200 wide. This society I would fain examine, at least such as it appears in the middle provinces; if it does not afford that variety of tinges and gradations which may be observed in Europe, we have colours peculiar to ourselves. For instance, it is natural to conceive that those who live near the sea must be very different from those who live in the woods; the intermediate space will afford a separate and distinct class.

Men are like plants; the goodness and flavour of the fruit proceeds from the peculiar soil and exposition in which they grow. We are nothing but what we derive from the air we breathe, the climate we inhabit, the government we obey, the system of religion we profess, and the nature of our employment. Here you will find but few crimes; these have acquired as yet no root among us. I wish I were able to trace all my ideas; if my ignorance prevents me from describing them properly, I hope I shall be able to delineate a few of the outlines, which is all I propose.

Those who live near the sea feed more on fish than on flesh and often encounter that boisterous element. This renders them more bold and enterprising; this leads them to neglect the confined occupations of the land. They see and converse with a variety of people; their intercourse with mankind becomes extensive. The sea inspires them with a love of traffic, a desire of transporting produce from one place to another, and leads them to a variety of resources which supply the place of labour. Those who inhabit the middle settlements, by far the most numerous, must be very different; the simple cultivation of the earth purifies them, but the indulgences of the government, the soft remonstrances of religion, the rank of independent freeholders, must necessarily inspire them with sentiments, very little known in Europe among a people of the same class. What do I say? Europe has no such class of men; the early knowledge they acquire, the early bargains they make, give them a great degree of sagacity. As freemen, they will be litigious; pride and obstinacy are often the cause of lawsuits; the nature of our laws and governments may be another. As citizens, it is easy to imagine that they will carefully read the newspapers, enter into every political disquisition, freely blame or censure governors and others. As farmers, they will be careful and anxious to get as much as they can, because what they get is their own. As northern men, they will love the cheerful cup. As Christians, religion curbs them not in their opinions; the general indulgence leaves every one to think for themselves in spiritual matters; the law inspects our actions; our thoughts are left to God. Industry, good living, selfishness, litigiousness, country politics, the pride of freemen, religious indifference, are their characteristics. If you recede still farther from the sea, you will come into more modern settlements; they exhibit the same strong lineaments, in a ruder appearance. Religion seems to have still less influence, and their manners are less improved.

Now we arrive near the great woods, near the last inhabited districts; there men seem to be placed still farther beyond the reach of government, which in some measure leaves them to themselves. How can it pervade every corner, as they were driven there by misfortunes, necessity of beginnings, desire of acquiring large tracks of land, idleness, frequent want of economy, ancient debts; the reunion of such people does not afford a very pleasing spectacle. When discord, want of unity and friendship, when either drunkenness or idleness prevail in such remote districts, contention, inactivity, and wretchedness must ensue. There are not the same remedies to these evils as in a long-established community. The few magistrates they have are in general little better than the rest; they are often in a perfect state of war; that of man against man, sometimes decided by blows, sometimes by means of the law; that of man against every wild inhabitant of these venerable woods, of which they are come to dispossess them. There men appear to be no better than carnivorous animals of a superior rank, living on the flesh of wild animals when they can catch them, and when they are not able, they subsist on grain. He who would wish to see America in its proper light and have a true idea of its feeble beginnings and barbarous rudiments must visit our extended line of frontiers, where the last settlers dwell and where he may see the first labours of settlement, the mode of clearing the earth, in all their different appearances, where men are wholly left dependent on their native tempers and on the spur of uncertain industry, which often fails when not sanctified by the efficacy of a few moral rules. There, remote from the power of example and check of shame, many families exhibit the most hideous parts of our society. They are a kind of forlorn hope, preceding by ten or twelve years the most respectable army of veterans which come after them. In that space, prosperity will polish some, vice and the law will drive off the rest, who, uniting again with others like themselves, will recede still farther, making room for more industrious people, who will finish their improvements, convert the log-house into a convenient habitation, and rejoicing that the first heavy labours are finished, will change in a few years that hitherto barbarous country into a fine, fertile, well-regulated district. Such is our progress; such is the march of the Europeans toward the interior parts of this continent. In all societies there are off-casts; this impure part serves as our precursors or pioneers; my father himself was one of that class, but he came upon honest principles and was therefore one of the few who held fast; by good conduct and temperance, he transmitted to me his fair inheritance, when not above one in fourteen of his contemporaries had the same good fortune.

Forty years ago, this smiling country was thus inhabited; it is now purged, a general decency of manners prevails throughout, and such has been the fate of our best countries.

Exclusive of those general characteristics, each province has its own, founded on the government, climate, mode of husbandry, customs, and peculiarity of circumstances. Europeans submit insensibly to these great powers and become, in the course of a few generations, not only Americans in general, but either Pennsylvanians, Virginians, or provincials under some other name. Whoever traverses the continent must easily observe those strong differences, which will grow more evident in time. The inhabitants of Canada, Massachusetts, the middle provinces, the southern ones, will be as different as their climates; their only points of unity will be those of religion and language.

As I have endeavoured to show you how Europeans become Americans, it may not be disagreeable to show you likewise how the various Christian sects introduced wear out and how religious indifference becomes prevalent. When any considerable number of a particular sect happen to dwell contiguous to each other, they immediately erect a temple and there worship the Divinity agreeably to their own peculiar ideas. Nobody disturbs them. If any new sect springs up in Europe, it may happen that many of its professors will come and settle in America. As they bring their zeal with them, they are at liberty to make proselytes if they can and to build a meeting and to follow the dictates of their consciences; for neither the government nor any other power interferes. If they are peaceable subjects and are industrious, what is it to their neighbours how and in what manner they think fit to address their prayers to the Supreme Being? But if the sectaries are not settled close together, if they are mixed with other denominations, their zeal will cool for want of fuel, and will be extinguished in a little time. Then, the Americans become as to religion what they are as to country, allied to all. In them the name of Englishman, Frenchman, and European is lost, and in like manner, the strict modes of Christianity as practised in Europe are lost also. This effect will extend itself still farther hereafter, and though this may appear to you as a strange idea, yet it is a very true one. I shall be able, perhaps, hereafter to explain myself better; in the meanwhile, let the following example serve as my first justification.

Let us suppose you and I to be travelling; we observe that in this house, to the right, lives a Catholic, who prays to God as he has been taught and believes in transsubstantiation; he works and raises wheat, he has a large family of children, all hale and robust; his belief, his prayers, offend nobody. About one mile farther on the same road, his next neighbour may be a good, honest, plodding German Lutheran, who addresses himself to the same God, the God of all, agreeably to the modes he has been educated in, and believes in consubstantiation; by so doing, he scandalizes nobody; he also works in his fields, embellishes the earth, clears swamps, etc. What has the world to do with his Lutheran principles? He persecutes nobody, and nobody persecutes him; he visits his neighbours, and his neighbours visit him. Next to him lives a seceder, the most enthusiastic of all sectaries; his zeal is hot and fiery, but separated as he is from others of the same complexion, he has no congregation of his own to resort to where he might cabal and mingle religious pride with worldly obstinacy. He likewise raises good crops, his house is handsomely painted, his orchard is one of the fairest in the neighbourhood. How does it concern the welfare of the country, or of the province at large, what this man's religious sentiments are, or really whether he has any at all? He is a good farmer, he is a sober, peaceable, good citizen; William Penn himself would not wish for more. This is the visible character; the invisible one is only guessed at, and is nobody's business. Next, again, lives a Low Dutchman, who implicitly believes the rules laid down by the synod of Dort. He conceives no other idea of a clergyman than that of an hired man; if he does his work well, he will pay him the stipulated sum; if not, he will dismiss him, and do without his sermons, and let his church be shut up for years. But notwithstanding this coarse idea, you will find his house and farm to be the neatest in all the country; and you will judge by his waggon and fat horses that he thinks more of the affairs of this world than of those of the next. He is sober and laborious; therefore, he is all he ought to be as to the affairs of this life. As for those of the next, he must trust to the great Creator. Each of these people instruct their children as well as they can, but these instructions are feeble compared to those which are given to the youth of the poorest class in Europe. Their children will therefore grow up less zealous and more indifferent in matters of religion than their parents. The foolish vanity or, rather, the fury of making proselytes is unknown here; they have no time, the seasons call for all their attention, and thus in a few years this mixed neighbourhood will exhibit a strange religious medley that will be neither pure Catholicism nor pure Calvinism. A very perceptible indifference, even in the first generation, will become apparent; and it may happen that the daughter of the Catholic will marry the son of the seceder and settle by themselves at a distance from their parents. What religious education will they give their children? A very imperfect one. If there happens to be in the neighbourhood any place of worship, we will suppose a Quaker's meeting; rather than not show their fine clothes, they will go to it, and some of them may perhaps attach themselves to that society. Others will remain in a perfect state of indifference; the children of these zealous parents will not be able to tell what their religious principles are, and their grandchildren still less. The neighbourhood of a place of worship generally leads them to it, and the action of going thither is the strongest evidence they can give of their attachment to any sect. The Quakers are the only people who retain a fondness for their own mode of worship; for be they ever so far separated from each other, they hold a sort of communion with the society and seldom depart from its rules, at least in this country. Thus all sects are mixed, as well as all nations; thus religious indifference is imperceptibly disseminated from one end of the continent to the other, which is at present one of the strongest characteristics of the Americans. Where this will reach no one can tell; perhaps it may leave a vacuum fit to receive other systems. Persecution, religious pride, the love of contradiction, are the food of what the world commonly calls religion. These motives have ceased here; zeal in Europe is confined; here it evaporates in the great distance it has to travel; there it is a grain of powder inclosed; here it burns away in the open air and consumes without effect.

But to return to our back settlers. I must tell you that there is something in the proximity of the woods which is very singular. It is with men as it is with the plants and animals that grow and live in the forests; they are entirely different from those that live in the plains. I will candidly tell you all my thoughts, but you are not to expect that I shall advance any reasons. By living in or near the woods, their actions are regulated by the wildness of the neighbourhood. The deer often come to eat their grain, the wolves to destroy their sheep, the bears to kill their hogs, the foxes to catch their poultry. This surrounding hostility immediately puts the gun into their hands; they watch these animals, they kill some; and thus by defending their property, they soon become professed hunters; this is the progress; once hunters, farewell to the plough. The chase renders them ferocious, gloomy, and unsocial; a hunter wants no neighbour, he rather hates them because he dreads the competition. In a little time, their success in the woods makes them neglect their tillage. They trust to the natural fecundity of the earth and therefore do little; carelessness in fencing often exposes what little they sow to destruction; they are not at home to watch; in order, therefore, to make up the deficiency, they go oftener to the woods. That new mode of life brings along with it a new set of manners, which I cannot easily describe. These new manners being grafted on the old stock produce a strange sort of lawless profligacy, the impressions of which are indelible. The manners of the Indian natives are respectable compared with this European medley. Their wives and children live in sloth and inactivity; and having no proper pursuits, you may judge what education the latter receive. Their tender minds have nothing else to contemplate but the example of their parents; like them, they grow up a mongrel breed, half civilized, half savage, except nature stamps on them some constitutional propensities. That rich, that voluptuous sentiment is gone that struck them so forcibly; the possession of their freeholds no longer conveys to their minds the same pleasure and pride. To all these reasons you must add their lonely situation, and you cannot imagine what an effect on manners the great distances they live from each other has! Consider one of the last settlements in its first view: of what is it composed? Europeans who have not that sufficient share of knowledge they ought to have in order to prosper; people who have suddenly passed from oppression, dread of government, and fear of laws into the unlimited freedom of the woods. This sudden change must have a very great effect on most men, and on that class particularly. Eating of wild meat, whatever you may think, tends to alter their temper, though all the proof I can adduce is that I have seen it, and having no place of worship to resort to, what little society this might afford is denied them. The Sunday meetings, exclusive of religious benefits, were the only social bonds that might have inspired them with some degree of emulation in neatness. Is it, then, surprising to see men thus situated, immersed in great and heavy labours, degenerate a little? It is rather a wonder the effect is not more diffusive. The Moravians and the Quakers are the only instances in exception to what I have advanced. The first never settle singly; it is a colony of the society which emigrates; they carry with them their forms, worship, rules, and decency. The others never begin so hard; they are always able to buy improvements, in which there is a great advantage, for by that time the country is recovered from its first barbarity. Thus our bad people are those who are half cultivators and half hunters; and the worst of them are those who have degenerated altogether into the hunting state. As old ploughmen and new men of the woods, as Europeans and new-made Indians, they contract the vices of both; they adopt the moroseness and ferocity of a native, without his mildness or even his industry at home. If manners are not refined, at least they are rendered simple and inoffensive by tilling the earth. All our wants are supplied by it; our time is divided between labour and rest, and leaves none for the commission of great misdeeds. As hunters, it is divided between the toil of the chase, the idleness of repose, or the indulgence of inebriation. Hunting is but a licentious idle life, and if it does not always pervert good dispositions, yet, when it is united with bad luck, it leads to want: want stimulates that propensity to rapacity and injustice, too natural to needy men, which is the fatal gradation. After this explanation of the effects which follow by living in the woods, shall we yet vainly flatter ourselves with the hope of converting the Indians? We should rather begin with converting our back-settlers; and now if I dare mention the name of religion, its sweet accents would be lost in the immensity of these woods. Men thus placed are not fit either to receive or remember its mild instructions; they want temples and ministers, but as soon as men cease to remain at home and begin to lead an erratic life, let them be either tawny or white, they cease to be its disciples.

Thus have I faintly and imperfectly endeavoured to trace our society from the sea to our woods! Yet you must not imagine that every person who moves back acts upon the same principles or falls into the same degeneracy. Many families carry with them all their decency of conduct, purity of morals, and respect of religion, but these are scarce; the power of example is sometimes irresistible. Even among these back-settlers, their depravity is greater or less according to what nation or province they belong. Were I to adduce proofs of this, I might be accused of partiality. If there happens to be some rich intervals, some fertile bottoms, in those remote districts, the people will there prefer tilling the land to hunting and will attach themselves to it; but even on these fertile spots you may plainly perceive the inhabitants to acquire a great degree of rusticity and selfishness.

It is in consequence of this straggling situation and the astonishing power it has on manners that the back-settlers of both the Carolinas, Virginia, and many other parts have been long a set of lawless people; it has been even dangerous to travel among them. Government can do nothing in so extensive a country; better it should wink at these irregularities than that it should use means inconsistent with its usual mildness. Time will efface those stains: in proportion as the great body of population approaches them they will reform and become polished and subordinate. Whatever has been said of the four New England provinces, no such degeneracy of manners has ever tarnished their annals; their back-settlers have been kept within the bounds of decency, and government, by means of wise laws, and by the influence of religion. What a detestable idea such people must have given to the natives of the Europeans! They trade with them; the worst of people are permitted to do that which none but persons of the best characters should be employed in. They get drunk with them and often defraud the Indians. Their avarice, removed from the eyes of their superiors, knows no bounds; and aided by a little superiority of knowledge, these traders deceive them and even sometimes shed blood. Hence those shocking violations, those sudden devastations which have so often stained our frontiers, when hundreds of innocent people have been sacrificed for the crimes of a few. It was in consequence of such behaviour that the Indians took the hatchet against the Virginians in 1774. Thus are our first steps trodden, thus are our first trees felled, in general, by the most vicious of our people; and thus the path is opened for the arrival of a second and better class, the true American freeholders, the most respectable set of people in this part of the world: respectable for their industry, their happy independence, the great share of freedom they possess, the good regulation of their families, and for extending the trade and the dominion of our mother country.

Europe contains hardly any other distinctions but lords and tenants; this fair country alone is settled by freeholders, the possessors of the soil they cultivate, members of the government they obey, and the framers of their own laws, by means of their representatives. This is a thought which you have taught me to cherish; our distance from Europe, far from diminishing, rather adds to our usefulness and consequence as men and subjects. Had our forefathers remained there, they would only have crowded it and perhaps prolonged those convulsions which had shaken it so long. Every industrious European who transports himself here may be compared to a sprout growing at the foot of a great tree; it enjoys and draws but a little portion of sap; wrench it from the parent roots, transplant it, and it will become a tree bearing fruit also. Colonists are therefore entitled to the consideration due to the most useful subjects; a hundred families barely existing in some parts of Scotland will here in six years cause an annual exportation of 10,000 bushels of wheat, 100 bushels being but a common quantity for an industrious family to sell if they cultivate good land. It is here, then, that the idle may be employed, the useless become useful, and the poor become rich; but by riches I do not mean gold and silver—we have but little of those metals; I mean a better sort of wealth—cleared lands, cattle, good houses, good clothes, and an increase of people to enjoy them.

There is no wonder that this country has so many charms and presents to Europeans so many temptations to remain in it. A traveller in Europe becomes a stranger as soon as he quits his own kingdom; but it is otherwise here. We know, properly speaking, no strangers; his is every person's country; the variety of our soils, situations, climates, governments, and produce hath something which must please everybody. No sooner does an European arrive, no matter of what condition, than his eyes are opened upon the fair prospect: he hears his language spoke; he retraces many of his own country manners; he perpetually hears the names of families and towns with which he is acquainted; he sees happiness and prosperity in all places disseminated; he meets with hospitality, kindness, and plenty everywhere; he beholds hardly any poor; he seldom hears of punishments and executions; and he wonders at the elegance of our towns, those miracles of industry and freedom. He cannot admire enough our rural districts, our convenient roads, good taverns, and our many accommodations; he involuntarily loves a country where everything is so lovely. When in England, he was a mere Englishman; here he stands on a larger portion of the globe, not less than its fourth part, and may see the productions of the north, in iron and naval stores; the provisions of Ireland; the grain of Egypt; the indigo, the rice of China. He does not find, as in Europe, a crowded society where every place is overstocked; he does not feel that perpetual collision of parties, that difficulty of beginning, that contention which oversets so many. There is room for everybody in America; has he any particular talent or industry? He exerts it in order to procure a livelihood, and it succeeds. Is he a merchant? The avenues of trade are infinite. Is he eminent in any respect? He will be employed and respected. Does he love a country life? Pleasant farms present themselves; he may purchase what he wants and thereby become an American farmer. Is he a labourer, sober and industrious? He need not go many miles nor receive many informations before he will be hired, well fed at the table of his employer, and paid four or five times more than he can get in Europe. Does he want uncultivated lands? Thousands of acres present themselves, which he may purchase cheap. Whatever be his talents or inclinations, if they are moderate, he may satisfy them. I do not mean that every one who comes will grow rich in a little time; no, but he may procure an easy, decent maintenance by his industry. Instead of starving, he will be fed; instead of being idle, he will have employment: and these are riches enough for such men as come over here. The rich stay in Europe; it is only the middling and poor that emigrate. Would you wish to travel in independent idleness, from north to south, you will find easy access, and the most cheerful reception at every house; society without ostentation; good cheer without pride; and every decent diversion which the country affords, with little expense. It is no wonder that the European who has lived here a few years is desirous to remain; Europe with all its pomp is not to be compared to this continent for men of middle stations or labourers.

An European, when he first arrives, seems limited in his intentions, as well as in his views; but he very suddenly alters his scale; two hundred miles formerly appeared a very great distance, it is now but a trifle; he no sooner breathes our air than he forms schemes and embarks in designs he never would have thought of in his own country. There the plenitude of society confines many useful ideas and often extinguishes the most laudable schemes, which here ripen into maturity. Thus Europeans become Americans.

But how is this accomplished in that crowd of low, indigent people who flock here every year from all parts of Europe? I will tell you; they no sooner arrive than they immediately feel the good effects of that plenty of provisions we possess: they fare on our best food, and are kindly entertained; their talents, character, and peculiar industry are immediately inquired into; they find countrymen everywhere disseminated, let them come from whatever part of Europe. Let me select one as an epitome of the rest: he is hired, he goes to work, and works moderately; instead of being employed by a haughty person, he finds himself with his equal, placed at the substantial table of the farmer, or else at an inferior one as good; his wages are high, his bed is not like that bed of sorrow on which he used to lie; if he behaves with propriety, and is faithful, he is caressed, and becomes as it were a member of the family. He begins to feel the effects of a sort of resurrection; hitherto he had not lived, but simply vegetated; he now feels himself a man because he is treated as such; the laws of his own country had overlooked him in his insignificancy; the laws of this cover him with their mantle. Judge what an alteration there must arise in the mind and the thoughts of this man. He begins to forget his former servitude and dependence; his heart involuntarily swells and glows; this first swell inspires him with those new thoughts which constitute an American. What love can he entertain for a country where his existence was a burthen to him; if he is a generous, good man, the love of this new adoptive parent will sink deep into his heart. He looks around and sees many a prosperous person who but a few years before was as poor as himself. This encourages him much; he begins to form some little scheme, the first, alas, he ever formed in his life. If he is wise, he thus spends two or three years, in which time he acquires knowledge, the use of tools, the modes of working the lands, felling trees, etc. This prepares the foundation of a good name, the most useful acquisition he can make. He is encouraged, he has gained friends; he is advised and directed; he feels bold, he purchases some land; he gives all the money he has brought over, as well as what he has earned, and trusts to the God of harvests for the discharge of the rest. His good name procures him credit. He is now possessed of the deed, conveying to him and his posterity the fee simple and absolute property of two hundred acres of land, situated on such a river. What an epocha in this man's life! He is become a freeholder, from perhaps a German boor. He is now an American, a Pennsylvanian, an English subject. He is naturalized; his name is enrolled with those of the other citizens of the province. Instead of being a vagrant, he has a place of residence; he is called the inhabitant of such a county, or of such a district, and for the first time in his life counts for something, for hitherto he had been a cypher. I only repeat what I have heard many say, and no wonder their hearts should glow and be agitated with a multitude of feelings, not easy to describe. From nothing to start into being; from a servant to the rank of a master; from being the slave of some despotic prince, to become a free man, invested with lands to which every municipal blessing is annexed! What a change indeed! It is in consequence of that change that he becomes an American. This great metamorphosis has a double effect: it extinguishes all his European prejudices, he forgets that mechanism of subordination, that servility of disposition which poverty had taught him; and sometimes he is apt to forget it too much, often passing from one extreme to the other. If he is a good man, he forms schemes of future prosperity, he proposes to educate his children better than he has been educated himself; he thinks of future modes of conduct, feels an ardour to labour he never felt before. Pride steps in and leads him to everything that the laws do not forbid; he respects them; with a heart-felt gratitude he looks toward the east, toward that insular government from whose wisdom all his new felicity is derived and under whose wings and protection he now lives. These reflections constitute him the good man and the good subject. Ye poor Europeans—ye who sweat

and work for the great; ye who are obliged to give so
many sheaves to the church, so many to your lords, so
many to your government, and have hardly any left for
yourselves; ye who are held in less estimation than favourite hunters or useless lap-dogs; ye who only breathe
the air of nature because it cannot be withholden from you
—it is here that ye can conceive the possibility of those
feelings I have been describing; it is here the laws of
naturalization invite every one to partake of our great
labours and felicity, to till unrented, untaxed lands!
Many, corrupted beyond the power of amendment, have
brought with them all their vices, and disregarding the
advantages held to them, have gone on in their former
career of iniquity until they have been overtaken and
punished by our laws. It is not every emigrant who succeeds; no, it is only the sober, the honest, and industrious. Happy those to whom this transition has served
as a powerful spur to labour, to prosperity, and to the
good establishment of children, born in the days of their
poverty and who had no other portion to expect but the
rags of their parents had it not been for their happy emigration. Others, again, have been led astray by this enchanting scene; their new pride, instead of leading them
to the fields, has kept them in idleness; the idea of possessing lands is all that satisfied them—though surrounded
with fertility, they have mouldered away their time in
inactivity, misinformed husbandry, and ineffectual endeavours. How much wiser, in general, the honest Germans than almost all other Europeans; they hire themselves to some of their wealthy landsmen, and in that apprenticeship learn everything that is necessary. They attentively consider the prosperous industry of others,
which imprints in their minds a strong desire of possessing the same advantages. This forcible idea never quits
them; they launch forth, and by dint of sobriety, rigid
parsimony, and the most persevering industry, they commonly succeed. Their astonishment at their first arrival
from Germany is very great—it is to them a dream; the
contrast must be very powerful indeed; they observe their
countrymen flourishing in every place; they travel through
whole counties where not a word of English is spoken;
and in the names and the language of the people, they
retrace Germany. They have been an useful acquisition

to this continent, and to Pennsylvania in particular; to them it owes some share of its prosperity: to their mechanical knowledge and patience it owes the finest mills in all America, the best teams of horses, and many other advantages. The recollection of their former poverty and slavery never quits them as long as they live.

The Scotch and the Irish might have lived in their own country perhaps as poor, but enjoying more civil advantages, the effects of their new situation do not strike them so forcibly, nor has it so lasting an effect. Whence the difference arises I know not, but out of twelve families of emigrants of each country, generally seven Scotch will succeed, nine German, and four Irish. The Scotch are frugal and laborious, but their wives cannot work so hard as German women, who on the contrary vie with their husbands, and often share with them the most severe toils of the field, which they understand better. They have therefore nothing to struggle against but the common casualties of nature. The Irish do not prosper so well; they love to drink and to quarrel; they are litigious and soon take to the gun, which is the ruin of everything; they seem beside to labour under a greater degree of ignorance in husbandry than the others; perhaps it is that their industry had less scope and was less exercised at home. I have heard many relate how the land was parcelled out in that kingdom; their ancient conquest has been a great detriment to them, by oversetting their landed property. The lands possessed by a few are leased down ad infinitum, and the occupiers often pay five guineas an acre. The poor are worse lodged there than anywhere else in Europe; their potatoes, which are easily raised, are perhaps an inducement to laziness: their wages are too low and their whisky too cheap.

There is no tracing observations of this kind without making at the same time very great allowances, as there are everywhere to be found a great many exceptions. The Irish themselves, from different parts of that kingdom, are very different. It is difficult to account for this surprising locality; one would think on so small an island an Irishman must be an Irishman. Yet it is not so; they are different in their aptitude to and in their love of labour.

The Scotch, on the contrary, are all industrious and

saving; they want nothing more than a field to exert themselves in, and they are commonly sure of succeeding. The only difficulty they labour under is that technical American knowledge which requires some time to obtain; it is not easy for those who seldom saw a tree to conceive how it is to be felled, cut up, and split into rails and posts.

As I am fond of seeing and talking of prosperous families, I intend to finish this letter by relating to you the history of an honest Scotch Hebridean who came here in 1774, which will show you in epitome what the Scotch can do wherever they have room for the exertion of their industry. Whenever I hear of any new settlement, I pay it a visit once or twice a year, on purpose to observe the different steps each settler takes; the gradual improvements; the different tempers of each family, on which their prosperity in a great measure depends; their different modifications of industry; their ingenuity and contrivance; for being all poor, their life requires sagacity and prudence. In an evening, I love to hear them tell their stories; they furnish me with new ideas; I sit still and listen to their ancient misfortunes, observing in many of them a strong degree of gratitude to God and the government. Many a well-meant sermon have I preached to some of them. When I found laziness and inattention prevail, who could refrain from wishing well to these new countrymen, after having undergone so many fatigues. Who could withhold good advice? What a happy change it must be to descend from the high, sterile, bleak lands of Scotland, where everything is barren and cold, and to rest on some fertile farms in these middle provinces! Such a transition must have afforded the most pleasing satisfaction.

The following dialogue passed at an out-settlement, where I lately paid a visit:

"Well, friend, how do you do now; I am come fifty odd miles on purpose to see you; how do you go on with your new cutting and slashing?" "Very well, good sir; we learn the use of the axe bravely, we shall make it out; we have a belly full of victuals every day; our cows run about and come home full of milk; our hogs get fat of themselves in the woods. Oh, this is a good country! God bless the king and William Penn; we shall do very well by and by, if we keep our healths." "Your log-house looks neat and light; where did you get these shingles?" "One of our neighbours is a New England man, and he showed us how to split them out of chestnut-trees. Now for a barn, but all in good time; here are fine trees to build it with." "Who is to frame it; sure you do not understand that work yet?" "A countryman of ours who has been in America these ten years offers to wait for his money until the second crop is lodged in it." "What did you give for your land?" "Thirty-five shillings per acre, payable in seven years." "How many acres have you got?" "A hundred and fifty." "That is enough to begin with; is not your land pretty hard to clear?" "Yes, sir, hard enough, but it would be harder still if it was already cleared, for then we should have no timber, and I love the woods much; the land is nothing without them." "Have not you found out any bees yet?" "No, sir; and if we had, we should not know what to do with them." "I will tell you by and by." "You are very kind." "Farewell, honest man; God prosper you; whenever you travel toward——, inquire for J. S. He will entertain you kindly, provided you bring him good tidings from your family and farm."

In this manner I often visit them and carefully examine their houses, their modes of ingenuity, their different ways; and make them relate all they know and describe all they feel. These are scenes which I believe you would willingly share with me. I well remember your philanthropic turn of mind. Is it not better to contemplate under these humble roofs the rudiments of future wealth and population than to behold the accumulated bundles of litigious papers in the office of a lawyer? To examine how the world is gradually settled, how the howling swamp is converted into a pleasing meadow, the rough ridge into a fine field; and to hear the cheerful whistling, the rural song, where there was no sound heard before, save the yell of the savage, the screech of the owl or the hissing of the snake? Here an European, fatigued with luxury, riches, and pleasures, may find a sweet relaxation in a series of interesting scenes, as affecting as they are new. England, which now contains so many domes, so many castles, was once like this: a place woody and marshy; its inhabitants, now the favourite nation for arts and commerce, were once painted like our neighbours. This country will flourish in its turn, and the same observations will be made which I have just delineated. Posterity will look back with avidity and pleasure to trace, if possible, the era of this or that particular settlement.

Pray, what is the reason that the Scots are in general more religious, more faithful, more honest, and industrious than the Irish? I do not mean to insinuate national reflections, God forbid! It ill becomes any man, and much less an American; but as I know men are nothing of themselves, and that they owe all their different modifications either to government or other local circumstances, there must be some powerful causes which constitute this great national difference.

Agreeable to the account which several Scotchmen have given me of the north of Britain, of the Orkneys, and the Hebride Islands, they seem, on many accounts, to be unfit for the habitation of men; they appear to be calculated only for great sheep pastures. Who, then, can blame the inhabitants of these countries for transporting themselves hither? This great continent must in time absorb the poorest part of Europe; and this will happen in proportion as it becomes better known and as war, taxation, oppression, and misery increase there. The Hebrides appear to be fit only for the residence of malefactors, and it would be much better to send felons there than either to Virginia or Maryland. What a strange compliment has our mother country paid to two of the finest provinces in America! England has entertained in that respect very mistaken ideas; what was intended as a punishment is become the good fortune of several; many of those who have been transported as felons are now rich, and strangers to the stings of those wants that urged them to violations of the laws: they are become industrious, exemplary, and useful citizens. The English government should purchase the most northern and barren of those islands; it should send over to us the honest, primitive Hebrideans, settle them here on good lands as a reward for their virtue and ancient poverty, and replace them with a colony of her wicked sons. The severity of the climate, the inclemency of the seasons, the sterility of the soil, the tempestuousness of the sea, would afflict and punish enough. Could there be found a spot better adapted to retaliate the injury it had received by their crimes? Some of those islands might be considered as the hell of Great Britain, where all evil spirits should be sent. Two essential ends would be answered by this simple operation: the good people, by emigration, would be rendered happier; the bad ones would be placed where they ought to be. In a few years the dread of being sent to that wintry region would have a much stronger effect than that of transportation. This is no place of punishment; were I a poor, hopeless, breadless Englishman, and not restrained by the power of shame, I should be very thankful for the passage. It is of very little importance how and in what manner an indigent man arrives; for if he is but sober, honest, and industrious, he has nothing more to ask of heaven. Let him go to work, he will have opportunities enough to earn a comfortable support, and even the means of procuring some land, which ought to be the utmost wish of every person who has health and hands to work. I knew a man who came to this country, in the literal sense of the expression, stark naked; I think he was a Frenchman and a sailor on board an English man-of-war. Being discontented, he had stripped himself and swam on-shore, where, finding clothes and friends, he settled afterwards at Maraneck, in the county of Chester, in the province of New York. He married and left a good farm to each of his sons. I knew another person who was but twelve years old when he was taken on the frontiers of Canada by the Indians; at his arrival at Albany, he was purchased by a gentleman who generously bound him apprentice to a tailor. He lived to the age of ninety and left behind him a fine estate and a numerous family, all well settled; many of them I am acquainted with. Where is, then, the industrious European who ought to despair?

After a foreigner from any part of Europe is arrived and become a citizen, let him devoutly listen to the voice of our great parent, which says to him, "Welcome to my shores, distressed European; bless the hour in which thou didst see my verdant fields, my fair navigable rivers, and my green mountains! If thou wilt work, I have bread for thee; if thou wilt be honest, sober, and industrious, I have greater rewards to confer on thee—ease and independence. I will give thee fields to feed and clothe thee, a comfortable fireside to sit by and tell thy children by what means thou hast prospered, and a decent bed to repose on. I shall endow thee beside with the immunities of a freeman. If thou wilt carefully educate thy children, teach them gratitude to God and reverence to that government, that philanthropic government, which has collected here so many men and made them happy, I will also provide for thy progeny; and to every good man this ought to be the most holy, the most powerful, the most earnest wish he can possibly form, as well as the most consolatory prospect when he dies. Go thou and work and till; thou shalt prosper, provided thou be just, grateful, and industrious."

HISTORY OF ANDREW, THE HEBRIDEAN

Let historians give the detail of our charters, the succession of our several governors and of their administrations, of our political struggles, and of the foundation of our towns; let annalists amuse themselves with collecting anecdotes of the establishment of our modern provinces: eagles soar high—I, a feebler bird, cheerfully content myself with skipping from bush to bush and living on insignificant insects. I am so habituated to draw all my food and pleasure from the surface of the earth which I till that I cannot, nor indeed am I able to, quit it. I therefore present you with the short history of a simple Scotchman, though it contain not a single remarkable event to amaze the reader, no tragical scene to convulse the heart, or pathetic narrative to draw tears from sympathetic eyes. All I wish to delineate is the progressive steps of a poor man, advancing from indigence to ease, from oppression to freedom, from obscurity and contumely to some degree of consequence—not by virtue of any freaks of fortune, but by the gradual operation of sobriety, honesty, and emigration. These are the limited fields through which I love to wander, sure to find in some parts the smile of new-born happiness, the glad heart, inspiring the cheerful song, the glow of manly pride excited by vivid hopes and rising independence. I always return from my neighbourly excursions extremely happy because there I see good living almost under every roof and prosperous endeavours almost in every field. But you may say, "Why don't you describe some of the more ancient, opulent settlements of our country, where even the eye of an European has something to admire?" It is true, our American fields are in general pleasing to behold, adorned and intermixed as they are with so many substantial houses, flourishing orchards, and coppices of woodlands: the pride of our farms, the source of every good we possess. But what I might observe there is but natural and common; for to draw comfortable subsistence from well-fenced, cultivated fields is easy to conceive. A father dies and leaves a decent house and rich farm to his son; the son modernizes the one and carefully tills the other; he marries the daughter of a friend and neighbour: this is the common prospect; but though it is rich and pleasant, yet it is far from being so entertaining and instructive as the one now in my view.

I had rather attend on the shore to welcome the poor European when he arrives; I observe him in his first moments of embarrassment, trace him throughout his primary difficulties, follow him step by step until he pitches his tent on some piece of land and realizes that energetic wish which has made him quit his native land, his kindred, and induced him to traverse a boisterous ocean. It is there I want to observe his first thoughts and feelings, the first essays of an industry, which hitherto has been suppressed. I wish to see men cut down the first trees, erect their new buildings, till their first fields, reap their first crops, and say for the first time in their lives, "This is our own grain, raised from American soil; on it we shall feed and grow fat and convert the rest into gold and silver." I want to see how the happy effects of their sobriety, honesty, and industry are first displayed; and who would not take a pleasure in seeing these strangers settling as new countrymen, struggling with arduous difficulties, overcoming them, and becoming happy?

Landing on this great continent is like going to sea; they must have a compass, some friendly directing needle, or else they will uselessly err and wander for a long time, even with a fair wind. Yet these are the struggles through which our forefathers have waded, and they have left us no other records of them but the possession of our farms. The reflections I make on these new settlers recall to my mind what my grandfather did in his days; they fill me with gratitude to his memory as well as to that government which invited him to come and helped him when he arrived, as well as many others. Can I pass over these reflections without remembering thy name, O Penn, thou best of legislators, who by the wisdom of thy laws hast endowed human nature, within the bounds of thy province, with every dignity it can possibly enjoy in a civilized state and showed by this singular establishment what all men might be if they would follow thy example!

In the year 1770, I purchased some lands in the county of——, which I intended for one of my sons, and was obliged to go there in order to see them properly surveyed and marked out: the soil is good, but the country has a very wild aspect. However, I observed with pleasure that land sells very fast, and I am in hopes when the lad gets a wife it will be a well-settled, decent country. Agreeable to our customs, which indeed are those of nature, it is our duty to provide for our eldest children while we live in order that our homesteads may be left to the youngest, who are the most helpless. Some people are apt to regard the portions given to daughters as so much lost to the family, but this is selfish and is not agreeable to my way of thinking; they cannot work as men do; they marry young: I have given an honest European a farm to till for himself, rent free, provided he clears an acre of swamp every year and that he quits it whenever my daughter shall marry. It will procure her a substantial husband, a good farmer—and that is all my ambition.

Whilst I was in the woods, I met with a party of Indians; I shook hands with them, and I perceived they had killed a cub; I had a little peach brandy; they perceived it also; we therefore joined company, kindled a large fire, and ate a hearty supper. I made their hearts glad, and we all reposed on good beds of leaves. Soon after dark, I was surprised to hear a prodigious hooting through the woods; the Indians laughed heartily. One of them, more skilful than the rest, mimicked the owls so exactly that a very large one perched on a high tree over our fire. We soon brought him down; he measured five feet seven inches from one extremity of the wings to the other. By Captain —— I have sent you the talons, on which I have had the heads of small candlesticks fixed. Pray keep them on the table of your study for my sake.

Contrary to my expectation, I found myself under the necessity of going to Philadelphia in order to pay the purchase money and to have the deeds properly recorded. I thought little of the journey, though it was above two hundred miles, because I was well acquainted with many friends, at whose houses I intended to stop. The third night after I left the woods, I put up at Mr. ——'s, the most worthy citizen I know; he happened to lodge at my house when you were there. He kindly inquired after your welfare and desired I would make a friendly mention of him to you. The neatness of these good people is no phenomenon, yet I think this excellent family surpasses everything I know. No sooner did I lie down to rest than I thought myself in a most odoriferous arbour, so sweet and fragrant were the sheets. Next morning I found my host in the orchard destroying caterpillars. "I think, friend B.," said I, "that thee art greatly departed from the good rules of the society; thee seemeth to have quitted that happy simplicity for which it hath hitherto been so remarkable." "Thy rebuke, friend James, is a pretty heavy one; what motive canst thee have for thus accusing us?" "Thy kind wife made a mistake last evening," I said; "she put me on a bed of roses instead of a common one; I am not used to such delicacies." "And is that all, friend James, that thee hast to reproach us with? Thee wilt not call it luxury I hope? Thee canst but know that it is the produce of our garden; and friend Pope sayeth that 'to enjoy is to obey.'" "This is a most learned excuse indeed, friend B., and must be valued because it is founded upon truth." "James, my wife hath done nothing more to thy bed than what is done all the year round to all the beds in the family; she sprinkles her linen with rose-water before she puts it under the press; it is her fancy, and I have nought to say. But thee shalt not escape so; verily I will send for her; thee and she must settle the matter whilst I proceed on my work before the sun gets too high.—Tom, go thou and call thy mistress, Philadelphia." "What," said I, "is thy wife called by

that name? I did not know that before." "I'll tell thee,
James, how it came to pass: her grandmother was the
first female child born after William Penn landed with the
rest of our brethren, and in compliment to the city he
intended to build, she was called after the name he intended to give it; and so there is always one of the
daughters of her family known by the name of Philadelphia." She soon came, and after a most friendly altercation, I gave up the point, breakfasted, departed, and in
four days reached the city.

A week after, news came that a vessel was arrived with
Scotch emigrants. Mr. C. and I went to the dock to see
them disembark. It was a scene which inspired me with a
variety of thoughts. "Here are," said I to my friend,
"a number of people driven by poverty and other adverse
causes to a foreign land in which they know nobody." The
name of a stranger, instead of implying relief, assistance,
and kindness, on the contrary, conveys very different
ideas. They are now distressed; their minds are racked
by a variety of apprehensions, fears, and hopes. It was
this last powerful sentiment which has brought them here.
If they are good people, I pray that heaven may realize
them. Whoever were to see them thus gathered again
in five or six years would behold a more pleasing sight,
to which this would serve as a very powerful contrast.
By their honesty, the vigour of their arms, and the benignity of government, their condition will be greatly
improved; they will be well clad, fat, possessed of that
manly confidence which property confers; they will
become useful citizens. Some of the posterity may act
conspicuous parts in our future American transactions.
Most of them appeared pale and emaciated, from the
length of the passage and the indifferent provision on
which they had lived. The number of children seemed as
great as that of the people; they had all paid for being
conveyed here. The captain told us they were a quiet,
peaceable, and harmless people who had never dwelt in
cities. This was a valuable cargo; they seemed, a few excepted, to be in the full vigour of their lives. Several
citizens, impelled either by spontaneous attachments or
motives of humanity, took many of them to their houses;
the city, agreeable to its usual wisdom and humanity,
ordered them all to be lodged in the barracks,

and plenty of provisions to be given them. My friend pitched upon one also and led him to his house, with his wife and a son about fourteen years of age. The majority of them had contracted for land the year before, by means of an agent; the rest depended entirely upon chance; and the one who followed us was of this last class. Poor man, he smiled on receiving the invitation, and gladly accepted it, bidding his wife and son do the same, in a language which I did not understand. He gazed with uninterrupted attention on everything he saw: the houses, the inhabitants, the Negroes, and carriages—everything appeared equally new to him; and we went slow in order to give him time to feed on this pleasing variety. "Good God!" said he, "is this Philadelphia, that blessed city of bread and provisions of which we have heard so much? I am told it was founded the same year in which my father was born; why, it is finer than Greenock and Glasgow, which are ten times as old." "It is so," said my friend to him; "and when thee hast been here a month, thee will soon see that it is the capital of a fine province, of which thee art going to be a citizen. Greenock enjoys neither such a climate nor such a soil." Thus we slowly proceeded along, when we met several large Lancaster six-horse waggons, just arrived from the country. At this stupendous sight, he stopped short and with great diffidence asked us what was the use of these great moving houses, and where those big horses came from? "Have you none such at home?" I asked him. "Oh, no; these huge animals would eat all the grass of our island!" We at last reached my friend's house, who, in the glow of well-meant hospitality, made them all three sit down to a good dinner and gave them as much cider as they could drink. "God bless the country and the good people it contains," said he; "this is the best meal's victuals I have made a long time. I thank you kindly."

"What part of Scotland dost thee come from, friend Andrew?" said Mr. C. "Some of us come from the main, some from the island of Barra," he answered; "I myself am a Barra man." I looked on the map, and by its latitude, easily guessed that it must be an inhospitable climate. "What sort of land have you got there?" I asked him. "Bad enough," said he; "we have no such trees as I

see here, no wheat, no kine, no apples." Then, I observed that it must be hard for the poor to live. "We
have no poor," he answered; "we are all alike, except
our laird; but he cannot help everybody." "Pray what
is the name of your laird?" "Mr. Neiel," said Andrew;
"the like of him is not to be found in any of the isles;
his forefathers have lived there thirty generations ago,
as we are told. Now, gentlemen, you may judge what
an ancient family estate it must be. But it is cold, the land
is thin, and there were too many of us, which are the
reasons that some are come to seek their fortunes here."
"Well, Andrew, what step do you intend to take in order
to become rich?" "I do not know, sir; I am but an
ignorant man, a stranger besides; I must rely on the
advice of good Christians: they would not deceive me, I
am sure. I have brought with me a character from our
Barra minister; can it do me any good here?" "Oh, yes;
but your future success will depend entirely on your own
conduct; if you are a sober man, as the certificate says,
laborious, and honest, there is no fear but that you will
do well. Have you brought any money with you, Andrew?" "Yes, sir, eleven guineas and an half." "Upon my
word, it is a considerable sum for a Barra man; how
came you by so much money?" "Why, seven years ago, I
received a legacy of thirty-seven pounds from an uncle
who loved me much; my wife brought me two guineas
when the laird gave her to me for a wife, which I have
saved ever since. I have sold all I had; I worked in
Glasgow for some time." "I am glad to hear you are so
saving and prudent; be so still; you must go and hire
yourself with some good people; what can you do?"
"I can thresh a little, and handle the spade." "Can you
plough?" "Yes, sir, with the little breast plough I have
brought with me." "These won't do here, Andrew; you
are an able man; if you are willing, you will soon learn.
I'll tell you what I intend to do: I'll send you to my
house, where you shall stay two or three weeks; there
you must exercise yourself with the axe; that is the principal tool the Americans want, and particularly the back-
settlers. Can your wife spin?" "Yes, she can." "Well then,
as soon as you are able to handle the axe, you shall go
and live with Mr. P. R., a particular friend of mine, who
will give you four dollars per month for the first six

and the usual price of five as long as you remain with him. I shall place your wife in another house, where she shall receive half a dollar a week for spinning, and your son a dollar a month to drive the team. You shall have, besides, good victuals to eat and good beds to lie on; will all this satisfy you, Andrew?" He hardly understood what I said; the honest tears of gratitude fell from his eyes as he looked at me, and its expressions seemed to quiver on his lips. Though silent, this was saying a great deal; there was, besides, something extremely moving to see a man six feet high thus shed tears, and they did not lessen the good opinion I had entertained of him. At last he told me that my offers were more than he deserved and that he would first begin to work for his victuals. "No, no," said I; "if you are careful and sober and do what you can, you shall receive what I told you, after you have served a short apprenticeship at my house." "May God repay you for all your kindnesses," said Andrew; "as long as I live, I shall thank you and do what I can for you." A few days after, I sent them all three to ——, by the return of some waggons, that he might have an opportunity of viewing and convincing himself of the utility of those machines which he had at first so much admired.

The farther descriptions he gave us of the Hebrides in general and of his native island in particular, of the customs and modes of living of the inhabitants, greatly entertained me. Pray, is the sterility of the soil the cause that there are no trees, or is it because there are none planted? What are the modern families of all the kings of the earth compared to the date of that of Mr. Neiel? Admitting that each generation should last but forty years, this makes a period of 1,200, an extraordinary duration for the uninterrupted descent of any family! Agreeably to the description he gave us of those countries, they seem to live according to the rules of nature, which gives them but bare subsistence; their constitutions are uncontaminated by any excess or effeminacy, which their soil refuses. If their allowance of food is not too scanty, they must all be healthy by perpetual temperance and exercise; if so, they are amply rewarded for their poverty. Could they have obtained but necessary food, they would not have left it; for it was not in consequence of oppression, either from their patriarch or the government, that they had emigrated. I wish we had a colony of these honest people settled in some parts of this province; their morals, their religion, seem to be as simple as their manners. This society would present an interesting spectacle could they be transported on a richer soil. But perhaps that soil would soon alter everything; for our opinions, vices, and virtues are altogether local: we are machines fashioned by every circumstance around us.

Andrew arrived at my house a week before I did, and I found my wife, agreeably to my instructions, had placed the axe in his hands as his first task. For some time, he was very awkward, but he was so docile, so willing, and grateful, as well as his wife, that I foresaw he would succeed. Agreeably to my promise, I put them all with different families, where they were well liked, and all parties were pleased. Andrew worked hard, lived well, grew fat, and every Sunday came to pay me a visit on a good horse, which Mr. P. R. lent him. Poor man, it took him a long time ere he could sit on the saddle and hold the bridle properly. I believe he had never before mounted such a beast, though I did not choose to ask him that question, for fear it might suggest some mortifying ideas. After having been twelve months at Mr. P. R.'s and having received his own and his family's wages, which amounted to eighty-four dollars, he came to see me on a weekday and told me that he was a man of middle age and would willingly have land of his own in order to procure him a home as a shelter against old age, that whenever this period should come, his son, to whom he would give his land, would then maintain him, and thus live altogether; he therefore required my advice and assistance. I thought his desire very natural and praiseworthy, and told him that I should think of it, but that he must remain one month longer with Mr. P. R., who had 3,000 rails to split. He immediately consented. The spring was not far advanced enough yet for Andrew to begin clearing any land, even supposing that he had made a purchase, as it is always necessary that the leaves should be out in order that this additional combustible may serve to burn the heaps of brush more readily.

A few days after, it happened that the whole family of Mr. P. R. went to meeting, and left Andrew to take care of the house. While he was at the door, attentively reading the Bible, nine Indians just come from the mountains suddenly made their appearance and unloaded their packs of furs on the floor of the piazza. Conceive, if you can, what was Andrew's consternation at this extraordinary sight! From the singular appearance of these people, the honest Hebridean took them for a lawless band come to rob his master's house. He therefore, like a faithful guardian, precipitately withdrew and shut the doors; but as most of our houses are without locks, he was reduced to the necessity of fixing his knife over the latch, and then flew upstairs in quest of a broadsword he had brought from Scotland. The Indians, who were Mr. P. R.'s particular friends, guessed at his suspicions and fears; they forcibly lifted the door and suddenly took possession of the house, got all the bread and meat they wanted, and sat themselves down by the fire. At this instant, Andrew, with his broadsword in his hand, entered the room, the Indians earnestly looking at him and attentively watching his motions. After a very few reflections, Andrew found that his weapon was useless when opposed to nine tomahawks, but this did not diminish his anger; on the contrary, it grew greater on observing the calm impudence with which they were devouring the family provisions. Unable to resist, he called them names in broad Scotch and ordered them to desist and be gone, to which the Indians (as they told me afterwards) replied in their equally broad idiom. It must have been a most unintelligible altercation between this honest Barra man and nine Indians who did not much care for anything he could say. At last he ventured to lay his hands on one of them in order to turn him out of the house. Here Andrew's fidelity got the better of his prudence, for the Indian, by his motions, threatened to scalp him, while the rest gave the war whoop. This horrid noise so effectually frightened poor Andrew that, unmindful of his courage, of his broadsword, and his intentions, he rushed out, left them masters of the house, and disappeared. I have heard one of the Indians say since that he never laughed so heartily in his life. Andrew, at a distance, soon recovered from the fears which had been in-

spired by this infernal yell and thought of no other remedy than to go to the meeting-house, which was about
two miles distant. In the eagerness of his honest intentions, with looks of affright still marked on his countenance, he called Mr. P. R. out and told him with great
vehemence of style that nine monsters were come to his
house—some blue, some red, and some black; that they
had little axes in their hands out of which they smoked;
and that like highlanders, they had no breeches; that they
were devouring all his victuals; and that God only knew
what they would do more. "Pacify yourself," said Mr.
P. R.; "my house is as safe with these people as if I was
there myself; as for the victuals, they are heartily welcome, honest Andrew; they are not people of much
ceremony; they help themselves thus whenever they are
among their friends; I do so too in their wigwams, whenever I go to their village; you had better therefore step
in and hear the remainder of the sermon, and when the
meeting is over, we will all go back in the waggon together."

At their return, Mr. P. R., who speaks the Indian language very well, explained the whole matter; the Indians
renewed their laugh and shook hands with honest Andrew, whom they made to smoke out of their pipes; and
thus peace was made and ratified according to the Indian custom, by the calumet.

Soon after this adventure, the time approached when
I had promised Andrew my best assistance to settle him;
for that purpose, I went to Mr. A. V., in the county of
———, who, I was informed, had purchased a track of
land contiguous to ——— settlement. I gave him a faithful detail of the progress Andrew had made in the rural
arts, of his honesty, sobriety, and gratitude; and
pressed him to sell him a hundred acres. "This I cannot comply with," said Mr. A. V.; "but at the same time
I will do better; I love to encourage honest Europeans
as much as you do and to see them prosper; you tell
me he has but one son; I will lease them a hundred
acres for any term of years you please, and make it
more valuable to your Scotchman than if he was possessed of the fee simple. By that means he may, with
that little money he has, buy a plough, a team, and
some stock; he will not be incumbered with debts and

mortgages; what he raises will be his own; had he two or three sons as able as himself, then I should think it more eligible for him to purchase the fee simple." "I join with you in opinion, and will bring Andrew along with me in a few days."

"Well, honest Andrew," said Mr. A. V., "in consideration of your good name, I will let you have a hundred acres of good arable land that shall be laid out along a new road; there is a bridge already erected on the creek that passes through the land, and a fine swamp of about twenty acres. These are my terms; I cannot sell, but I will lease you the quantity that Mr. James, your friend, has asked; the first seven years you shall pay no rent; whatever you sow and reap, and plant and gather, shall be entirely your own; neither the king, government, nor church will have any claim on your future property. The remaining part of the time, you must give me twelve dollars and a half a year; and that is all you will have to pay me. Within the three first years, you must plant fifty apple trees and clear seven acres of swamp within the first part of the lease; it will be your own advantage; whatever you do more within that time, I will pay you for it, at the common rate of the country. The term of the lease shall be thirty years; how do you like it, Andrew?" "Oh, sir, it is very good, but I am afraid that the king or his ministers, or the governor, or some of our great men will come and take the land from me; your son may say to me, by and by, 'This is my father's land, Andrew, you must quit it.' " "No, no," said Mr. A. V.; "there is no such danger; the king and his ministers are too just to take the labour of a poor settler; here we have no great men, but what are subordinate to our laws; but to calm all your fears, I will give you a lease so that none can make you afraid. If ever you are dissatisfied with the land, a jury of your own neighbourhood shall value all your improvements, and you shall be paid agreeably to their verdict. You may sell the lease, or if you die, you may previously dispose of it as if the land was your own." Expressive yet inarticulate joy was mixed in his countenance, which seemed impressed with astonishment and confusion. "Do you understand me well?" said Mr. A. V. "No, sir," replied Andrew; "I know nothing of what you mean about lease, improvement, will, jury, etc." "That is honest; we will explain these things to you by and by." It must be confessed that those were hard words, which he had never heard in his life; for by his own account, the ideas they convey would be totally useless in the island of Barra. No wonder, therefore, that he was embarrassed; for how could the man who had hardly a will of his own since he was born imagine he could have one after his death? How could the person who never possessed anything conceive that he could extend his new dominion over this land, even after he should be laid in his grave? For my part, I think Andrew's amazement did not imply any extraordinary degree of ignorance: he was an actor introduced upon a new scene; it required some time ere he could reconcile himself to the part he was to perform. However, he was soon enlightened and introduced into those mysteries with which we native Americans are but too well acquainted.

Here, then, is honest Andrew, invested with every municipal advantage they confer, become a freeholder, possessed of a vote, of a place of residence, a citizen of the province of Pennsylvania. Andrew's original hopes and the distant prospects he had formed in the island of Barra were at the eve of being realized; we therefore can easily forgive him a few spontaneous ejaculations, which would be useless to repeat. This short tale is easily told; few words are sufficient to describe this sudden change of situation; but in his mind it was gradual, and took him above a week before he could be sure that without disbursing any money he could possess lands. Soon after he prepared himself, I lent him a barrel of pork and 200-lb. weight of meal and made him purchase what was necessary besides.

He set out, and hired a room in the house of a settler who lived the most contiguous to his own land. His first work was to clear some acres of swamp, that he might have a supply of hay the following year for his two horses and cows. From the first day he began to work, he was indefatigable; his honesty procured him friends, and his industry the esteem of his new neighbours. One of them offered him two acres of cleared land whereon he might plant corn, pompions, squashes, and a few potatoes that very season. It is astonishing how quick men will learn when they work for themselves. I saw with pleasure, two months after, Andrew holding a two-horse plough and tracing his furrows quite straight; thus the spademan of the island of Barra was become the tiller of American soil. "Well done," said I; "Andrew, well done; I see that God speeds and directs your works; I see prosperity delineated in all your furrows and headlands. Raise this crop of corn with attention and care, and then you will be master of the art."

As he had neither mowing nor reaping to do that year, I told him that the time was come to build his house; and that for the purpose I would myself invite the neighbourhood to a frolic; that thus he would have a large dwelling erected and some upland cleared in one day. Mr. P. R., his old friend, came at the time appointed, with all his hands, and brought victuals in plenty; I did the same. About forty people repaired to the spot; the songs and merry stories went round the woods from cluster to cluster, as the people had gathered to their different works; trees fell on all sides, bushes were cut up and heaped; and while many were thus employed, others with their teams hauled the big logs to the spot which Andrew had pitched upon for the erection of his new dwelling. We all dined in the woods; in the afternoon, the logs were placed with skids and the usual contrivances; thus the rude house was raised and above two acres of land cut up, cleared, and heaped.

Whilst all these different operations were performing, Andrew was absolutely incapable of working; it was to him the most solemn holiday he had ever seen; it would have been sacrilegious in him to have defiled it with menial labour. Poor man, he sanctified it with joy and thanksgiving and honest libations: he went from one to the other with the bottle in his hand, pressing everybody to drink, and drinking himself to show the example. He spent the whole day in smiling, laughing, and uttering monosyllables; his wife and son were there also, but as they could not understand the language, their pleasure must have been altogether that of the imagination. The powerful lord, the wealthy merchant, on seeing the superb mansion finished, never can feel half the joy and real happiness which was felt and enjoyed on that day by this honest Hebridean, though this new dwelling, erected in the midst of the woods, was nothing more than a square inclosure, composed of twenty-four large, clumsy logs, let in at the ends. When the work was finished, the company made the woods resound with the noise of their three cheers and the honest wishes they formed for Andrew's prosperity. He could say nothing, but with thankful tears he shook hands with them all. Thus, from the first day he had landed, Andrew marched towards this important event; this memorable day made the sun shine on that land on which he was to sow wheat and other grain. What swamp he had cleared lay before his door; the essence of future bread, milk, and meat were scattered all round him. Soon after, he hired a carpenter, who put on a roof and laid the floors; in a week more, the house was properly plastered and the chimney finished. He moved into it, and purchased two cows, which found plenty of food in the woods; his hogs had the same advantage. That very year, he and his son sowed three bushels of wheat, from which he reaped ninety-one and a half; for I had ordered him to keep an exact account of all he should raise. His first crop of other corn would have been as good had it not been for the squirrels, which were enemies not to be dispersed by the broadsword. The fourth year, I took an inventory of the wheat this man possessed, which I send you. Soon after, farther settlements were made on that road, and Andrew, instead of being the last man towards the wilderness, found himself in a few years in the middle of a numerous society. He helped others as generously as others had helped him, and I have dined many times at his table with several of his neighbours. The second year, he was made overseer of the road and served on two petty juries, performing as a citizen all the duties required of him. The historiographer of some great prince or general does not bring his hero victorious to the end of a successful campaign with one half of the heart-felt pleasure with which I have conducted Andrew to the situation he now enjoys: he is independent and easy. Triumph and military honours do not always imply those two blessings. He is unencumbered with debts, services, rents, or any other dues; the successes of a campaign, the laurels of war, must be purchased at the dearest rate, which makes every cool, reflecting citizen to tremble and shudder. By the literal account hereunto annexed, you will easily be made acquainted with the happy effects which constantly flow, in this country, from sobriety and industry, when united with good land and freedom.

The account of the property he acquired with his own hands and those of his son, in four years, is as under:

	Dollars
The value of his improvements and lease . .	225
Six cows, at 13 dollars	78
Two breeding mares	50
The rest of the stock	100
Seventy-three bushels of wheat	66
Money due to him on notes	43
Pork and beef in his cellar	28
Wool and flax	19
Ploughs and other utensils of husbandry . .	31
£240 Pennsylvania currency—dollars .	640

LETTER IV

DESCRIPTION OF THE ISLAND OF NANTUCKET, WITH THE MANNERS, CUSTOMS, POLICY, AND TRADE OF THE INHABITANTS

The greatest compliment that can be paid to the best of kings, to the wisest ministers, or the most patriotic rulers is to think that the reformation of political abuses and the happiness of their people are the primary objects of their attention. But alas! How disagreeable must the work of reformation be, how dreaded the operation, for we hear of no amendment; on the contrary, the great number of European emigrants yearly coming over here informs us that the severity of taxes, the injustice of laws, the tyranny of the rich, and the oppressive avarice of the church are as intolerable as ever. Will these calamities have no end? Are not the great rulers of the earth afraid of losing, by degrees, their most useful subjects? This country, providentially intended for the general asylum of the world, will flourish by the oppression of other people; they will every day become better acquainted with the happiness we enjoy and seek for the means of transporting themselves here, in spite of all obstacles and laws. To what purpose, then, have so many useful books and divine maxims been transmitted to us from preceding ages? Are they all vain, all useless? Must human nature ever be the sport of the few, and its many wounds remain unhealed? How happy are we here in having fortunately escaped the miseries which attended our fathers; how thankful ought we to be that they reared us in a land where sobriety and industry never fail to meet with the most ample rewards! You have, no doubt, read several histories of this continent, yet there are a thousand facts, a thousand explanations, overlooked. Authors will certainly convey to you a geographical knowledge of this country; they will acquaint you with the eras of the several settlements, the foundations of our towns, the spirit of our different charters, etc., yet they do not sufficiently disclose the genius of the people, their various customs, their modes of agriculture, the innumerable resources which the industrious have of raising themselves to a comfortable and easy situation. Few of these writers have resided here, and those who have, had not pervaded every part of the country nor carefully examined the nature and principles of our association. It would be a task worthy a speculative genius to enter intimately into the situation and characters of the people from Nova Scotia to West Florida; and surely history cannot possibly present any subject more pleasing to behold. Sensible how unable I am to lead you through so vast a maze, let us look attentively for some small unnoticed corner; but where shall we go in quest of such a one? Numberless settlements, each distinguished by some peculiarities, present themselves on every side; all seem to realize the most sanguine wishes that a good man could form for the happiness of his race. Here they live by fishing on the most plentiful coasts in the world; there they fell trees by the sides of large rivers for masts and lumber; here others convert innumerable logs into the best boards; there, again, others cultivate the land, rear cattle, and clear large fields. Yet I have a spot in my view, where none of these occupations are performed, which will, I hope, reward us for the trouble of inspection; but though it is barren in its soil, insignificant in its extent, inconvenient in its situation, deprived of materials for building, it seems to have been inhabited merely to prove what mankind can do when happily governed! Here I can point out to you exertions of the most successful industry, instances of native sagacity unassisted by science, the happy fruits of a well-directed perseverance. It is always a refreshing spectacle to me when in my review of the various component parts of this immense *whole,* I observe the labours of its inhabitants singularly rewarded by nature; when I see them emerged out of their first difficulties, living with decency and ease, and conveying to their posterity that plentiful subsistence which their fathers have so deservedly earned. But when their prosperity arises from the goodness of the climate and fertility of the soil, I partake of their happiness it is true, yet stay but a little while with them, as they exhibit nothing but what is natural and common. On the contrary, when I meet with barren spots fertilized, grass growing where none grew before, grain gathered from fields which had hitherto produced nothing better than brambles, dwellings raised where no building materials were to be found, wealth acquired by the most uncommon means—there I pause to dwell on the favourite object of my speculative inquiries. Willingly do I leave the former to enjoy the odoriferous furrow or their rich valleys, with anxiety repairing to the spot where so many difficulties have been overcome, where extraordinary exertions have produced extraordinary effects, and where every natural obstacle has been removed by a vigorous industry.

I want not to record the annals of the island of Nantucket; its inhabitants have no annals, for they are not a race of warriors. My simple wish is to trace them throughout their progressive steps from their arrival here to this present hour; to inquire by what means they have raised themselves from the most humble, the most insignificant beginnings, to the ease and the wealth they now possess; and to give you some idea of their customs, religion, manners, policy, and mode of living.

This happy settlement was not founded on intrusion, forcible entries, or blood, as so many others have been; it drew its origin from necessity on the one side and from good will on the other; and ever since, all has been a scene of uninterrupted harmony. Neither political nor religious broils, neither disputes with the natives, nor any other contentions, have in the least agitated or disturbed its detached society. Yet the first founders knew nothing either of Lycurgus or Solon, for this settlement has not been the work of eminent men or powerful legislators forcing nature by the accumulated labours of art. This singular establishment has been effected by means of that native industry and perseverance common to all men when they are protected by a government which demands but little for its protection, when they are permitted to enjoy a system of rational laws founded on perfect freedom. The mildness and humanity of such a government necessarily implies that confidence which is the source of the most arduous undertakings and permanent success. Would you believe that a sandy spot of about twenty-three thousand acres, affording neither stones nor timber, meadows nor arable, yet can boast of a handsome town consisting of more than 500 houses, should possess above 200 sail of vessels; constantly employ upwards of 2,000 seamen; feed more than 15,000 sheep, 500 cows, 200 horses; and has several citizens worth £20,000 sterling! Yet all these facts are uncontroverted. Who would have imagined that any people should have abandoned a fruitful and extensive continent filled with the riches which the most ample vegetation affords; replete with good soil, enamelled meadows, rich pastures, every kind of timber, and with all other materials necessary to render life happy and comfortable, to come and inhabit a little sandbank to which nature had refused those advantages, to dwell on a spot where there scarcely grew a shrub to announce, by the budding of its leaves, the arrival of the spring and to warn by their fall the proximity of winter? Had this island been contiguous to the shores of some ancient monarchy, it would only have been occupied by a few wretched fishermen, who, oppressed by poverty, would hardly have been able to purchase or build little fishing barks, always dreading the weight of taxes or the servitude of men-of-war. Instead of that boldness of speculation for which the inhabitants of this island are so remarkable, they would fearfully have confined themselves within the narrow limits of the most trifling attempts; timid in their excursions, they never could have extricated themselves from their first difficulties. This island, on the contrary, contains 5,000 hardy people who boldly derive their riches from the element that surrounds them and have been compelled by the sterility of the soil to seek abroad for the means of subsistence. You must not imagine, from the recital of these facts, that they enjoyed any exclusive privileges or royal charters or that they were nursed by particular immunities in the infancy of their settlement. No, their freedom, their skill, their probity, and perseverance have accomplished everything and brought them by degrees to the rank they now hold.

From this first sketch, I hope that my partiality to this island will be justified. Perhaps you hardly know that such an one exists in the neighbourhood of Cape Cod. What has happened here has and will happen everywhere else. Give mankind the full rewards of their industry, allow them to enjoy the fruit of their labour under the peaceable shade of their vines and fig-trees, leave their native activity unshackled and free, like a fair stream without dams or other obstacles; the first will fertilize the very sand on which they tread, the other exhibit a navigable river, spreading plenty and cheerfulness wherever the declivity of the ground leads it. If these people are not famous for tracing the fragrant furrow on the plain, they plough the rougher ocean, they gather from its surface, at an immense distance and with Herculean labours, the riches it affords; they go to hunt and catch that huge fish which by its strength and velocity one would imagine ought to be beyond the reach of man. This island has nothing deserving of notice but its inhabitants; here you meet with neither ancient monuments, spacious halls, solemn temples, nor elegant dwellings; not a citadel, nor any kind of fortification, not even a battery to rend the air with its loud peals on any solemn occasion. As for their rural improvements, they are many, but all of the most simple and useful kind.

The island of Nantucket lies in latitude 41°10'; 60 miles N.E. from Cape Cod; 27 N. from Hyannis, or Barnstable, a town on the most contiguous part of the great peninsula; 21 miles W. by N. from Cape Poge, on the vineyard; 50 W. by N. from Woods Hole, on Elizabeth Island; 80 miles N. from Boston; 120 from Rhode Island; 800 S. from Bermuda.* Sherborn is the only town on the island, which consists of about 530 houses, that have been framed on the main; they are lathed and plastered within, handsomely painted and boarded without; each has a cellar underneath, built with stones fetched also from the main; they are all of a similar construction and appearance, plain and entirely devoid of exterior or in-

* This information is incorrect, as the reader can ascertain by consulting a map of the area.——Ed.

terior ornament. I observed but one which was built of
bricks, belonging to Mr. ———, but like the rest, it is unadorned. The town stands on a rising sandbank on the
west side of the harbour, which is very safe from all
winds. There are two places of worship, one for the Society of Friends, the other for that of Presbyterians; and
in the middle of the town, near the market-place, stands
a simple building which is the county court-house. The
town regularly ascends toward the country, and in its
vicinage they have several small fields and gardens yearly
manured with the dung of their cows and the soil of
their streets. There are a good many cherry- and peach-
trees planted in their streets and in many other places.
The apple-tree does not thrive well; they have therefore
planted but few. The island contains no mountains, yet
is very uneven, and the many rising grounds and emi-
nences with which it is filled have formed in the several
valleys a great variety of swamps, where the Indian
grass and the blue bent, peculiar to such soils, grow with
tolerable luxuriancy. Some of the swamps abound with
peat, which serves the poor instead of firewood. There
are fourteen ponds on this island, all extremely useful,
some lying transversely, almost across it, which greatly
help to divide it into partitions for the use of their cattle; others abound with peculiar fish and sea fowls. Their
streets are not paved, but this is attended with little
inconvenience, as it is never crowded with country carriages; and those they have in the town are seldom made
use of but in the time of coming in and before the
sailing of their fleets. At my first landing, I was much
surprised at the disagreeable smell which struck me in
many parts of the town; it is caused by the whale oil
and is unavoidable; the neatness peculiar to these people
can neither remove or prevent it. There are near the
wharfs a great many storehouses, where their staple
commodity is deposited, as well as the innumerable
materials which are always wanted to repair and fit out
so many whalemen. They have three docks, each three
hundred feet long and extremely convenient, at the head
of which there are ten feet of water. These docks are
built like those in Boston, of logs fetched from the continent, filled with stones, and covered with sand. Between
these docks and the town there is room sufficient for the

landing of goods and for the passage of their numerous carts; for almost every man here has one. The wharfs to the north and south of the docks are built of the same materials and give a stranger, at his first landing, a high idea of the prosperity of these people; and there is room around these three docks for 300 sail of vessels. When their fleets have been successful, the bustle and hurry of business on this spot for some days after their arrival would make you imagine that Sherborn is the capital of a very opulent and large province. On that point of land which forms the west side of the harbour stands a very neat lighthouse; the opposite peninsula, called Coitou, secures it from the most dangerous winds. There are but few gardens and arable fields in the neighbourhood of the town, for nothing can be more sterile and sandy than this part of the island; they have, however, with unwearied perseverance, by bringing a variety of manure and by cow-penning, enriched several spots, where they raised Indian corn, potatoes, pompions, turnips, etc. On the highest part of this sandy eminence, four windmills grind the grain they raise to export; and contiguous to them, their rope walk is to be seen, where full half of their cordage is manufactured. Between the shores of the harbour, the docks, and the town, there is a most excellent piece of meadow, inclosed and manured with such cost and pains as show how necessary and precious grass is at Nantucket. Toward the point of Shèmàh, the island is more level and the soil bettèr; and there they have considerable lots, well fenced and richly manured, where they diligently raise their yearly crops. There are but very few farms on this island because there are but very few spots that will admit of cultivation without the assistance of dung and other manure, which is very expensive to fetch from the main. This island was patented in the year 1671 by twenty-seven proprietors, under the province of New York, which then claimed all the islands from the Neway Sink to Cape Cod. They found it so universally barren and so unfit for cultivation that they mutually agreed not to divide it, as each could neither live on nor improve that lot which might fall to his share. They then cast their eyes on the sea, and finding themselves obliged to become fishermen, they looked for a harbour, and having found one, they determined to build a town in its neighbourhood and to dwell together. For that purpose, they surveyed as much ground as would afford to each what is generally called here a home lot. Forty acres were thought sufficient to answer this double purpose, for to what end should they covet more land than they could improve, or even inclose, not being possessed of a single tree, in the whole extent of their new dominion. This was all the territorial property they allotted; the rest they agreed to hold in common, and seeing that the scanty grass of the island might feed sheep, they agreed that each proprietor should be entitled to feed on it, if he pleased, 560 sheep. By this agreement, the national flock was to consist of 15,120; that is, the undivided part of the island was by such means ideally divisible into as many parts, or shares, to which nevertheless no certain determinate quantity of land was affixed: for they knew not how much the island contained, nor could the most judicious surveyor fix this small quota as to quality and quantity. Farther, they agreed, in case the grass should grow better by seeding, that then four sheep should represent a cow, and two cows a horse: such was the method this wise people took to enjoy in common their new settlement; such was the mode of their first establishment, which may be truly and literally called a pastoral one. Several hundred of sheep-pasture titles have since been divided on those different tracks, which are now cultivated; the rest by inheritance and intermarriages have been so subdivided that it is very common for a girl to have no other portion but her outset and four sheep pastures or the privilege of feeding a cow. But as this privilege is founded on an ideal though real title to some unknown piece of land, which one day or another may be ascertained, these sheep-pasture titles should convey to your imagination something more valuable and of greater credit than the mere advantage arising from the benefit of a cow, which in that case would be no more than a right of commonage. Whereas, here as labour grows cheaper, as misfortunes from their sea adventures may happen, each person possessed of a sufficient number of these sheep-pasture titles may one day realize them on some peculiar spot such as shall be adjudged by the council of the proprietors to be adequate to their value; and this is the reason that these people very unwillingly sell those small rights and esteem them more than you would imagine. They are the representation of a future freehold; they cherish in the mind of the possessor a latent, though distant, hope that by his success in his next whale season he may be able to pitch on some predilected spot and there build himself a home, to which he may retire and spend the latter end of his days in peace. A council of proprietors always exists in this island who decide their territorial differences; their titles are recorded in the books of the county which this town represents, as well as every conveyance of lands and other sales.

This island furnishes the naturalist with few or no objects worthy observation: it appears to be the uneven summit of a sandy submarine mountain, covered here and there with sorrel, grass, a few cedar bushes, and scrubby oaks; their swamps are much more valuable for the peat they contain than for the trifling pasture of their surface; those declining grounds which lead to the sea-shores abound with beach grass, a light fodder when cut and cured, but very good when fed green. On the east side of the island, they have several tracks of salt grasses, which, being carefully fenced, yield a considerable quantity of that wholesome fodder. Among the many ponds or lakes with which this island abounds, there are some which have been made by the intrusion of the sea, such as Wiwidiah, the Long, the Narrow, and several others; consequently, those are salt and the others fresh. The former answer two considerable purposes: first by enabling them to fence the island with greater facility; at peculiar high tides, a great number of fish enter into them, where they feed and grow large, and at some known seasons of the year the inhabitants assemble and cut down the small bars which the waves always throw up. By these easy means, the waters of the pond are let out, and as the fish follow their native element, the inhabitants with proper nets catch as many as they want, in their way out, without any other trouble. Those which are most common are the streaked bass, the blue-fish, the tom-cod, the mackerel, the tew-tag, the herring, the flounder, eel, etc. Fishing is one of the greatest diversions the island affords. At the west end lies the harbour of Mardiket, formed by Smith Point on the south-west, by

Eel Point on the north, and Tuckernut Island on the north-west; but it is neither so safe nor has it so good anchoring ground as that near which the town stands. Three small creeks run into it which yield the bitterest eels I have ever tasted. Between the lots of Palpus on the east, Barry's Valley and Miacomet pond on the south, and the narrow pond on the west, not far from Shèmah Point, they have a considerable track of even ground, being the least sandy and the best on the island. It is divided into seven fields, one of which is planted by that part of the community which are entitled to it. This is called the common plantation, a simple but useful expedient, for were each holder of this track to fence his property, it would require a prodigious quantity of posts and rails, which you must remember are to be purchased and fetched from the main. Instead of those private subdivisions, each man's allotment of land is thrown into the general field, which is fenced at the expense of the parties; within it, every one does with his own portion of the ground whatever he pleases. This apparent community saves a very material expense, a great deal of labour, and perhaps raises a sort of emulation among them which urges every one to fertilize his share with the greatest care and attention. Thus every seven years the whole of this track is under cultivation, and enriched by manure and ploughing, yields afterwards excellent pasture, to which the town cows, amounting to 500, are daily led by the town shepherd and as regularly drove back in the evening. There each animal easily finds the house to which it belongs, where they are sure to be well rewarded for the milk they give by a present of bran, grain, or some farinaceous preparation, their economy being very great in that respect. These are commonly called Tètoukèmah lots. You must not imagine that every person on the island is either a landholder or concerned in rural operations; no, the greater part are at sea, busily employed in their different fisheries; others are mere strangers who come to settle as handicrafts, mechanics, etc., and even among the natives, few are possessed of determinate shares of land: for engaged in sea affairs or trade, they are satisfied with possessing a few sheep pastures, by means of which they may have perhaps one or two cows. Many have but one, for the great number of

children they have has caused such subdivisions of the
original proprietorship as is sometimes puzzling to trace;
and several of the most fortunate at sea have purchased
and realized a great number of these original pasture
titles. The best land on the island is at Palpus, remarkable for nothing but a house of entertainment. Quayes is
a small but valuable track, long since purchased by Mr.
Coffin, where he has erected the best house on the island.
By long attention, proximity of the sea, etc., this fertile
spot has been well manured and is now the garden of
Nantucket. Adjoining to it on the west side there is a
small stream on which they have erected a fulling mill; on
the east side is the lot, known by the name of Squam, watered likewise by a small rivulet on which stands another
fulling mill. Here is fine loamy soil, producing excellent
clover, which is mowed twice a year. These mills prepare
all the cloth which is made here: you may easily suppose
that having so large a flock of sheep, they abound in wool;
part of this they export, and the rest is spun by their industrious wives and converted into substantial garments.
To the south-east is a great division of the island, fenced
by itself, known by the name of Siasconcet lot. It is a
very uneven track of ground, abounding with swamps;
here they turn in their fat cattle, or such as they intend
to stall-feed, for their winter's provisions. It is on the
shores of this part of the island, near Pochick Rip, where
they catch their best fish, such as sea bass, tew-tag, or
black fish, cod, smelt, perch, shadine, pike, etc. They
have erected a few fishing houses on this shore, as well
as at Sankate's Head and Suffakatchè Beach, where the
fishermen dwell in the fishing season. Many red cedar
bushes and beach grass grow on the peninsula of Coitou;
the soil is light and sandy and serves as a receptacle for
rabbits. It is here that their sheep find shelter in the
snow-storms of the winter. At the north end of Nantucket, there is a long point of land projecting far into
the sea, called Sandy Point; nothing grows on it but
plain grass; and this is the place whence they often
catch porpoises and sharks by a very ingenious method. On this point they commonly drive their horses
in the spring of the year in order to feed on the grass it
bears,. which is useless when arrived at maturity. Between that point and the main island, they have a valua-

ble salt meadow, called Croskaty, with a pond of the
same name famous for black ducks. Hence we must return to Squam, which abounds in clover and herds grass;
those who possess it follow no maritime occupation and
therefore neglect nothing that can render it fertile and
profitable. The rest of the undescribed part of the island
is open and serves as a common pasture for their sheep.
To the west of the island is that of Tuckernut, where in
the spring their young cattle are driven to feed; it has a
few oak bushes and two freshwater ponds, abounding
with teals, brandts, and many other sea fowls, brought
to this island by the proximity of their sandbanks and
shallows, where thousands are seen feeding at low water.
Here they have neither wolves nor foxes; those inhabitants, therefore, who live out of town raise with all security as much poultry as they want; their turkeys are very
large and excellent. In summer this climate is extremely
pleasant; they are not exposed to the scorching sun of
the continent, the heats being tempered by the sea breezes,
with which they are perpetually refreshed. In the winter, however, they pay severely for those advantages; it
is extremely cold; the north-west wind, the tyrant of this
country, after having escaped from our mountains and
forests, free from all impediment in its short passage,
blows with redoubled force and renders this island bleak
and uncomfortable. On the other hand, the goodness of
their houses, the social hospitality of their firesides, and
their good cheer make them ample amends for the severity of the season; nor are the snows so deep as on the
main. The necessary and unavoidable inactivity of that
season, combined with the vegetative rest of nature,
force mankind to suspend their toils: often at this season
more than half the inhabitants of the island are at sea,
fishing in milder latitudes.

This island, as has been already hinted, appears to be
the summit of some huge sandy mountain, affording
some acres of dry land for the habitation of man; other
submarine ones lie to the southward of this, at different
depths and different distances. This dangerous region is
well known to the mariners by the name of Nantucket
shoals: these are the bulwarks which so powerfully defend this island from the impulse of the mighty ocean
and repel the force of its waves, which, but for the ac-

cumulated barriers, would ere now have dissolved its foundations and torn it in pieces. These are the banks which afforded to the first inhabitants of Nantucket their daily subsistence, as it was from these shoals that they drew the origin of that wealth which they now possess, and was the school where they first learned how to venture farther, as the fish of their coast receded. The shores of this island abound with the soft-shelled, the hard-shelled, and the great sea clams, a most nutritious shell-fish. Their sands, their shallows, are covered with them; they multiply so fast that they are a never-failing resource. These and the great variety of fish they catch constitute the principal food of the inhabitants. It was likewise that of the aborigines, whom the first settlers found here, the posterity of whom still live together in decent houses along the shores of Miacomet pond, on the south side of the island. They are an industrious, harmless race, as expert and as fond of a seafaring life as their fellow inhabitants, the whites. Long before their arrival, they had been engaged in petty wars against one another; the latter brought them peace, for it was in quest of peace that they abandoned the main. This island was then supposed to be under the jurisdiction of New York, as well as the islands of the Vineyard, Elizabeth's, etc., but have been since adjudged to be a part of the province of Massachusetts Bay. This change of jurisdiction procured them that peace they wanted, and which their brethren had so long refused them in the days of their religious frenzy; thus have enthusiasm and persecution, both in Europe as well as here, been the cause of the most arduous undertakings and the means of those rapid settlements which have been made along these extended sea-shores. This island, having been since incorporated with the neighbouring province, is become one of its counties, known by the name of Nantucket, as well as the island of the Vineyard, by that of Dukes County. They enjoy here the same municipal establishment in common with the rest, and therefore every requisite officer, such as sheriff, justice of the peace, supervisors, assessors, constables, overseer of the poor, etc. Their taxes are proportioned to those of the metropolis; they are levied as with us by valuations, agreed on and fixed, according to the laws of the province, and by assessments formed by the assessors, who are yearly chosen by the people and whose office obliges them to take either an oath or an affirmation. Two thirds of the magistrates they have here are of the Society of Friends.

Before I enter into the further detail of this people's government, industry, mode of living, etc., I think it necessary to give you a short sketch of the political state the natives had been in a few years preceding the arrival of the whites among them. They are hastening towards a total annihilation, and this may be perhaps the last compliment that will ever be paid them by any traveller. They were not extirpated by fraud, violence, or injustice, as hath been the case in so many provinces; on the contrary, they have been treated by these people as brethren, the peculiar genius of their sect inspiring them with the same spirit of moderation which was exhibited at Pennsylvania. Before the arrival of the Europeans, they lived on the fish of their shores, and it was from the same resources the first settlers were compelled to draw their first subsistence. It is uncertain whether the original right of the Earl of Sterling or that of the Duke of York was founded on a fair purchase of the soil or not; whatever injustice might have been committed in that respect cannot be charged to the account of those Friends who purchased from others who no doubt founded their right on Indian grants; and if their numbers are now so decreased, it must not be attributed either to tyranny or violence, but to some of those causes, which have uninterruptedly produced the same effects from one end of the continent to the other, wherever both nations have been mixed. This insignificant spot, like the sea-shores of the great peninsula, was filled with these people; the great plenty of clams, oysters, and other fish on which they lived, and which they easily catched, had prodigiously increased their numbers. History does not inform us what particular nation the aborigines of Nantucket were of; it is, however, very probable that they anciently emigrated from the opposite coast, perhaps from Hyannis, which is but twenty-seven miles distant. As they then spoke and still speak the Nattic, it is reasonable to suppose that they must have had some affinity with that nation, or else that the Nattic, like the Huron, in the north-western parts of this continent, must have been

the most prevailing one in this region. Mr. Elliot, an eminent New England divine and one of the first founders
of that great colony, translated the Bible into this language in the year 1666, which was printed soon after at
Cambridge, near Boston; he translated also the catechism
and many other useful books, which are still very common on this island and are daily made use of by those
Indians who are taught to read. The young Europeans
learn it with the same facility as their own tongues and
ever after speak it both with ease and fluency. Whether
the present Indians are the descendants of the ancient
natives of the island, or whether they are the remains of
the many different nations which once inhabited the regions of Mashpè and Nobscusset, in the peninsula now
known by the name of Cape Cod, no one can positively
tell, not even themselves. The last opinion seems to be
that of the most sensible people of the island. So prevailing is the disposition of man to quarrel and shed
blood, so prone is he to divisions and parties, that even
the ancient natives of this little spot were separated into
two communities, inveterately waging war against each
other like the more powerful tribes of the continent. What
do you imagine was the cause of this national quarrel?
All the coast of their island equally abounded with the
same quantity of fish and clams; in that instance, there
could be no jealousy, no motives to anger; the country afforded them no game; one would think this ought to have
been the country of harmony and peace. But behold the
singular destiny of the human kind, ever inferior in many
instances to the more certain instinct of animals,
among which the individuals of the same species are always friends, though reared in different climates; they
understand the same language, they shed not each other's
blood, they eat not each other's flesh. That part of these
rude people who lived on the eastern shores of the island
had from time immemorial tried to destroy those who
lived on the west; those latter, inspired with the same
evil genius, had not been behind hand in retaliating:
thus was a perpetual war subsisting between these people, founded on no other reason but the adventitious
place of their nativity and residence. In process of time,
both parties became so thin and depopulated that the
few who remained, fearing lest their race should become

totally extinct, fortunately thought of an expedient which prevented their entire annihilation. Some years before the Europeans came, they mutually agreed to settle a partition line which should divide the island from north to south; the people of the west agreed not to kill those of the east, except they were found transgressing over the western part of the line; those of the last entered into a reciprocal agreement. By these simple means, peace was established among them, and this is the only record which seems to entitle them to the denomination of men. This happy settlement put a stop to their sanguinary depredations; none fell afterward but a few rash, imprudent individuals; on the contrary, they multiplied greatly. But another misfortune awaited them: when the Europeans came, they caught the smallpox, and their improper treatment of that disorder swept away great numbers. This calamity was succeeded by the use of rum; and these are the two principal causes which so much diminished their numbers, not only here but all over the continent. In some places, whole nations have disappeared. Some years ago, three Indian canoes, on their return to Detroit from the falls of Niagara, unluckily got the smallpox from the Europeans with whom they had traded. It broke out near the long point on Lake Erie; there they all perished; their canoes and their goods were afterwards found by some travellers journeying the same way; their dogs were still alive. Besides the smallpox and the use of spirituous liquors, the two greatest curses they have received from us, there is a sort of physical antipathy, which is equally powerful from one end of the continent to the other. Wherever they happen to be mixed, or even to live in the neighbourhood of the Europeans, they become exposed to a variety of accidents and misfortunes to which they always fall victims: such are particular fevers, to which they were strangers before, and sinking into a singular sort of indolence and sloth. This has been invariably the case wherever the same association has taken place, as at Nattic, Mashpè, Soccanoket in the bounds of Falmouth, Nobscusset, Houratonick, Monhauset, and the Vineyard. Even the Mohawks themselves, who were once so populous and such renowned warriors, are now reduced to less than 200 since the European settlements have circumscribed the

territories which their ancestors had reserved. Three
years before the arrival of the Europeans at Cape Cod,
a frightful distemper had swept away a great many along
its coasts, which made the landing and intrusion of our
forefathers much easier than it otherwise might have
been. In the year 1763, above half of the Indians of this
island perished by a strange fever, which the Europeans
who nursed them never caught; they appear to be a race
doomed to recede and disappear before the superior
genius of the Europeans. The only ancient custom of
these people that is remembered is that in their mutual
exchanges, forty sun-dried clams, strung on a string,
passed for the value of what might be called a copper.
They were strangers to the use and value of wampum,
so well known to those of the main. The few families
now remaining are meek and harmless; their ancient ferocity is gone; they were early Christianized by the New
England missionaries, as well as those of the Vineyard
and of several other parts of Massachusetts, and to this
day they remain strict observers of the laws and customs of that religion, being carefully taught while young.
Their sedentary life has led them to this degree of civilization much more effectually than if they had still remained hunters. They are fond of the sea, and expert
mariners. They have learned from the Quakers the art
of catching both the cod and whale, in consequence of
which five of them always make part of the complement
of men requisite to fit out a whale-boat. Many have removed hither from the Vineyard, on which account
they are more numerous on Nantucket than anywhere
else.

It is strange what revolution has happened among them
in less than two hundred years! What is become of those
numerous tribes which formerly inhabited the extensive
shores of the great bay of Massachusetts? Even from
Numkeag (Salem), Saugus (Lynn), Shawmut (Boston),
Pataxet, Napouset (Milton), Matapan (Dorchester),
Winèsimèt (Chelsea), Poïasset, Pokànoket (New Plymouth), Suecanosset (Falmouth), Titicut (Chatham),
Nobscusset (Yarmouth), Naussit (Eastham), Hyanneès
(Barnstable), etc., and many others who lived on sea-
shores of above three hundred miles in length; without
mentioning those powerful tribes which once dwelt be-

tween the rivers Hudson, Connecticut, Piscataqua, and
Kennebec, the Mèhikaudret, Mohiguine, Pequots, Narragansets, Niantics, Massachusetts, Wampanoags, Nipnets,
Tarrateens, etc.—They are gone, and every memorial of
them is lost; no vestiges whatever are left of those
swarms which once inhabited this country and replenished both sides of the great peninsula of Cape Cod: not
even one of the posterity of the famous Masconomèo is
left (the sachem of Cape Ann); not one of the descendants
of Massasoit, father of Mètacomèt (Philip), and Wam-
sutta (Alexander), he who first conveyed some lands to
the Plymouth Company. They have all disappeared either
in the wars which the Europeans carried on against them,
or else they have mouldered away, gathered in some of
their ancient towns, in contempt and oblivion; nothing
remains of them all, but one extraordinary monument,
and even this they owe to the industry and religious zeal
of the Europeans, I mean, the Bible translated into the
Nattic tongue. Many of these tribes, giving way to the
superior power of the whites, retired to their ancient villages, collecting the scattered remains of nations once
populous, and in their grant of lands reserved to themselves and posterity certain portions which lay contiguous
to them. There forgetting their ancient manners, they
dwelt in peace; in a few years, their territories were
surrounded by the improvements of the Europeans, in
consequence of which they grew lazy, inactive, unwilling, and unapt to imitate or to follow any of our trades,
and in a few generations either totally perished or else
came over to the Vineyard, or to this island, to reunite
themselves with such societies of their countrymen as
would receive them. Such has been the fate of many nations, once warlike and independent; what we see now
on the main or on those islands may be justly considered
as the only remains of those ancient tribes. Might I be
permitted to pay perhaps a very useless compliment to
those at least who inhabit the great peninsula of Namset, now Cape Cod, with whose names and ancient situation I am well acquainted. This peninsula was divided into
two great regions: that on the side of the bay was known
by the name of Nobscusset, from one of its towns; the
capital was called Nausit (now Eastham); hence the Indians of that region were called Nausit Indians, though

they dwelt in the villages of Pamet, Nosset, Pashée, Potomaket, Soktoowoket, Nobscusset (Yarmouth).

The region on the Atlantic side was called Mashpèe, and contained the tribes of Haynnèes, Costowet, Waquoit, Scootin, Saconasset, Mashpèe, and Namset. Several of these Indian towns have been since converted into flourishing European settlements, known by different names; for as the natives were excellent judges of land, which they had fertilized besides with the shells of their fish, etc., the latter could not make a better choice, though in general this great peninsula is but a sandy pine track, a few good spots excepted. It is divided into seven townships, viz., Barnstable, Yarmouth, Harwich, Chatham, Eastham, Pamet, Namset, or Provincetown, at the extremity of the Cape. Yet these are very populous, though I am at a loss to conceive on what the inhabitants live besides clams, oysters, and fish, their piny lands being the most ungrateful soil in the world. The minister of Namset, or Provincetown, receives from the government of Massachusetts a salary of fifty pounds per annum; and such is the poverty of the inhabitants of that place that, unable to pay him any money, each master of a family is obliged to allow him two hundred horse feet (sea spin), with which this primitive priest fertilizes the land of his glebe, which he tills himself: for nothing will grow on these hungry soils without the assistance of this extraordinary manure, fourteen bushels of Indian corn being looked upon as a good crop. But it is time to return from a digression, which I hope you will pardon. Nantucket is a great nursery of seamen, pilots, coasters, and bank-fishermen; as a country belonging to the province of Massachusetts, it has yearly the benefit of a court of common pleas, and their appeal lies to the supreme court at Boston. I observed before that the Friends compose two thirds of the magistracy of this island; thus they are the proprietors of its territory and the principal rulers of its inhabitants; but with all this apparatus of law, its coercive powers are seldom wanted or required. Seldom is it that any individual is amerced or punished; their jail conveys no terror; no man has lost his life here judicially since the foundation of this town, which is upwards of a hundred years. Solemn tribunals, public executions, humiliating punishments, are altogether unknown. I saw neither governors nor any pageantry of state, neither ostentatious magistrates nor any individuals clothed with useless dignity: no artificial phantoms subsist here, either civil or religious; no gibbets loaded with guilty citizens offer themselves to your view; no soldiers are appointed to bayonet their compatriots into servile compliance. But how is a society composed of 5,000 individuals preserved in the bonds of peace and tranquillity? How are the weak protected from the strong? I will tell you. Idleness and poverty, the causes of so many crimes, are unknown here; each seeks in the prosecution of his lawful business that honest gain which supports them; every period of their time is full, either on shore or at sea. A probable expectation of reasonable profits or of kindly assistance if they fail of success renders them strangers to licentious expedients. The simplicity of their manners shortens the catalogues of their wants; the law, at a distance, is ever ready to exert itself in the protection of those who stand in need of its assistance. The greatest part of them are always at sea, pursuing the whale or raising the cod from the surface of the banks; some cultivate their little farms with the utmost diligence; some are employed in exercising various trades; others, again, in providing every necessary resource in order to refit their vessels or repair what misfortunes may happen, looking out for future markets, etc. Such is the rotation of those different scenes of business which fill the measure of their days, of that part of their lives at least which is enlivened by health, spirits, and vigour. It is but seldom that vice grows on a barren sand like this, which produces nothing without extreme labour. How could the common follies of society take root in so despicable a soil; they generally thrive on its exuberant juices; here there are none but those which administer to the useful, to the necessary, and to the indispensable comforts of life. This land must necessarily either produce health, temperance, and a great equality of conditions, or the most abject misery. Could the manners of luxurious countries be imported here, like an epidemical disorder they would destroy everything; the majority of them could not exist a month; they would be obliged to emigrate. As in all societies except that of the natives, some difference must necessarily exist between individual and individual, for there must be some more exalted than the rest either by their riches or their talents; so in *this*, there are what you might call the high, the middling, and the low; and this difference will always be more remarkable among people who live by sea excursions than among those who live by the cultivation of their land. The first run greater hazard, and adventure more; the profits and the misfortunes attending this mode of life must necessarily introduce a greater disparity than among the latter, where the equal division of the land offers no short road to superior riches. The only difference that may arise among them is that of industry, and perhaps of superior goodness of soil: the gradations I observed here are founded on nothing more than the good or ill success of their maritime enterprises and do not proceed from education; that is the same throughout every class, simple, useful, and unadorned like their dress and their houses. This necessary difference in their fortunes does not, however, cause those heart burnings which in other societies generate crimes. The sea which surrounds them is equally open to all and presents to all an equal title to the chance of good fortune. A collector from Boston is the only king's officer who appears on these shores to receive the trifling duties which this community owes to those who protect them, and under the shadow of whose wings they navigate to all parts of the world.

LETTER V

The easiest way of becoming acquainted with the modes
of thinking, the rules of conduct, and the prevailing manners of any people is to examine what sort of education
they give their children, how they treat them at home,
and what they are taught in their places of public worship. At home their tender minds must be early struck
with the gravity, the serious though cheerful deportment
of their parents; they are inured to a principle of subordination, arising neither from sudden passions nor inconsiderate pleasure; they are gently holden by an uniform
silk cord, which unites softness and strength. A perfect
equanimity prevails in most of their families, and bad
example hardly ever sows in their hearts the seeds of
future and similar faults. They are corrected with tenderness, nursed with the most affectionate care, clad with
that decent plainness from which they observe their parents never to depart: in short, by the force of example,
which is superior even to the strongest instinct of nature, more than by precepts, they learn to follow the
steps of their parents, to despise ostentatiousness as being
sinful. They acquire a taste for that neatness for which their
fathers are so conspicuous; they learn to be prudent and
saving; the very tone of voice with which they are always addressed establishes in them that softness of dic-

127

tion which ever after becomes habitual. Frugal, sober, orderly parents, attached to their business, constantly following some useful occupation, never guilty of riot, dissipation, or other irregularities, cannot fail of training up children to the same uniformity of life and manners. If they are left with fortunes, they are taught how to save them and how to enjoy them with moderation and decency; if they have none, they know how to venture, how to work and toil as their fathers have done before them. If they fail of success. there are always in this island (and wherever this society prevails) established resources, founded on the most benevolent principles. At their meetings they are taught the few, the simple tenets of their sect, tenets as fit to render men sober, industrious, just, and merciful as those delivered in the most magnificent churches and cathedrals; they are instructed in the most essential duties of Christianity so as not to offend the Divinity by the commission of evil deeds, to dread His wrath and the punishments He has denounced; they are taught at the same time to have a proper confidence in His mercy while they deprecate His justice. As every sect, from their different modes of worship and their different interpretations of some parts of the Scriptures, necessarily have various opinions and prejudices which contribute something in forming their characteristics in society, so those of the Friends are well known: obedience to the laws, even to non-resistance, justice, good will to all, benevolence at home, sobriety, meekness, neatness, love of order, fondness and appetite for commerce. They are as remarkable here for those virtues as at Philadelphia, which is their American cradle and the boast of that society. At schools they learn to read and write a good hand, until they are twelve years old; they are then in general put apprentices to the cooper's trade, which is the second essential branch of business followed here; at fourteen they are sent to sea, where in their leisure hours their companions teach them the art of navigation, which they have an opportunity of practising on the spot. They learn the great and useful art of working a ship in all the different situations which the sea and wind so often require, and surely there cannot be a better or a more useful school of that kind in the world. They then go gradually through every station of rowers, steersmen, and harpooners; thus they learn to attack, to pursue, to overtake, to cut, to dress their huge game; and after having performed several such voyages and perfected themselves in this business, they are fit either for the counting-house or the chase.

The first proprietors of this island, or rather the first founders of this town, began their career of industry with a single whale-boat, with which they went to fish for cod; the small distance from their shores at which they caught it enabled them soon to increase their business, and those early successes first led them to conceive that they might likewise catch the whales, which hitherto sported undisturbed on their banks. After many trials and several miscarriages, they succeeded; thus they proceeded, step by step; the profits of one successful enterprise helped them to purchase and prepare better materials for a more extensive one; as these were attended with little costs, their profits grew greater. The south sides of the island, from east to west, were divided into four equal parts, and each part was assigned to a company of six, which, though thus separated, still carried on their business in common. In the middle of this distance, they erected a mast provided with a sufficient number of rounds, and near it they built a temporary hut, where five of the associates lived, whilst the sixth from his high station carefully looked toward the sea in order to observe the spouting of the whales. As soon as any were discovered, the sentinel descended, the whale-boat was launched, and the company went forth in quest of their game. It may appear strange to you, that so slender a vessel as an American whale-boat, containing six diminutive beings, should dare to pursue and to attack, in its native element, the largest and strongest fish that Nature has created. Yet by the exertions of an admirable dexterity, improved by a long practice, in which these people are become superior to any other whalemen, by knowing the temper of the whale after her first movement, and by many other useful observations, they seldom failed to harpoon it and to bring the huge leviathan on the shores. Thus they went on until the profits they made enabled them to purchase larger vessels, and to pursue them farther when the whales quitted their coasts; those who failed in their enterprises returned to the cod-fisheries, which had been their first school and their first resource; they even began to visit the banks of Cape Breton, the Isle of Sable and all the other fishing places with which this coast of America abounds. By degrees they went a-whaling to Newfoundland, to the Gulf of St. Lawrence, to the Straits of Belle Isle, the coast of Labrador, Davis Straits, even to Cape Desolation, in 70° of latitude, where the Danes carry on some fisheries in spite of the perpetual severities of that inhospitable climate. In process of time, they visited the western islands, the latitude of 34° famous for that fish, the Brazils, the coast of Guinea. Would you believe that they have already gone to the Falkland Islands and that I have heard several of them talk of going to the South Sea! Their confidence is so great and their knowledge of this branch of business so superior to that of any other people that they have acquired a monopoly of this commodity. Such were their feeble beginnings, such the infancy and the progress of their maritime schemes; such is now the degree of boldness and activity to which they are arrived in their manhood. After their examples, several companies have been formed in many of our capitals, where every necessary article of provisions, implements, and timber are to be found. But the industry exerted by the people of Nantucket hath hitherto enabled them to rival all their competitors; consequently, this is the greatest mart for oil, whalebone, and spermaceti on the continent. It does not follow, however, that they are always successful; this would be an extraordinary field indeed where the crops should never fail; many voyages do not repay the original cost of fitting out; they bear such misfortunes like true merchants, and as they never venture their all like gamesters, they try their fortunes again; the latter hope to win by chance alone, the former by industry, well-judged speculation, and some hazard. I was there when Mr. —— had missed one of his vessels; she had been given over for lost by everybody, but happily arrived before I came away, after an absence of thirteen months. She had met with a variety of disappointments on the station she was ordered to, and rather than return empty, the people steered for the coast of Guinea, where they fortunately fell in with several whales, and brought home upward of 600 barrels of oil, beside bone. Those returns are sometimes disposed of in the towns of the continent, where they are exchanged for such commodities as are wanted; but they are most commonly sent to England, where they always sell for cash. When this is intended, a vessel larger than the rest is fitted out to be filled with oil on the spot where it is found and made, and thence she sails immediately for London. This expedient saves time, freight, and expense; and from that capital they bring back whatever they want. They employ also several vessels in transporting lumber to the West Indian Islands, from whence they procure in return the various productions of the country, which they afterwards exchange wherever they can hear of an advantageous market. Being extremely acute, they well know how to improve all the advantages which the combination of so many branches of business constantly affords; the spirit of commerce, which is the simple art of a reciprocal supply of wants, is well understood here by everybody. They possess, like the generality of the Americans, a large share of native penetration, activity, and good sense, which leads them to a variety of other secondary schemes too tedious to mention; they are well acquainted with the cheapest method of procuring lumber from Kennebec River, Penobscot, etc.; pitch and tar from North Carolina; flour and biscuit from Philadelphia; beef and pork from Connecticut. They know how to exchange their cod-fish and West Indian produce for those articles which they are continually either bringing to their island or sending off to other places where they are wanted. By means of all these commercial negotiations, they have greatly cheapened the fitting out of their whaling fleets and therefore much improved their fisheries. They are indebted for all these advantages not only to their national genius but to the poverty of their soil; and as a proof of what I have so often advanced, look at the Vineyard (their neighbouring island), which is inhabited by a set of people as keen and as sagacious as themselves. Their soil being in general extremely fertile, they have fewer navigators, though they are equally well situated for the fishing business. As in my way back to Falmouth, on the main, I visited this sister island, permit me to give you as concisely as I can a short but true description of it; I am not so limited in the principal object of this journey as to wish to confine myself to the single spot of Nantucket.

LETTER VI

DESCRIPTION OF THE ISLAND OF MARTHA'S VINEYARD AND OF THE WHALE FISHERY

This island is twenty miles in length and from seven to eight miles in breadth. It lies nine miles from the continent and with the Elizabeth Island forms one of the counties of Massachusetts Bay, known by the name of Dukes County. Those latter, which are six in number, are about nine miles distant from the Vineyard, and are all famous for excellent dairies. A good ferry is established between Edgartown and Falmouth, on the main, the distance being nine miles. Martha's Vineyard is divided into three townships, viz., Edgar, Chilmark, and Tisbury; the number of inhabitants is computed at about 4,000, 300 of which are Indians. Edgar is the best seaport and the shire town, and as its soil is light and sandy, many of its inhabitants follow the example of the people of Nantucket. The town of Chilmark has no good harbour, but the land is excellent and no way inferior to any on the continent: it contains excellent pastures, convenient brooks for mills, stone for fencing, etc. The town of Tisbury is remarkable for the excellence of its timber and has a harbour where the water is deep enough for ships of the line. The stock of the island is 20,000 sheep, 2,000 neat cattle, beside horses and goats; they have also some deer and abundance of sea-fowls. This has been from the beginning and is to this day the principal seminary of the Indians; they live on that part of the island which is called Chappaquiddick and were very early Christianized by the respectable family of the Mahews, the first proprietors of it. The first settler of that name conveyed by will to a favourite daughter a certain part of it, on which there grew many wild vines; thence it was called Martha's Vineyard, after her name, which in process of time extended to the whole island. The posterity of the ancient aborigines remain here to this day, on lands which their forefathers reserved for themselves and which are religiously kept from any encroachments. The New England people are remarkable for the honesty with which they have fulfilled, all over that province, those ancient covenants which in many others have been disregarded, to the scandal of those governments. The Indians there appeared, by the decency of their manners, their industry, and neatness, to be wholly Europeans and no way inferior to many of the inhabitants. Like them, they are sober, laborious, and religious, which are the principal characteristics of the four New England provinces. They often go, like the young men of the Vineyard, to Nantucket and hire themselves for whalemen or fishermen; and indeed their skill and dexterity in all sea affairs is nothing inferior to that of the whites. The latter are divided into two classes: the first occupy the land, which they till with admirable care and knowledge; the second, who are possessed of none, apply themselves to the sea, the general resource of mankind in this part of the world. This island therefore, like Nantucket, is become a great nursery which supplies with pilots and seamen the numerous coasters with which this extended part of America abounds. Go where you will from Nova Scotia to the Mississippi, you will find almost everywhere some natives of these two islands employed in seafaring occupations. Their climate is so favourable to population that marriage is the object of every man's earliest wish; and it is a blessing so easily obtained that great numbers are obliged to quit their native land and go to some other countries in quest of subsistence. The inhabitants are all Presbyterians, which is the established religion of Massachusetts; and here let me remember with gratitude the hospitable treatment

I received from B. Norton, Esq., the colonel of the island, as well as from Dr. Mahew, the lineal descendant of the first proprietor. Here are to be found the most expert pilots, either for the great bay, their sound, Nantucket shoals, or the different ports in their neighbourhood. In stormy weather they are always at sea, looking out for vessels, which they board with singular dexterity, and hardly ever fail to bring safe to their intended harbour. Gay-Head, the western point of this island, abounds with a variety of ochres of different colours, with which the inhabitants paint their houses.

The vessels most proper for whale fishing are brigs of about 150 tons burthen, particularly when they are intended for distant latitudes; they always man them with thirteen hands in order that they may row two whale-boats, the crews of which must necessarily consist of six, four at the oars, one standing on the bows with the harpoon, and the other at the helm. It is also necessary that there should be two of these boats, that if one should be destroyed in attacking the whale, the other, which is never engaged at the same time, may be ready to save the hands. Five of the thirteen are always Indians; the last of the complement remains on board to steer the vessel during the action. They have no wages; each draws a certain established share in partnership with the proprietor of the vessel, by which economy they are all proportionably concerned in the success of the enterprise and all equally alert and vigilant. None of these whalemen ever exceed the age of forty; they look on those who are past that period not to be possessed of all that vigour and agility which so adventurous a business requires. Indeed, if you attentively consider the immense disproportion between the object assailed and the assailants, if you think of the diminutive size and weakness of their frail vehicle, if you recollect the treachery of the element on which this scene is transacted, the sudden and unforeseen accidents of winds, etc., you will readily acknowledge that it must require the most consummate exertion of all the strength, agility, and judgement of which the bodies and the minds of men are capable to undertake these adventurous encounters.

As soon as they arrive in those latitudes where they

expect to meet with whales, a man is sent up to the masthead; if he sees one, he immediately cries out AWAITE PAWANA, *here is a whale;* they all remain still and silent until he repeats PAWANA, *a whale,* when in less than six minutes the two boats are launched, filled with every implement necessary for the attack. They row toward the whale with astonishing velocity; and as the Indians early became their fellow-labourers in this new warfare, you can easily conceive how the Nattic expressions became familiar on board the whale-boats. Formerly it often happened that whale vessels were manned with none but Indians and the master; recollect also that the Nantucket people understand the Nattic and that there are always five of these people on board. There are various ways of approaching the whale, according to their peculiar species; and this previous knowledge is of the utmost consequence. When these boats are arrived at a reasonable distance, one of them rests on its oars and stands off as a witness of the approaching engagement; near the bows of the other, the harpooner stands up, and on him principally depends the success of the enterprise. He wears a jacket, closely buttoned, and round his head a handkerchief, tightly bound; in his hands he holds the dreadful weapon, made of the best steel, marked sometimes with the name of their town and sometimes with that of their vessel, to the shaft of which the end of a cord of due strength, coiled up with the utmost care in the middle of the boat, is firmly tied; the other end is fastened to the bottom of the boat. Thus prepared, they row in profound silence, leaving the whole conduct of the enterprise to the harpooner and to the steersman, attentively following their directions. When the former judges himself to be near enough to the whale, that is, at the distance of about fifteen feet, he bids them stop; perhaps she has a calf, whose safety attracts all the attention of the dam, which is a favourable circumstance; perhaps she is of a dangerous species, and it is safest to retire, though their ardour will seldom permit them; perhaps she is asleep—in that case he balances high the harpoon, trying in this important moment to collect all the energy of which he is capable. He launches it forth; she is struck; from her first movement they judge of her temper, as well as of their future success. Sometimes, in the immediate im-

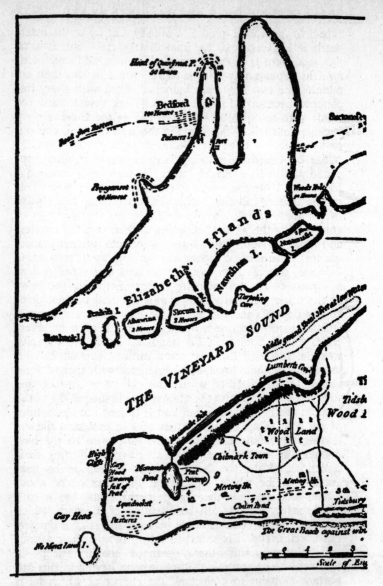

Island of Quainnut P.
34 Houses

Bedford
100 Houses

Sacharnet

Road from Barton

Palmers I.

Port

Froganset
44 Houses

Woods Hole
or Bourne

Elizabeth   Islands

Nanshon I.

Nashawinah

Turpking Cove

Pescaba I.

Slocum I.
2 Houses

Athewine
2 Houses

Nashawek

THE   VINEYARD   SOUND

Middle ground Shoal & Rocks at low water

Lumberts Cove

Ti

Tisbu
Wood I.

Wood   Land

High
Cliff

Gay
Head
Swamp
full of
Peat

Nomans
Pond

Peat
Swamp

9

Chilmark Town

Meeting Ho.

Meeting Ho.

Squidnokset
Pastures

Chilm Pond

3 Ch.
Tisbury

Gay Head

The Great Beach against wit

No Mens Land I.

Scale of Eng

1. Starbuck Point; 2. Beniah Norton's house, the colonel of the island;
3. the house of James Athearn, Esq.; 4. Dr. Mahew's house; 5. iron-mine,
the ore of which is carried to the forges at Taunton; 6. lagoon, famous for

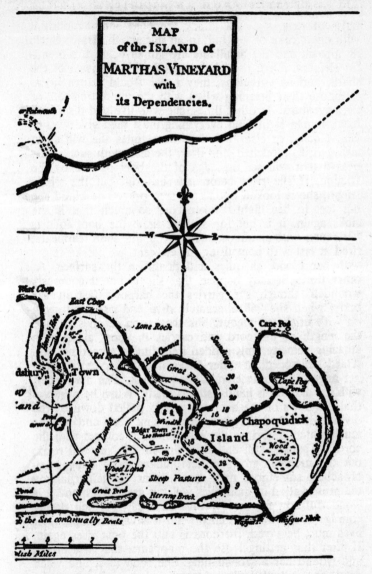

MAP
of the ISLAND of
MARTHAS VINEYARD
with
its Dependencies.

catching bass under the ice; 7. the best mowing grounds in the island, yielding four tons of black grass per acre; 8. excellent planting ground; 9. a mine of good pipe-clay.

pulse of rage, she will attack the boat and demolish it with one stroke of her tail; in an instant, the frail vehicle disappears and the assailants are immersed in the dreadful element. Were the whale armed with the jaws of the shark, and as voracious, they never would return home to amuse their listening wives with the interesting tale of the adventure. At other times, she will dive and disappear from human sight; and everything must then give way to her velocity, or else all is lost. Sometimes she will swim away, as if untouched, and draw the cord with such swiftness that it will set the edge of the boat on fire by the friction. If she rises before she has run out the whole length, she is looked upon as a sure prey. The blood she has lost in her flight weakens her so much that if she sinks again, it is but for a short time; the boat follows her course with an almost equal speed. She soon reappears; tired at last with convulsing the element, which she tinges with her blood, she dies and floats on the surface. At other times, it may happen that she is not dangerously wounded, though she carries the harpoon fast in her body, when she will alternately dive and rise, and swim on with unabated vigour. She then soon reaches beyond the length of the cord and carries the boat along with amazing velocity: this sudden impediment sometimes will retard her speed; at other times it only serves to rouse her anger and to accelerate her progress. The harpooner, with the axe in his hands, stands ready. When he observes that the bows of the boat are greatly pulled down by the diving whale and that it begins to sink deep and to take much water, he brings the axe almost in contact with the cord; he pauses, still flattering himself that she will relax; but the moment grows critical; unavoidable danger approaches; sometimes men more intent on gain than on the preservation of their lives will run great risks; and it is wonderful how far these people have carried their daring courage at this awful moment! But it is vain to hope; their lives must be saved; the cord is cut; the boat rises again. If after thus getting loose she reappears, they will attack and wound her a second time. She soon dies, and when dead, she is towed alongside of their vessel, where she is fastened.

The next operation is to cut with axes and spades every part of her body which yields oil; the kettles are set a-boiling; they fill their barrels as fast as it is made; but as this operation is much slower than that of cutting up, they fill the hold of their ship with those fragments, lest a storm should arise and oblige them to abandon their prize. It is astonishing what a quantity of oil some of these fish will yield and what profit it affords to those who are fortunate enough to overtake them. The river St. Lawrence whale, which is the only one I am well acquainted with, is seventy-five feet long, sixteen deep, twelve in the length of its bone, which commonly weighs 3,000 lb., twenty in the breadth of their tails, and produces 180 barrels of oil: I once saw 16 boiled out of the tongue only. After having once vanquished this leviathan, there are two enemies to be dreaded beside the wind, the first of which is the shark: that fierce, voracious fish, to which nature has given such dreadful offensive weapons, often comes alongside, and in spite of the people's endeavours, will share with them in their prey, at night particularly. They are very mischievous, but the second enemy is much more terrible and irresistible; it is the killer, sometimes called the thrasher, a species of whales about thirty feet long. They are possessed of such a degree of agility and fierceness as often to attack the largest spermaceti whales, and not seldom to rob the fishermen of their prey; nor are there any means of defence against so potent an adversary. When all their barrels are full, for everything is done at sea, or when their limited time is expired and their stores almost expended, they return home, freighted with their valuable cargo, unless they have put it on board a vessel for the European market. Such are, as briefly as I can relate them, the different branches of the economy practised by these bold navigators and the method with which they go such distances from their island to catch this huge game.

The following are the names and principal characteristics of the various species of whales known to these people:

The river St. Lawrence whale, just described.

The disko, or Greenland ditto.

The right whale, or seven feet bone, common on the coasts of this country, about sixty feet long.

The spermaceti whale, found all over the world and

of all sizes; the longest are sixty feet and yield about 100 barrels of oil.

The hump-backs, on the coast of Newfoundland, from forty to seventy feet in length.

The finn-back, an American whale, never killed, as being too swift.

The sulphur-bottom, river St. Lawrence, ninety feet long; they are but seldom killed, as being extremely swift.

The grampus, thirty feet long, never killed, on the same account.

The killer, or thrasher, about thirty feet; they often kill the other whales, with which they are at perpetual war.

The black fish whale, twenty feet; yields from eight to ten barrels.

The porpoise, weighing about 160 lb.

In 1769 they fitted out 125 whalemen; the first fifty that returned brought with them 11,000 barrels of oil. In 1770 they fitted out 135 vessels for the fisheries, at thirteen hands each; four West-Indiamen, twelve hands; twenty-five wood vessels, four hands; eighteen coasters, five hands; fifteen London traders, eleven hands. All these amount to 2,158 hands, employed in 197 vessels. Trace their progressive steps between the possession of a few whale-boats, and that of such a fleet!

The moral conduct, prejudices, and customs of a people who live two thirds of their time at sea, must naturally be very different from those of their neighbours, who live by cultivating the earth. That long abstemiousness to which the former are exposed, the breathing of saline air, the frequent repetitions of danger, the boldness acquired in surmounting them, the very impulse of the winds, to which they are exposed—all these, one would imagine, must lead them, when on shore, to no small desire of ine-briation and a more eager pursuit of those pleasures, of which they have been so long deprived and which they must soon forego. There are many appetites that may be gratified on shore, even by the poorest man, but which must remain unsatisfied at sea. Yet, notwithstanding the powerful effects of all these causes, I observe here, at the return of their fleets, no material irregularities, no tumultuous drinking assemblies; whereas in our continental towns, the thoughtless seaman indulges himself in the coarsest pleasures and, vainly thinking that a week of debauchery can compensate for months of abstinence, foolishly lavishes in a few days of intoxication the fruits of half a year's labour. On the contrary, all was peace here, and a general decency prevailed throughout; the reason, I believe, is that almost everybody here is married, for they get wives very young; and the pleasure of returning to their families absorbs every other desire. The motives that lead them to the sea are very different from those of most other sea-faring men; it is neither idleness nor profligacy that sends them to that element; it is a settled plan of life, a well-founded hope of earning a livelihood; it is because their soil is bad, that they are early initiated to this profession; and were they to stay at home, what could they do? The sea therefore becomes to them a kind of patrimony; they go to whaling with as much pleasure and tranquil indifference, with as strong an expectation of success, as a landman undertakes to clear a piece of swamp. The first is obliged to advance his time and labour to procure oil on the surface of the sea; the second advances the same to procure himself grass from grounds that produced nothing before but hassocks and bogs. Among those who do not use the sea, I observed the same calm appearance as among the inhabitants on the continent; here I found, without gloom, a decorum and reserve so natural to them that I thought myself in Philadelphia. At my landing I was cordially received by those to whom I was recommended and treated with unaffected hospitality by such others with whom I became acquainted; and I can tell you that it is impossible for any traveller to dwell here one month without knowing the heads of the principal families. Wherever I went I found simplicity of diction and manners, rather more primitive and rigid than I expected; and I soon perceived that it proceeded from their secluded situation, which has prevented them from mixing with others. It is therefore easy to conceive how they have retained every degree of peculiarity for which this sect was formerly distinguished. Never was a beehive more faithfully employed in gathering wax, beebread, and honey from all the neighbouring fields than are the members of this society; every one in the town follows some particular occupation with great diligence, but without that servil-

ity of labour which I am informed prevails in Europe. The
mechanic seemed to be descended from as good parent-
age, was as well dressed and fed, and held in as much
estimation as those who employed him; they were once
nearly related; their different degrees of prosperity is
what has caused the various shades of their community.
But this accidental difference has introduced, as yet,
neither arrogance nor pride on the one part, nor meanness and servility on the other. All their houses are neat,
convenient, and comfortable; some of them are filled with
two families, for when the husbands are at sea, the wives
require less house-room. They all abound with the most
substantial furniture, more valuable from its usefulness
than from any ornamental appearance. Wherever I went
I found good cheer, a welcome reception; and after the
second visit, I felt myself as much at my ease as if I had
been an old acquaintance of the family. They had as great
plenty of everything as if their island had been part
of the golden quarter of Virginia (a valuable track of land
on Cape Charles); I could hardly persuade myself that
I had quitted the adjacent continent, where everything
abounds, and that I was on a barren sandbank, fertilized
with whale-oil only. As their rural improvements are but
trifling, and only of the useful kind, and as the best of
them are at a considerable distance from the town, I
amused myself for several days in conversing with the
most intelligent of the inhabitants of both sexes and
making myself acquainted with the various branches of
their industry; the different objects of their trade; the nature of that sagacity which, deprived as they are of
every necessary material, produce, etc., yet enables them
to flourish, to live well, and sometimes to make considerable fortunes. The whole is an enigma to be solved only
by coming to the spot and observing the national genius
which the original founders brought with them, as well
as their unwearied patience and perseverance. They
have all, from the highest to the lowest, a singular
keenness of judgement, unassisted by any academical light;
they all possess a large share of good sense, improved
upon the experience of their fathers; and this is the surest
and best guide to lead us through the path of life, because
it approaches nearest to the infallibility of instinct. Shining
talents and university knowledge would be entirely useless

here, nay, would be dangerous; it would pervert their plain judgement, it would lead them out of that useful path which is so well adapted to their situation; it would make them more adventurous, more presumptuous, much less cautious, and therefore less successful. It is pleasing to hear some of them tracing a father's progress and their own through the different vicissitudes of good and adverse fortune. I have often, by their firesides, travelled with them the whole length of their career, from their earliest steps, from their first commercial adventure, from the possession of a single whale-boat, up to that of a dozen large vessels! This does not imply, however, that every one who began with a whale-boat has ascended to a like pitch of fortune; by no means the same casualty, the same combination of good and evil which attends human affairs in every other part of the globe, prevails here: great prosperity is not the lot of every man, but there are many and various gradations; if they all do not attain riches, they all attain an easy subsistence. After all, is it not better to be possessed of a single whale-boat or a few sheep pastures, to live free and independent under the mildest government, in a healthy climate, in a land of charity and benevolence, than to be wretched as so many are in Europe, possessing nothing but their industry; tossed from one rough wave to another; engaged either in the most servile labours for the smallest pittance or fettered with the links of the most irksome dependence, even without the hopes of rising?

The majority of those inferior hands which are employed in this fishery, many of the mechanics, such as coopers, smiths, caulkers, carpenters, etc., who do not belong to the Society of Friends, are Presbyterians and originally came from the main. Those who are possessed of the greatest fortunes at present belong to the former, but they all began as simple whalemen: it is even looked upon as honourable and necessary for the son of the wealthiest man to serve an apprenticeship to the same bold, adventurous business which has enriched his father; they go several voyages, and these early excursions never fail to harden their constitutions and introduce them to the knowledge of their future means of subsistence.

LETTER VII

As I observed before, every man takes a wife as soon as
he chooses, and that is generally very early; no portion
is required, none is expected; no marriage articles are
drawn up among us by skilful lawyers to puzzle and lead
posterity to the bar or to satisfy the pride of the parties.
We give nothing with our daughters; their education, their
health, and the customary outset are all that the fathers
of numerous families can afford. As the wife's fortune
consists principally in her future economy, modesty, and
skilful management, so the husband's is founded on his
abilities to labour, on his health, and the knowledge of
some trade or business. Their mutual endeavours, after a
few years of constant application, seldom fail of success
and of bringing them the means to rear and support the
new race which accompanies the nuptial bed. Those children born by the sea-side hear the roaring of its waves
as soon as they are able to listen; it is the first noise
with which they become acquainted, and by early plunging in it they acquire that boldness, that presence of
mind, and dexterity which make them ever after such
expert seamen. They often hear their fathers recount the
adventures of their youth, their combats with the whales,
and these recitals imprint on their opening minds an

144

early curiosity and taste for the same life. They often cross the sea to go to the main and learn even in those short voyages how to qualify themselves for longer and more dangerous ones; they are therefore deservedly conspicuous for their maritime knowledge and experience all over the continent. A man born here is distinguishable by his gait from among a hundred other men, so remarkable are they for a pliability of sinews and a peculiar agility, which attends them even to old age. I have heard some persons attribute this to the effects of the whale-oil with which they are so copiously anointed in the various operations it must undergo ere it is fit either for the European market or the candle manufactory.

But you may perhaps be solicitous to ask what becomes of that exuberancy of population which must arise from so much temperance, from healthiness of climate, and from early marriage? You may justly conclude that their native island and town can contain but a limited number. Emigration is both natural and easy to a maritime people, and that is the very reason why they are always populous, problematical as it may appear. They yearly go to different parts of this continent, constantly engaged in sea affairs; as our internal riches increase, so does our external trade, which consequently requires more ships and more men: sometimes they have emigrated like bees, in regular and connected swarms. Some of the Friends (by which word I always mean the people called Quakers), fond of a contemplative life, yearly visit the several congregations which this society has formed throughout the continent. By their means, a sort of correspondence is kept up among them all; they are generally good preachers, friendly censors, checking vice wherever they find it predominating, preventing relaxations in any parts of their ancient customs and worship. They everywhere carry admonition and useful advice; and by thus travelling, they unavoidably gather the most necessary observations concerning the various situations of particular districts, their soils, their produce, their distance from navigable rivers, the price of the land, etc. In consequence of informations of this kind, received at Nantucket in the year 1766, a considerable number of them purchased a large track of land in the county of Orange, in North Carolina, situated on the several spring heads of Deep River, which is the western branch of Cape Fear, or North-West River. The advantage of being able to convey themselves by sea to within forty miles of the spot, the richness of the soil, etc., made them cheerfully quit an island on which there was no longer any room for them. There they have founded a beautiful settlement, known by the name of New Garden, contiguous to the famous one which the Moravians have at Bethabara, Bethamia, and Salem, on Yadkin River. No spot of earth can be more beautiful; it is composed of gentle hills, of easy declivities, excellent lowlands, accompanied by different brooks which traverse this settlement. I never saw a soil that rewards men so early for their labours and disbursements; such in general, with very few exceptions, are the lands which adjoin the innumerable heads of all the large rivers which fall into the Chesapeake, or flow through the provinces of North and South Carolina, Georgia, etc. It is perhaps the most pleasing, the most bewitching country which the continent affords, because while it preserves an easy communication with the seaport towns at some seasons of the year, it is perfectly free from the contagious air often breathed in those flat countries which are more contiguous to the Atlantic. These lands are as rich as those over the Alleghany; the people of New Garden are situated at the distance of between 200 and 300 miles from Cape Fear; Cape Fear is at least 450 from Nantucket: you may judge therefore that they have but little correspondence with this their little metropolis except it is by means of the itinerant Friends. Others have settled on the famous river Kennebec, in that territory of the province of Massachusetts which is known by the name of Sagadahock. Here they have softened the labours of clearing the heaviest timbered land in America by means of several branches of trade which their fair river and proximity to the sea afford them. Instead of entirely consuming the timber, as we are obliged to do, some parts of it are converted into useful articles for exportation, such as staves, scantlings, boards, hoops, poles, etc. For that purpose they keep a correspondence with their native island, and I know many of the principal inhabitants of Sherborn, who, though merchants and living at Nantucket, yet possess valuable farms on that river, from whence they draw great part of their subsistence, meat, grain, fire-wood, etc. The title of these lands is vested in the ancient Plymouth Company, under the powers of which the Massachusetts was settled; and that company, which resides in Boston, are still the granters of all the vacant lands within their limits.

Although this part of the province is so fruitful and so happily situated, yet it has been singularly overlooked and neglected; it is surprising that the excellence of that soil which lies on the river should not have caused it to be filled before now with inhabitants, for the settlements from thence to Penobscot are as yet but in their infancy. It is true that immense labour is required to make room for the plough, but the peculiar strength and quality of the soil never fails most amply to reward the industrious possessor; I know of no soil in this country more rich or more fertile. I do not mean that sort of transitory fertility which evaporates with the sun and disappears in a few years; here, on the contrary, even their highest grounds are covered with a rich moist swamp mould, which bears the most luxuriant grass and never-failing crops of grain.

If New Garden exceeds this settlement by the softness of its climate, the fecundity of its soil, and a greater variety of produce from less labour, it does not breed men equally hardy, nor capable to encounter dangers and fatigues. It leads too much to idleness and effeminacy, for great is the luxuriance of that part of America and the ease with which the earth is cultivated. Were I to begin life again, I would prefer the country of Kennebec to the other, however bewitching; the navigation of the river for above 200 miles, the great abundance of fish it contains, the constant healthiness of the climate, the happy severities of the winters always sheltering the earth with a voluminous coat of snow, the equally happy necessity of labour—all these reasons would greatly preponderate against the softer situations of Carolina, where mankind reap too much, do not toil enough, and are liable to enjoy too fast the benefits of life. There are many I know who would despise my opinion and think me a bad judge; let those go and settle at the Ohio, the Monongahela, Red Stone Creek, etc.; let them go and inhabit the extended shores of that superlative river; I with equal cheerfulness would pitch my tent on the rougher shores of Kennebec; this will always be a country of health, labour, and strong activity, and those are characteristics of society which I value more than greater opulence and voluptuous ease.

Thus, though this fruitful hive constantly sends out swarms, as industrious as themselves, yet it always remains full without having any useless drones; on the contrary, it exhibits constant scenes of business and new schemes; the richer an individual grows, the more extensive his field of action becomes; he that is near ending his career drudges on as well as he who has just begun it; nobody stands still. But is it not strange that after having accumulated riches, they should never wish to exchange their barren situation for a more sheltered, more pleasant one on the main? Is it not strange that after having spent the morning and the meridian of their days amidst the jarring waves, weary with the toils of a laborious life, they should not wish to enjoy the evenings of those days of industry in a larger society on some spots of terra firma where the severity of the winters is balanced by a variety of more pleasing scenes, not to be found here? But the same magical power of habit and custom which makes the Laplander, the Siberian, the Hottentot, prefer their climates, their occupations, and their soil to more beneficial situations leads these good people to think that no other spot on the globe is so analogous to their inclinations as Nantucket. Here their connexions are formed; what would they do at a distance removed from them? Live sumptuously, you will say, procure themselves new friends, new acquaintances, by their splendid tables, by their ostentatious generosity, and by affected hospitality. These are thoughts that have never entered into their heads; they would be filled with horror at the thought of forming wishes and plans so different from that simplicity which is their general standard in affluence as well as in poverty. They abhor the very idea of expending in useless waste and vain luxuries the fruits of prosperous labour; they are employed in establishing their sons and in many other useful purposes; strangers to the honours of monarchy, they do not aspire to the possession of affluent fortunes with which to purchase sounding titles and frivolous names!

Yet there are not at Nantucket so many wealthy people as one would imagine after having considered their great successes, their industry, and their knowledge. Many die poor, though hardly able to reproach Fortune with a frown; others leave not behind them that affluence which the circle of their business and of their prosperity naturally promised. The reason of this is, I believe, the peculiar expense necessarily attending their tables; for as their island supplies the town with little or nothing (a few families excepted), every one must procure what they want from the main. The very hay their horses consume, and every other article necessary to support a family, though cheap in a country of so great abundance as Massachusetts, yet the necessary waste and expense attending their transport render these commodities dear. A vast number of little vessels from the main, and from the Vineyard, are constantly resorting here, as to a market. Sherborn is extremely well supplied with everything, but this very constancy of supply necessarily drains off a great deal of money. The first use they make of their oil and bone is to exchange it for bread and meat and whatever else they want; the necessities of a large family are very great and numerous, let its economy be what it will; they are so often repeated that they perpetually draw off a considerable branch of the profits. If by any accidents those profits are interrupted, the capital must suffer; and it very often happens that the greatest part of their property is floating on the sea.

There are but two congregations in this town. They assemble every Sunday in meeting-houses as simple as the dwellings of the people; and there is but one priest on the whole island. What would a good Portuguese observe? But one single priest to instruct a whole island, and to direct their consciences! It is even so; each individual knows how to guide his own and is content to do it as well as he can. This lonely clergyman is a Presbyterian minister, who has a very large and respectable congregation; the other is composed of Quakers, who you know admit of no particular person, who in consequence of being ordained becomes exclusively entitled to preach, to catechize, and to receive certain salaries for his trouble. Among them, every one may expound the Scriptures who thinks he is called so to do; beside, as they admit of neither sacrament, baptism, nor any other outward forms whatever, such a man would be useless. Most of these people are continually at sea and have often the most urgent reasons to worship the Parent of Nature in the midst of the storms which they encounter. These two sects live in perfect peace and harmony with each other; those ancient times of religious discords are now gone (I hope never to return) when each thought it meritorious not only to damn the other, which would have been nothing, but to persecute and murther one another for the glory of that Being who requires no more of us than that we should love one another and live! Every one goes to that place of worship which he likes best, and thinks not that his neighbour does wrong by not following him; each, busily employed in their temporal affairs, is less vehement about spiritual ones, and fortunately you will find at Nantucket neither idle drones, voluptuous devotees, ranting enthusiasts, nor sour demagogues. I wish I had it in my power to send the most persecuting bigot I could find in —— to the whale fisheries; in less than three or four years you would find him a much more tractable man and therefore a better Christian.

Singular as it may appear to you, there are but two medical professors on the island; for of what service can physic be in a primitive society, where the excesses of inebriation are so rare? What need of galenical medicines where fevers and stomachs loaded by the loss of the digestive powers are so few? Temperance, the calm of passions, frugality, and continual exercise keep them healthy and preserve unimpaired that constitution which they have received from parents as healthy as themselves, who in the unpolluted embraces of the earliest and chastest love conveyed to them the soundest bodily frame which nature could give. But as no habitable part of this globe is exempt from some diseases, proceeding either from climate or modes of living, here they are sometimes subject to consumptions and to fevers. Since the foundation of that town no epidemical distempers have appeared, which at times cause such depopulations in other countries; many of them are extremely well acquainted with the Indian methods of curing simple diseases and practise them with success. You will hardly find anywhere a community composed of the same number of individuals possessing such uninterrupted health and exhibiting so many green old men who show their advanced age by the maturity of their wisdom rather than by the wrinkles of their faces; and this is indeed one of the principal blessings of the island, which richly compensates their want of the richer soils of the south, where iliac complaints and bilious fevers grow by the side of the sugar-cane, the ambrosial ananas, etc. The situation of this island, the purity of the air, the nature of their marine occupations, their virtue and moderation, are the causes of that vigour and health which they possess. The poverty of their soil has placed them, I hope, beyond the danger of conquest or the wanton desire of extirpation. Were they to be driven from this spot, the only acquisition of the conquerors would be a few acres of land, enclosed and cultivated, a few houses, and some movables. The genius, the industry of the inhabitants would accompany them; and it is those alone which constitute the sole wealth of their island. Its present fame would perish, and in a few years it would return to its pristine state of barrenness and poverty; they might perhaps be allowed to transport themselves in their own vessels to some other spot or island, which they would soon fertilize by the same means with which they have fertilized this.

One single lawyer has of late years found means to live here, but his best fortune proceeds more from having married one of the wealthiest heiresses of the island than from the emoluments of his practice; however, he is sometimes employed in recovering money lent on the main or in preventing those accidents to which the contentious propensity of its inhabitants may sometimes expose them. He is seldom employed as the means of self-defence and much seldomer as the channel of attack, to which they are strangers, except the fraud is manifest and the danger imminent. Lawyers are so numerous in all our populous towns that I am surprised they never thought before of establishing themselves here; they are plants that will grow in any soil that is cultivated by the hands of others; and when once they have taken root, they will extinguish every other vegetable that grows around them. The fortunes they daily acquire in every

Lawyers

province from the misfortunes of their fellow-citizens are surprising! The most ignorant, the most bungling member of that profession will, if placed in the most obscure part of the country, promote litigiousness and amass more wealth without labour than the most opulent farmer with all his toils. They have so dexterously interwoven their doctrines and quirks with the laws of the land, or rather they are become so necessary an evil in our present constitutions, that it seems unavoidable and past all remedy. What a pity that our forefathers, who happily extinguished so many fatal customs and expunged from their new government so many errors and abuses, both religious and civil, did not also prevent the introduction of a set of men so dangerous! In some provinces where every inhabitant is constantly employed in tilling and cultivating the earth, they are the only members of society who have any knowledge; let these provinces attest what iniquitous use they have made of that knowledge. They are here what the clergy were in past centuries with you; the reformation which clipped the clerical wings is the boast of that age, and the happiest event that could possibly happen; a reformation equally useful is now wanted to relieve us from the shameful shackles and the oppressive burthen under which we groan; this perhaps is impossible; but if mankind would not become too happy, it were an event most devoutly to be wished.

Here, happily, unoppressed with any civil bondage, this society of fishermen and merchants live without any military establishments, without governors or any masters but the laws; and their civil code is so light that it is never felt. A man may pass (as many have done whom I am acquainted with) through the various scenes of a long life, may struggle against a variety of adverse fortune, peaceably enjoy the good when it comes, and never in that long interval apply to the law either for redress or assistance. The principal benefit it confers is the general protection of individuals, and this protection is purchased by the most moderate taxes, which are cheerfully paid, and by the trifling duties incident in the course of their lawful trade (for they despise contraband). Nothing can be more simple than their municipal regulations, though similar to those of the other counties of the same province, because they are more detached from the rest, more distinct in their manners, as well as in the nature of the business they pursue, and more unconnected with the populous province to which they belong. The same simplicity attends the worship they pay to the Divinity; their elders are the only teachers of their congregations, the instructors of their youth, and often the example of their flock. They visit and comfort the sick; after death, the society bury them with their fathers, without pomp, prayers, or ceremonies; not a stone or monument is erected to tell where any person was buried; their memory is preserved by tradition. The only essential memorial that is left of them is their former industry, their kindness, their charity, or else their most conspicuous faults.

The Presbyterians live in great charity with them and with one another; their minister, as a true pastor of the gospel, inculcates to them the doctrines it contains, the rewards it promises, the punishments it holds out to those who shall commit injustice. Nothing can be more disencumbered likewise from useless ceremonies and trifling forms than their mode of worship; it might with great propriety have been called a truly primitive one had that of the Quakers never appeared. As fellow Christians, obeying the same legislator, they love and mutually assist each other in all their wants; as fellow labourers, they unite with cordiality and without the least rancour in all their temporal schemes; no other emulation appears among them but in their sea excursions, in the art of fitting out their vessels; in that of sailing, in harpooning the whale, and in bringing home the greatest harvest. As fellow subjects, they cheerfully obey the same laws and pay the same duties: but let me not forget another peculiar characteristic of this community: there is not a slave I believe on the whole island, at least among the Friends; whilst slavery prevails all around them, this society alone, lamenting that shocking insult offered to humanity, have given the world a singular example of moderation, disinterestedness, and Christian charity in emancipating their Negroes. I shall explain to you farther the singular virtue and merit to which it is so justly entitled by having set before the rest of their fellow-subjects, so pleasing, so edifying a reformation. Happy the people who are subject to so mild a government; happy the government which has to rule over such harmless and such industrious subjects!

While we are clearing forests, making the face of Nature smile, draining marshes, cultivating wheat, and converting it into flour, they yearly skim from the surface of the sea riches equally necessary. Thus, had I leisure and abilities to lead you through this continent, I could show you an astonishing prospect very little known in Europe, one diffusive scene of happiness reaching from the sea-shores to the last settlements on the borders of the wilderness: a happiness, interrupted only by the folly of individuals, by our spirit of litigiousness, and by those unforeseen calamities from which no human society can possibly be exempted. May the citizens of Nantucket dwell long here in uninterrupted peace, undisturbed either by the waves of the surrounding element or the political commotions which sometimes agitate our continent.

LETTER VIII

PECULIAR CUSTOMS AT NANTUCKET

The manners of the Friends are entirely founded on that simplicity which is their boast and their most distinguished characteristic, and those manners have acquired the authority of laws. Here they are strongly attached to plainness of dress, as well as to that of language; insomuch that though some part of it may be ungrammatical, yet should any person who was born and brought up here attempt to speak more correctly, he would be looked upon as a fop or an innovator. On the other hand, should a stranger come here and adopt their idiom in all its purity (as they deem it), this accomplishment would immediately procure him the most cordial reception, and they would cherish him like an ancient member of their society. So many impositions have they suffered on this account that they begin now indeed to grow more cautious. They are so tenacious of their ancient habits of industry and frugality that if any of them were to be seen with a long coat made of English cloth on any other than the First Day (Sunday), he would be greatly ridiculed and censured; he would be looked upon as a careless spendthrift, whom it would be unsafe to trust and in vain to relieve. A few years ago, two single-horse chairs were imported from Boston, to the great offence of these prudent citizens;

nothing appeared to them more culpable than the use of such gaudy painted vehicles, in contempt of the more useful and more simple single-horse carts of their fathers. This piece of extravagant and unknown luxury almost caused a schism, and set every tongue a-going; some predicted the approaching ruin of those families that had imported them; others feared the dangers of example; never since the foundation of the town had there happened anything which so much alarmed this primitive community. One of the possessors of these profane chairs, filled with repentance, wisely sent it back to the continent; the other, more obstinate and perverse, in defiance of all remonstrances, persisted in the use of his chair until by degrees they became more reconciled to it, though I observed that the wealthiest and the most respectable people still go to meeting or to their farms in a single-horse cart with a decent awning fixed over it; indeed, if you consider their sandy soil and the badness of their roads, these appear to be the best contrived vehicles for this island.

Idleness is the most heinous sin that can be committed in Nantucket: an idle man would soon be pointed out as an object of compassion, for idleness is considered as another word for want and hunger. This principle is so thoroughly well understood and is become so universal, so prevailing a prejudice, that, literally speaking, they are never idle. Even if they go to the market-place, which is (if I may be allowed the expression) the coffee-house of the town, either to transact business or to converse with their friends, they always have a piece of cedar in their hands, and while they are talking, they will, as it were, instinctively employ themselves in converting it into something useful, either in making bungs or spoyls for their oil casks, or other useful articles. I must confess that I have never seen more ingenuity in the use of the knife; thus the most idle moments of their lives become usefully employed. In the many hours of leisure which their long cruises afford them, they cut and carve a variety of boxes and pretty toys, in wood, adapted to different uses, which they bring home as testimonies of remembrance to their wives or sweethearts. They have shown me a variety of little bowls and other implements, executed cooper-wise, with the greatest neatness and elegance. You will be pleased to remember they are all brought up to the trade of coopers, be their future intentions or fortunes what they may; therefore, almost every man in this island has always two knives in his pocket, one much larger than the other; and though they hold everything that is called *fashion* in the utmost contempt, yet they are as difficult to please and as extravagant in the choice and price of their knives as any young buck in Boston would be about his hat, buckles, or coat. As soon as a knife is injured or superseded by a more convenient one, it is carefully laid up in some corner of their desk. I once saw upwards of fifty thus preserved at Mr. ———'s, one of the worthiest men on this island; and among the whole, there was not one that perfectly resembled another. As the sea excursions are often very long, their wives in their absence are necessarily obliged to transact business, to settle accounts, and, in short, to rule and provide for their families. These circumstances, being often repeated, give women the abilities as well as a taste for that kind of superintendency, to which, by their prudence and good management, they seem to be in general very equal. This employment ripens their judgement and justly entitles them to a rank superior to that of other wives; and this is the principal reason why those of Nantucket as well as those of Montreal are so fond of society, so affable, and so conversant with the affairs of the world. The men at their return, weary with the fatigues of the sea, full of confidence and love, cheerfully give their consent to every transaction that has happened during their absence, and all is joy and peace. "Wife, thee hast done well," is the general approbation they receive for their application and industry. What would the men do without the agency of these faithful mates? The absence of so many of them at particular seasons leaves the town quite desolate; and this mournful situation disposes the women to go to each other's house much oftener than when their husbands are at home: hence the custom of incessant visiting has infected every one, and even those whose husbands do not go abroad. The house is always cleaned before they set out, and with peculiar alacrity they pursue their intended visit, which consists of a social chat, a dish of tea, and a hearty supper. When the good man of the house returns from his labour, he peaceably goes after his wife and brings her home; meanwhile, the young fellows, equally vigilant, easily find out which is the most convenient house, and there they assemble with the girls of the neighbourhood. Instead of cards, musical instruments, or songs, they relate stories of their whaling voyages, their various sea adventures, and talk of the different coasts and people they have visited. "The island of Catharine in the Brazil," says one, "is a very droll island; it is inhabited by none but men; women are not permitted to come in sight of it; not a woman is there on the whole island. Who among us is not glad it is not so here? The Nantucket girls and boys beat the world." At this innocent sally, the titter goes round; they whisper to one another their spontaneous reflections: puddings, pies, and custards never fail to be produced on such occasions; for I believe there never were any people in their circumstances, who live so well, even to superabundance. As inebriation is unknown, and music, singing, and dancing are holden in equal detestation, they never could fill all the vacant hours of their lives without the repast of the table. Thus these young people sit and talk and divert themselves as well as they can; if any one has lately returned from a cruise, he is generally the speaker of the night; they often all laugh and talk together, but they are happy and would not exchange their pleasures for those of the most brilliant assemblies in Europe. This lasts until the father and mother return, when all retire to their respective homes, the men reconducting the partners of their affections.

Thus they spend many of the youthful evenings of their lives; no wonder, therefore, that they marry so early. But no sooner have they undergone this ceremony than they cease to appear so cheerful and gay; the new rank they hold in the society impresses them with more serious ideas than were entertained before. The title of master of a family necessarily requires more solid behaviour and deportment; the new wife follows in the trammels of custom, which are as powerful as the tyranny of fashion; she gradually advises and directs; the new husband soon goes to sea; he leaves her to learn and exercise the new government in which she is entered. Those who stay at home are full as passive in general, at least with regard to the inferior departments of the family. But you must not imagine from this account that the Nantucket wives are turbulent, of high temper, and difficult to be ruled; on the contrary, the wives of Sherborn, in so doing, comply only with the prevailing custom of the island; the husbands, equally submissive to the ancient and respectable manners of their country, submit, without ever suspecting that there can be any impropriety. Were they to behave otherwise, they would be afraid of subverting the principles of their society by altering its ancient rules; thus both parties are perfectly satisfied, and all is peace and concord. The richest person now in the island owes all his present prosperity and success to the ingenuity of his wife; this is a known fact which is well recorded, for while he was performing his first cruises, she traded with pins and needles and kept a school. Afterward she purchased more considerable articles, which she sold with so much judgement that she laid the foundation of a system of business that she has ever since prosecuted with equal dexterity and success. She wrote to London, formed connexions, and, in short, became the only ostensible instrument of that house, both at home and abroad. Who is he in this country and who is a citizen of Nantucket or Boston who does not know Aunt Kesiah? I must tell you that she is the wife of Mr. C——n, a very respectable man, who, well pleased with all her schemes, trusts to her judgement and relies on her sagacity with so entire a confidence as to be altogether passive to the concerns of his family. They have the best country seat on the island, at Quayes, where they live with hospitality and in perfect union. He seems to be altogether the contemplative man.

To this dexterity in managing the husband's business whilst he is absent the Nantucket wives unite a great deal of industry. They spin, or cause to be spun in their houses, abundance of wool and flax, and would be forever disgraced and looked upon as idlers if all the family were not clad in good, neat, and sufficient homespun cloth. First Days are the only seasons when it is lawful for both sexes to exhibit some garments of English manufacture; even these are of the most moderate price and of the gravest colours: there is no kind of difference in their dress; they are all clad alike and resemble in that respect the members of one family.

A singular custom prevails here among the women, at which I was greatly surprised and am really at a loss how to account for the original cause that has introduced in this primitive society so remarkable a fashion, or rather so extraordinary a want. They have adopted these many years the Asiatic custom of taking a dose of opium every morning, and so deeply rooted is it that they would be at a loss how to live without this indulgence; they would rather be deprived of any necessary than forego their favourite luxury. This is much more prevailing among the women than the men, few of the latter having caught the contagion, though the sheriff, whom I may call the first person in the island, who is an eminent physician beside and whom I had the pleasure of being well acquainted with, has for many years submitted to this custom. He takes three grains of it every day after breakfast, without the effects of which, he often told me, he was not able to transact any business.

It is hard to conceive how a people always happy and healthy, in consequence of the exercise and labour they undergo, never oppressed with the vapours of idleness, yet should want the fictitious effects of opium to preserve that cheerfulness to which their temperance, their climate, their happy situation, so justly entitle them. But where is the society perfectly free from error or folly; the least imperfect is undoubtedly that where the greatest good preponderates; and agreeable to this rule, I can truly say, that I never was acquainted with a less vicious or more harmless one.

The majority of the present inhabitants are the descendants of the twenty-seven first proprietors who patented the island; of the rest, many others have since come over amongst them, chiefly from the Massachusetts: here are neither Scotch, Irish, nor French, as is the case in most other settlements; they are an unmixed English breed. The consequence of this extended connexion is that they are all in some degree related to each other; you must not be surprised, therefore, when I tell you that they always call each other cousin, uncle, or aunt, which are become such common appellations that no other are made use of in their daily intercourse; you would be deemed stiff and affected were you to refuse conforming yourself to this ancient custom, which truly depicts the image of a large family. The many who reside here that have not the least claim of relationship with any one in the town, yet by the power of custom make use of no other address in their conversation. Were you here yourself but a few days, you would be obliged to adopt the same phraseology, which is far from being disagreeable, as it implies a general acquaintance and friendship, which connects them all in unity and peace.

Their taste for fishing has been so prevailing that it has engrossed all their attention and even prevented them from introducing some higher degree of perfection in their agriculture. There are many useful improvements which might have meliorated their soil; there are many trees which if transplanted here would have thriven extremely well and would have served to shelter as well as decorate the favourite spots they have so carefully manured. The red cedar, the locust, the buttonwood, I am persuaded, would have grown here rapidly and to a great size, with many others; but their thoughts are turned altogether toward the sea. The Indian corn begins to yield them considerable crops, and the wheat sown on its stocks is become a very profitable grain; rye will grow with little care; they might raise, if they would, an immense quantity of buckwheat.

Such an island, inhabited as I have described, is not the place where gay travellers should resort in order to enjoy that variety of pleasures the more splendid towns of this continent afford. Not that they are wholly deprived of what we might call recreations and innocent pastimes, but opulence, instead of luxuries and extravagancies, produces nothing more here than an increase of business, an additional degree of hospitality, greater neatness in the preparation of dishes, and better wines. They often walk and converse with each other, as I have observed before, and upon extraordinary occasions will take a ride to Palpus, where there is a house of entertainment; but these rural amusements are conducted upon the same plan of moderation as those in town. They are so simple as hardly to be described; the pleasure of going and returning together, of chatting and walking about, of throwing the bar, heaving stones, etc., are the only entertainments they are acquainted with. This is all they practise and all they seem to desire. The house at Palpus is the general resort of those who possess the luxury of a horse and chaise, as well as of those who still retain, as the majority do, a predilection for their primitive vehicle. By resorting to that place, they enjoy a change of air, they taste the pleasures of exercise; perhaps an exhilarating bowl, not at all improper in this climate, affords the chief indulgence known to these people on the days of their greatest festivity. The mounting a horse must afford a most pleasing exercise to those men who are so much at sea. I was once invited to that house, and had the satisfaction of conducting thither one of the many beauties of that island (for it abounds with handsome women), dressed in all the betwitching attire of the most charming simplicity; like the rest of the company, she was cheerful without loud laughs, and smiling without affectation. They all appeared gay without levity. I had never before in my life seen so much unaffected mirth, mixed with so much modesty. The pleasures of the day were enjoyed with the greatest liveliness and the most innocent freedom; no disgusting pruderies, no coquettish airs, tarnished this enlivening assembly; they behaved according to their native dispositions, the only rules of decorum with which they were acquainted. What would an European visitor have done here without a fiddle, without a dance, without cards? He would have called it an insipid assembly and ranked this among the dullest days he had ever spent. This rural excursion had a very great affinity to those practised in our province, with this difference only that we have no objection to the sportive dance, though conducted by the rough accents of some self-taught African fiddler. We returned as happy as we went; and the brightness of the moon kindly lengthened a day which had passed, like other agreeable ones, with singular rapidity.

In order to view the island in its longest direction from the town, I took a ride to the easternmost parts of it, remarkable only for the Pochick Rip, where their best fish are caught. I passed by the Tetoukèmah lots, which are the fields of the community; the fences were made of cedar posts and rails, and looked perfectly straight and neat; the various crops they enclosed were flourishing; thence I descended into Barry's Valley, where the blue and the spear grass looked more abundant than I had seen on any other part of the island; thence to Gib's Pond; and arrived at last at Siasconcet. Several dwellings had been erected on this wild shore for the purpose of sheltering the fishermen in the season of fishing; I found them all empty, except that particular one to which I had been directed. It was like the others, built on the highest part of the shore, in the face of the great ocean; the soil appeared to be composed of no other stratum but sand, covered with a thinly scattered herbage. What rendered this house still more worthy of notice in my eyes was that it had been built on the ruins of one of the ancient huts erected by the first settlers for observing the appearance of the whales. Here lived a single family without a neighbour; I had never before seen a spot better calculated to cherish contemplative ideas, perfectly unconnected with the great world, and far removed from its perturbations. The ever-raging ocean was all that presented itself to the view of this family; it irresistibly attracted my whole attention: my eyes were involuntarily directed to the horizontal line of that watery surface, which is ever in motion and ever threatening destruction to these shores. My ears were stunned with the roar of its waves rolling one over the other, as if impelled by a superior force to overwhelm the spot on which I stood. My nostrils involuntarily inhaled the saline vapours which arose from the dispersed particles of the foaming billows or from the weeds scattered on the shores. My mind suggested a thousand vague reflections, pleasing in the hour of their spontaneous birth, but now half forgotten, and all indistinct; and who is the landman that can behold without affright so singular an element, which by its impetuosity seems to be the destroyer of this poor planet, yet at particular times accumulates the scattered fragments and produces islands and continents fit for men to dwell on! Who can observe the regular vicissitudes of its waters without astonishment, now swelling themselves in order to penetrate through every river and opening and thereby facilitate navigation, at other times retiring from the shores to permit man to collect that variety of shell-fish which is the support of the poor? Who can see the storms of wind, blowing sometimes with an impetuosity sufficiently strong even to move the earth, without feeling himself affected beyond the sphere of common ideas? Can this wind which but a few days ago refreshed our American fields and cooled us in the shade be the same element which now and then so powerfully convulses the waters of the sea, dismasts vessels, causes so many shipwrecks and such extensive desolations? How diminutive does a man appear to himself when filled with these thoughts, and standing as I did on the verge of the ocean! This family lived entirely by fishing, for the plough has not dared yet to disturb the parched surface of the neighbouring plain; and to what purpose could this operation be performed! Where is it that mankind will not find safety, peace, and abundance, with freedom and civil happiness? Nothing was wanting here to make this a most philosophical retreat but a few ancient trees to shelter contemplation in its beloved solitude. There I saw a numerous family of children of various ages—the blessings of an early marriage; they were ruddy as the cherry, healthy as the fish they lived on, hardy as the pine knots; the eldest were already able to encounter the boisterous waves and shuddered not at their approach, early initiating themselves in the mysteries of that seafaring career, for which they were all intended; the younger, timid as yet, on the edge of a less agitated pool, were teaching themselves with nut-shells and pieces of wood, in imitation of boats, how to navigate in a future day the larger vessels of their father through a rougher and deeper ocean. I stayed two days there on purpose to become acquainted with the different branches of their economy and their manner of living in this singular retreat. The clams, the oysters of the shores, with the addition of Indian dumplings, constituted their daily and most substantial food. Larger fish were often caught on the neighbouring rip; these afforded them their greatest dainties; they had likewise plenty of smoked bacon. The noise of the wheels announced the industry of the mother and daughters; one of them had been bred a weaver, and having a loom in the house, found means of clothing the whole family; they were perfectly at ease and seemed to want for nothing. I found very few books among these people, who have very little time for reading; the Bible and a few school tracts, both in the Nattic and English languages, constituted their most numerous libraries. I saw indeed several copies of Hudibras and Josephus, but no one knows who first imported them. It is something extraordinary to see this people, professedly so grave and strangers to every branch of literature, reading with pleasure the former work, which should seem to require some degree of taste and antecedent historical knowledge. They all read it much and can by memory repeat many passages, which yet I could not discover that they understood the beauties of. Is it not a little singular to see these books in the hands of fishermen, who are perfect strangers almost to any other? Josephus' history is indeed intelligible and much fitter for their modes of education and taste, as it describes the history of a people from whom we have received the prophecies which we believe and the religious laws which we follow.

Learned travellers, returned from seeing the paintings and antiquities of Rome and Italy, still filled with the admiration and reverence they inspire, would hardly be persuaded that so contemptible a spot, which contains nothing remarkable but the genius and the industry of its inhabitants, could ever be an object worthy attention. But I, having never seen the beauties which Europe contains, cheerfully satisfy myself with attentively examining what my native country exhibits; if we have neither ancient amphitheatres, gilded palaces, nor elevated spires, we enjoy in our woods a substantial happiness which the wonders of art cannot communicate. None among us suffer oppression either from government or religion; there are very few poor except the idle, and fortunately the force of example and the most ample encouragement soon create a new principle of activity, which had been extinguished perhaps in their native country for want of those opportunities which so often compel honest Europeans to seek shelter among us. The means of procuring subsistence in Europe are limited; the army may be full, the navy may abound with seamen, the land perhaps wants no additional labourers, the manufacturer is overcharged with supernumerary hands; what, then, must become of the unemployed? Here, on the contrary, human industry has acquired a boundless field to exert itself in—a field which will not be fully cultivated in many ages!

LETTER IX

DESCRIPTION OF CHARLES TOWN; THOUGHTS ON SLAVERY; ON PHYSICAL EVIL; A MELANCHOLY SCENE

Charles Town is, in the north, what Lima is in the south; both are capitals of the richest provinces of their respective hemispheres; you may therefore conjecture that both cities must exhibit the appearances necessarily resulting from riches. Peru abounding in gold, Lima is filled with inhabitants who enjoy all those gradations of pleasure, refinement, and luxury which proceed from wealth. Carolina produces commodities more valuable perhaps than gold because they are gained by greater industry; it exhibits also on our northern stage a display of riches and luxury, inferior indeed to the former, but far superior to what are to be seen in our northern towns. Its situation is admirable, being built at the confluence of two large rivers, which receive in their course a great number of inferior streams, all navigable in the spring for flat boats. Here the produce of this extensive territory concentres; here therefore is the seat of the most valuable exportation; their wharfs, their docks, their magazines, are extremely convenient to facilitate this great commercial business. The inhabitants are the gayest in America; it is called the centre of our beau monde and is always filled with the richest planters in the province, who resort hither in quest of health and pleasure. Here is always to be seen a great number of valetudinarians from the West Indies, seeking for the renovation of health, exhausted by the debilitating nature of their sun, air, and modes of living. Many of these West Indians have I seen, at thirty, loaded with the infirmities of old age; for nothing is more common in those countries of wealth than for persons to lose the abilities of enjoying the comforts of life at a time when we northern men just begin to taste the fruits of our labour and prudence. The round of pleasure and the expenses of those citizens' tables are much superior to what you would imagine; indeed, the growth of this town and province has been astonishingly rapid. It is pity that the narrowness of the neck on which it stands prevents it from increasing; and which is the reason why houses are so dear. The heat of the climate, which is sometimes very great in the interior parts of the country, is always temperate in Charles Town, though sometimes when they have no sea breezes, the sun is too powerful. The climate renders excesses of all kinds very dangerous, particularly those of the table; and yet, insensible or fearless of danger, they live on and enjoy a short and a merry life. The rays of their sun seem to urge them irresistibly to dissipation and pleasure: on the contrary, the women, from being abstemious, reach to a longer period of life and seldom die without having had several husbands. An European at his first arrival must be greatly surprised when he sees the elegance of their houses, their sumptuous furniture, as well as the magnificence of their tables. Can he imagine himself in a country the establishment of which is so recent?

The three principal classes of inhabitants are lawyers, planters, and merchants; this is the province which has afforded to the first the richest spoils, for nothing can exceed their wealth, their power, and their influence. They have reached the *ne plus ultra* of worldly felicity; no plantation is secured, no title is good, no will is valid, but what they dictate, regulate, and approve. The whole mass of provincial property is become tributary to this society, which, far above priests and bishops, disdain to be satisfied with the poor Mosaical portion of the tenth. I appeal to the many inhabitants who, while contending perhaps for their right to a few hundred acres, have lost by the mazes of the law their whole patrimony. These men are more properly lawgivers than interpreters of the law and have united here, as well as in most other provinces, the skill and dexterity of the scribe with the power and ambition of the prince; who can tell where this may lead in a future day? The nature of our laws and the spirit of freedom, which often tends to make us litigious, must necessarily throw the greatest part of the property of the colonies into the hands of these gentlemen. In another century, the law will possess in the north what now the church possesses in Peru and Mexico.

While all is joy, festivity, and happiness in Charles Town, would you imagine that scenes of misery overspread in the country? Their ears by habit are become deaf, their hearts are hardened; they neither see, hear, nor feel for the woes of their poor slaves, from whose painful labours all their wealth proceeds. Here the horrors of slavery, the hardship of incessant toils, are unseen; and no one thinks with compassion of those showers of sweat and of tears which from the bodies of Africans daily drop and moisten the ground they till. The cracks of the whip urging these miserable beings to excessive labour are far too distant from the gay capital to be heard. The chosen race eat, drink, and live happy, while the unfortunate one grubs up the ground, raises indigo, or husks the rice, exposed to a sun full as scorching as their native one, without the support of good food, without the cordials of any cheering liquor. This great contrast has often afforded me subjects of the most afflicting meditations. On the one side, behold a people enjoying all that life affords most bewitching and pleasurable, without labour, without fatigue, hardly subjected to the trouble of wishing. With gold, dug from Peruvian mountains, they order vessels to the coasts of Guinea; by virtue of that gold, wars, murders, and devastations are committed in some harmless, peaceable African neighbourhood where dwelt innocent people who even knew not but that all men were black. The daughter torn from her weeping mother, the child from the wretched parents, the wife from the loving husband; whole families swept away and brought through storms and tempests to this rich metropolis! There, arranged like horses at a fair, they are branded like cattle and then driven to toil, to starve,

and to languish for a few years on the different plantations of these citizens. And for whom must they work?
For persons they know not, and who have no other power
over them than that of violence, no other right than what
this accursed metal has given them! Strange order of
things! Oh, Nature, where art thou? Are not these blacks
thy children as well as we? On the other side, nothing is to
be seen but the most diffusive misery and wretchedness,
unrelieved even in thought or wish! Day after day they
drudge on without any prospect of ever reaping for
themselves; they are obliged to devote their lives, their
limbs, their will, and every vital exertion to swell the
wealth of masters who look not upon them with half the
kindness and affection with which they consider their dogs
and horses. Kindness and affection are not the portion
of those who till the earth, who carry burthens, who
convert the logs into useful boards. This reward, simple
and natural as one would conceive it, would border on
humanity; and planters must have none of it!

If Negroes are permitted to become fathers, this fatal
indulgence only tends to increase their misery; the poor
companions of their scanty pleasures are likewise the companions of their labours; and when at some critical
seasons they could wish to see them relieved, with tears
in their eyes they behold them perhaps doubly oppressed,
obliged to bear the burden of Nature—a fatal present—as
well as that of unabated tasks. How many have I seen
cursing the irresistible propensity and regretting that by
having tasted of those harmless joys they had become
the authors of double misery to their wives. Like their
masters, they are not permitted to partake of those
ineffable sensations with which Nature inspires the hearts
of fathers and mothers; they must repel them all and
become callous and passive. This unnatural state often
occasions the most acute, the most pungent of their
afflictions; they have no time, like us, tenderly to rear
their helpless offspring, to nurse them on their knees, to
enjoy the delight of being parents. Their paternal fondness is embittered by considering that if their children
live, they must live to be slaves like themselves; no time
is allowed them to exercise their pious office; the mothers
must fasten them on their backs and, with this double
load, follow their husbands in the fields, where they too

often hear no other sound than that of the voice or whip of the taskmaster and the cries of their infants, broiling in the sun. These unfortunate creatures cry and weep like their parents, without a possibility of relief; the very instinct of the brute, so laudable, so irresistible, runs counter here to their master's interest; and to that god, all the laws of Nature must give way. Thus planters get rich; so raw, so inexperienced am I in this mode of life that were I to be possessed of a plantation, and my slaves treated as in general they are here, never could I rest in peace; my sleep would be perpetually disturbed by a retrospect of the frauds committed in Africa in order to entrap them, frauds surpassing in enormity everything which a common mind can possibly conceive. I should be thinking of the barbarous treatment they meet with on shipboard, of their anguish, of the despair necessarily inspired by their situation, when torn from their friends and relations, when delivered into the hands of a people differently coloured, whom they cannot understand, carried in a strange machine over an ever agitated element, which they had never seen before, and finally delivered over to the severities of the whippers and the excessive labours of the field. Can it be possible that the force of custom should ever make me deaf to all these reflections and as insensible to the injustice of that trade and to their miseries as the rich inhabitants of this town seem to be? What, then, is man, this being who boasts so much of the excellence and dignity of his nature among that variety of unscrutable mysteries, of unsolvable problems, with which he is surrounded? The reason why man has been thus created is not the least astonishing! It is said, I know, that they are much happier here than in the West Indies because, land being cheaper upon this continent than in those islands, the fields allowed them to raise their subsistence from are in general more extensive. The only possible chance of any alleviation depends on the humour of the planters, who, bred in the midst of slaves, learn from the example of their parents to despise them and seldom conceive either from religion or philosophy any ideas that tend to make their fate less calamitous, except some strong native tenderness of heart, some rays of philanthropy, overcome the obduracy contracted by habit.

I have not resided here long enough to become insensible of pain for the objects which I every day behold. In the choice of my friends and acquaintance, I always endeavour to find out those whose dispositions are somewhat congenial with my own. We have slaves likewise in our northern provinces; I hope the time draws near when they will be all emancipated, but how different their lot, how different their situation, in every possible respect! They enjoy as much liberty as their masters; they are as well clad and as well fed; in health and sickness, they are tenderly taken care of; they live under the same roof and are, truly speaking, a part of our families. Many of them are taught to read and write, and are well instructed in the principles of religion; they are the companions of our labours, and treated as such; they enjoy many perquisites, many established holidays, and are not obliged to work more than white people. They marry where inclination leads them, visit their wives every week, are as decently clad as the common people; they are indulged in educating, cherishing, and chastising their children, who are taught subordination to them as to their lawful parents: in short, they participate in many of the benefits of our society without being obliged to bear any of its burthens. They are fat, healthy, and hearty; and far from repining at their fate, they think themselves happier than many of the lower class of whites; they share with their masters the wheat and meat provision they help to raise; many of those whom the good Quakers have emancipated have received that great benefit with tears of regret and have never quitted, though free, their former masters and benefactors.

But is it really true, as I have heard it asserted here, that those blacks are incapable of feeling the spurs of emulation and the cheerful sound of encouragement? By no means; there are a thousand proofs existing of their gratitude and fidelity: those hearts in which such noble dispositions can grow are then like ours; they are susceptible of every generous sentiment, of every useful motive of action; they are capable of receiving lights, of imbibing ideas that would greatly alleviate the weight of their miseries. But what methods have in general been made use of to obtain so desirable an end? None; the day in which they arrive and are sold is the first of their labours, labours which from that hour admit of no respite; for though indulged by law with relaxation on Sundays, they are obliged to employ that time which is intended for rest to till their little plantations. What can be expected from wretches in such circumstances? Forced from their native country, cruelly treated when on board, and not less so on the plantations to which they are driven, is there anything in this treatment but what must kindle all the passions, sow the seeds of inveterate resentment, and nourish a wish of perpetual revenge? They are left to the irresistible effects of those strong and natural propensities; the blows they receive, are they conducive to extinguish them or to win their affections? They are neither soothed by the hopes that their slavery will ever terminate but with their lives or yet encouraged by the goodness of their food or the mildness of their treatment. The very hopes held out to mankind by religion, that consolatory system, so useful to the miserable, are never presented to them; neither moral nor physical means are made use of to soften their chains; they are left in their original and untutored state, that very state wherein the natural propensities of revenge and warm passions are so soon kindled. Cheered by no one single motive that can impel the will or excite their efforts, nothing but terrors and punishments are presented to them; death is denounced if they run away; horrid delaceration if they speak with their native freedom; perpetually awed by the terrible cracks of whips or by the fear of capital punishments, while even those punishments often fail of their purpose.

A clergyman settled a few years ago at George Town, and feeling as I do now, warmly recommended to the planters, from the pulpit, a relaxation of severity; he introduced the benignity of Christianity and pathetically made use of the admirable precepts of that system to melt the hearts of his congregation into a greater degree of compassion toward their slaves than had been hitherto customary. "Sir," said one of his hearers, "we pay you a genteel salary to read to us the prayers of the liturgy and to explain to us such parts of the Gospel as the rule of the church directs, but we do not want you to teach us what we are to do with our blacks." The clergyman found it prudent to withhold any farther ad-

monition. Whence this astonishing right, or rather this
barbarous custom, for most certainly we have no kind
of right beyond that of force? We are told, it is true,
that slavery cannot be so repugnant to human-nature as
we at first imagine because it has been practised in all
ages and in all nations; the Lacedaemonians themselves,
those great asserters of liberty, conquered the Helotes
with the design of making them their slaves; the Romans, whom we consider as our masters in civil and
military policy, lived in the exercise of the most horrid
oppression; they conquered to plunder and to enslave.
What a hideous aspect the face of the earth must then
have exhibited! Provinces, towns, districts, often depopulated! Their inhabitants driven to Rome, the greatest
market in the world, and there sold by thousands! The
Roman dominions were tilled by the hands of unfortunate people who had once been, like their victors, free,
rich, and possessed of every benefit society can confer,
until they became subject to the cruel right of war and
to lawless force. Is there, then, no superintending power
who conducts the moral operations of the world, as well
as the physical? The same sublime hand which guides
the planets round the sun with so much exactness, which
preserves the arrangement of the whole with such exalted wisdom and paternal care, and prevents the vast
system from falling into confusion—doth it abandon mankind to all the errors, the follies, and the miseries, which
their most frantic rage and their most dangerous vices
and passions can produce?

The history of the earth! Doth it present anything but
crimes of the most heinous nature, committed from one
end of the world to the other? We observe avarice, rapine, and murder, equally prevailing in all parts. History
perpetually tells us of millions of people abandoned to
the caprice of the maddest princes, and of whole nations
devoted to the blind fury of tyrants. Countries destroyed,
nations alternately buried in ruins by other nations, some
parts of the world beautifully cultivated, returned again
into their pristine state, the fruits of ages of industry, the
toil of thousands in a short time destroyed by few! If
one corner breathes in peace for a few years, it is, in
turn subjected, torn, and levelled; one would almost believe the principles of action in man, considered as the

first agent of this planet, to be poisoned in their most essential parts. We certainly are not that class of beings which we vainly think ourselves to be; man, an animal of prey, seems to have rapine and the love of bloodshed implanted in his heart, nay, to hold it the most honourable occupation in society; we never speak of a hero of mathematics, a hero of knowledge or humanity, no, this illustrious appellation is reserved for the most successful butchers of the world. If Nature has given us a fruitful soil to inhabit, she has refused us such inclinations and propensities as would afford us the full enjoyment of it. Extensive as the surface of this planet is, not one half of it is yet cultivated, not half replenished; she created man and placed him either in the woods or plains and provided him with passions which must forever oppose his happiness; everything is submitted to the power of the strongest; men, like the elements, are always at war; the weakest yield to the most potent; force, subtlety, and malice always triumph over unguarded honesty and simplicity. Benignity, moderation, and justice are virtues adapted only to the humble paths of life; we love to talk of virtue and to admire its beauty while in the shade of solitude and retirement, but when we step forth into active life, if it happen to be in competition with any passion or desire, do we observe it to prevail? Hence so many religious impostors have triumphed over the credulity of mankind and have rendered their frauds the creeds of succeeding generations during the course of many ages until, worn away by time, they have been replaced by new ones. Hence the most unjust war, if supported by the greatest force, always succeeds; hence the most just ones, when supported only by their justice, as often fail. Such is the ascendancy of power, the supreme arbiter of all the revolutions which we observe in this planet; so irresistible is power that it often thwarts the tendency of the most forcible causes and prevents their subsequent salutary effects, though ordained for the good of man by the Governor of the universe. Such is the perverseness of human nature; who can describe it in all its latitude?

In the moments of our philanthropy, we often talk of an indulgent nature, a kind parent, who for the benefit of mankind has taken singular pains to vary the genera of plants, fruits, grain, and the different productions of the earth and has spread peculiar blessings in each climate. This is undoubtedly an object of contemplation which calls forth our warmest gratitude; for so singularly benevolent have those paternal intentions been, that where barrenness of soil or severity of climate prevail, there she has implanted in the heart of man sentiments which overbalance every misery and supply the place of every want. She has given to the inhabitants of these regions an attachment to their savage rocks and wild shores, unknown to those who inhabit the fertile fields of the temperate zone. Yet if we attentively view this globe, will it not appear rather a place of punishment than of delight? And what misfortune that those punishments should fall on the innocent, and its few delights be enjoyed by the most unworthy! Famine, diseases, elementary convulsions, human feuds, dissensions, etc., are the produce of every climate; each climate produces, besides, vices and miseries peculiar to its latitude. View the frigid sterility of the north, whose famished inhabitants, hardly acquainted with the sun, live and fare worse than the bears they hunt and to which they are superior only in the faculty of speaking. View the arctic and antarctic regions, those huge voids where nothing lives, regions of eternal snow where winter in all his horrors has established his throne and arrested every creative power of nature. Will you call the miserable stragglers in these countries by the name of men? Now contrast this frigid power of the north and south with that of the sun; examine the parched lands of the torrid zone, replete with sulphureous exhalations; view those countries of Asia subject to pestilential infections which lay Nature waste; view this globe, often convulsed both from within and without, pouring forth from several mouths rivers of boiling matter which are imperceptibly leaving immense subterranean graves wherein millions will one day perish! Look at the poisonous soil of the equator, at those putrid slimy tracks, teeming with horrid monsters, the enemies of the human race; look next at the sandy continent, scorched perhaps by the fatal approach of some ancient comet, now the abode of desolation. Examine the rains, the convulsive storms of those climates, where masses of sulphur, bitumen, and electrical fire, combining their dreadful powers, are incessantly hovering and bursting over a globe threatened with dissolution. On this little shell, how very few are the spots where man can live and flourish? Even under those mild climates which seem to breathe peace and happiness, the poison of slavery, the fury of despotism, and the rage of superstition are all combined against man! There only the few live and rule whilst the many starve and utter ineffectual complaints; there human nature appears more debased, perhaps, than in the less favoured climates. The fertile plains of Asia, the rich lowlands of Egypt and of Diarbeck, the fruitful fields bordering on the Tigris and the Euphrates, the extensive country of the East Indies in all its separate districts—all these must to the geographical eye seem as if intended for terrestrial paradises; but though surrounded with the spontaneous riches of nature, though her kindest favours seem to be shed on those beautiful regions with the most profuse hand, yet there in general we find the most wretched people in the world. Almost everywhere, liberty so natural to mankind is refused, or rather enjoyed but by their tyrants; the word slave is the appellation of every rank who adore as a divinity a being worse' than themselves, subject to every caprice and to every lawless rage which unrestrained power can give. Tears are shed, perpetual groans are heard, where only the accents of peace, alacrity, and gratitude should resound. There the very delirium of tyranny tramples on the best gifts of nature and sports with the fate, the happiness, the lives of millions; there the extreme fertility of the ground always indicates the extreme misery of the inhabitants!

Everywhere one part of the human species is taught the art of shedding the blood of the other, of setting fire to their dwellings, of levelling the works of their industry: half of the existence of nations regularly employed in destroying other nations. What little political felicity is to be met with here and there has cost oceans of blood to purchase, as if good was never to be the portion of unhappy man. Republics, kingdoms, monarchies, founded either on fraud or successful violence, increase by pursuing the steps of the same policy until they are destroyed in their turn, either by the influence of their own crimes or by more successful but equally criminal enemies.

If from this general review of human nature we descend to the examination of what is called civilized society, there the combination of every natural and artificial want makes us pay very dear for what little share of political felicity we enjoy. It is a strange heterogeneous assemblage of vices and virtues and of a variety of other principles, forever at war, forever jarring, forever producing some dangerous, some distressing extreme. Where do you conceive, then, that nature intended we should be happy? Would you prefer the state of men in the woods to that of men in a more improved situation? Evil preponderates in both; in the first they often eat each other for want of food, and in the other they often starve each other for want of room. For my part, I think the vices and miseries to be found in the latter exceed those of the former, in which real evil is more scarce, more supportable, and less enormous. Yet we wish to see the earth peopled, to accomplish the happiness of kingdoms, which is said to consist in numbers. Gracious God! To what end is the introduction of so many beings into a mode of existence in which they must grope amidst as many errors, commit as many crimes, and meet with as many diseases, wants, and sufferings!

The following scene will, I hope, account for these melancholy reflections and apologize for the gloomy thoughts with which I have filled this letter: my mind is, and always has been, oppressed since I became a witness to it. I was not long since invited to dine with a planter who lived three miles from ——, where he then resided. In order to avoid the heat of the sun, I resolved to go on foot, sheltered in a small path leading through a pleasant wood. I was leisurely travelling along, attentively examining some peculiar plants which I had collected, when all at once I felt the air strongly agitated, though the day was perfectly calm and sultry. I immediately cast my eyes toward the cleared ground, from which I was but a small distance, in order to see whether it was not occasioned by a sudden shower, when at that instant a sound resembling a deep rough voice, uttered, as I thought, a few inarticulate monosyllables. Alarmed and surprised, I precipitately looked all round, when I

perceived at about six rods distance something resembling
a cage, suspended to the limbs of a tree, all the branches
of which appeared covered with large birds of prey, flut-
tering about and anxiously endeavouring to perch on the
cage. Actuated by an involuntary motion of my hands
more than by any design of my mind, I fired at them; they
all flew to a short distance, with a most hideous noise,
when, horrid to think and painful to repeat, I perceived
a Negro, suspended in the cage and left there to expire!
I shudder when I recollect that the birds had already
picked out his eyes; his cheek-bones were bare; his arms
had been attacked in several places; and his body seemed
covered with a multitude of wounds. From the edges of
the hollow sockets and from the lacerations with which
he was disfigured, the blood slowly dropped and tinged
the ground beneath. No sooner were the birds flown than
swarms of insects covered the whole body of this unfortunate wretch, eager to feed on his mangled flesh and
to drink his blood. I found myself suddenly arrested by
the power of affright and terror; my nerves were convulsed; I trembled; I stood motionless, involuntarily contemplating the fate of this Negro in all its dismal latitude.
The living spectre, though deprived of his eyes, could still
distinctly hear, and in his uncouth dialect begged me to
give him some water to allay his thirst. Humanity herself would have recoiled back with horror; she would have
balanced whether to lessen such reliefless distress or
mercifully with one blow to end this dreadful scene of
agonizing torture! Had I had a ball in my gun, I certainly
should have dispatched him, but finding myself unable to
perform so kind an office, I sought, though trembling, to
relieve him as well as I could. A shell ready fixed to a
pole, which had been used by some Negroes, presented
itself to me; filled it with water, and with trembling hands
I guided it to the quivering lips of the wretched sufferer.
Urged by the irresistible power of thirst, he endeavoured
to meet it, as he instinctively guessed its approach by the
noise it made in passing through the bars of the cage.
"Tanky you, white man; tanky you; puta some poison
and give me." "How long have you been hanging there?"
I asked him. "Two days, and me no die; the birds, the
birds; aaah me!" Oppressed with the reflections which
this shocking spectacle afforded me, I mustered strength

enough to walk away and soon reached the house at which I intended to dine. There I heard that the reason for this slave's being thus punished was on account of his having killed the overseer of the plantation. They told me that the laws of self-preservation rendered such executions necessary, and supported the doctrine of slavery with the arguments generally made use of to justify the practice, with the repetition of which I shall not trouble you at present. Adieu.

LETTER X

ON SNAKES; AND ON THE HUMMING-BIRD

Why would you prescribe this task; you know that what we take up ourselves seems always lighter than what is imposed on us by others. You insist on my saying something about our snakes; and in relating what I know concerning them, were it not for two singularities, the one of which I saw and the other I received from an eyewitness, I should have but very little to observe. The southern provinces are the countries where Nature has formed the greatest variety of alligators, snakes, serpents, and scorpions from the smallest size up to the pine barren, the largest species known here. We have but two, whose stings are mortal, which deserve to be mentioned; as for the black one, it is remarkable for nothing but its industry, agility, beauty, and the art of enticing birds by the power of its eyes. I admire it much and never kill it, though its formidable length and appearance often get the better of the philosophy of some people, particularly Europeans. The most dangerous one is the pilot, or copperhead, for the poison of which no remedy has yet been discovered. It bears the first name because it always precedes the rattlesnake, that is, quits its state of torpidity in the spring a week before the other. It bears the second name on account of its head being adorned with many copper-coloured spots. It lurks in rocks near the water and is extremely active and dangerous. Let man beware of it! I have heard only of one person who was stung by a copperhead in this country. The poor wretch instantly swelled in a most dreadful manner; a multitude of spots of different hues alternately appeared and vanished on different parts of his body; his eyes were filled with madness and rage; he cast them on all present with the most vindictive looks; he thrust out his tongue as the snakes do; he hissed through his teeth with inconceivable strength and became an object of terror to all bystanders. To the lividness of a corpse he united the desperate force of a maniac; they hardly were able to fasten him so as to guard themselves from his attacks, when in the space of two hours death relieved the poor wretch from his struggles and the spectators from their apprehensions. The poison of the rattlesnake is not mortal in so short a space, and hence there is more time to procure relief; we are acquainted with several antidotes with which almost every family is provided. They are extremely inactive, and if not touched, are perfectly inoffensive. I once saw, as I was travelling, a great cliff which was full of them; I handled several, and they appeared to be dead; they were all entwined together, and thus they remain until the return of the sun. I found them out by following the track of some wild hogs which had fed on them; and even the Indians often regale on them. When they find them asleep, they put a small forked stick over their necks, which they keep immovably fixed on the ground, giving the snake a piece of leather to bite; and this they pull back several times with great force until they observe their two poisonous fangs torn out. Then they cut off the head, skin the body, and cook it as we do eels; and their flesh is extremely sweet and white. I once saw a *tamed one,* as gentle as you can possibly conceive a reptile to be; it took to the water and swam whenever it pleased; and when the boys to whom it belonged called it back, their summons was readily obeyed. It had been deprived of its fangs by the preceding method; they often stroked it with a soft brush, and this friction seemed to cause the most pleasing sensations, for it would turn on its back to enjoy it, as a cat does before the fire. One of this species was the cause, some years ago, of a most deplorable acci-

dent, which I shall relate to you as I had it from the
widow and mother of the victims. A Dutch farmer of the
Minisink went to mowing, with his Negroes, in his boots,
a precaution used to prevent being stung. Inadvertently
he trod on a snake, which immediately flew at his legs;
and as it drew back in order to renew its blow, one of his
Negroes cut it in two with his scythe. They prosecuted
their work and returned home; at night the farmer pulled
off his boots and went to bed, and was soon after attacked with a strange sickness at his stomach; he swelled,
and before a physician could be sent for, died. The sudden death of this man did not cause much inquiry; the
neighbourhood wondered, as is usual in such cases, and
without any further examination, the corpse was buried.
A few days after, the son put on his father's boots and
went to the meadow; at night he pulled them off, went to
bed, and was attacked with the same symptoms about the
same time, and died in the morning. A little before he
expired, the doctor came, but was not able to assign what
could be the cause of so singular a disorder; however,
rather than appear wholly at a loss before the country
people, he pronounced both father and son to have been
bewitched. Some weeks after, the widow sold all the
movables for the benefit of the younger children, and the
farm was leased. One of the neighbours, who bought the
boots, presently put them on, and was attacked in the
same manner as the other two had been; but this man's
wife, being alarmed by what had happened in the former
family, despatched one of her Negroes for an eminent
physician, who, fortunately having heard something of
the dreadful affair, guessed at the cause, applied oil, etc.,
and recovered the man. The boots which had been so
fatal were then carefully examined, and he found that the
two fangs of the snake had been left in the leather after
being wrenched out of their sockets. by the strength
with which the snake had drawn back its head. The blad-
ders which contained the poison and several of the small
nerves were still fresh and adhered to the boot. The unfortunate father and son had been poisoned by pulling
off these boots, in which action they imperceptibly
scratched their legs with the points of the fangs, through
the hollow of which some of this astonishing poison was
conveyed. You have no doubt heard of their rattles if

you have not seen them; the only observation I wish to make is that the rattling is loud and distinct when they are angry and, on the contrary, when pleased, it sounds like a distant trepidation, in which nothing distinct is heard. In the thick settlements, they are now become very scarce, for wherever they are met with, open war is declared against them, so that in a few years there will be none left but on our mountains. The black snake, on the contrary, always diverts me because it excites no idea of danger. Their swiftness is astonishing; they will sometimes equal that of a horse; at other times they will climb up trees in quest of our tree toads or glide on the ground at full length. On some occasions they present themselves half in the reptile state, half erect; their eyes and their heads in the erect posture appear to great advantage; the former display a fire which I have often admired, and it is by these they are enabled to fascinate birds and squirrels. When they have fixed their eyes on an animal, they become immovable, only turning their head sometimes to the right and sometimes to the left, but still with their sight invariably directed to the object. The distracted victim, instead of flying its enemy, seems to be arrested by some invincible power; it screams; now approaches and then recedes; and after skipping about with unaccountable agitation, finally rushes into the jaws of the snake and is swallowed, as soon as it is covered with a slime or glue to make it slide easily down the throat of the devourer.

One anecdote I must relate, the circumstances of which are as true as they are singular. One of my constant walks when I am at leisure is in my lowlands, where I have the pleasure of seeing my cattle, horses, and colts. Exuberant grass replenishes all my fields, the best representative of our wealth; in the middle of that track I have cut a ditch eight feet wide, the banks of which Nature adorns every spring with the wild salendine and other flowering weeds, which on these luxuriant grounds shoot up to a great height. Over this ditch I have erected a bridge, capable of bearing a loaded waggon; on each side I carefully sow every year some grains of hemp, which rise to the height of fifteen feet, so strong and so full of limbs as to resemble young trees; I once ascended one of them four feet above the ground. These produce natural arbours, rendered often still more compact by the assistance of an annual creeping plant, which we call a vine, that never fails to entwine itself among their branches and always produces a very desirable shade. From this simple grove I have amused myself a hundred times in observing the great number of humming-birds with which our country abounds: the wild blossoms everywhere attract the attention of these birds, which like bees subsist by suction. From this retreat I distinctly watch them in all their various attitudes, but their flight is so rapid that you cannot distinguish the motion of their wings. On this little bird Nature has profusely lavished her most splendid colours; the most perfect azure, the most beautiful gold, the most dazzling red, are forever in contrast and help to embellish the plumes of his majestic head. The richest palette of the most luxuriant painter could never invent anything to be compared to the variegated tints with which this insect bird is arrayed. Its bill is as long and as sharp as a coarse sewing needle; like the bee, Nature has taught it to find out in the calyx of flowers and blossoms those mellifluous particles that serve it for sufficient food; and yet it seems to leave them untouched, undeprived of anything that our eyes can possibly distinguish. When it feeds, it appears as if immovable, though continually on the wing; and sometimes, from what motives I know not, it will tear and lacerate flowers into a hundred pieces, for, strange to tell, they are the most irascible of the feathered tribe. Where do passions find room in so diminutive a body? They often fight with the fury of lions until one of the combatants falls a sacrifice and dies. When fatigued, it has often perched within a few feet of me, and on such favourable opportunities I have surveyed it with the most minute attention. Its little eyes appear like diamonds, reflecting light on every side; most elegantly finished in all parts, it is a miniature work of our Great Parent, who seems to have formed it the smallest, and at the same time the most beautiful of the winged species.

As I was one day sitting solitary and pensive in my primitive arbour, my attention was engaged by a strange sort of rustling noise at some paces distant. I looked all around without distinguishing anything, until I climbed one of my great hemp stalks, when to my astonishment

I beheld two snakes of considerable length, the one pursuing the other with great celerity through a hemp-stubble field. The aggressor was of the black kind, six feet long; the fugitive was a water snake, nearly of equal dimensions. They soon met, and in the fury of their first encounter, they appeared in an instant firmly twisted together; and whilst their united tails beat the ground, they mutually tried with open jaws to lacerate each other. What a fell aspect did they present! Their heads were compressed to a very small size, their eyes flashed fire; and after this conflict had lasted about five minutes, the second found means to disengage itself from the first and hurried toward the ditch. Its antagonist instantly assumed a new posture, and half creeping and half erect, with a majestic mien, overtook and attacked the other again, which placed itself in the same attitude and prepared to resist. The scene was uncommon and beautiful; for thus opposed, they fought with their jaws, biting each other with the utmost rage; but notwithstanding this appearance of mutual courage and fury, the water snake still seemed desirous of retreating toward the ditch, its natural element. This was no sooner perceived by the keen-eyed black one, than twisting its tail twice round a stalk of hemp and seizing its adversary by the throat, not by means of its jaws but by twisting its own neck twice round that of the water snake, pulled it back from the ditch. To prevent a defeat, the latter took hold likewise of a stalk on the bank, and by the acquisition of that point of resistance, became a match for its fierce antagonist. Strange was this to behold; two great snakes strongly adhering to the ground, mutually fastened together by means of the writhings which lashed them to each other, and stretched at their full length, they pulled but pulled in vain; and in the moments of greatest exertions, that part of their bodies which was entwined seemed extremely small, while the rest appeared inflated and now and then convulsed with strong undulations, rapidly following each other. Their eyes seemed on fire and ready to start out of their heads; at one time the conflict seemed decided; the water snake bent itself into two great folds and by that operation rendered the other more than commonly outstretched; the next minute the new struggles of the black one gained an unexpected superiority; it acquired two great folds likewise, which necessarily extended the body of its adversary in proportion as it had contracted its own. These efforts were alternate; victory seemed doubtful, inclining sometimes to the one side and sometimes to the other, until at last the stalk to which the black snake fastened suddenly gave way, and in consequence of this accident they both plunged into the ditch. The water did not extinguish their vindictive rage; for by their agitations I could trace, though not distinguish, their mutual attacks. They soon reappeared on the surface twisted together, as in their first onset; but the black snake seemed to retain its wonted superiority, for its head was exactly fixed above that of the other, which it incessantly pressed down under the water, until it was stifled and sunk. The victor no sooner perceived its enemy incapable of farther resistance than, abandoning it to the current, it returned on shore and disappeared.

LETTER XI

FROM MR. IW—N AL—Z,
A RUSSIAN GENTLEMAN,
DESCRIBING THE VISIT
HE PAID AT MY REQUEST
TO MR. JOHN BERTRAM,
THE CELEBRATED
PENNSYLVANIAN BOTANIST

Examine this flourishing province in whatever light you will, the eyes as well as the mind of an European traveller are equally delighted because a diffusive happiness appears in every part, happiness which is established on the broadest basis. The wisdom of Lycurgus and Solon never conferred on man one half of the blessings and uninterrupted prosperity which the Pennsylvanians now possess; the name of Penn, that simple but illustrious citizen, does more honour to the English nation than those of many of their kings.

In order to convince you that I have not bestowed undeserved praises in my former letters on this celebrated government, and that either nature or the climate seems to be more favourable here to the arts and sciences than to any other American province, let us together, agreeable to your desire, pay a visit to Mr. John Bertram, the first botanist in this new hemisphere, become such by a native impulse of disposition. It is to this simple man that America is indebted for several useful discoveries and the knowledge of many new plants. I had been greatly prepossessed in his favour by the extensive correspondence which I knew he held with the most eminent Scotch and French botanists; I knew also that he had been honoured with that of Queen Ulrica of Sweden.

His house is small but decent; there was something peculiar in its first appearance which seemed to distinguish it from those of his neighbours: a small tower in the middle of it not only helped to strengthen it but afforded convenient room for a staircase. Every disposition of the fields, fences, and trees seemed to bear the marks of perfect order and regularity, which in rural affairs always indicate a prosperous industry.

I was received at the door by a woman dressed extremely neat and simple, who, without courtesying or any other ceremonial, asked me, with an air of benignity, whom I wanted. I answered, "I should be glad to see Mr. Bertram." "If thee wilt step in and take a chair, I will send for him." "No," I said, "I had rather have the pleasure of walking through his farm; I shall easily find him out with your directions." After a little time I perceived the Schuylkill, winding through delightful meadows, and soon cast my eyes on a new-made bank, which seemed greatly to confine its stream. After having walked on its top a considerable way, I at last reached the place where ten men were at work. I asked, if any of them could tell me where Mr. Bertram was. An elderly looking man with wide trousers and a large leather apron on, looking at me, said, "My name is Bertram; dost thee want me?" "Sir, I am come on purpose to converse with you, if you can be spared from your labour." "Very easily," he answered; "I direct and advise more than I work." We walked toward the house, where he made me take a chair while he went to put on clean clothes, after which he returned and sat down by me. "The fame of your knowledge," said I, "in American botany and your well-known hospitality have induced me to pay you a visit, which I hope you will not think troublesome; I should be glad to spend a few hours in your garden." "The greatest advantage," replied he, "which I receive from what thee callest my botanical fame is the pleasure which it often procureth me in receiving the visits of friends and foreigners; but our jaunt into the garden must be postponed for the present, as the bell is ringing for dinner." We entered into a large hall, where there was a long table full of victuals; at the lowest part sat his Negroes; his hired men were next, then the family and myself; and at the head, the venerable father and his wife presided. Each reclined his head and said his prayers, divested of the tedious cant of some and of the ostentatious style of others. "After the luxuries of our cities," observed he, "this plain fare must appear to thee a severe fast." "By no means, Mr. Bertram; this honest country dinner convinces me that you receive me as a friend and an old acquaintance." "I am glad of it, for thee art heartily welcome. I never knew how to use ceremonies; they are insufficient proofs of sincerity; our society, besides, are utterly strangers to what the world calleth polite expressions. We treat others as we treat ourselves. I received yesterday a letter from Philadelphia, by which I understand thee art a Russian; what motives can possibly have induced thee to quit thy native country and to come so far in quest of knowledge or pleasure? Verily it is a great compliment thee payest to this our young province, to think that anything it exhibiteth may be worthy thy attention." "I have been most amply repaid for the trouble of the passage. I view the present Americans as the seed of future nations, which will replenish this boundless continent; the Russians may be in some respects compared to you; we likewise are a new people, new, I mean, in knowledge, arts, and improvements. Who knows what revolutions Russia and America may one day bring about; we are perhaps nearer neighbours than we imagine. I view with peculiar attention all your towns, I examine their situation and the police, for which many are already famous. Though their foundations are now so recent and so well remembered, yet their origin will puzzle posterity as much as we are now puzzled to ascertain the beginning of those which time has in some measure destroyed. Your new buildings, your streets, put me in mind of those of the city of Pompeii, where I was a few years ago; I attentively examined everything there, particularly the foot-path which runs along the houses. They appeared to have been considerably worn by the great number of people which had once travelled over them. But now how distant; neither builder nor proprietors remain; nothing is known!" "Why, thee hast been a great traveller for a man of thy years." "Few years, sir, will enable anybody to journey over a great track of country; but it requires a superior degree of knowledge to gather harvests as we go. Pray, Mr. Bertram, what banks are those which you are making; to what purpose is so much expense and so much labour bestowed?" "Friend Iwan, no branch of industry was ever more profitable to any country, as well as to the proprietors; the Schuylkill in its many windings once covered a great extent of ground, though its waters were but shallow even in our highest tides; and though some parts were always dry, yet the whole of this great track presented to the eye nothing but a putrid swampy soil, useless either for the plough or for the scythe. The proprietors of these grounds are now incorporated; we yearly pay to the treasurer of the company a certain sum, which makes an aggregate, superior to the casualties that generally happen either by inundations or the musk squash. It is owing to this happy contrivance that so many thousand acres of meadows have been rescued from the Schuylkill, which now both enricheth and embellisheth so much of the neighbourhood of our city. Our brethren of Salem in New Jersey have carried the art of banking to a still higher degree of perfection." "It is really an admirable contrivance, which greatly redounds to the honour of the parties concerned and shows a spirit of discernment and perseverance which is highly praiseworthy; if the Virginians would imitate your example, the state of their husbandry would greatly improve. I have not heard of any such association in any other parts of the continent; Pennsylvania hitherto seems to reign the unrivalled queen of these fair provinces. Pray, sir, what expenses are you at ere these grounds be fit for the scythe?" "The expenses are very considerable, particularly when we have land, brooks, trees, and brush to clear away. But such is the excellence of these bottoms and the goodness of the grass for fattening of cattle that the produce of three years pays all advances." "Happy the country where Nature has bestowed such rich treasures, treasures superior to mines," said I; "if all this fair province is thus cultivated, no wonder it has acquired such reputation for the prosperity and the industry of its inhabitants."

By this time the working part of the family had finished their dinner and had retired with a decency and silence which pleased me much. Soon after, I heard, as I thought, a distant concert of instruments. "However simple and pastoral your fare was, Mr. Bertram, this is the dessert of a prince; pray what is this I hear?" "Thee must not be alarmed; it is of a piece with the rest of thy treatment, friend Iwan." Anxious, I followed the sound, and by ascending the staircase, found that it was the effect of the wind through the strings of an Eolian harp, an instrument which I had never before seen. After dinner we quaffed an honest bottle of Madeira wine, without the irksome labour of toasts, healths, or sentiments and then retired into his study.

I was no sooner entered than I observed a coat of arms in a gilt frame with the name of John Bertram. The novelty of such a decoration in such a place struck me; I could not avoid asking, "Does the Society of Friends take any pride in those armorial bearings, which sometimes serve as marks of distinction between families, and much oftener as food for pride and ostentation?" "Thee must know," said he, "that my father was a Frenchman; he brought this piece of painting over with him; I keep it as a piece of family furniture, and as a memorial of his removal hither." From his study we went into the garden, which contained a great variety of curious plants and shrubs; some grew in a greenhouse, over the door of which were written these lines:

> Slave to no sect, who takes no private road,
> But looks through nature, up to nature's God!

He informed me that he had often followed General Bouquet to Pittsburgh, with the view of herbarizing, that he had made useful collections in Virginia, and that he had been employed by the king of England to visit the two Floridas.

Our walks and botanical observations engrossed so much of our time that the sun was almost down ere I thought of returning to Philadelphia; I regretted that the day had been so short, as I had not spent so rational an one for a long time before. I wanted to stay, yet was doubtful whether it would not appear improper, being an utter stranger. Knowing, however, that I was visiting the least ceremonious people in the world, I bluntly informed him of the pleasure I had enjoyed, and with the desire I had of staying a few days with him. "Thee art as welcome as if I was thy father; thee art no stranger; thy desire of knowledge, thy being a foreigner besides, entitleth thee to consider my house as thine own as long as thee pleaseth; use thy time with the most perfect freedom; I too shall do so myself." I thankfully accepted the kind invitation.

We went to view his favourite bank; he showed me the principles and method on which it was erected, and we walked over the grounds which had been already drained. The whole store of Nature's kind luxuriance seemed to have been exhausted on these beautiful meadows; he made me count the amazing number of cattle and horses now feeding on solid bottoms, which but a few years before had been covered with water. Thence we rambled through his fields, where the right-angular fences, the heaps of pitched stones, the flourishing clover, announced the best husbandry, as well as the most assiduous attention. His cows were then returning home, deep-bellied, short-legged, having udders ready to burst, seeking with seeming toil to be delivered from the great exuberance they contained; he next showed me his orchard, formerly planted on a barren sandy soil, but long since converted into one of the richest spots in that vicinage.

"This," said he, "is altogether the fruit of my own contrivance; I purchased some years ago the privilege of a small spring, about a mile and a half from hence, which at a considerable expense I have brought to this reservoir; therein I throw old lime, ashes, horse dung, etc., and twice a week I let it run, thus impregnated; I regularly spread on this ground in the fall old hay, straw, and whatever damaged fodder I have about my barn. By these simple means I mow, one year with another, fifty-three hundreds of excellent hay per acre from a soil which scarcely produced five-fingers [a small plant resembling strawberries] some years before." "This is, sir, a miracle in husbandry; happy the country which is cultivated by a society of men whose application and taste lead them to prosecute and accomplish useful works." "I am not the only person who do these things," he said; "wherever water can be had, it is always turned to that important use; wherever a farmer can water his meadows, the greatest crops of the best hay and excellent after-grass are the sure rewards of his labours. With the banks of my meadow ditches, I have greatly enriched my upland fields; those which I intend to rest for a few years, I constantly sow with red clover, which is the greatest meliorator of our lands. For three years after, they yield abundant pasture; when I want to break up my clover fields, I give them a good coat of mud, which hath been exposed to the severities of three or four of our winters. This is the reason that I commonly reap from twenty-eight to thirty-six bushels of wheat an acre; my flax, oats, and Indian corn I raise in the same proportion. Would'st thee inform me whether the inhabitants of thy country follow the same methods of husbandry?" "No, sir; in the neighbourhood of our towns, there are indeed some intelligent farmers who prosecute their rural schemes with attention, but we should be too numerous, too happy, too powerful a people if it were possible for the whole Russian empire to be cultivated like the province of Pennsylvania. Our lands are so unequally divided and so few of our farmers are possessors of the soil they till that they cannot execute plans of husbandry with the same vigour as you do, who hold yours, as it were, from the Master of Nature, unencumbered and free. Oh, America!" exclaimed I, "thou knowest not as yet the whole extent of thy happiness: the foundation of thy civil polity must lead thee in a few years to a degree of population and power which Europe little thinks of!" "Long before this happen," answered the good man, "we shall rest beneath the turf; it is vain for mortals to be presumptuous in their conjectures; our country is, no doubt, the cradle of an extensive future population; the old world is growing weary of its inhabitants; they must come here to flee from the tyranny of the great. But doth not thee imagine that the great will, in the course of years, come over here also; for it is the misfortune of all societies everywhere to hear of great men, great rulers, and of great tyrants." "My dear sir," I replied, "tyranny never can take a strong hold in this country; the land is too widely distributed; it is poverty in Europe that makes slaves." "Friend Iwan, as I make no doubt that thee understandest the Latin tongue, read this kind epistle which the good Queen of Sweden, Ulrica, sent me a few years ago. Good woman! That she should think in her palace at Stockholm of poor John Bertram, on the banks of the Schuylkill, appeareth to me very strange." "Not in the least, dear sir; you are the first man whose name as a botanist has done honour to America; it is very natural, at the same time, to imagine that so extensive a continent must contain many curious plants and trees; is it, then, surprising to see a princess, fond of useful knowledge, descend sometimes from the throne to walk in the gardens of Linnaeus?" " 'Tis to the directions of that learned man," said Mr. Bertram, "that I am indebted for the method which has led me to the knowledge I now possess; the science of botany is so diffusive that a proper thread is absolutely wanted to conduct the beginner." "Pray, Mr. Bertram, when did you imbibe the first wish to cultivate the science of botany; was you regularly bred to it in Philadelphia?" "I have never received any other education than barely reading and writing; this small farm was all the patrimony my father left me; certain debts and the want of meadows kept me rather low in the beginning of my life; my wife brought me nothing in money; all her riches consisted in her good temper and great knowledge of housewifery. I scarcely know how to trace my steps in the botanical career; they appear to me now like unto a dream, but thee mayest rely on what I shall relate, though I know that some of our friends have laughed at it." "I am not one of those people, Mr. Bertram, who aim at finding out the ridiculous in what is sincerely and honestly averred." "Well, then, I'll tell thee: one day I was very busy in holding my plough (for thee see'st that I am but a ploughman), and being weary, I ran under the shade of a tree to repose myself. I cast my eyes on a daisy; I plucked it mechanically and viewed it with more curiosity than common country farmers are wont to do, and observed therein very many distinct parts, some perpendicular, some horizontal. 'What a shame,' said my mind, or something that inspired my mind, 'that thee shouldest have employed so many years in tilling the earth and destroying so many flowers and plants without being acquainted with their structures and their uses!' This seeming inspiration suddenly awakened my curiosity, for these were not thoughts to which I had been accustomed. I returned to my team, but this new desire did not quit my mind; I mentioned it to my wife, who greatly discouraged me from prosecuting my new scheme, as she called it; I was not opulent enough, she said, to dedicate much of my time to studies and labours which might rob me of that portion of it which is the only wealth of the American farmer. However, her prudent caution did not discourage me; I thought about it continually, at supper, in bed, and wherever I went. At last I could not resist the impulse; for on the fourth day of the following week, I hired a man to plough for me and went to Philadelphia. Though I knew not what book to call for, I ingenuously told the bookseller my errand, who provided me with such as he thought best and a Latin grammar beside. Next I applied to a neigh-bouring schoolmaster, who in three months taught me Latin enough to understand Linnaeus, which I purchased afterward. Then I began to botanize all over my farm; in a little time I became acquainted with every vegetable that grew in my neighbourhood and next ventured into Maryland, living among the Friends; in proportion as I thought myself more learned, I proceeded farther, and by a steady application of several years, I have acquired a pretty general knowledge of every plant and tree to be found in our continent. In process of time I was applied to from the old countries, whither I every year send many collections. Being now made easy in my cir-cumstances, I have ceased to labour, and am never so happy as when I see and converse with my friends. If among the many plants or shrubs I am acquainted with there are any thee wantest to send to thy native coun-try, I will cheerfully procure them and give thee, more-over, whatever directions thee mayest want."

Thus I passed several days in ease, improvement, and pleasure; I observed in all the operations of his farm, as well as in the mutual correspondence between the master and the inferior members of his family, the greatest ease and decorum; not a word like command seemed to exceed the tone of a simple wish. The very Negroes themselves appeared to partake of such a de-cency of behaviour and modesty of countenance as I had never before observed. "By what means," said I, "Mr. Bertram, do you rule your slaves so well, that they seem to do their work with the cheerfulness of white men?" "Though our erroneous prejudices and opinions once induced us to look upon them as fit only for slavery, though ancient custom had very unfortunately taught us to keep them in bondage, yet of late, in consequence of the remonstrances of several Friends and of the good books they have published on that subject, our society treats them very differently. With us they are now free. I give those whom thee didst see at my table eighteen pounds a year, with victuals and clothes and all other privileges which the white men enjoy. Our society treats them now as the companions of our labours; and by this management, as well as by means of the education we have given them, they are in general become a new set of beings. Those whom I admit to my table I have found to be good, trusty, moral men; when they do not what we think they should do, we dismiss them, which is all the punishment we inflict. Other societies of Christians keep them still as slaves, without teaching them any kind of religious principles; what motive beside fear can they have to behave well? In the first settlement of this province, we employed them as slaves, I acknowledge; but when we found that good example, gentle admonition, and religious principles could lead them to subordination and sobriety, we relinquished a method so contrary to the profession of Christianity. We gave them freedom, and yet few have quitted their ancient masters. The women breed in our families, and we become attached to one another. I taught mine to read and to write; they love God and fear His judgements. The oldest person among them transacts my business in Philadelphia with a punctuality from which he has never deviated. They constantly attend our meetings; they participate in health and sickness, infancy and old age, in the advantages our society affords. Such are the means we have made use of to relieve them from that bondage and ignorance in which they were kept before. Thee perhaps hast been surprised to see them at my table, but by elevating them to the rank of freemen, they necessarily acquire that emulation without which we ourselves should fall into debasement and profligate ways." "Mr. Bertram, this is the most philosophical treatment of Negroes that I have heard of; happy would it be for America would other denominations of Christians imbibe the same principles and follow the same admirable rules. A great number of men would be relieved from those cruel shackles under which they now groan; and under this impression, I cannot endure to spend more time in the southern provinces. The method with which they are treated there, the meanness of their food, the severity of their tasks, are spectacles I have not patience to behold." "I am glad to see that thee hast so much compassion; are there any slaves in thy country?" "Yes, unfortunately, but they are more properly civil than domestic slaves; they are attached to the soil on which they live; it is the remains of ancient barbarous customs established in the days of the greatest ignorance and savageness of manners and preserved notwithstanding the repeated tears of humanity, the loud calls of policy, and the commands of religion. The pride of great men, with the avarice of landholders, make them look on this class as necessary tools of husbandry, as if freemen could not cultivate the ground." "And is it really so, Friend Iwan? To be poor, to be wretched, to be a slave, is hard indeed; existence is not worth enjoying on these terms. I am afraid the country can never flourish under such impolitic government." "I am very much of your opinion, Mr. Bertram, though I am in hopes that the present reign, illustrious by so many acts of the soundest policy, will not expire without this salutary, this necessary emancipation, which would fill the Russian empire with tears of gratitude." "How long hast thee been in this country?" "Four years, sir." "Why thee speakest English almost like a native; what a toil a traveller must undergo to learn various languages, to divest himself of his native prejudices, and to accommodate himself to the customs of all those among whom he chooseth to reside."

Thus I spent my time with this enlightened botanist, this worthy citizen who united all the simplicity of rustic manner to the most useful learning. Various and extensive were the conversations that filled the measure of my visit. I accompanied him to his fields, to his barn, to his bank, to his garden, to his study, and at the last to the meeting of the society on the Sunday following. It was at the town of Chester, whither the whole family went in two waggons, Mr. Bertram and I on horseback.

When I entered the house where the Friends were assembled, who might be about two hundred men and women, the involuntary impulse of ancient custom made me pull off my hat; but soon recovering myself, I sat with it on, at the end of a bench. The meeting-house was a square building devoid of any ornament whatever; the whiteness of the walls, the conveniency of seats, that of a large stove, which in cold weather keeps the whole house warm, were the only essential things which I observed. Neither pulpit nor desk, font nor altar, tabernacle nor organ, were there to be seen; it is merely a spacious room, in which these good people meet every Sunday. A profound silence ensued, which lasted about half an hour; every one had his head reclined and seemed absorbed in profound meditation, when a female Friend arose and declared with a most engaging modesty that the spirit moved her to entertain them on the subject she had chosen. She treated it with great propriety, as a moral useful discourse, and delivered it without theological parade or the ostentation of learning. Either she must have been a great adept in public speaking or had studiously prepared herself, a circumstance that cannot well be supposed, as it is a point, in their profession, to utter nothing but what arises from spontaneous impulse; or else the Great Spirit of the World, the patronage and influence of which they all came to invoke, must have inspired her with the soundest morality. Her discourse lasted three quarters of an hour. I did not observe one single face turned toward her; never before had I seen a congregation listening with so much attention to a public oration. I observed neither contortions of body nor any kind of affectation in her face, style, or manner of utterance; everything was natural, and therefore pleasing, and shall I tell you more, she was very handsome, although upward of forty. As soon as she had finished, every one seemed to return to their former meditation for about a quarter of an hour, when they rose up by common consent and after some general conversation departed.

How simple their precepts, how unadorned their religious system, how few the ceremonies through which they pass during the course of their lives! At their deaths they are interred by the fraternity, without pomp, without prayers, thinking it then too late to alter the course of God's eternal decrees, and as you well know, without either monument or tombstone. Thus after having lived under the mildest government, after having been guided by the mildest doctrine, they die just as peaceably as those who, being educated in more pompous religions, pass through a variety of sacraments, subscribe to complicated creeds, and enjoy the benefits of a church establishment. These good people flatter themselves with following the doctrines of Jesus Christ in that simplicity with which they were delivered; a happier system could not have been devised for the use of mankind. It appears to be entirely free from those ornaments and political additions which each country and each government hath fashioned after its own manners.

At the door of this meeting-house, I had been invited to spend some days at the houses of some respectable farmers in the neighbourhood. The reception I met with everywhere insensibly led me to spend two months among these good people; and I must say they were the golden days of my riper years. I never shall forget the gratitude I owe them for the innumerable kindnesses they heaped on me; it was to the letter you gave me that I am indebted for the extensive acquaintance I now have throughout Pennsylvania. I must defer thanking you as I ought until I see you again. Before that time comes, I may perhaps entertain you with more curious anecdotes than this letter affords. Farewell. I——n Al——z.

LETTER XII

DISTRESSES OF A FRONTIER MAN

I wish for a change of place; the hour is come at last
that I must fly from my house and abandon my farm!
But what course shall I steer, inclosed as I am? The
climate best adapted to my present situation and humour
would be the polar regions, where six months' day and six
months' night divide the dull year; nay, a simple aurora
borealis would suffice me and greatly refresh my eyes,
fatigued now by so many disagreeable objects. The
severity of those climates, that great gloom where
melancholy dwells, would be perfectly analogous to the
turn of my mind. Oh, could I remove my plantation to
the shores of the Obi, willingly would I dwell in the hut
of a Samoyed; with cheerfulness would I go and bury
myself in the cavern of a Laplander. Could I but carry
my family along with me, I would winter at Pello, or
Tobolsk, in order to enjoy the peace and innocence of
that country. But let me arrive under the pole, or reach
the antipodes, I never can leave behind me the remembrance of the dreadful scenes to which I have been
witness; therefore, never can I be happy! Happy—why
would I mention that sweet, that enchanting word? Once
happiness was our portion; now it is gone from us, and
I am afraid not to be enjoyed again by the present

generation! Whichever way I look, nothing but the most
frightful precipices present themselves to my view, in
which hundreds of my friends and acquaintances have
already perished; of all animals that live on the surface
of this planet, what is man when no longer connected
with society, or when he finds himself surrounded by a
convulsed and a half-dissolved one? He cannot live in
solitude; he must belong to some community bound by
some ties, however imperfect. Men mutually support and
add to the boldness and confidence of each other; the
weakness of each is strengthened by the force of the
whole. I had never before these calamitous times formed
any such ideas; I lived on, laboured and prospered, without having ever studied on what the security of my life
and the foundation of my prosperity were established;
I perceived them just as they left me. Never was a situation so singularly terrible as mine, in every possible respect, as a member of an extensive society, as a citizen
of an inferior division of the same society, as a husband,
as a father, as a man who exquisitely feels for the miseries of others as well as for his own! But alas! So
much is everything now subverted among us that the
very word *misery*, with which we were hardly acquainted
before, no longer conveys the same ideas, or, rather,
tired with feeling for the miseries of others, every one
feels now for himself alone. When I consider myself as
connected in all these characters, as bound by so many
cords, all uniting in my heart, I am seized with a fever
of the mind, I am transported beyond that degree of
calmness which is necessary to delineate our thoughts.
I feel as if my reason wanted to leave me, as if it
would burst its poor weak tenement; again, I try to compose myself, I grow cool, and preconceiving the dreadful loss, I endeavour to retain the useful guest.

You know the position of our settlement; I need not
therefore describe it. To the west it is inclosed by a
chain of mountains, reaching to ——; to the east, the
country is as yet but thinly inhabited; we are almost
insulated, and the houses are at a considerable distance
from each other. From the mountains we have but too
much reason to expect our dreadful enemy; the wilderness is a harbour where it is impossible to find them.
It is a door through which they can enter our country

whenever they please; and, as they seem determined to destroy the whole chain of frontiers, our fate cannot be far distant: from Lake Champlain, almost all has been conflagrated one after another. What renders these incursions still more terrible is that they most commonly take place in the dead of the night; we never go to our fields but we are seized with an involuntary fear, which lessens our strength and weakens our labour. No other subject of conversation intervenes between the different accounts, which spread through the country, of successive acts of devastation, and these, told in chimney-corners, swell themselves in our affrighted imaginations into the most terrific ideas! We never sit down either to dinner or supper but the least noise immediately spreads a general alarm and prevents us from enjoying the comfort of our meals. The very appetite proceeding from labour and peace of mind is gone; we eat just enough to keep us alive; our sleep is disturbed by the most frightful dreams; sometimes I start awake, as if the great hour of danger was come; at other times the howling of our dogs seems to announce the arrival of our enemy; we leap out of bed and run to arms; my poor wife, with panting bosom and silent tears, takes leave of me, as if we were to see each other no more; she snatches the youngest children from their beds, who, suddenly awakened, increase by their innocent questions the horror of the dreadful moment. She tries to hide them in the cellar, as if our cellar was inaccessible to the fire. I place all my servants at the windows and myself at the door, where I am determined to perish. Fear industriously increases every sound; we all listen; each communicates to the other his ideas and conjectures. We remain thus sometimes for whole hours, our hearts and our minds racked by the most anxious suspense: what a dreadful situation, a thousand times worse than that of a soldier engaged in the midst of the most severe conflict! Sometimes feeling the spontaneous courage of a man, I seem to wish for the decisive minute; the next instant a message from my wife, sent by one of the children, puzzling me beside with their little questions, unmans me; away goes my courage, and I descend again into the deepest despondency. At last, finding that it was a false alarm, we return once more to our beds; but what good can the kind of sleep of Nature do to us when interrupted by such scenes! Securely placed as you are, you can have no idea of our agitations, but by hearsay; no relation can be equal to what we suffer and to what we feel. Every morning my youngest children are sure to have frightful dreams to relate; in vain I exert my authority to keep them silent; it is not in my power; and these images of their disturbed imagination, instead of being frivolously looked upon as in the days of our happiness, are on the contrary considered as warnings and sure prognostics of our future fate. I am not a superstitious man, but since our misfortunes, I am grown more timid and less disposed to treat the doctrine of omens with contempt.

Though these evils have been gradual, yet they do not become habitual like other incidental evils. The nearer I view the end of this catastrophe, the more I shudder. But why should I trouble you with such unconnected accounts; men secure and out of danger are soon fatigued with mournful details: can you enter with me into fellowship with all these afflictive sensations; have you a tear ready to shed over the approaching ruin of a once opulent and substantial family? Read this, I pray, with the eyes of sympathy, with a tender sorrow; pity the lot of those whom you once called your friends, who were once surrounded with plenty, ease, and perfect security, but who now expect every night to be their last, and who are as wretched as criminals under an impending sentence of the law.

As a member of a large society which extends to many parts of the world, my connexion with it is too distant to be as strong as that which binds me to the inferior division in the midst of which I live. I am told that the great nation of which we are a part is just, wise, and free beyond any other on earth, within its own insular boundaries, but not always so to its distant conquests; I shall not repeat all I have heard because I cannot believe half of it. As a citizen of a smaller society, I find that any kind of opposition to its now prevailing sentiments immediately begets hatred; how easily do men pass from loving to hating and cursing one another! I am a lover of peace; what must I do? I am divided between the respect I feel for the ancient connexion and the fear of innovations, with the consequence of which I am not well acquainted, as they are embraced by my own countrymen. I am conscious that I was happy before this unfortunate revolution. I feel that I am no longer so; therefore I regret the change. This is the only mode of reasoning adapted to persons in my situation. If I attach myself to the mother country, which is 3,000 miles from me, I become what is called an enemy to my own region; if I follow the rest of my countrymen, I become opposed to our ancient masters: both extremes appear equally dangerous to a person of so little weight and consequence as I am, whose energy and example are of no avail. As to the argument on which the dispute is founded, I know little about it. Much has been said and written on both sides, but who has a judgement capacious and clear enough to decide? The great moving principles which actuate both parties are much hid from vulgar eyes, like mine; nothing but the plausible and the probable are offered to our contemplation. The innocent class are always the victims of the few; they are in all countries and at all times the inferior agents on which the popular phantom is erected; they clamour and must toil and bleed, and are always sure of meeting with oppression and rebuke. It is for the sake of the great leaders on both sides that so much blood must be spilt; that of the people is counted as nothing. Great events are not achieved for us, though it is by us that they are principally accomplished, by the arms, the sweat, the lives of the people. Books tell me so much that they inform me of nothing. Sophistry, the bane of freemen, launches forth in all her deceiving attire! After all, most men reason from passions; and shall such an ignorant individual as I am decide and say this side is right, that side is wrong? Sentiment and feeling are the only guides I know. Alas, how should I unravel an argument in which Reason herself has given way to brutality and bloodshed! What then must I do? I ask the wisest lawyers, the ablest casuists, the warmest patriots; for I mean honestly. Great Source of wisdom! Inspire me with light sufficient to guide my benighted steps out of this intricate maze! Shall I discard all my ancient principles, shall I renounce that name, that nation which I held once so respectable? I feel the powerful attraction; the sentiments they inspired grew with my

earliest knowledge and were grafted upon the first rudiments of my education. On the other hand, shall I arm
myself against that country where I first drew breath,
against the playmates of my youth, my bosom friends,
my acquaintance? The idea makes me shudder! Must I
be called a parricide, a traitor, a villain, lose the esteem
of all those whom I love to preserve my own, be shunned
like a rattlesnake, or be pointed at like a bear? I have
neither heroism not magnanimity enough to make so
great a sacrifice. Here I am tied, I am fastened by numerous strings, nor do I repine at the pressure they cause;
ignorant as I am, I can pervade the utmost extent of the
calamities which have already overtaken our poor afflicted country. I can see the great and accumulated ruin
yet extending itself as far as the theatre of war has
reached; I hear the groans of thousands of families now
ruined and desolated by our aggressors. I cannot count
the multitude of orphans this war has made nor ascertain
the immensity of blood we have lost. Some have asked
whether it was a crime to resist, to repel some parts of
this evil. Others have asserted that a resistance so general makes pardon unattainable and repentance useless,
and dividing the crime among so many renders it imperceptible. What one party calls meritorious, the other
denominates flagitious. These opinions vary, contract, or
expand, like the events of the war on which they are
founded. What can an insignificant man do in the midst
of these jarring contradictory parties, equally hostile to
persons situated as I am? And after all, who will be the
really guilty? Those most certainly who fail of success.
Our fate, the fate of thousands, is, then, necessarily involved in the dark wheel of fortune. Why, then, so many
useless reasonings; we are the sport of fate. Farewell education, principles, love of our country, farewell; all are
become useless to the generality of us: he who governs
himself according to what he calls his principles may be
punished either by one party or the other for those very
principles. He who proceeds without principle, as chance,
timidity, or self-preservation directs, will not perhaps fare
better, but he will be less blamed. What are *we* in the
great scale of events, we poor defenceless frontier inhabitants? What is it to the gazing world whether we breathe
or whether we die? Whatever virtue, whatever merit and

disinterestedness we may exhibit in our secluded re-treats, of what avail? We are like the pismires destroyed by the plough, whose destruction prevents not the future crop. Self-preservation, therefore, the rule of Nature, seems to be the best rule of conduct; what good can we do by vain resistance, by useless efforts? The cool, the distant spectator, placed in safety, may arraign me for ingrati-tude, may bring forth the principles of Solon or Mon-tesquieu; he may look on me as wilfully guilty; he may call me by the most opprobrious names. Secure from personal danger, his warm imagination, undisturbed by the least agitation of the heart, will expatiate freely on this grand question and will consider this extended field but as exhibiting the double scene of attack and defence. To him the object becomes abstracted; the intermediate glares; the perspective distance and a variety of opinions, unimpaired by affections, present to his mind but one set of ideas. Here he proclaims the high guilt of the one, and there the right of the other. But let him come and reside with us one single month; let him pass with us through all the successive hours of necessary toil, terror, and affright; let him watch with us, his musket in his hand, through tedious, sleepless nights, his imagination furrowed by the keen chisel of every passion; let his wife and his children become exposed to the most dread-ful hazards of death; let the existence of his property depend on a single spark, blown by the breath of an enemy; let him tremble with us in our fields, shudder at the rustling of every leaf; let his heart, the seat of the most affecting passions, be powerfully wrung by hearing the melancholy end of his relations and friends; let him trace on the map the progress of these desolations; let his alarmed imagination predict to him the night, the dreadful night when it may be his turn to perish, as so many have perished before. Observe, then, whether the man will not get the better of the citizen, whether his political maxims will not vanish! Yes, he will cease to glow so warmly with the glory of the metropolis; all his wishes will be turned toward the preservation of his fam-ily! Oh, were he situated where I am, were his house perpetually filled, as mine is, with miserable victims just escaped from the flames and the scalping knife, telling of barbarities and murders that make human nature tremble, his situation would suspend every political reflection and expel every abstract idea. My heart is full and involuntarily takes hold of any notion from whence it can receive ideal ease or relief. I am informed that the king has the most numerous, as well as the fairest, progeny of children of any potentate now in the world; he may be a great king, but he must feel as we common mortals do in the good wishes he forms for their lives and prosperity. His mind no doubt often springs forward on the wings of anticipation and contemplates us as happily settled in the world. If a poor frontier inhabitant may be allowed to suppose this great personage the first in our system to be exposed but for one hour to the exquisite pangs we so often feel, would not the preservation of so numerous a family engross all his thoughts; would not the ideas of dominion and other felicities attendant on royalty all vanish in the hour of danger? The regal character, however sacred, would be superseded by the stronger, because more natural one of man and father. Oh! Did he but know the circumstances of this horrid war, I am sure he would put a stop to that long destruction of parents and children. I am sure that while he turned his ears to state policy, he would attentively listen also to the dictates of Nature, that great parent; for, as a good king, he no doubt wishes to create, to spare, and to protect, as she does. Must I then, in order to be called a faithful subject, coolly and philosophically say it is necessary for the good of Britain that my children's brains should be dashed against the walls of the house in which they were reared; that my wife should be stabbed and scalped before my face; that I should be either murthered or captivated; or that for greater expedition we should all be locked up and burnt to ashes as the family of the B———n was? Must I with meekness wait for that last pitch of desolation and receive with perfect resignation so hard a fate from ruffians acting at such a distance from the eyes of any superior, monsters left to the wild impulses of the wildest nature? Could the lions of Africa be transported here and let loose, they would no doubt kill us in order to prey upon our carcasses! But their appetites would not require so many victims. Shall I wait to be punished with death, or else to be stripped of all food and raiment, reduced to despair without redress and without hope? Shall those who may escape see everything they hold dear destroyed and gone? Shall those few survivors, lurking in some obscure corner, deplore in vain the fate of their families, mourn over parents either captivated, butchered, or burnt; roam among our wilds and wait for death at the foot of some tree, without a murmur or without a sigh, for the good of the cause? No, it is impossible! So astonishing a sacrifice is not to be expected from human nature; it must belong to beings of an inferior or superior order, actuated by less or by more refined principles. Even those great personages who are so far elevated above the common ranks of men, those, I mean, who wield and direct so many thunders, those who have let loose against us these demons of war, could they be transported here and metamorphosed into simple planters as we are—they would, from being the arbiters of human destiny, sink into miserable victims; they would feel and exclaim as we do, and be as much at a loss what line of conduct to prosecute. Do you well comprehend the difficulties of our situation? If we stay we are sure to perish at one time or another; no vigilance on our part can save us; if we retire, we know not where to go; every house is filled with refugees as wretched as ourselves; and if we remove, we become beggars. The property of farmers is not like that of merchants, and absolute poverty is worse than death. If we take up arms to defend ourselves, we are denominated rebels; should we not be rebels against Nature, could we be shamefully passive? Shall we, then, like martyrs, glory in an allegiance now become useless, and voluntarily expose ourselves to a species of desolation which, though it ruin us entirely, yet enriches not our ancient masters. By this inflexible and sullen attachment, we shall be despised by our countrymen and destroyed by our ancient friends; whatever we may say, whatever merit we may claim, will not shelter us from those indiscriminate blows, given by hired banditti, animated by all those passions which urge men to shed the blood of others; how bitter the thought! On the contrary, blows received by the hands of those from whom we expected protection extinguish ancient respect and urge us to self-defence—perhaps to revenge; this is the path which Nature herself points out, as well to the civilized as to the uncivilized. The Creator of hearts has himself stamped on them those propensities at their first formation; and must we then daily receive this treatment from a power once so loved? The fox flies or deceives the hounds that pursue him; the bear, when overtaken, boldly resists and attacks them; the hen, the very timid hen, fights for the preservation of her chicken, nor does she decline to attack and to meet on the wing even the swift kite. Shall man, then, provided both with instinct and reason, unmoved, unconcerned, and passive see his subsistence consumed and his progeny either ravished from him or murdered? Shall fictitious reason extinguish the unerring impulse of instinct? No; my former respect, my former attachment, vanishes with my safety; that respect and attachment were purchased by protection, and it has ceased. Could not the great nation we belong to have accomplished her designs by means of her numerous armies, by means of those fleets which cover the ocean? Must those who are masters of two thirds of the trade of the world, who have in their hands the power which almighty gold can give, who possess a species of wealth that increases with their desires—must they establish their conquest with our insignificant, innocent blood!

Must I, then, bid farewell to Britain, to that renowned country? Must I renounce a name so ancient and so venerable? Alas, she herself, that once indulgent parent, forces me to take up arms against her. She herself first inspired the most unhappy citizens of our remote districts with the thoughts of shedding the blood of those whom they used to call by the name of friends and brethren. That great nation which now convulses the world, which hardly knows the extent of her Indian kingdoms, which looks toward the universal monarchy of trade, of industry, of riches, of power: why must she strew our poor frontiers with the carcasses of her friends, with the wrecks of our insignificant villages, in which there is no gold? When, oppressed by painful recollection, I revolve all these scattered ideas in my mind, when I contemplate my situation and the thousand streams of evil with which I am surrounded, when I descend into the particular tendency even of the remedy I have proposed, I am convulsed—convulsed sometimes to that degree as to be tempted to exclaim, "Why has the Master of the world permitted so much indiscriminate evil throughout every part of this poor planet, at all times, and among all kinds of people?" It ought surely to be the punishment of the wicked only. I bring that cup to my lips, of which I must soon taste, and shudder at its bitterness. What, then, is life, I ask myself; is it a gracious gift? No, it is too bitter; a gift means something valuable conferred, but life appears to be a mere accident, and of the worst kind: we are born to be victims of diseases and passions, of mischances and death; better not to be than to be miserable. Thus, impiously I roam, I fly from one erratic thought to another, and my mind, irritated by these acrimonious reflections, is ready sometimes to lead me to dangerous extremes of violence. When I recollect that I am a father and a husband, the return of these endearing ideas strikes deep into my heart. Alas! They once made it glow with pleasure and with every ravishing exultation; but now they fill it with sorrow. At other times, my wife industriously rouses me out of these dreadful meditations and soothes me by all the reasoning she is mistress of; but her endeavours only serve to make me more miserable by reflecting that she must share with me all these calamities the bare apprehensions of which I am afraid will subvert her reason. Nor can I with patience think that a beloved wife, my faithful helpmate, throughout all my rural schemes the principal hand which has assisted me in rearing the prosperous fabric of ease and independence I lately possessed, as well as my children, those tenants of my heart, should daily and nightly be exposed to such a cruel fate. Self-preservation is above all political precepts and rules, and even superior to the dearest opinions of our minds; a reasonable accommodation of ourselves to the various exigencies of the times in which we live is the most irresistible precept. To this great evil I must seek some sort of remedy adapted to remove or to palliate it; situated as I am, what steps should I take that will neither injure nor insult any of the parties, and at the same time save my family from that certain destruction which awaits it if I remain here much longer. Could I ensure them bread, safety, and subsistence, not the bread of idleness, but that earned by proper labour as heretofore; could this be accomplished by the sacrifice of my life, I would willingly give it up. I attest before heaven that it is only for these I would wish to live and toil, for these whom I have brought into this miserable existence. I resemble, methinks, one of the stones of a ruined arch, still retaining that pristine form which anciently fitted the place I occupied, but the centre is tumbled down; I can be nothing until I am replaced, either in the former circle or in some stronger one. I see one on a smaller scale, and at a considerable distance, but it is within my power to reach it; and since I have ceased to consider myself as a member of the ancient state now convulsed, I willingly descend into an inferior one. I will revert into a state approaching nearer to that of nature, unencumbered either with voluminous laws or contradictory codes, often galling the very necks of those whom they protect, and at the same time sufficiently remote from the brutality of unconnected savage nature. Do you, my friend, perceive the path I have found out? It is that which leads to the tenants of the great ———— village of ————, where, far removed from the accursed neighbourhood of Europeans, its inhabitants live with more ease, decency, and peace than you imagine; who, though governed by no laws, yet find in uncontaminated simple manners all that laws can afford. Their system is sufficiently complete to answer all the primary wants of man and to constitute him a social being such as he ought to be in the great forest of Nature. There it is that I have resolved at any rate to transport myself and family: an eccentric thought, you may say, thus to cut asunder all former connexions and to form new ones with a people whom Nature has stamped with such different characteristics! But as the happiness of my family is the only object of my wishes, I care very little where we are or where we go, provided that we are safe and all united together. Our new calamities, being shared equally by all, will become lighter; our mutual affection for each other will in this great transmutation become the strongest link of our new society, will afford us every joy we can receive on a foreign soil, and preserve us in unity as the gravity and coherency of matter prevent the world from dissolution. Blame me not; it would be cruel in you, it would beside be entirely useless; for when you receive this, we shall be on the wing. When we think all hopes are gone, must we,

like poor pusillanimous wretches, despair and die? No;
I perceive before me a few resources, though through
many dangers, which I will explain to you hereafter. It
is not, believe me, a disappointed ambition which leads
me to take this step; it is the bitterness of my situation,
it is the impossibility of knowing what better measure to
adopt: my education fitted me for nothing more than
the most simple occupations of life; I am but a feller of
trees, a cultivator of lands, the most honourable title an
American can have. I have no exploits, no discoveries,
no inventions to boast of; I have cleared about 370 acres
of land, some for the plough, some for the scythe, and
this has occupied many years of my life. I have never
possessed or wish to possess anything more than what
could be earned or produced by the united industry
of my family. I wanted nothing more than to live at home
independent and tranquil and to teach my children how
to provide the means of a future ample subsistence,
founded on labour, like that of their father. This is the
career of life I have pursued and that which I had
marked out for them and for which they seemed to be so
well calculated by their inclinations and by their constitutions. But now these pleasing expectations are gone;
we must abandon the accumulated industry of nineteen
years; we must fly we hardly know whither, through the
most impervious paths, and become members of a new
and strange community. Oh, virtue! Is this all the reward
thou hast to confer on thy votaries? Either thou art only
a chimera, or thou art a timid, useless being; soon affrighted, when ambition, thy great adversary, dictates,
when war re-echoes the dreadful sounds and poor helpless individuals are mowed down by its cruel reapers like
useless grass. I have at all times generously relieved what
few distressed people I have met with; I have encouraged
the industrious; my house has always been opened to
travellers; I have not lost a month in illness since I have
been a man; I have caused upwards of a hundred and
twenty families to remove hither. Many of them I have
led by the hand in the days of their first trial; distant as
I am from any places of worship or school of education,
I have been the pastor of my family and the teacher of
many of my neighbours. I have learnt them as well as I
could the gratitude they owe to God, the Father of har-

vests, and their duties to man; I have been an useful
subject, ever obedient to the laws, ever vigilant to see
them respected and observed. My wife hath faithfully
followed the same line within her province; no woman
was ever a better economist or spun or wove better
linen; yet we must perish, perish like wild beasts, included within a ring of fire!

Yes, I will cheerfully embrace that resource; it is a
holy inspiration; by night and by day, it presents itself
to my mind; I have carefully revolved the scheme; I
have considered in all its future effects and tendencies
the new mode of living we must pursue, without salt,
without spices, without linen, and with little other clothing; the art of hunting we must acquire, the new manners
we must adopt, the new language we must speak; the
dangers attending the education of my children we must
endure. These changes may appear more terrific at a
distance perhaps than when grown familiar by practice;
what is it to us whether we eat well-made pastry or
pounded àlagrichés, well-roasted beef or smoked venison, cabbages or squashes? Whether we wear neat homespun or good beaver, whether we sleep on feather-beds
or on bearskins? The difference is not worth attending
to. The difficulty of the language, the fear of some great
intoxication among the Indians, finally the apprehension
lest my younger children should be caught by that singular charm, so dangerous at their tender years, are the
only considerations that startle me. By what power does
it come to pass that children who have been adopted
when young among these people can never be prevailed
on to readopt European manners? Many an anxious parent have I seen last war who at the return of the peace
went to the Indian villages where they knew their children had been carried in captivity, when to their inexpressible sorrow they found them so perfectly Indianized that
many knew them no longer, and those whose more
advanced ages permitted them to recollect their fathers
and mothers absolutely refused to follow them and ran
to their adoptive parents for protection against the
effusions of love their unhappy real parents lavished
on them! Incredible as this may appear, I have heard
it asserted in a thousand instances, among persons of
credit. In the village of ———, where I purpose to go,

there lived, about fifteen years ago, an Englishman and a Swede, whose history would appear moving had I time to relate it. They were grown to the age of men when they were taken; they happily escaped the great punishment of war captives and were obliged to marry the squaws who had saved their lives by adoption. By the force of habit, they became at last thoroughly naturalized to this wild course of life. While I was there, their friends sent them a considerable sum of money to ransom themselves with. The Indians, their old masters, gave them their choice, and without requiring any consideration, told them that they had been long as free as themselves. They chose to remain, and the reasons they gave me would greatly surprise you: the most perfect freedom, the ease of living, the absence of those cares and corroding solicitudes which so often prevail with us, the peculiar goodness of the soil they cultivated, for they did not trust altogether to hunting—all these and many more motives which I have forgot made them prefer that life of which we entertain such dreadful opinions. It cannot be, therefore, so bad as we generally conceive it to be; there must be in their social bond something singularly captivating and far superior to anything to be boasted of among us; for thousands of Europeans are Indians, and we have no examples of even one of those aborigines having from choice become Europeans! There must be something more congenial to our native dispositions than the fictitious society in which we live; or else why should children, and even grown persons, become in a short time so invincibly attached to it? There must be something very bewitching in their manners, something very indelible and marked by the very hands of Nature. For, take a young Indian lad, give him the best education you possibly can, load him with your bounty, with presents, nay with riches, yet he would secretly long for his native woods, which you would imagine he must have long since forgot; and on the first opportunity he can possibly find, you will see him voluntarily leave behind all you have given him and return with inexpressible joy to lie on the mats of his fathers. Mr. —— some years ago received from a good old Indian, who died in his house, a young lad of nine years of age, his grandson. He kindly educated

him with his children and bestowed on him the same
care and attention in respect to the memory of his
venerable grandfather, who was a worthy man. He intended to give him a genteel trade, but in the spring
season when all the family went to the woods to make
their maple sugar, he suddenly disappeared, and it was
not until seventeen months after that his benefactor
heard he had reached the village of Bald Eagle, where
he still dwelt. Let us say what we will of them, of their
inferior organs, of their want of bread, etc., they are
as stout and well made as the Europeans. Without
temples, without priests, without kings, and without laws,
they are in many instances superior to us; and the proofs
of what I advance are that they live without care, sleep
without inquietude, take life as it comes, bearing all its
asperities with unparalleled patience, and die without any
kind of apprehension for what they have done or for
what they expect to meet with hereafter. What system
of philosophy can give us so many necessary qualifications for happiness? They most certainly are much more
closely connected with Nature than we are; they are her
immediate children: the inhabitants of the woods are her
undefiled offspring; those of the plains are her degenerated breed, far, very far removed from her primitive
laws, from her original design. It is therefore resolved on,
I will either die in the attempt or succeed; better perish
all together in one fatal hour than to suffer what we
daily endure. I do not expect to enjoy in the village of
——— an uninterrupted happiness; it cannot be our
lot, let us live where we will; I am not founding my
future prosperity on golden dreams. Place mankind where
you will, they must always have adverse circumstances
to struggle with; from nature, accidents, constitution;
from seasons, from that great combination of mischances which perpetually leads us to diseases, to
poverty, etc. Who knows but I may meet in this new
situation some accident whence may spring up new
sources of unexpected prosperity? Who can be presumptuous enough to predict all the good? Who can
foresee all the evils which strew the paths of our lives?
But after all, I cannot but recollect what sacrifice I am
going to make, what amputation I am going to suffer,
what transition I am going to experience. Pardon my

repetitions, my wild, my trifling reflections; they proceed from the agitations of my mind and the fulness of my heart; the action of thus retracing them seems to lighten the burthen and to exhilarate my spirits; this is, besides, the last letter you will receive from me; I would fain tell you all, though I hardly know how. Oh! In the hours, in the moments of my greatest anguish, could I intuitively represent to you that variety of thought which crowds on my mind, you would have reason to be surprised and to doubt of their possibility. Shall we ever meet again? If we should, where will it be? On the wild shores of ———. If it be my doom to end my days there, I will greatly improve them and perhaps make room for a few more families who will choose to retire from the fury of a storm, the agitated billows of which will yet roar for many years on our extended shores. Perhaps I may repossess my house, if it be not burnt down; but how will my improvements look? Why, half defaced, bearing the strong marks of abandonment and of the ravages of war. However, at present I give everything over for lost; I will bid a long farewell to what I leave behind. If ever I repossess it, I shall receive it as a gift, as a reward for my conduct and fortitude. Do not imagine, however, that I am a stoic—by no means: I must, on the contrary, confess to you that I feel the keenest regret at abandoning a house which I have in some measure reared with my own hands. Yes, perhaps I may never revisit those fields which I have cleared, those trees which I have planted, those meadows which, in my youth, were a hideous wilderness, now converted by my industry into rich pastures and pleasant lawns. If in Europe it is praiseworthy to be attached to paternal inheritances, how much more natural, how much more powerful must the tie be with us, who, if I may be permitted the expression, are the founders, the creators, of our own farms! When I see my table surrounded with my blooming offspring, all united in the bonds of the strongest affection, it kindles in my paternal heart a variety of tumultuous sentiments which none but a father and a husband in my situation can feel or describe. Perhaps I may see my wife, my children, often distressed, involuntarily recalling to their minds the ease and abundance which they enjoyed under the paternal roof. Perhaps I may see them want that bread which I now leave behind, overtaken by diseases and penury, rendered more bitter by the recollection of former days of opulence and plenty. Perhaps I may be assailed on every side by unforeseen accidents which I shall not be able to prevent or to alleviate. Can I contemplate such images without the most unutterable emotions? My fate is determined; but I have not determined it, you may assure yourself, without having undergone the most painful conflicts of a variety of passions—interest, love of ease, disappointed views, and pleasing expectations frustrated —I shuddered at the review! Would to God I was master of the stoical tranquillity of that magnanimous sect; oh, that I were possessed of those sublime lessons which Appollonius of Chalcis gave to the Emperor Antoninus! I could then with much more propriety guide the helm of my little bark, which is soon to be freighted with all that I possess most dear on earth, through this stormy passage to a safe harbour, and when there, become to my fellow-passengers a surer guide, a brighter example, a pattern more worthy of imitation, throughout all the new scenes they must pass and the new career they must traverse. I have observed, notwithstanding, the means hitherto made use of to arm the principal nations against our frontiers. Yet they have not, they will not take up the hatchet against a people who have done them no harm. The passions necessary to urge these people to war cannot be roused; they cannot feel the stings of vengeance, the thirst of which alone can impel them to shed blood: far superior in their motives of action to the Europeans who, for sixpence per day, may be engaged to shed that of any people on earth. They know nothing of the nature of our disputes; they have no ideas of such revolutions as this; a civil division of a village or tribe are events which have never been recorded in their traditions; many of them know very well that they have too long been the dupes and the victims of both parties, foolishly arming for our sakes, sometimes against each other, sometimes against our white enemies. They consider us as born on the same land, and, though they have no reasons to love us, yet they seem carefully to avoid entering into this quarrel, from whatever motives. I am speaking of those nations with which I am best acquainted; a few hundreds of the worst kind mixed with whites worse than themselves are now hired by Great Britain to perpetuate those dreadful incursions. In my youth I traded with the ———, under the conduct of my uncle, and always traded justly and equitably; some of them remember it to this day. Happily their village is far removed from the dangerous neighbourhood of the whites; I sent a man last spring to it who understands the woods extremely well and who speaks their language; he is just returned, after several weeks' absence, and has brought me, as I had flattered myself, a string of thirty purple wampum as a token that their honest chief will spare us half of his wigwam until we have time to erect one. He has sent me word that they have land in plenty, of which they are not so covetous as the whites; that we may plant for ourselves, and that in the meantime he will procure us some corn and meat; that fish is plenty in the waters of ———, and that the village to which he had laid open my proposals have no objection to our becoming dwellers with them. I have not yet communicated these glad tidings to my wife, nor do I know how to do it; I tremble lest she should refuse to follow me, lest the sudden idea of this removal rushing on her mind might be too powerful. I flatter myself I shall be able to accomplish it and to prevail on her; I fear nothing but the effects of her strong attachment to her relations. I would willingly let you know how I purpose to remove my family to so great a distance, but it would become unintelligible to you because you are not acquainted with the geographical situation of this part of the country. Suffice it for you to know that with about twenty-three miles land carriage, I am enabled to perform the rest by water; and when once afloat, I care not whether it be two or three hundred miles. I propose to send all our provisions, furniture, and clothes to my wife's father, who approves of the scheme, and to reserve nothing but a few necessary articles of covering, trusting to the furs of the chase for our future apparel. Were we imprudently to encumber ourselves too much with baggage, we should never reach to the waters of ———, which is the most dangerous as well as the most difficult part of our journey, and yet but a trifle in point of distance. I intend to say to my Negroes, "In the name of God, be free, my honest lads; I thank you for your past services; go, from henceforth, and work for yourselves; look on me as your old friend and fellow-labourer; be sober, frugal, and industrious, and you need not fear earning a comfortable subsistence." Lest my countrymen should think that I am gone to join the incendiaries of our frontiers, I intend to write a letter to Mr. —— to inform him of our retreat and of the reasons that have urged me to it. The man whom I sent to —— village is to accompany us also, and a very useful companion he will be on every account.

You may therefore, by means of anticipation, behold me under the wigwam; I am so well acquainted with the principal manners of these people that I entertain not the least apprehension from them. I rely more securely on their strong hospitality than on the witnessed compacts of many Europeans. As soon as possible after my arrival, I design to build myself a wigwam, after the same manner and size with the rest in order to avoid being thought singular or giving occasion for any railleries, though these people are seldom guilty of such European follies. I shall erect it hard by the lands which they propose to allot me, and will endeavour that my wife, my children, and myself may be adopted soon after our arrival. Thus becoming truly inhabitants of their village, we shall immediately occupy that rank within the pale of their society, which will afford us all the amends we can possibly expect for the loss we have met with by the convulsions of our own. According to their customs, we shall likewise receive names from them, by which we shall always be known. My youngest children shall learn to swim and to shoot with the bow, that they may acquire such talents as will necessarily raise them into some degree of esteem among the Indian lads of their own age; the rest of us must hunt with the hunter. I have been for several years an expert marksman; but I dread lest the imperceptible charm of Indian education may seize my younger children and give them such a propensity to that mode of life as may preclude their returning to the manners and customs of their parents. I have but one remedy to prevent this great evil, and that is to employ them in the labour of the fields as much as I can; I have even resolved to make their daily subsistence depend altogether on it. As long as we keep ourselves busy in tilling the earth, there is no fear of any of us becoming wild; it is the chase and the food it procures that have this strange effect. Excuse a simile —those hogs which range in the woods, and to whom grain is given once a week, preserve their former degree of tameness; but if, on the contrary, they are reduced to live on ground nuts and on what they can get, they soon become wild and fierce. For my part, I can plough, sow, and hunt, as occasion may require; but my wife, deprived of wool and flax, will have no room for industry; what is she then to do? Like the other squaws, she must cook for us the nasaump, the ninchickè, and such other preparations of corn as are customary among these people. She must learn to bake squashes and pompions under the ashes, to slice and smoke the meat of our own killing in order to preserve it; she must cheerfully adopt the manners and customs of her neighbours, in their dress, deportment, conduct, and internal economy, in all respects. Surely if we can have fortitude enough to quit all we have, to remove so far, and to associate with people so different from us, these necessary compliances are but subordinate parts of the scheme. The change of garments, when those they carry with them are worn out, will not be the least of my wife's and daughter's concerns, though I am in hopes that self-love will invent some sort of reparation. Perhaps you would not believe that there are in the woods looking-glasses and paint of every colour; and that the inhabitants take as much pains to adorn their faces and their bodies, to fix their bracelets of silver, and plait their hair as our forefathers the Picts used to do in the time of the Romans. Not that I would wish to see either my wife or daughter adopt those savage customs; we can live in great peace and harmony with them without descending to every article; the interruption of trade hath, I hope, suspended this mode of dress. My wife understands inoculation perfectly well; she inoculated all our children one after another and has successfully performed the operation on several scores of people, who, scattered here and there through our woods, were too far removed from all medical assistance. If we can persuade but one family to submit to it, and it succeeds, we shall then be as happy as our situation will admit of; it will raise her into some degree of consideration, for whoever is useful in any society will always be respected. If we are so fortunate as to carry one family through a disorder, which is the plague among these people, I trust to the force of example we shall then become truly necessary, valued, and beloved; we indeed owe every kind office to a society of men who so readily offer to admit us into their social partnership and to extend to my family the shelter of their village, the strength of their adoption, and even the dignity of their names. God grant us a prosperous beginning; we may then hope to be of more service to them than even missionaries who have been sent to preach to them a Gospel they cannot understand.

As to religion, our mode of worship will not suffer much by this removal from a cultivated country into the bosom of the woods; for it cannot be much simpler than that which we have followed here these many years, and I will with as much care as I can redouble my attention and twice a week retrace to them the great outlines of their duty to God and to man. I will read and expound to them some part of the decalogue, which is the method I have pursued ever since I married.

Half a dozen of acres on the shores of ——, the soil of which I know well, will yield us a great abundance of all we want; I will make it a point to give the overplus to such Indians as shall be most unfortunate in their huntings; I will persuade them, if I can, to till a little more land than they do and not to trust so much to the produce of the chase. To encourage them still farther, I will give a quirn to every six families; I have built many for our poor back-settlers, it being often the want of mills which prevents them from raising grain. As I am a carpenter, I can build my own plough and can be of great service to many of them; my example alone may rouse the industry of some and serve to direct others in their labours. The difficulties of the language will soon be removed; in my evening conversations, I will endeavour to make them regulate the trade of their village in such a manner as that those pests of the continent, those Indian-traders, may not come within a certain distance; and there they shall be obliged to transact their business before the old people. I am in hopes that the constant respect which is paid to the elders, and shame, may prevent the young hunters from infringing this regulation. The son of —— will soon be made acquainted with our schemes, and I trust that the power of love and the strong attachment he professes for my daughter may bring him along with us; he will make an excellent hunter; young and vigorous, he will equal in dexterity the stoutest man in the village. Had it not been for this fortunate circumstance, there would have been the greatest danger; for however I respect the simple, the inoffensive society of these people in their villages, the strongest prejudices would make me abhor any alliance with them in blood, disagreeable no doubt to Nature's intentions, which have strongly divided us by so many indelible characters. In the days of our sickness, we shall have recourse to their medical knowledge, which is well calculated for the simple diseases to which they are subject. Thus shall we metamorphose ourselves from neat, decent, opulent planters, surrounded with every conveniency which our external labour and internal industry could give, into a still simpler people divested of everything beside hope, food, and the raiment of the woods: abandoning the large framed house to dwell under the wigwam, and the featherbed to lie on the mat or bear's skin. There shall we sleep undisturbed by frightful dreams and apprehensions; rest and peace of mind will make us the most ample amends for what we shall leave behind. These blessings cannot be purchased too dear; too long have we been deprived of them. I would cheerfully go even to the Mississippi to find that repose to which we have been so long strangers. My heart sometimes seems tired with beating; it wants rest like my eyelids, which feel oppressed with so many watchings.

These are the component parts of my scheme, the success of each of which appears feasible, whence I flatter myself with the probable success of the whole. Still, the danger of Indian education returns to my mind and alarms me much; then again, I contrast it with the education of the times; both appear to be equally pregnant with evils. Reason points out the necessity of choosing the least dangerous, which I must consider as the only good within my reach; I persuade myself that industry and labour will be a sovereign preservative against the dangers of the former; but I consider, at the same time, that the share of labour and industry which is intended to procure but a simple subsistence, with hardly any superfluity, cannot have the same restrictive effects on our minds as when we tilled the earth on a more extensive scale. The surplus could be then realized into solid wealth, and at the same time that this realization rewarded our past labours, it engrossed and fixed the attention of the labourer and cherished in his mind the hope of future riches. In order to supply this great deficiency of industrious motives and to hold out to them a real object to prevent the fatal consequences of this sort of apathy, I will keep an exact account of all that shall be gathered and give each of them a regular credit for the amount of it, to be paid them in real property at the return of peace. Thus, though seemingly toiling for bare subsistence on a foreign land, they shall entertain the pleasing prospect of seeing the sum of their labours one day realized either in legacies or gifts, equal if not superior to it. The yearly expense of the clothes which they would have received at home, and of which they will then be deprived, shall likewise be added to their credit; thus I flatter myself that they will more cheerfully wear the blanket, the matchcoat, and the moccasins. Whatever success they may meet with in hunting or fishing shall be only considered as recreation and pastime; I shall thereby prevent them from estimating their skill in the chase as an important and necessary accomplishment. I mean to say to them: "You shall hunt and fish merely to show your new companions that you are not inferior to them in point of sagacity and dexterity." Were I to send them to such schools as the interior parts of our settlements afford at present, what can they learn there? How could I support them there? What must become of me; am I to proceed on my voyage and leave them? That I never could submit to. Instead of the perpetual discordant noise of disputes so common among us, instead of those scolding scenes, frequent in every house, they will observe nothing but silence at home and abroad: a singular appearance of peace and concord are the first characteristics which strike you in the villages of these people. Nothing can be more pleasing, nothing surprises an European so much, as the silence and harmony which prevail among them, and in each family, except when disturbed by that accursed spirit given them by the wood rangers in exchange for their furs. If my children learn nothing of geometrical rules, the use of the compass, or of the Latin tongue, they will learn and practise sobriety, for rum can no longer be sent to these people; they will learn that modesty and diffidence for which the young Indians are so remarkable; they will consider labour as the most essential qualification, hunting as the second. They will prepare themselves in the prosecution of our small rural schemes, carried on for the benefit of our little community, to extend them farther when each shall receive his inheritance. Their tender minds will cease to be agitated by perpetual alarms, to be made cowards by continual terrors; if they acquire in the village of —— such an awkwardness of deportment and appearance as would render them ridiculous in our gay capitals, they will imbibe, I hope, a confirmed taste for that simplicity which so well becomes the cultivators of the land. If I cannot teach them any of those professions which sometimes embellish and support our society, I will show them how to hew wood, how to construct their own ploughs, and with a few tools how to supply themselves with every necessary implement, both in the house and in the field. If they are hereafter obliged to confess that they belong to no one particular church, I shall have the consolation of teaching them that great, that primary worship which is the foundation of all others. If they do not fear God according to the tenets of any one seminary, they shall learn to worship Him upon the broad scale of nature. The Supreme Being does not reside in peculiar churches or communities; He is equally the great Manitou of the woods and of the plains; and even in the gloom, the obscurity of those very woods, His justice may be as well understood and felt as in the most sumptuous temples. Each worship with us hath, you know, its peculiar political tendency; there it has none but to inspire gratitude and truth: their tender minds shall receive no other idea of the Supreme Being than that of the Father of all men, who requires nothing more of us than what tends to make each other happy. We shall say with them: "Soungwanèha, èsa caurounkyawga, nughwonshauza neattèwek, nèsalanga." Our Father, be thy will done in earth as it is in great heaven.

Perhaps my imagination gilds too strongly this distant prospect; yet it appears founded on so few and simple principles that there is not the same probability of adverse incidents as in more complex schemes. These vague rambling contemplations which I here faithfully retrace carry me sometimes to a great distance; I am lost in the anticipation of the various circumstances attending this proposed metamorphosis! Many unforeseen accidents may doubtless arise. Alas! It is easier for me in all the glow of paternal anxiety, reclined on my bed, to form the theory of my future conduct than to reduce my schemes into practice. But when once secluded from the great society to which we now belong, we shall unite closer together, and there will be less room for jealousies or contentions. As I intend my children neither for the law nor the church, but for the cultivation of the land, I wish them no literary accomplishments; I pray heaven that they may be one day nothing more than expert scholars in husbandry: this is the science which made our continent to flourish more rapidly than any other. Were they to grow up where I am now situated, even admitting that we were in safety; two of them are verging toward that period of their lives when they must necessarily take up the musket and learn, in that new school, all the vices which are so common in armies. Great God! Close my eyes forever rather than I should live to see this calamity! May they rather become inhabitants of the woods.

Thus then in the village of ——, in the bosom of that peace it has enjoyed ever since I have known it, connected with mild, hospitable people, strangers to *our* political disputes and having none among themselves; on the shores of a fine river, surrounded with woods, abounding with game, our little society, united in perfect harmony with the new adoptive one, in which we shall be incorporated, shall rest, I hope, from all fatigues, from all apprehensions, from our present terrors, and from our long watchings. Not a word of politics shall cloud our simple conversation; tired either with the chase or the labours of the field, we shall sleep on our mats without any distressing want, having learnt to retrench every superfluous one; we shall have but two prayers to make to the Supreme Being, that He may shed His fertilizing dew on our little crops and that He will be pleased to restore peace to our unhappy country. These shall be the only subject of our nightly prayers and of our daily ejaculations; and if the labour, the industry, the frugality, the union of men, can be an agreeable offering to Him, we shall not fail to receive His paternal blessings. There I shall contemplate Nature in her most wild and ample extent; I shall carefully study a species of society of which I have at present but very imperfect ideas; I will endeavour to occupy with propriety that place which will enable me to enjoy the few and sufficient benefits it confers. The solitary and unconnected mode of life I have lived in my youth must fit me for this trial; I am not the first who has attempted it; Europeans did not, it is true, carry to the wilderness numerous families; they went there as mere speculators, I as a man seeking a refuge from the desolation of war. They went there to study the manner of the aborigines, I to conform to them, whatever they are; some went as visitors, as travellers; I, as a sojourner, as a fellow-hunter and labourer, go determined industriously to work up among them such a system of happiness as may be adequate to my future situation and may be a sufficient compensation for all my fatigues and for the misfortunes I have borne: I have always found it at home; I may hope likewise to find it under the humble roof of my wigwam.

O Supreme Being! If among the immense variety of planets, inhabited by thy creative power, thy paternal and omnipotent care deigns to extend to all the individuals they contain, if it be not beneath thy infinite dignity to cast thy eye on us wretched mortals, if my future felicity is not contrary to the necessary effects of those secret causes which thou hast appointed, receive the supplications of a man to whom in thy kindness thou hast given a wife and an offspring; view us all with benignity, sanctify this strong conflict of regrets, wishes, and other natural passions; guide our steps through these unknown paths and bless our future mode of life. If it is good and well meant, it must proceed from thee; thou knowest, O Lord, our enterprise contains neither fraud nor malice nor revenge. Bestow on me that energy of conduct now become so necessary that it may be in my power to carry the young family thou hast given me through this great trial with safety and in thy peace. Inspire me with such intentions and such rules of conduct as may be most acceptable to thee. Preserve, O God, preserve the companion of my bosom, the best gift thou hast given me; endue her with courage and strength sufficient to accomplish this perilous journey. Bless the children of our love, those portions of our hearts; I implore thy divine assistance, speak to their tender minds and inspire them with the love of that virtue which alone can serve as the basis of their conduct in this world and of their happiness with thee. Restore peace and concord to our poor afflicted country; assuage the fierce storm which has so long ravaged it. Permit, I beseech thee, O Father of nature, that our ancient virtues and our industry may not be totally lost and that as a reward for the great toils we have made on this new land, we may be restored to our ancient tranquillity and enabled to fill it with successive generations that will constantly thank thee for the ample subsistence thou hast given them.

The unreserved manner in which I have written must give you a convincing proof of that friendship and esteem of which I am sure you never yet doubted. As members of the same society, as mutually bound by the ties of affection and old acquaintance, you certainly cannot avoid feeling for my distresses; you cannot avoid mourning with me over that load of physical and moral evil with which we are all oppressed. My own share of it I often overlook when I minutely contemplate all that hath befallen our native country.

Sketches of Eighteenth-century America

CHAPTER I

A SNOW-STORM AS IT AFFECTS THE AMERICAN FARMER

No man of the least degree of sensibility can journey through any number of years in whatever climate without often being compelled to make many useful observations on the different phenomena of Nature which surround him and without involuntarily being struck either with awe or admiration in beholding some of the elementary conflicts in the midst of which he lives. A great thunder-storm, an extensive flood, a desolating hurricane, a sudden and intense frost, an overwhelming snow-storm, a sultry day—each of these different scenes exhibits singular beauties even in spite of the damage they cause. Often whilst the heart laments the loss to the citizen, the enlightened mind, seeking for the natural causes, and astonished at the effects, awakes itself to surprise and wonder.

Of all the scenes which this climate offers, none has struck me with a greater degree of admiration than the ushering in of our winters, and the vehemence with which their first rigour seizes and covers the earth; a rigour which, when once descended, becomes one of the principal favours and blessings this climate has to boast of. I mean to view it as connected with the welfare of husbandry—as a great flood of congealed water sheltering the grass and the grains of our fields and overwhelming men, beasts, birds living under the care of man. [He] in the midst of this sudden alteration has to provide food and shelter for so many animals, on the preservation of which the husbandman's welfare entirely depends. This single thought is really tremendous: from grass and pastures growing in our meadows and in our fields; from various other means by which the tenants of our farms lived before, they must suddenly pass to provenders, to grains, and to other resources gathered by Man when the face of the earth teemed with a luxuriant vegetation.

'Tis at this period that the functions of a great farmer become more extended and more difficult. 'Tis from his stores that all must draw their subsistence. He must know whether they will be sufficient to reach the other end of the wintry career. He must see whether all have a sufficient quantity daily delivered to them, whether each class is properly divided, whether water can be procured, what diseases and accidents may happen. These are a few sketches of that energetic circle of foresight, knowledge, and activity which fill the space of five months, to which you must add the care of a large family as to raiment, fuel, and victuals.

The tenants of his house, like the beasts of his farm, must now depend on the collected stores of the preceding season, sagaciously distributed and prepared by the industry of his wife. There lies the "aurum potabile" of an American farmer. He may work and gather the choicest fruits of his farm; but if female economy fails, he loses the comfort of good victuals. He sees wholesome meats, excellent flours converted into indifferent food; whilst his neighbour, more happy, though less rich, feeds on well-cooked dishes, well-composed puddings. For such is our lot: if we are blessed with a good wife, we may boast of living better than any people of the same rank on the globe.

Various tokens, long since known, guide the farmer in his daily progress and various occupations from the autumnal fall of the leaves. If he is prudent and active, he makes himself ready against the worst which Nature can give. Sheds, stables, barn-yards, partitions, racks, and mangers must be carefully reviewed and repaired; the stores of corn-stalks, straw, and hay must be securely placed where neither rain nor snow can damage them.

Great rains at last replenish the springs, the brooks, the swamps, and impregnate the earth. Then a severe frost succeeds which prepares it to receive the voluminous coat of snow which is soon to follow, though it is often preceded by a short interval of smoke and mildness, called the Indian Summer. This is in general the invariable rule: winter is not said properly to begin until these few moderate days and the rising of the waters have announced it to Man. This great mass of liquid, once frozen, spreads everywhere natural bridges, opens communications impassible before. The man of foresight neglects nothing; he has saved every object which might be damaged or lost; he is ready.

The wind, which is a great regulator of the weather, shifts to the north-east; the air becomes bleak and then intensely cold; the light of the sun becomes dimmed as if an eclipse had happened; a general night seems coming on. At last, imperceptible atoms make their appearance; they are few and descend slowly, a sure prognostic of a great snow. Little or no wind is as yet felt. By degrees the number as well as the size of these white particles is increased; they descend in larger flakes; a distant wind is heard; the noise swells and seems to advance; the new element at last appears and overspreads everything. In a little time the heavy clouds seem to approach nearer the earth and discharge a winged flood, driving along towards the south-west, howling at every door, roaring in every chimney, whistling with asperous sound through the naked limbs of the trees; these are the shrill notes which mark the weight of the storm. Still the storm increases as the night approaches, and its great obscurity greatly adds to the solemnity of the scene.

Sometimes the snow is preceded by melted hail which, like a shining varnish, covers and adorns the whole surface of the earth, of buildings and trees; a hurtful time for the cattle, which it chills and oppresses. Mournful and solitary, they retire to what shelter they can get; and, forgetting to eat, they wait with instinctive patience until the storm is over. How amazingly changed is the aspect of Nature! From the dusky hues of the autumnal shades, everything becomes refulgently white; from soft, miry roads, we pass all at once to solid icy bridges. What could an inhabitant of Africa say or think in contemplating this northern phenomenon? Would not it raise in his mind a greater degree of astonishment than his thunder-storms and his vertical suns?

A general alarm is spread through the farm. The master calls all his hands, opens the gates, lets down the bars, calls and counts all his stock as they come along. The oxen, the cows, remembering ancient experience, repair to the place where they were foddered the preceding winter; the colts wild, whilst they could unrestrained bound on the grassy fields, suddenly deprived of that liberty, become tame and docile to the hands which stroke and feed them. The sheep, more encumbered than the rest, slowly creep along and by their incessant bleating show their instinctive apprehension; they are generally the first which attract our attention and care. The horses are led to their stables, the oxen to their stalls; the rest are confined under their proper sheds and districts. All is safe, but no fodder need be given them yet; the stings of hunger are necessary to make them eat cheerfully the dried herbage and forget the green one on which they so lately fed. Heaven be praised, no accident has happened; all is secured from the inclemency of the storm. The farmer's vigilant eye has seen every operation performed; has numbered every head; and, as a good master, provided for the good welfare of all.

At last he returns home, loaded with hail and snow melting on his rough but warm clothes; his face is red with the repeated injury occasioned by the driving wind. His cheerful wife, not less pleased, welcomes him home with a mug of gingered cider; and whilst she helps him to dried and more comfortable clothes, she recounts to him the successful pains she has taken also in collecting all her ducks, geese, and all the rest of her numerous poultry, a province less extensive indeed but not less useful. But no sooner this simple tale is told than the cheerfulness of her mind is clouded by a sudden thought. Her children went to a distant school early in the morning whilst the sun shone and ere any ideas were formed of this storm. They are not yet returned. What is become of them? Has the master had tenderness enough to tarry awhile and watch over his little flock until the arrival of some relief? Or has he rudely dismissed them in quest of his own safety?

These alarming thoughts are soon communicated to her husband, who, starting up in all the glow of paternal anxiety, orders one of his Negroes to repair to the school-house with Bonny, the old faithful mare, who, like his wife, by her fecundity has replenished his farm. 'Tis done; she is mounted bareback and hurried through the storm to the school-house, at the door of which each child is impatiently waiting for this paternal assistance. At the sight of honest Tom, the Negro, their joy is increased by the pleasure of going home on horse-back. One is mounted before and two behind. Rachel, the poor widow's little daughter, with tears in her eyes, sees her playmates, just before her equals, as she thought, now provided with a horse and an attendant—a sad mortification. This is the first time she ever became sensible of the difference of her situation. Her distressed mother, not less anxious to fetch her child, prays to heaven that some charitable neighbour may bring her along. She, too, has a cow to take care of; a couple of pigs hitherto tenderly fed at the door; three or four ewes, perhaps, demanding her shelter round some part of her lonely log-house. Kind heaven hears her prayers. Honest Tom lifts her [Rachel] up and, for want of room, places her on Bonny's neck; there she is upheld by the oldest boy. Thus fixed with difficulty, they turn about and boldly face the driving storm; they all scream and are afraid of falling; at last they clinch together and are hushed. With cheerfulness and instinctive patience, Bonny proceeds along; and, sensible of the valuable cargo, highly lifting her legs, she securely treads along, shaking now and then her ears as the drifted snow penetrates into them.

A joyful meeting ensues. The thoughts of avoided danger increase the pleasure of the family. The milk-biscuit, the short-cake, the newly baked apple-pie are immediately produced; and the sudden joy these presents occasion expels every idea of cold and snow. In this country of hospitality and plenty, it would be a wonder indeed if little Rachel had not partaken of the same bounty. She is fed, made to warm herself; she has forgot the little reflections she had made at the school-house door; she is happy; and, to complete the goodly act, she is sent home on the same vehicle. The unfeigned thanks, the honest blessings of the poor widow, who was just going to set out, amply repays the trouble that has been taken—happy wages of this charitable attention.

The messenger returns. Everything is safe both within and without. At that instant the careful Negro, Jack, who has been busily employed in carrying wood to the shed that he may not be at a loss to kindle fire in the morning, comes into his master's room carrying on his hip an enormous back-log without which a fire is supposed to be imperfectly made and to be devoid of heat. All hands rise; the fire is made to blaze; the hearth is cleaned; and all the cheerful family sit around. Rest after so many laborious operations brings along with it an involuntary silence, even among the children, who grow sleepy, with their victuals in their hands, as they grow warm. "Lord, hear, how it blows!" says one. "My God, what a storm!" says another. "Mammy, where does all this snow come from?" asks a third. "Last year's storm, I think, was nothing to this," observes the wife. "I hope all is fast about the house. How happy it is for us that we had daylight to prepare us for it."

The father now and then opens the door to pass judgement and to contemplate the progress of the storm: " 'Tis dark, 'tis pitch-dark," he says; "a fence four rods off cannot be distinguished. The locust-trees hard by the door bend under the pressure of the loaded blast. Thank God, all is secured. I'll fodder my poor cattle well in the morning if it please Him I should live to see it." And this pious sentiment serves him as a reward for all his former industry, vigilance, and care. The Negroes, friends to the fire, smoke and crack some coarse jokes; and, well fed and clad, they contentedly make their brooms and ladles without any further concerns on their minds. Thus the industrious family, all gathered together under one roof, eat their wholesome supper, drink their mugs of cider, and grow imperceptibly less talkative and more thoughtless as they grow more sleepy. Now and then, when the redoubled fury of the storm rattles in the chimney, they seem to awake. They look at the door again and again, but 'tis the work of omnipotence; it is unavoidable; their neighbours feel it as well as themselves. Finally they go to bed, not to that bed of slavery or sorrow as is the

case in Europe with people of their class, but on the
substantial collection of honest feathers picked and provided by the industrious wife. There, stretched between
flannel sheets and covered with warm blankets made of
their own sheep's wool, they enjoy the luxury of sound,
undisturbed repose, earned by the fatigues of the preceding day. The Almighty has no crime to punish in this
innocent family; why should He permit ominous dreams
and terrific visions to disturb the imaginations of these
good people?

As soon as day reappears, the American farmer awakes
and calls all his hands. While some are busy in kindling
the fires, the rest with anxiety repair to the barns and
sheds. What a dismal aspect presents itself to their view!
The roads, the paths are no longer visible. The drifted
snow presents obstacles which must be removed with the
shovel. The fences and the trees, bending under the weight
of snow which encumbers them, bend in a thousand
shapes; but by a lucky blast of wind they are discharged;
and they immediately recover their natural situation.
The cattle, who had hitherto remained immovable,
their tails to the wind, appear strangely disfigured by the
long accession and adherence of the snow to their bodies.
On the sight of the master, suddenly animated, they
heavily shake themselves clean and crowd from all parts
in expectation of that fodder which the industry of Man
has provided for them. Where their number is extensive,
various and often distant are their allotments, which
are generally in the vicinity of the stacks of hay. In
that case, when the barn-yard work is done, the farmer
mounts his horse, followed by his men armed with pitch-
forks. He counts again the number of each sort and sees
that each receives a sufficient quantity. The strong are
separated from the weak, oxen with oxen, yearlings with
yearlings, and so on through every class. For cattle, like
men, conscious of their superior force will abuse it when
unrestrained by any law, and often live on their neighbour's property.

What a care, what an assiduity does this life require!
Who on contemplating the great and important field of
action performed every year by a large farmer can refrain from valuing and praising as they ought this useful, this dignified class of men? These are the people who,

scattered on the edge of this great continent, have made it to flourish, and have, without the dangerous assistance of mines, gathered, by the sweat of their honest brows and by the help of their ploughs, such a harvest of commercial emoluments for their country, uncontaminated either by spoils or rapine. These are the men who in future will replenish this huge continent, even to its utmost unknown limits, and render this new-found part of the world by far the happiest, the most potent as well as the most populous of any. Happy people! May the poor, the wretched of Europe, animated by our example, invited by our laws, avoid the fetters of their country and come in shoals to partake of our toils as well as of our happiness!

The next operation is to seek for convenient watering-places. Holes must be cut through the ice; 'tis done. The veteran, experienced cattle lead the way, tread down the snow, and form a path; the rest soon follow. Two days' experience [teaches] them all the way to this place as well as the station they must occupy in their progress thither; the stoutest marching first and the weakest closing the rear. The succeeding operations, with regard to the preservation of the cattle, entirely depend on the judgement of the farmer. He knows, according to the weather, when it is best to give them either straw, cornstalks, or hay. In very hard weather they are more hungry and better able to consume the coarse fodder; corn stalks are reserved for sheep and young cattle; hay is given to all in thaws.

Soon after this great fall of snow, the wind shifts to the north-west and blows with great impetuosity; it gathers and drives the loose element. Everything seems to be involved a second time in a general whirlwind of white atoms, not so dangerous, indeed, as those clouds of sand raised in the deserts of Arabia. This second scourge is rather worse than the first because it renders parts of the roads seemingly impassable. 'Tis then that with empty sleighs the neighbourhood gather and by their united efforts open a communication along the road. If new snow falls, new endeavours must be made use of to guard against the worst of inconveniences. For, to live, it is necessary to go to market, to mill, to the woods. This is, besides, the season of merriment and mutual visiting. All the labours of the farm are now reduced to those of the barn, to the fetching of fuel and to cleaning their own flax. The fatigues of the preceding summer require now some relaxation. What can be more conducive to it than the great plenty of wholesome food we all have? Cider is to be found in every house. The convenience of travelling invites the whole country to society, pleasure, and visiting. Bees are made, by which a number of people with their sleighs resort to the inviter's house, and there in one day haul him as much wood as will serve him a whole year. Next day 'tis another man's turn; admirable contrivance which promotes good-will, kindness, and mutual assistance. By means of these associations, often the widows and orphans are relieved.

After two or three falls of snow, the weather becomes serene, though cold. New communications are opened over lakes and rivers and through forests hitherto impassable. The ox rests from his summer labour; and the horse, amply fed, now does all the work. His celerity is strengthened by the steel shoes with which his hoofs are armed; he is fit to draw on the snow as well as on the ice. Immense is the value of this season: logs for future buildings are easily drawn to the saw-mills; ready-piled stones are with equal ease brought to the intended spot; grain is conveyed to the different landings on our small rivers, from whence in the spring small vessels carry it to the sea-port towns, and from which, again, larger ones convey it away to the different marts of the world. The constancy of this serenely cold weather is one of the greatest blessings which seldom fails us. More to the southward, their winters are often interrupted by thaws and rains, which are unfavourable to transportation as well as to the cattle. [This is] a happy suspension of toils and labours, happy rest without which the vegetation of our cold climates would soon be exhausted. On the other hand, 'tis an expensive season in every respect: nothing profitable can be done, and clothes of the warmest sorts must be provided for everyone. Great parts of the profits of summer are expended in carrying a family through this wintry career—but let not that reflection diminish our happiness! We are robust, healthy, and strong; the milder climates of the South have nothing that can compensate for these advantages. It is true that the class of men who work for the farmers have less employment, but nevertheless they live with comfort and in such abundance as is proportioned to their situation; everyone has bread and meat. As for the real poor, we have none in this happy country; those who through age and infirmities are past labour are provided for by the township to which they belong. Such are the Mohawk and Canadian winters. . . . A long ramble like this through a cold Canadian storm requires rest, silence, and sleep. After so long an excursion we may with propriety wish each other good night.

CHAPTER II

ANT-HILL TOWN

I am now sitting under one of the most enchanting groves of Virginia; 'tis the work of art, but executed with so much simplicity as greatly to resemble that of Nature. 'Tis an octagon frame round which vines and honeysuckles have been planted. They have grown with such luxuriancy; their limbs and foliage are so interwoven as to refuse all admittance to the rays of the sun, yet leave a free passage to the air. Round this verdant temple, at an equal distance, stands a double row of the mellifluous locusts, the umbrageous catalpas, and the soft magnolias. Alternately planted, they expand their friendly limbs all round and repel the scorching rays of the sun. 'Tis a grove of Tempé; 'tis a Druidical temple, in point of gloom, shade, and solitude.

From this predilected spot, which is my daily resort, an avenue leads to the house, a second to a private garden, and a third to a bath; while the front expands towards an extensive lawn, a very rare thing here, and opens the view to a variety of luxuriant fields of tobacco, corn, etc., reaching to the very shores of that noble river which is the boundary of this province. By extending [the view] beyond the Potomac, the country rises into a most delightful perspective, composed of plantations, buildings intermixed with copses of trees, peach orchards, etc. There is still something wanting: the pride and principal ornaments of more moist, more northern climates. Here they want the verdant lawns of England, of Ireland, and Normandy; all their art cannot produce that which Nature and the soil seem to refuse. To the south, you have an imperfect view of that great and capacious bay where all the great rivers of this province disembogue themselves. The great number of small gulfs, of bays, islands, and shoals formed by the confluence of so many streams affords food and asylum to an amazing number of ducks, of geese, swans, etc. This is the place where the sport they afford presents itself to all those who care not what fatigues they undergo provided that pleasure is annexed to it.

This rural scene where I am now, this sylvan bower, appears to me so much the more enchanting on account of the cool, the calm, the placid retreat it affords because I contrast it with the scorching fury of their sun, which is now ripening with its fullest energy their extensive harvests. Here it is that I forget the toils of my late journey; the fatigues it occasioned seem now but a moderate purchase for the ease I feel. I am in that state which conveys the most harmless and indefinable happiness. The feelings of [pleasure] and ease encompass me all around. I am perfectly inactive, yet I am anxious to transmit to you some little memorial of friendship by the ——, which is to sail for England from —— in a few days. I cannot at present be very serious. Harvest and the joys it spreads are themes which ought to inspire me with the rural song. Unfortunately it is not very applicable to this country where the grain is gathered by slaves and where their daily toils absorb the very idea of joys.

What revolutions do we experience in great as well as in small concerns! Life is but a checkered surface, every step of which is perpetually diversified. 'Tis not two months ago that in the province of Massachusetts I thought myself happy to sit by the comfortable fireside of ——; and I thought his warm room, his clean hearth afforded the greatest felicity and amply supplied the place of their then heatless sun. 'Tis not two months since his potent Madeira, his enlivening pipe afforded me a fund of cheerfulness that now would be improper. There, reading their provincial newspapers, I beheld with pleasure a fictitious renovation of the spring in the growth of the evergreen which overran his mantle-piece. Now, on the contrary, I stand surrounded with these southern blasts, big with igneous particles and ready to inflame one of the most irascible of matters. We had, three days ago, a most solemn trial, one of the most awful thunder-storms ever remembered.

But, however agreeable this part of America is in consequence of the hospitality of its inhabitants, the temperate zones of Europe are much superior to it. There it is that mankind enjoy a gentleness of seasons which is much more favourable to the increase of mankind and to the preservation of their health. There, husbandry may be displayed in all its perfection and beauty; here, one sees and feels nothing but extremes. But exclusive of those primary advantages to be enjoyed, nowhere but in the country is there a great variety of other pleasing sensations which never entered into the head of an inhabitant of cities. I don't mean those belonging to the well-pursued plan of an extensive rural economy, which govern and pursue the useful labours of a large landed estate; much less do I mean those fantastic ones often transplanted from the bosom of cities. No, those I mean are those which indeed I have often felt. They, properly speaking, afford no vulgar enjoyment; 'tis a multitude of pleasing sensations from whence one may collect instruction, morality, rectitude of judgement, motives of gratitude.

Here, they have no towns of any note, and I am glad of it. How I hate to dwell in these accumulated and crowded cities! They are but the confined theatre of cupidity; they exhibit nothing but the action and reaction of a variety of passions which, being confined within narrower channels, impel one another with the greatest vigour. The same passions are more rare in the country; and, from their greater extent and expansion, they are but necessary gales. I always delighted to live in the country. Have you never felt at the returning of spring a glow of general pleasure, an indiscernible something that pervades our whole frame, an inward involuntary admiration of everything which surrounds us? 'Tis then the beauties of Nature, everywhere spread, seem to swell every sentiment as she swells every juice. She dissolves herself in universal love and seems to lead us to the same sentiments. Did you ever, unmoved, pass by a large orchard in full bloom without feeling an uncommon ravishment, not only arising from the exquisite perfumes surrounding you on all sides, but from the very splendour of the scene? Who can at this time of the year observe the ushering in of buds, the unfolding of leaves, the appearance of flowers, the whole progress of vegetation, and remain insensible? The well-known industry of bees, that excellent government which pervades their habitations, that never-ceasing industry by which they are actuated, though sung by so many poets and long since become the subject of so many allusions, metaphors, and the theme of so many orators—yet 'tis a subject ever new. Set yourself down under some trees in their neighbourhood; see them arriving with the spoils of the fields; observe the digested dews, the concocted ethereal particles of flowers and blossoms converted by them into honey. When these industrious citizens are all out, open one of their hives and see the wonderful instinct which leads them by the most invariable rules to project and to execute with so much regularity that variety of cells calculated to contain their honey, their coarser food, as well as the eggs from whence new swarms are to arise.

Have not the regular arrival and departure of certain birds ever set you a-thinking whence they came? Have you never reflected on the sublimity of the knowledge they possess in order to overcome so many difficulties, to steer so invariable a course to other more favourable regions unseen by men, either in their flight or return? When in the spring you happen to revisit some trees of your own planting, have you never felt something of the paternal affection, of that peculiar satisfaction which attends viewing the works of our hands? Have you never enjoyed as you ought the transcendent pleasure attending that magnificent scene—unheeded, alas, by most men—because it is often repeated? Have you never worshipped the Master of Nature in the most august of all temples, in that extensive one of His own framing where He no doubt presides as the great invisible Pontiff but where He permits His awful representative to become visible in order to bless mankind with light and life? Have you never observed the sun rising on a calm morning? What majesty pervades, then, all Nature when the variegated aspect of the heavens, when those mixed tinges of emerging light and vanishing shades, united with that diffusive [pleasure] issuing from the fecundated earth, exhibit the most august spectacle which this transitory life affords!

How often have I viewed with admiration that sublime gradation of objects reaching and filling the whole extent of my perception: from the refulgent luminary to the fainting moon, to the dimmed stars, down to the vocal choir, even to the polygonal cobweb, perpendicularly hung or horizontally suspended—all bespangled with dewdrops refulgent as the diamond, waving to the raptured eyes! 'Tis not that I would mean to recommend to you the worship of fire in this solar appearance. I am far from believing with the disciples of Zoroaster, that the sun is the true Shekinah of the divine presence, the grand tabernacle, the Keblah where He alone resides. No, but relegated as we are at such a distance from the great Author of all, is not it a consolation to view scenes of this nature, by which we are elevated and permitted in thought to approach nearer to His throne? 'Tis in the country alone that you can follow this rotation of objects which feeds contemplation, which delights, improves, and often assuages the pains of an afflicted mind. Even the approach of a thunder-storm, though so dreaded by the generality of mankind—how solemn, how awful, what reverence does it not inspire us with! Nature seems angry. Yes, but it is for our good, and she wisely draws from that strife of elements the salubrity of the air we breathe.

As soon as the sea breeze came, I took a walk towards the shores of the river. As I was searching for the most convenient spot to descend to the shores, I perceived a large flat stone lying on the ground. As they are very scarce in this part of the country, I stopped to view it and to consider whether it had not been left there on some peculiar account. On looking at it more attentively, I perceived the marks of ancient sea-shells encrusted on its surface. How could this stone have received these marine impressions? How could it be brought here where stones are so scarce? Hoping to find some of these shell fragments better preserved on the opposite side, I lifted it up with some difficulty, when to my great surprise and amusement I found that it served as a roof to a subterranean structure of a very singular appearance. It covered the upper walks of a town seemingly composed of arches, of vaults, of a multitude of passages intermixed throughout the whole. From these obscure mansions there were a number of apertures leading to the excavated surface which was covered by the stone. It was cut into a great number of streets, sometimes contiguous and parallel to each other, sometimes receding in various directions. These streets were divided from each other by little banks of earth of a different thickness, as is the case in winter-time in the streets of Quebec. The whole surface was about thirty-five inches long and about twenty-three broad. It contained seventy-one streets and had fourteen subterraneous openings. The first idea it conveyed was that of a labyrinth; but on following with attention any one of the streets, the intricacy vanished.

In order to have a fuller view of this scene of mysterious ingenuity, I removed the stone with the utmost care. On the south-east and north-west sides, I perceived two considerable breaches full three inches wide gradually sloping from the surface of the ground to the subterranean avenues. These were, I suppose, the two great communications to fetch their foods and to carry off their unnecessary materials.

Here lived thousands of ants of the pismire class. But no pen can delineate the seeming confusion and affright which my bold intrusion caused among them; it was a whole republic thrown into the most imminent danger. The never-failing impulse of instinct immediately led them to provide for the preservation of their young. They appeared to be as big as small grains of wheat and seemed to have been brought up from the lower habitations in order to receive more immediately the prolific effects of the sun's heat and to swell their limbs into life and action. These embryos appeared to be in a different degree of animal advancement. Some seemed quite torpid and lifeless; others showed marks of feeling and pains on being suddenly seized, though by maternal claws. No sooner was the first effect of their panic over than they hurried away their young out of my sight; but as they were more numerous than the parents, more assistance immediately came from below, or else the same individuals returned to the pious office. In about five minutes, not the least vestiges were left of that numerous society, and no one could have believed that it had been replenished with so many inhabitants. In this great national dismay, no one quitted the mansion or attempted to make his escape although they knew not what sort of enemy I was. The whole community, bound by the ties of the firmest confederacy, unanimously went down, trusting, perhaps, to their works of defence or to my inability to pursue them where all appeared so dark and so intricate.

What a situation for this Virginia republic when the refulgent sun at once pervaded every corner of their habitation, where his rays had never reached before! We may, then, pronounce that what the stone covered were their paths of life and health, the cradles of their rising generations. Their other and invisible recesses must have far exceeded this little insignificant surface; for, no doubt, it must have afforded them convenient rooms for their winter-stores, receptacles for their daily food, besides capacious lodgings for so many thousand inhabitants.

Should I turn up and destroy so fair a monument of industry? Should I overwhelm in death and desolation so many harmless animals? No, I could not permit myself to satisfy so impious a curiosity at the expense of so much evil and to pollute my hands by the commission of so atrocious a deed; on the contrary, I replaced the stone.

A few days afterwards, I paid them a second visit, when I observed a great number of ants decorated with wings. But this gaudy attire did not appear to add any celerity to their flight; they never expanded them. Like the preposterous dress of some ladies it served only to render them more conspicuous than the rest. Upon a closer inspection, they appeared more inactive and wholly deprived of that quickness of motion for which the unwinged sort are so remarkable. Perhaps they were the matrons of the republic, never departing from that for-

mal gravity appointed to the rank by Nature; perhaps
they were young damsels embarrassed by the rule of
modesty and decorum; perhaps they were young ones
just hatched, not having as yet ventured to traverse the
air in order to harden their limbs in the aspect of the
sun. How sorry [I am] that I never have read Buffon!
I could have explained myself technically, whereas I am
now speaking to you in the language of a schoolboy who
possesses as yet nothing of knowledge besides curiosity.

Within a few rods and nearer to the river were erected
eleven great conical buildings three feet high and two
and a half broad at the bottom. They were perforated
with an immense number of holes. The whole appeared
to be built of slight materials; yet, by means of sticks
and straws, the ends of which only were visible, they
had given it a great degree of stability. The inhabitants
of this second colony appeared to be of a much larger
size, much stronger, and more capable of lifting heavy
burthens. What surprised me was that although so near
this subterranean settlement, yet there appeared no kind
of communication between them. Weak and defenceless
as the first were, a perfect peace and tranquillity prevailed, a most marvellous thing considering the superiority which the one had over the other species. This harmony
must have arisen from their feeding on different things.
In this case, there could be no room either for contention or competition, no cause that could influence
their little passions and produce those sanguinary commotions so frequent among mankind. The circumjacent
ground which surrounded these eleven pyramids was
perfectly cleaned; neither bush, shrub, nor herbage, or
any foliage whatever grew nigh that might conceal or
harbour any enemy. They had made considerable paths
to the waterside, as well as to different fields in which
they invariably travelled; but I never followed them in
any of their excursions.

The same Pythagorean disposition which prevented me
from turning up the bowels of the first republic in order
to satisfy a vain curiosity made me refrain from tumbling down one of these cones which might have showed
me the structure within. Whether these serve them only
as summer habitations and are but a collection of materials excavated from below, I dare not ascertain. Such

as it presented itself to my view, it seems to answer all their purposes and to preserve them from the inclemency of the air, wind, and rain. What other casual accidents may happen is no doubt quickly repaired by the mutual assistance of so many alert and vigorous insects.

When some of your friends hear of your having received a letter from North America, they will perhaps expect to hear some learned accounts of natural knowledge, botany, etc. What will they think of your correspondent when, instead of useful discoveries, important dissertations, they hear you read this trifling incident not worth its passage over the Atlantic? For your sake, make some sort of apology which will palliate their disappointment without lessening your dignity. And, after all, is it not in the course of a long correspondence sometimes necessary to write as we feel? Premeditated subjects become a laborious task, and the communicating of those impulses when they arise is truly pleasurable. Indeed, had I my choice, I'd much rather amuse myself with these objects of instinctive economy, knowledge, and industry than to wade over fields of battle strewn with the carcasses of friends and foes, the victims of so many phantoms. Such as this is, pray receive it, agreeable to your ancient custom for better, for worse. Adieu.

CHAPTER III

In my preceding letters, I have endeavoured to show you that the prevailing modes of religion which are taught in this country, a few sects excepted, are propagated in such a manner as to preclude that particular efficacy which might be its triumph. The situation and extent of parishes are a very great impediment. That mixture of opinions which every member of society is at liberty to follow causes in some districts a total indifference about any.

Let us follow one of these colonists in his progress towards the wilderness; he may well serve as an epitome by which we may judge of the rest. For we have all been emigrants in our turns, from the first families who planted the sea-shores to these last ones, the labours of which I wish to describe. This man was perhaps known in the place where he was bred as a Presbyterian. It may have happened that his children have gone through a slight course of catechism, but what does it teach them that can cause a lasting impression, that can give them a permanent idea of their duties to their Creator and of their various obligations to Man? The strongest part of their belief, the most certain idea they have of their profession, arises often from this: that they remember having several times gone to meeting in company with their parents. If, therefore, any one asks them in the new country of what profession they are, they will readily answer: "We were bred Presbyterians." This answer supplies the place of all other knowledge. If their parents are descended from progenitors among whom there prevailed some extraordinary zeal, that [causes] the contempt and jealousy of other sects. This sentiment may perhaps descend to the present generation. However, these questions are seldom asked, for the people in general, particularly in newly settled countries, care very little what the religious opinions of new-comers are. Be they what they will, they are sure to find in this new district some one or another that entertains and cherishes the same.

It may be easily supposed that in all these new establishments, often formed by chance, it must take a number of years ere a proper religious one can take place. This delay may proceed from many causes. These are always voluntary, excepting in some parts of New England. For its completion, therefore, it requires the consent of a sufficient number of wills and the assistance of a certain number of purses, as well to erect the new temple as to support its minister. If the settlers happen to be greatly divided in their religious opinions, there will not be enough of any one denomination to support the establishment. None, therefore, will take place, for no family whatever is obliged to contribute unless agreeable to their will and pleasure. If in process of time any sect becomes numerous enough to attempt it, the temple will be fixed in that part of the settlement where the greatest number of this sect happens to reside. The government, unconcerned, sees and observes this great deficiency; but it cannot remedy it without departing from that system of toleration which serves as a foundation for their laws and pervades every part of their organization. It can't put itself to the expense of building, at the public charge, religious edifices for every sect which inhabits the new country. The matter is, therefore, left to the people's zeal and to time.

But if among these new colonists there happens to be a considerable number who still entertain some degree of affection for those opinions they brought with them, these people will once in a while assemble themselves in the most convenient house among their own people. There the greatest scholar will undertake to read some part of the Scriptures, to say some extempore prayers and perhaps expound a text. This happy succedaneum is all they can get, and they are satisfied. This temporary priest assumes neither new airs nor new clothes in consequence of the new office. This gives him no other consequence than what he enjoyed before. The rest of the inhabitants, either more careless or lukewarm, will pass all the days of their lives in the prosecution of their labours, reading or saying prayers morning and evening to their families, industrious and peaceable, and in the most perfect religious apathy. Their children, bred still further from any religious education than their parents, must necessarily acquire a greater degree of indifference.

These people will, notwithstanding, clear these rough forests; they will enrich the soil with cattle, meadows, and buildings; they will make every vale to smile under their feet. They will fill this new country with children who perhaps never will be baptized. They will attain to a good old age, some of them with the most respectable characters. They may be raised to civil employments or to various other municipal functions. They will discharge their duty to society and to the government like the best of subjects; and, notwithstanding their having remained so many years utter strangers to the practice of any other religious duties than those I have mentioned, and perhaps to none, they will die at last in the bosoms of their families without any perturbation of mind and without any remorse of conscience. Though thus unassisted by any ministerial exhortations, prayers, or religious ceremonies, they will quit this world which they have embellished as peaceably and with more confidence and tranquillity than a Spaniard who receives daily visits from his confessor, and whose room is filled with every vehicle of assistance his church can confer. Such is the situation of many even in more ancient, more flourishing settlements.

With regard to the real religious knowledge of these new settlers, a short retrospect of what it was ere they left their ancient habitations will not be improper in order to complete the picture. The parishes are in gen-

eral very extensive. The minister, often occupied with
the cares and solicitudes of a large family with a small
stipend and a farm (for every one tills the earth), cannot attend to every distance, to every circumstance, and
to every call. He may, therefore, recommend it to all
heads of families to watch over the religious principles
of their children. But these have their labours to prosecute. Perhaps they are not well instructed themselves.
Perhaps they may want zeal, and that is very common.
Thus these children will grow up. I don't mean that it
is so in all families and in all settlements. No, but it is
the prevailing method in many.

This apathy may be attributed likewise to that general
happiness which proceeds from a government which does
everything for us and requires little or nothing. It may
be attributed to that great stream of prosperity, of
which everyone here receives his full share. 'Tis only
when we feel sorrow and misfortunes that we love to
pray and to take refuge in the arms of a Superior Being.
Few accidents oblige us to think of God and of His
judgements, except it is in consequence of a better and
happier education. On the other hand, the simplicity of
our worship scarcely leaves any impressions on the imagination of the vulgar. 'Tis but a mixture of theoretical
divinity, ancient history, and singing. The morality of the
New Testament is not taught separately but is involved
in the different chapters which are read to us. The
whole is intermixed with extempore prayers, dictated
agreeable to the imagination of the minister. It would
require more constancy and application than most of
these working-men can bestow to conceive and enter
into the general views of this simplified system. Some
part of the innovation is too spiritual for coarse understandings; some part is too controversial; some part
purely anticeremonial; other parts abstruse and not easily brought to the standard of daily use and vulgar con-
ceptions. 'Tis a knowledge, or rather a study, well
enough adapted to contemplative minds, but not so well
fitted for the measure of these people who must toil,
sweat, and labour the whole year. But 'tis hard to reconcile a useful, simple, rational worship, happily deprived of that mechanism which inspires but a fictitious
religion, with the coarse organs of the majority of man-

kind. Such in general was the situation of most of these people when they left their native habitations to go to form new settlements.

Let us view now the new colonist as possessed of property. This has a great weight and a mighty influence. From earliest infancy we are accustomed to a greater exchange of things, a greater transfer of property than the people of the same class in Europe. Whether it is occasioned by that perpetual and necessary emigrating genius which constantly sends the exuberancy of full societies to replenish new tracts; whether it proceeds from our being richer; whether it is that we are fonder of trade, which is but an exchange—I cannot ascertain. This man, thus bred, from a variety of reasons is determined to improve his fortune by removing to a new district and resolves to purchase as much land as will afford substantial farms to every one of his children—a pious thought which causes so many even wealthy people to sell their patrimonial estates to enlarge their sphere of action and leave a sufficient inheritance to their progeny.

No sooner he is resolved than he takes all the information he can with regard to the country he proposes to go to inhabit. He finds out all travellers who have been on the spot; he views maps; attentively weighs the benefits and disadvantages of climate, seasons, situation, etc.; he compares it with his own. A world of the most ponderous reflections must needs fill his mind. He at last goes to the capital and applies to some great landholders. He wants to make a purchase. Each party sets forth the peculiar goodness of its tracts in all the various possible circumstances of health; soil; proximity of lakes, rivers, roads, etc. Maps are presented to him; various lots are spread before him as pieces of linen in the shop of a draper. What a sagacity must this common farmer have, first to enable him to choose the province, the country, the peculiar tract most agreeable to his fortune; then to resist, to withstand the sophistry of these learned men armed with all the pomp of their city arguments! Yet he is a match for them all. These mathematical lines and sheets of paper would represent nothing to a man of his class in Europe; yet he understands their meaning, even the various courses by which

the rivers and mountains are known. He remembers
them while in the woods and is not at a loss to trace
them through the impervious forest and to reason ac-
curately upon the errors and mistakes which may have
been made by the surveyor's neglect or ignorance in the
representation of them. He receives proper directions
and departs for the intended place, for he wants to view
and examine ere he purchases.

When near the spot, he hires a man, perhaps a
hunter, of which all the frontiers are full; and instead
of being lost and amazed in the middle of these gloomy
retreats, he finds the place of beginning on which the
whole survey is founded. This is all the difficulty he was
afraid of; he follows the ancient blazed trees with a
sagacity and quickness of sight which have many times
astonished me, though bred in the woods. Next he judges
of the soil by the size and the appearance of the trees;
next he judges of the goodness of the timber by that
of the soil. The humble bush which delights in the shade,
the wild ginseng, the spignet, the weeds on which he
treads teach him all he wants to know. He observes the
springs, the moisture of the earth, the range of the mountains, the course of the brooks. He returns at last; he
has formed his judgement as to his future buildings, their
situation, future roads, cultivation, etc. He has properly
combined the future mixture of conveniences and inconveniences which he expects to meet with. In short,
the complicated arrangement of a great machine would
not do greater honour to the most skilful artist than the
reduction and digesting of so many thoughts and calcula-
tions by this hitherto obscure man.

He meets once more the land-proprietors; a new scene
ensues. He is startled at the price. He altercates with
them, for now he has something to say, having well explored the country. Now he makes them an offer; now
he seems to recede; now wholly indifferent about the
bargain; now willing to fulfil it if the terms are reasonable. If not, he can't but stay where he is, or perhaps
accept of better offers which have been made to him
by another person. He relinquishes, he pursues his object—that is his advantage—through a more complex
labyrinth than a European could well imagine. He is
diffident; he is mistrustful as to the title, ancientness of

patent, priority of claim, etc. The idea that would occur to an Englishman of his class would be that such great and good men would not deceive such a poor farmer as he is; he would feel an inward shame to doubt their assertions. You are wrong, my friends; these are not your country parish-squires who would by so gross a deceit defame their characters and lose your vote. Besides, the price of things is better ascertained there in all possible bargains than here. This is a land-merchant who, like all other merchants, has no other rule than to get what he can. This is the general standard except where there is some competition. The native sagacity of this American colonist carries him at last through the whole bargain. He purchases fifteen hundred acres at three dollars per acre to be paid in three equal yearly payments. He gives his bond for the same, and the whole tract is mortgaged as a security. On the other hand, he obtains bonds of indemnity to secure him against the miscarriages of the patent and other claims.

He departs with all his family, and great and many are the expenses and fatigues of this removal with cows and cattle. He at last arrives on the spot. He finds himself suddenly deprived of the assistance of friends, neighbours, tradesmen, and of all those inferior links which make a well-established society so beautiful and pleasing. He and his family are now alone. On their courage, perseverance, and skill their success depends. There is now no retreating; shame and ruin would infallibly overtake them. What is he to do in all possible cases of accidents, sickness, and other casualties which may befall his family, his cattle and horses; breaking of the implements of husbandry, etc.? A complicated scene presents itself to the contemplative mind, which does the Americans a superlative honour. Whence proceed that vigour and energy, those resources which they never fail to show on these trying occasions? From the singularity of their situation, from that locality of existence which is peculiar to themselves as a new people improving a new country?

I have purposely visited many who have spent the earliest part of their lives in this manner, now ploughmen, now mechanics, sometimes even physicians. They are and must be everything. Nay, who would believe it?

This new man will commence as a hunter and learn in these woods how to pursue and overtake the game with which it abounds. He will in a short time become master of that necessary dexterity which this solitary life inspires. Husband, father, priest, principal governor—he fills up all these stations, though in the humble vale of life. Are there any of his family taken sick, either he or his wife must recollect ancient directions received from aged people, from doctors, from a skilful grandmother, perhaps, who formerly learned of the Indians of her neighborhood how to cure simple diseases by means of simple medicines. The swamps and woods are ransacked to find the plants, the bark, the roots prescribed. An ancient almanac, constituting perhaps all his library, with his Bible, may chance to direct him to some more-learned ways.

Has he a cow or an ox sick, his anxiety is not less, for they constitute part of his riches. He applies what recipes he possesses: he bleeds, he foments; he has no farrier at hand to assist him. Does either his plough or his cart break, he runs to his tools; he repairs them as well as he can. Do they finally break down, with reluctance he undertakes to rebuild them, though he doubts of his success. This was an occupation committed before to the mechanic of his neighbourhood; but necessity gives him invention, teaches him to imitate, to recollect what he has seen. Somehow or another 'tis done, and happily there is no traveller, no inquisitive eye to grin and criticize his work. It answers the purposes for the present. Next time, he arrives nearer perfection. Behold him henceforth a sort of intuitive carpenter! Happy man, thou hast nothing to demand of propitious heaven but a long life to enable thee to finish the most material part of thy labours in order to leave each of thy children an improved inheritance. Thank God and thy fate; thy wife can weave. This happy talent constitutes the most useful part of her portion. Then all is with thee as well as it can be. The yarn which thy daughters have spun will now be converted into coarse but substantial cloth. Thus his flax and the wool clothes all the family; most women are something of tailors. Thus if they are healthy, these settlers find within themselves a resource against all probable accidents.

His ingenuity in the fields is not less remarkable in executing his rural work in the most expeditious manner. He naturally understands the use of levers, handspikes, etc. He studies how to catch the most favourable seasons for each task. This great field of action deters him not. But what [shall] he do for shoes? Never before did he find himself so near going bare-footed. Long wintry nights come on. It ought to be a time of inactivity and repose, considering the amazing fatigues of the summer. The great fire warms the whole house, cheers all the family; it makes them think less of the severity of the season. He hugs himself with an involuntary feeling; he is conscious of present ease and security. He hears the great snow-storm driving by his door; he hears the impotent wind roaring in his chimney. If he regrets his ancient connections, the mug of cider and other conveniences he enjoyed before, he finds himself amply remunerated by the plenty of fuel he now possesses, etc. The rosy children sitting round the hearth sweat and sleep with their basins of samp on their laps; the industrious mother is rattling at her loom, avariciously improving every minute of her time. Shall the master, the example of so happy a family, smoke and sleep and be idle? No, he has heard the children complain of sores and chilblains for want of shoes; he has leather, but no shoemaker at hand. A secret wish arises, natural enough to a father's heart: he wants to see them all happy. So noble a motive can't but have a successful end. He has, perhaps, a few lasts and some old tools; he tries to mend an old pair. Heaven be praised! The child can walk with them and boast to the others of his new acquisition. A second pair is attempted; he succeeds as well. He ventures at last to make a new one. They are coarse, heavy, ponderous, and clumsy; but they are tight and strong and answer all the intended purposes. What more can he want? If his gears break, he can easily repair them. Every man here understands how to spin his own yarn and to [make] his own ropes. He is a universal fabricator like Crusoe. With bark and splinters, the oldest of the children amuse themselves by making little baskets. The hint being praised by the father is further improved, and in a little time they are supplied with what baskets they want.

Casks require too much labour and particular ingenuity. He in vain attempts it; he cannot succeed, but indulgent Nature offers him a sufficient compensation. In the woods which surround him, hollow trees present themselves to him; he can easily distinguish them by the sound they yield when struck with the axe. They have long served as winter habitations to squirrels and other animals. Now they are cut into proper lengths, smoothed on the inside. They are placed on the floor and [are] ready to contain anything but liquids. Tight vessels are not wanted as yet, for he has no fermented liquor to preserve (save spruce beer) until his young orchard begins to bear, and by that time the natural improvement of the country will bring the necessary tradesmen into his neighbourhood.

Happy man, did'st thou but know the extent of thy good fortune! Permit me to hold for a minute the sketch of thy political felicity, that thou mayest never forget that share of gratitude which thou owest to the mild government under which thou livest. Thou hast no church-dues to pay derived from the most unaccountable donations, the pious offerings of rough ignorance or mistaken zeal; those ancient calamities are unknown to thy land. Thou mayest go to toil and exert the whole energy and circle of thy industry, and try the activity of human nature in all situations. Fear not that a clergyman whom thou never hearest, or any other, shall demand the tenth part of thy labour. Thy land, descended from its great Creator, holds not its precarious tenure either from a supercilious prince or a proud lord. Thou need'st not dread any contradictions in thy government and laws of thy country; they are simple and natural, and if they are sometimes burdensome in the execution, 'tis the fault of men. Thou need'st not fear those absurd ordinances alternately puzzling the understanding and the reason of subjects and crushing all national industry. Thou need'st not tremble lest the most incomprehensible prohibitions shall rob thee of that sacred immunity with which the produce of thy farm may circulate from hand to hand until it reaches those of the final exporter. 'Tis all as free as the air which thou breathest. Thy land, thy canton, is not claimed by any neighbouring monarch who, anxious for the new dominion, ravages, devastates, and despoils its peaceable inhabitants. Rest secure: no cruel militia-laws shall be enacted to ravish from thee thy son and to make him serve an unknown master in his wars; to enrich a foreign land with his carcass, unrelieved in his pains and agonies, unpitied in his death. The produce of thy loins shall not feed foreign wolves and vultures.

No, undisturbed, this offspring of thine shall remain with thee to co-operate in that family partnership of which thou art the first director and manager. At a proper season thou shalt see him marry, perhaps thy neighbour's daughter. Thou then shalt have the pleasure of settling him on that land which he has helped thee to earn and to clear; henceforth he shall become also a new neighbour to thee, still remaining thy son and friend. Thy heart shall swell with inward exultation when thou shalt see him prosper and flourish, for his future prosperity will be a part of thine in the same proportion as thy family happiness is a part of that diffusive one which overspreads thy country's. In the future extensive harvests thou shalt raise; and other laborious undertakings which the seasons and the elements bid thee execute quickly. The reunited aid of the combined family by a reciprocal assistance will often throughout the year combine together to accomplish the most painful tasks.

Humanity is not obliged here, as in the old world, to pass through the slow windings of the alembic. Here 'tis an abundant spring, running and dividing itself everywhere agreeable to the nature and declivity of the ground. Neither dams nor mounds nor any other obstructions restrain it; 'tis never artificially gathered as a turbid flood to exhale in the sun, nor sunken under ground for some sinister purposes. 'Tis a regular fecundating stream left to the laws of declivity and invariably pursuing its course.

Thus this man devoid of society learns more than ever to center every idea within that of his own welfare. To him, all that appears good, just, equitable has a necessary relation to himself and family. He has been so long alone that he has almost forgot the rest of mankind, except it is when he carries his crops on the snow to some distant market.

The country, however, fills with new inhabitants. His granary is resorted to from all parts by other beginners, who did not come so well prepared. How will he sell his grain to these people who are strangers to him? Shall he deduct the expense of carrying it to a distant mill? This would appear just; but where is the necessity of this justice? His neighbours absolutely want his supply; they can't go to other places. He therefore concludes upon having the full price. He remembers his former difficulties; no one assisted him then. Why should he assist others? They are all able to work for themselves. He has a large family, and it would be giving its lawful substance away; he cannot do it. How should he be charitable? He has scarcely seen a poor man in his life. How should he be merciful, except from native instinct? He has never heard that it was a necessary qualification, and he has never seen objects that required the benefits of his sympathy. He has had to struggle alone through numbers of difficult situations and inconveniences; he therefore deals hardly with his new neighbours. If they are not punctual in their payment, he prosecutes them at law, for by this time its benefits have reached him. 'Tis laid out into a new county and divided into townships. Perhaps he takes a mortgage on his neighbour's land. But it may happen that it is already encumbered by anterior and more ponderous debts. He knows instinctively the coercive power of the laws: he impeaches the cattle; he has proper writings drawn; he gets bonds in judgement. He secures himself, and all this is done from native knowledge; he has neither counsellor nor adviser. Who can be wiser than himself in this half-cultivated country? The sagacity peculiar to the American never forsakes him; it may slumber sometimes, but upon the appearance of danger, it arises again as vigorous as ever.

But behold him happily passed through the course of many laborious years; his wealth and, therefore, his consequence increase with the progress of the settlement. If he is litigious, overbearing, purse-proud, which will very probably be the bent of his mind, he has a large field. Among so many beginners there need be many needy, inconsiderate, drunken, and lazy. He may bring the necessary severity of the law to flourish even in these wilds. Well may we be subjects to its lash, or else we would be too happy, for this is almost all the tribute we pay.

Now advanced in life and grown rich, he builds a good substantial stone or frame house; and the humble log one, under which he has so much prospered, becomes the kitchen. Several roads intersect and meet near this spot, which he has contrived on purpose. He becomes an innholder and a country merchant. This introduces him into all the little mysteries of self-interest, clothed under the general name of profits and emoluments. He sells for good that which perhaps he knows to be indifferent because he also knows that the ashes he has collected, the wheat he has taken in may not be so good or so clean as it was asserted. Fearful of fraud in all his dealings and transactions, he arms himself, therefore, with it. Strict integrity is not much wanted, as each is on his guard in his daily intercourse; and this mode of thinking and acting becomes habitual. If any one is detected in anything too glaring but without the reach of the law, where is the recollection of ancient principles, either civil or religious, that can raise the blush of conscious shame? No minister is at hand by his daily admonitions to put him in remembrance of a vindictive God punishing all frauds and bad intentions, rewarding rectitude and justice. Whatever ideas of this kind they might have imbibed when young, whatever conscience may say, these voices have been so long silent that they are no longer heard. The law, therefore, and its plain meaning are the only forcible standards which strike and guide their senses and become their rule of action. 'Tis to them an armour serving as well for attack as for defence; 'tis all that seems useful and pervading. Its penalties and benefits are the only thing feared and remembered, and this fearful remembrance is what we might call in the closet a reverence for the law.

With such principles of conduct as these, follow him in all these situations which link men in society, in that vast variety of bargains, exchanges, barters, sales, etc., and adduce the effects which must follow. If it is not *bellum omnium contra omnes,* 'tis a general mass of keenness and sagacious acting against another mass of equal sagacity; 'tis caution against caution. Happy, when it does not degenerate into fraud against fraud! The law, which cannot pervade and direct every action, here leaves her children to themselves and abandons those peccadilloes (which convulse not though they may [dim] some of the most beautiful colours of society) to the more invisible efficacy of religion.

But here this great resource fails in some measure, at least with a great many of them, from the weakness of their religious education, from a long inattention, from the paucity of instructions received. Is it a wonder that new rules of action should arise? It must constitute a new set of opinions, the parent of manners. You have already observed this colonist is necessarily different from what he was in the more ancient settlements he originally came from—become such by his new local situation, his new industry, that share of cunning which was absolutely necessary in consequence of his intercourse with his new neighbours.

CHAPTER IV

**THOUGHTS OF AN AMERICAN FARMER ON VARIOUS
RURAL SUBJECTS**

I. FARM LIFE

I am perfectly sensible of the superiority of your agriculture. England surpasses all the world for the perfection of mechanism and the peculiar excellence with which
all its tools and implements are finished. We are but
children and they [the English] our parents. The immense difference, therefore, ought not to make us blush.
We have the same blood in our veins. In time we shall
arrive likewise at perfection. All the praises we at present deserve ought to be bestowed on that strength, fortitude, and perseverance which have been requisite to
clear so many fields, to drain so many swamps. Great
parts of the colony of Massachusetts and Connecticut
have cost more in clearing than the land was worth.
The native industry of the English is nowhere more manifest than in the settlement and cultivation of those two
provinces. They had every species of difficulty to struggle
with: climate, stubbornness of soil, amazing trees, stones,
etc. And yet, now some parts of these countries, I am
informed, are not inferior to the best cultivated spots in
Europe, considering the short space of time in which
these great works have been accomplished.

However inferior in all these rural respects we are to
England, yet you seem to confess with pleasure the sur-

prise you felt in travelling from New Hampshire to this place. Everywhere, you saw good houses, well-fenced fields, ample barns, large orchards. Everywhere, you saw the people busy either at home or on their farms. Everywhere they seemed contented and happy. You no sooner quitted the sight of an orchard but another presented itself to your view. Everywhere tolerable roads, pretty towns, good bridges forced you to ask yourself: When is it that these people have had time and abilities to perform so many labours? Everywhere you inform me that you met with the most cordial hospitality. Tell me in what part of Europe you could have travelled three hundred and sixty miles for four dollars? I feel proud and happy that the various accounts I gave you of this part of America did not fall short of what you have experienced. The people of New England had been represented to you in a strange light, yet I know no province which is so justly entitled to the respect of the world on many accounts. They are the true and unmixed descendants of Englishmen, and surely there is no country in America where an Englishman ought to travel with more pleasure. Here he may find the names of almost all the towns in his country and those of many families with which he is acquainted.

Some people, without knowing why, look with disdain on their democratic government. They do not consider that this was the very rule which prevailed in England when they left it and that nothing more than the blessings it confers could possibly have animated these people and urged them on to undertake such labours. Slaves may cultivate the smooth and fertile plains of the South. It is the hands of freemen only that could till this asperous soil. Had they laboured under an oppressive form of government, it is very probable that Massachusetts and Connecticut would have been possessed yet by the Pequots, the Narragansets, and the Wampanoags, the ancient lords of these rough countries. There is not a province in the whole continent which does not exhibit to the contemplative traveller something highly praiseworthy and highly deserving the attention of a stranger. Everywhere, you find the strongest marks of industry, of activity, and of prosperous boldness. When an Englishman arrives here, he should quit his insular prejudices.

He should procure a small book wherein he should carefully set down the date of every establishment; and thus furnished, he might travel with more satisfaction to himself and do more justice to the inhabitants. This is the rule I always observe. For instance, who can visit some of the modern settlements in the New Hampshire grants without amazement and surprise? I know many townships that are but twelve years old which contain inhabitants worth two thousand pounds, all acquired by their labours and good contrivance in that short space of time. The English farmer, when he purchases his farm, finds it already cleared, already fenced, already ditched. His ploughs are excellent, his horses good, his servants humble and subordinate. No wonder indeed that he can perform all the operations with so much neatness and accuracy!

Our present modes of making fences are very bad, though they are the only ones we can possibly make use of. They decay so fast, they are so subject to be hove up by the frost, it is inconceivable the cost and care which a large farm requires in that single article. I have often observed whole lengths of posts and rails raised from the ground in the spring, and the labours of weeks thus destroyed. Often when the frost quits the earth, the stakes of our worn fences are entirely lifted up. Then the riders tumble down, and the strength, the stability they gave them is gone.

These repairs take up, every spring, abundance of time; and, after all, it is impossible to stop up every hole so carefully as to prevent the intrusion of hogs and pigs. Their inclination to mischief and their singular ingenuity in finding out these vacancies are such that, properly speaking, no crops are secured except the fields are surrounded with stone fences. This is a blessing which every country has not. Our sheep will often learn to jump, and no obstacle can possibly prevent them. I have found out, however, one method which entirely puts a stop to their boldness and activity. I carefully cut one of the sinews which passes through their hind fetlocks. The damage done by the hogs is sometimes astonishing. If we yoke them, it greatly retards their growth. To prevent them from rooting, I cut the two sinews to which their snouts hang. If this simple operation is performed while

they are young, for ever afterwards it disables them from
doing any mischief with that pernicious instrument. The
English farmer, on the contrary, whose fields are surrounded with impenetrable fences, rests secure. He feels
not on his mind that concern which so often afflicts the
American. When the country becomes older and the
price of labour somewhat less, we shall likewise be enabled to plant good thorn fences. The American thorn
is excellent for that purpose and inexpugnable. I know
already many farms that are thus defended. I wish I
were able to do the same.

As to labour and labourers—what difference! When
we hire any of these people we rather pray and entreat
them. You must give them what they ask: three shillings
per day in common wages and five or six shillings in
harvest. They must be at your table and feed, as you saw
it at my house, on the best you have. I have often seen
Irishmen just landed, inconceivably hard to please and
as greedy as wolves. These are a few of the many reasons
why we can't bring anything to perfection. The few Negroes we have are at best but our friends and companions. Their original cost is very high. Their clothing and
their victuals amount to a great sum, besides the risk of
losing them. Our mechanics and tradesmen are very dear
and sometimes great bunglers. Our winters are so severe
and so long that we are obliged to consume during that
season a great part of what we earn in the summer. This
is, sir, but a feeble sketch of that great picture I might
draw of the amazing inconveniences to which the locality
of our situation exposes us.

Last year Mr. ——, the first man in our country, our
first judge and assemblyman, received in harvest a large
company from the town of ——. He immediately ordered two tables in two different rooms, for he always
eats with his workpeople. The reapers, perceiving the new
distinction which he was going to establish, quitted him
after having made very severe reflections; and it was
not without great difficulties that he was enabled to finish
his harvest with his own people. What would one of your
country squires say to this? Whether this gentleman was
entitled to the appellation or not, I cannot tell, but sure I
am that he possesses fifteen hundred acres of excellent
land and [belongs to] one of the most respectable fam-

ilies we have. We should be too happy were it otherwise. And indeed the present constitution of things: our government, modes of religion, our manners, the scarcity of people, the ease with which they may live and have lands of their own—all these reasons must necessarily tend to subject us to these inconveniences. Better put up with them than with high taxes, encroachment of lords, free passage of hounds and huntsmen, tithes, etc.

Farming in the northern provinces is, therefore, not so advantageous as a European might at first imagine. These are fit only for people who are capable of working, the southern ones for those who have capital and can purchase Negroes. I could mention to you a thousand other details, but they would be useless and perhaps tiresome. The proper distinction of ranks in England procures to the rich, servants who know their places; to the farmers, workmen who are afraid of losing their bread. Very different is our lot. A particular friend of mine who possesses a large farm and mows every year about one hundred and twenty acres of meadow, and keeps one hundred head of horned cattle, sheep, and horses in proportion, came the other day to dine with me. "How happily, how peaceably you live here," he said. "Your farm is not so large as mine and yet brings you all you want. You have time to rest and to think. For my part, I am weary. I must be in the fields with the hired men; nothing is done except I am there. I must not find fault with them or else they will quit me and give me a bad name. I am but the first slave on my farm." Nor is his case uncommon; it is that of every person who tills the earth upon a large scale. This gentleman's farm in Europe would constitute him an opulent man without giving himself any trouble besides a general oversight of the whole.

When I am considering myself thus injudiciously, delineating several of our usages and customs, I blush at the task you have imposed on me and at the readiness with which I have accepted it. There is something truly ridiculous in a farmer quitting his plough or his axe and then flying to his pen. His hands, as well as his mind, do not seem well calculated for this new employment. The consequences may be doubly disadvantageous. This may induce me to become careless and remiss in the due prosecution of my daily labour and [the writing] must, when gathered together in your hands, form a strange assemblage of incoherent reflections, trifling thoughts, and useless paintings. 'Tis not from a principle of vanity that I am induced to make these observations, but from a sincere regret that I am not capable of doing better. My wife herself, who has never seen me handle the pen so much in all my life, helps to confound me; she laughs at my folly. What, then, is it that makes me prosecute this theme? Your positive injunctions, my solemn promise, and the desire that you may be enabled to give your friends in Europe a more certain account of our modes of cultivating the earth, as well as of the great advances we must make, and of the inconveniences we labour under.

I hope that in your travels through Virginia you'll find some planter who will inform you of every detail relating to their mode of planting. You'll then possess the two extremes and be better able to judge in what part it will be best for your friends to come and settle. Here we enjoy a happy poverty and a strong health. There riches are attainable, but the necessary intemperance of the climate leads to many diseases which northern farmers are strangers to. The good is always mixed with the evil. The matter is how to choose the least. Were I to begin the world again, I would go and pitch my tent either in a severe climate where the frost is never interrupted by pernicious thaws, or else at the foot of the Alleghenies, where they almost enjoy a perpetual summer. Either of these extremes would suit me better than the climate of these middle colonies. Give me either a Canadian or a Mohawk winter, or else none at all.

Nor have I related you the tenth part of the inconveniences to which we are subject. Our country teems with more destructive insects and animals than Europe. 'Tis difficult for us to guard against them all. What man sows must be done here, as well as everywhere else, at the sweat of his brows; and here he has many more enemies to defend himself from than you have in Europe. The great woods with which our country is replenished affords them a shelter from which we cannot drive them. Such is the nature of man's labours and that of the grain he lives on that he is obliged to declare war against every ancient inhabitant of this country. Strange state of things! First by trials, by fraud, by a thousand artifices he drives away the ancient inhabitants. Then he is obliged to hunt the bear, the wolf, and the fox. The bear loves his apples, often climbs into our trees, and by his weight tears their limbs. The wolves, finding the deer becoming scarce, have learned how to feed on our sheep. The fox, for want of pheasants and partridges, lives on our poultry; the squirrels on our corn. The crows and the blackbirds know how to eradicate it out of the ground, even when it is four inches high. Caterpillars, an awful progeny, sometimes spontaneously arise in some countries and travel in quest of their particular food. Some attack the black oak, on the leaves of which they feed and entirely destroy them. Others attack our grass, eat every leaf, and leave nothing but the bare stalk. Others again spring up from the ground in imitation of the locust and enter into the heart of our corn, blasting the hopes of the farmer. Others climb into our apple trees and, if not prevented, eat all their leaves and buds and blossoms and render a flourishing orchard a sad picture of ruin, sterility, and desolation. At other times, innumerable swarms of grasshoppers arise and indiscriminately feed on all they find: grain, grass, turnips, etc. I had once a field of four acres of hemp seven feet high, which they entirely stripped of all the leaves and rendered useless, whereby I lost at least a ton of that commodity.

Man sows and tills, and Nature from her great lap of fecundity often produces those swarms of beings, those great exuberances of life, which seem to threaten us with destruction. If these were general and not transitory, man would soon fall a victim to their devouring jaws; and, small as they are, they become by their numbers powerful agents of desolation. I have heard many people call them the avengers of the Almighty, created to punish men for their iniquities. This cannot be, for they eat the substance of the good and the wicked indiscriminately. They appear in certain districts or follow certain courses which they invariably pursue. What greater crimes do we commit than the Europeans? It is a local evil, and this evil is nothing among us to what you'll observe in the southern provinces. The heat and the moisture of their climates spread everywhere a disposition in matter to form itself into organized bodies. There their fields teem with ten thousand different species with which I am not acquainted. Strange that you should have in England so many learned and wise men and that none should ever have come over here to describe some part of this great field which Nature presents. I have heard several Virginians say that when their wheat is ripe, a peculiar sort of winged weevil attacks it in the fields. The heads of this grain seem all alive, and it is with the utmost difficulty that they can save it. When in the barn, it becomes subject to the depredations of another sort [of insect], which, though deprived of wings, is equally terrible in the mischief it causes. Our very peas are subject to the attack of a fly which deposits an egg, imperceptible in the middle of its blossoms. This egg grows with the peas, which serve him as a cradle, but he does not touch them until towards the spring. Then he has acquired a degree of strength sufficient to eat the meat of the two lobes. The fly then bores a hole through which it quits its ancient habitation. The peas, reduced to this hollow state, will grow again, but are unfit for any culinary uses. There is no other remedy but to place them as soon as threshed in an oven half heated. The heat will parch and kill the worms.

Now if you unite the damages which we yearly suffer from all these enemies, to the badness of our fences, to the want of subordinate workmen, to the high price of our labour, to the ignorance of our tradesmen, to the severities of our winters, to the great labours we must undergo, to the celerity with which the rapid seasons hurry all our rural operations, you'll have a more complete idea of our situation as farmers than you had before. Some part of the rich landscape will gradually fail, and you'll soon perceive that the lot of the American farmer is very often unjustly envied by many Europeans who wish to see us taxed, and think that we live too well. It is true that no people feed on better pork and bread, but these are in general dearly earned.

He that is just arrived and sees a fine, smooth plantation with a good house or a flourishing orchard, and hears that the proprietor pays but a small tax, immediately thinks: this man is too happy. His imagination presents him with such images and ideas as are suggested to

him by what he has seen in Europe. He sees not that
sea of trouble, of labour, and expense which have been
lavished on this farm. He forgets the fortitude, and the
regrets with which the first emigrant left his friends, his
relations, and his native land. He is unacquainted with
the immense difficulties of first settlement, with the sums
borrowed, with the many years of interest paid, with the
various shifts these first people have been obliged to make
use of. The original log-house, the cradle of the American, is now gone and has made room for the more elegant
framed one. Is there no credit to be given to these first
cultivators, who by their sweat, their toil, and their perseverance have come over a sea of three thousand miles
to till a new soil? Thereby they have enlarged the trade,
the power, the riches of the mother country.

No, these just ideas seldom enter into the heads of
such Europeans or visitors. They come to trade and to
get rich and very often at their return do not do us that
justice which we deserve. The title of Yankee is given to
one province; other contemptuous reflections are made
on others. Yet to a philosophic eye, to a heart full of
philanthropy, where is that part of the world that can
supply an enlightened traveller with more pleasing ideas?
The American farmer has his peculiar degree of happiness
without which he could not subsist. His toils and situation
are such that he cannot afford to pay the taxes of Europe.
If he is kept poor, how is he to purchase more lands
rough as his own were and there place his children, whom
he has taught to work as hard as himself? If he is possessed of but the bare means of subsistence, he must
send his children to sea, or to trade, or let them live in
idleness. Lands are not purchased for nothing. A man
must have a beginning, a certain capital without which he
may languish and vegetate simply all the days of his
life. Let this European censor quit the sea-shore and go
three hundred miles into the wilderness and see how men
begin the world. The credit of England enables our merchants to trade and to get rich. The credit and wealth of
the fathers enable our children to form new settlements.
Were these two sources suspended only for ten years,
you would soon see a death of enterprises, a spirit of
inaction, a general languor diffuse itself throughout the
continent. That bold activity, that spirit of emigration

which is the source of our prosperity, would soon cease. I speak not through the narrow channel of a partial American. I speak the language of truth, and I hope that one year of observation will convince you of the propriety of what I have said.

Flourishing as we may appear to a superficial observer, yet there are many dark spots which, on due consideration, greatly lessen that show of happiness which the Europeans think we possess. The number of debts which one part of the country owes to the other would greatly astonish you. The younger a country is, the more it is oppressed, for new settlements are always made by people who do not possess much. They are obliged to borrow; and, if any accidents intervene, they are not enabled to repay that money in many years. The interest is a cankerworm which consumes their yearly industry. Many never can surmount these difficulties. The land is sold, their labours are lost, and they are obliged to begin the world anew. Oh, could I have the map of the county wherein I live; could I point out the different farms on which several families have struggled for many years; [could I] open the great book of mortgages and show you the immense encumbrances, the ramifications of which are spread and felt everywhere—you would be surprised! Yes, I am sure that the sum total of what is due for the original cost of the land, and what the people owe to each other, would not fall very short of seven hundred [?].

It is vain to say: Why do they borrow? I answer that it is impossible in America to till a farm without it. After being possessed of the land, one must have a team and a Negro. Three or four hundred pounds is but a trifling sum to what is sometimes requisite. It is very true that with industry and health, [settlers] will be enabled to pay off the greatest part of these sums in a few years, but life is so full of accidents that out of twelve that begin the world with a debt of three hundred pounds, not above six perhaps will be able to pay it all in the first generation. These encumbrances, therefore, descend with the land, aye, even to the third generation. Happy [are they] when their pressure is such that they can be borne without selling the lands! Whoever, therefore, cursorily judges of our riches by the appearance of our farms, of our houses, of our fields, without descending to deeper particulars, judges imperfectly. He should feel the pulse of every farmer, and know whether he is perfectly free.

These are, sir, the great and the enormous taxes which we are obliged to pay, one to another. Our very merchants are obliged to follow the same system. Had it not been for the generous credit of England, how could they have traded? It is a rule which extends itself to every part of this great continent, from the poor, barren fields of Nova Scotia to the slimy plains of the Mississippi. The evil is unavoidable. My father began the world seven hundred and fifty pounds in debt. He had received from my grandfather very ample beginnings, yet it took him eleven years of the most prosperous industry ere he could call himself a freeman. Nor could he have even succeeded so rapidly but for a legacy of one hundred and fifty pounds, which was left him by a relation. Never was a man who enjoyed the pleasure of owing nothing with more heartfelt joy than he. He and my mother had hitherto toiled night and day. He had taken a solemn vow to buy nothing of English manufacture until he could buy it with his own money, and never before that time had he worn a yard of English cloth. He was perfectly sober and industrious. His wife was prudent; and had it not been for these favourable circumstances, some part of the load must have descended to me. Thank God, I owe nothing, but I can tell you that there are not one hundred besides me in the county who can say that all they have is their own. Are there no praises for, is there no good will due towards a set of men who labour under these excessive burthens, whose toils serve to enrich their mother country? Every bushel of wheat which we raise, every yard of calico, every lock or nail we purchase tend to promote the happiness and the trade of England.

It may appear a very odd sort of speculation, yet I often amuse myself with it: the poor beginner toiling in the woods, peeling the bark of trees to cover his house, stubbing up the heavy ground to produce bread is very similar and greatly resembles the situation of the English manufacturer. The one works for the other to supply mutual wants. The odds, however, are in favour of the American. With good luck and perseverance, he may live to clear his lands of useless wood as well as his title of heavy encumbrances. If he does that, he may then die with a peaceable conscience. He has acted his part as a good American ought to do. He has left an ample provision for his children. Who can wish for more in a country where we have neither bishops, counts, nor marquises? If he leaves them land paid for, and ability to work, they have the most ample inheritance. If it please God that I should live long enough, this will be one day my great happiness; and if I can see [my children] possessed of the proper qualifications requisite to make them good farmers, I shall close my eyes in peace. They won't be apt to say that I have not trained them up to the plough, for I fix them on it, even from the breast.

But to convince you still further of what I have but imperfectly sketched, I will take you to Mr. ———'s office, who is our clerk, and there you'll see the many wounds and bleeding places which this county suffers, even though it is fifty-three years old. These ulcers generally heal in proportion to the age of the country. It is now much less in debt than it was formerly, and the reason that it owes yet so much money is on account of the many swamps it contains. This may surprise you. They are in general so expensive and difficult to clear that it cannot be done in the ordinary course of husbandry. It is generally done by the acre; and, in order to pay these extraordinary expenses, the proprietors are obliged to borrow money. It is indeed very well laid out. A swamp in five years will repay the cost of clearing. Could these great works be all accomplished, you would then see how quickly the people would extricate themselves out of all their difficulties. Another reason which keeps us in debt is the multiplicity of shops with English goods. These present irresistible temptations. It is so much easier to buy than it is to spin. The allurement of fineries is so powerful with our young girls that they must be philosophers indeed to abstain from them. Thus one fifth part of all our labours every year is laid out in English commodities. These are the taxes that we pay.

Another is that most of the articles they send us from England are extremely bad. What is intended for exportation is good enough when there are no rival merchants. Their linens and their duffle and their wool cards are much worse now than they were ten years ago. The prosperity of our different counties depends besides on the general qualities of the soil. The more they abound in swamps, the richer they are. It greatly depends also on the genius of the inhabitants. By some chance or other the character of the first settlers imprints a kind of spirit which becomes prevalent by example and remains ever after the distinguishing characteristic. For instance, the county of —— is famous for the litigious spirit of its inhabitants. There the lawyers will have all. The sheriff told me not long since that the whole set of its inhabitants had almost changed in eighteen years; that is, their farms in that space of time were sold in consequence of mortgages unpaid, and they were obliged to remove. That of ——, on the contrary, is remarkable for its peace, tranquillity, and industry. Many of its inhabitants are Dutch, who are so attached to their interest that they never squander any part of it to feed the ravens of the law. I wish we were all like them. Others are remarkable for the goodness of their roads and that of their bridges, and so it is throughout the continent. Every province is as different in staple and in the different manners of its inhabitants.

No country ever was so flourishing and happy as to have no poor; there are unfortunate men in all countries. This county is famous for taking good care of those we have. They are placed with some able farmer who feeds and clothes them and receives from the town or precinct from twenty to thirty pounds per annum for their support. We have abundance of roads, and they are repaired not by a tax, which would be better, but by six days' labour of the people. We hate taxes so much that our assemblies dare not venture upon the expedient, though I must confess that I had rather give twenty shillings a year than be obliged to work six days, and these moneys properly laid out would do more good. But we cannot expect to enjoy every advantage. I think we have made most rapid strides, considering that the county was but a huge wilderness fifty years ago without a path. You'd be astonished were I to tell you the extent of its cleared ground, of its meadows, the number of its houses, inhabitants, etc. I have often amused myself with making an estimate of the sum of labour and then comparing it with the original and present value of the land. This fair estimate would be the strongest proof of our industry, an industry which the people of the South cannot boast of, for the evenness and fertility of their land are very superior to ours. There they labour with slaves; here we do everything ourselves. There they enjoy a variety of pleasures and pastimes; here we know of none except our frolics and going to the meeting on a Sunday.

The name "frolic" may perhaps scandalize you and make you imagine that we meet to riot together. Lest you should misunderstand me, give me leave to explain myself. I really know among us of no custom which is so useful and tends so much to establish the union and the little society which subsists among us. Poor as we are, if we have not the gorgeous balls, the harmonious concerts, the shrill horn of Europe, yet we dilate our hearts as well with the simple Negro fiddle, and with our rum and water, as you do with your delicious wines. In the summer, it often happens that either through sickness or accident, some families are not able to do all they must do. Are we afraid, for instance, that we shall not be able to break up our summer fallow? In due time we invite a dozen neighbours, who will come with their teams and finish it all in one day. At dinner we give them the best victuals our farm affords; these are feasts the goodness of which greatly depends on the knowledge and ability of our wives. Pies; puddings; fowls, roasted and boiled—nothing is spared that can evince our gratitude. In the evening, the same care is repeated, after which young girls and lads generally come from all parts to unite themselves to the assembly. As they have done no work, they generally come after supper and partake of the general dance. I have never been so happy in my life as when I have assisted at these simple merriments, and indeed they are the only ones I know. Each returns home happy and is satisfied, and our work is done.

If any of our wives are unable to spin that quantity of flax which was intended, they give out one pound to every one of their acquaintances. The youngsters take the same quantity, which they get spun by their sweethearts. The day is fixed when they all bring home the yarn to the house and receive in return a hearty supper and a dance. Can there be anything more harmless or more useful? The same is done for every species of labour. When my father built his house, he had had the stones previously pitched in large heaps; and the winter following, he invited upwards of thirty people, who came with their sleighs and horses and brought him in one day upwards of five hundred loads. Had he been obliged to have done that himself or to have hired it done, it would have cost him more than the house. We generally invite the minister of the precinct, who partakes with us of the pleasure of the day and who sanctifies by his presence the well-meant labours of our people. Thus we help one another; thus by our single toils at home and by our collective strength we remove many obstacles which no single family could do. Many swamps have been cleared in this manner to the great joy of the possessors, who were not able to hire the work done.

I could have wished when you were with me that I could have carried you to such an assembly. There you would have seen better what the American farmers are than by seeing them singly in their homes. The cheerful glass, the warmth of their country politics, the ruddy faces of their daughters, the goodness of their horses would give you a more lively idea of their happiness as men, of their native pride as freeholders than anything I could tell you. At these assemblies they forget all their cares, all their labours. They bring their governors and assemblymen to a severe account; they boldly blame them or censure them for such measures as they dislike. Here you might see the American freeman in all the latitude of his political felicity, a felicity—alas!—of which they are not so sensible as they ought to be. Your picture of the poor Germans and Russians makes me shudder. It is, then, to England we owe this elevated rank we possess, these noble appellations of freemen, freeholders, citizens; yes, it is to that wise people we owe our freedom. Had we been planted by some great monarchy, we should have been but the mean slaves of some distant monarch. Our great distance from him would have constituted the only happiness we should enjoy.

The small present of maple sugar which my wife sends you by this opportunity obliges me to [describe] to you another pleasurable scene, in which I always spend a week or ten days every spring. In clearing his farm, my father very prudently saved all the maple trees he found, which fortunately are all placed together in the middle of our woodland; and by his particular caution in bleeding them, they yield sap as plentifully as ever. The common method is to notch them with an axe. This operation, after a few years, destroys the tree entirely. That which my father followed is much easier and gives these trees wounds which are almost imperceptible. The best time to make this sugar is between the months of March and April, according to the season. There must be snow on the ground, and it must freeze at night and thaw in the day. These three circumstances are absolutely requisite to make the sap run in abundance. But as my trees are but a little way from my house, I now and then go to try them; and as soon as the time is come, then I bring all my hands, and we go to work. Nothing can be simpler than this operation. I previously provide myself with as many trays as I have trees. These I bore with a large gimlet. I then fix a spile made of elder, through which the sap runs into the trays. From them it is carried into the boiler, which is already fixed on the fire. If the evaporation is slow, we are provided with barrels to receive it. In a little time it becomes of the consistency of syrup. Then it is put into another vessel and made to granulate. When in that state, we cast it into little moulds made according to the fancy of the farmer. Some persons know how to purify it, and I am told that there are people at Montreal who excel in this branch. For my part, I am perfectly well satisfied with the colour and taste which Nature has given it. When the trees have ceased to run, we stop the holes with pegs made of the same wood. We cut them close to the bark, and in a little time the cicatrix becomes imperceptible. By these simple means our trees will afford sugar for a long time, nor have I ever observed that it impaired their growth in the least degree. They will run every year, according to the seasons, from six to fifteen days, until their buds fill. They do not yield every year the same quantity, but as I regularly bleed two hundred trees, which are all I have, I have commonly received six barrels of sap in twenty-four hours, which have yielded me from twelve to eighteen [pounds of sugar].

Thus, without the assistance of the West Indies, by the help of my trees and of my bees, we yearly procure the sweetening we want; and it is not a small quantity, you know, that satisfies the wants of a tolerable American family. I have several times made sugar with the sap of the birch; though it seldom runs in any quantity, it is sweeter, richer, and makes stronger sugar. These trees, however, are so rare among us that they are never made use of for that purpose. By way of imitating in some respects my provident father, who so religiously saved this small sugar plantation, I have cleared about a half acre of land adjoining it, on which I have planted above seventy young maples, which I have raised in a nursery. As that part of my woods is extremely moist, I propose to enlarge this useful plantation as fast as I can raise trees big enough for transplantation.

II. ENEMIES OF THE FARMER

What, still the same subject? This is really kind; you could not have pitched upon a more proper one for a farmer, [one] with which you know I am best acquainted. Yet, upon a proper recollection, this is the very reason why I am more at a loss. I am afraid of not being able to distinguish the useful from the useless, that which might be worthy of your perusal from what might be trifling. To a farmer everything appears important. Besides, what we are familiarly acquainted with does not strike our imagination so forcibly, though necessary to be known, as what we but seldom see. This is the greatest impediment I have to struggle against. This prevents me from arranging my thoughts with that propriety I could wish to possess. You want genuine details of all the benefits we enjoy as farmers; of all the inconveniences to which we are exposed, from birds, insects, animals, from seasons, and climates; of our peculiar modes of living. You wish that I should give you as complete a picture as I am able to draw of our lives and occupations, both at home and in the fields. In my preceding letters, I have already sketched some of the principal outlines, and without any further ceremony shall proceed on as my well-meant desire may lead me.

Nor are those which I have mentioned before the only

adverse circumstances which we have to struggle with. Many more call for our care and vigilance almost the whole year. Each season brings along with it its pains, pleasures, toils, and unavoidable losses. Often Nature herself opposes us. What, then, can we do? She is irresistible; I mean the uncertainty of the snows in the winter and the dryness of our summers. It is astonishing how variable the former grows, much more so indeed than formerly; and I make no doubt but that in a few hundred years they will be very different from what they are at present. That mildness, when interrupted by transitory frosts and thaws, will become very detrimental to our husbandry. For though the quantity of snow may diminish, yet it cannot be entirely so with the frost. Our proximity to the horrid mountainous waste which overspreads our north will always expose us to the severe blasts which often nip all our hopes and destroy the fairest and most promising expectations of the farmer, like a merchant losing his vessel in sight of the harbour. Last spring all my apples dropped in consequence of such an accident, although they were grown to the size of nutmegs. Nor could it be prevented, though it was foreseen.

Had my father been as wise as Mr. ——, this would not have been the case. This gentleman was very knowing and attentive for a first settler. He planted his orchard on the north side of a hill. This exposure commonly causes the difference of a fortnight in the opening of the blossoms, and this artificial delay always saves his apples. I could wish that [my orchard] had been thus situated, though it is so great an ornament to a farm that most people plant it either on one side of their house or on the other. How naked my settlement would look [were mine] removed! I am surprised, however, that this simple idea has not been more generally extended. The hint, I am sure, was not new, for most people plant their peach orchards in the most northern situation they have in order to avoid the same inconveniences. You must remember my situation. My loss in apples last year was the greater because of its being the bearing year; for you must know that all our trees (both in the forest and elsewhere) bear but every other year. In a little time I am in hopes to remedy this inconvenience, having planted in the fall a new apple orchard of five acres, con-

sisting of three hundred and fifty-eight trees. That of my
father was planted in the spring, and by their not bearing at the same time, I shall have a yearly supply of apples.

Perhaps you may want to know what it is we want to
do with so many apples. It is not for cider, God knows!
Situated as we are, it would not quit cost to transport
it even twenty miles. Many a barrel have I sold at the
press for a half-dollar. As soon as our hogs have done with
the peaches, we turn them into our orchards. The [apples],
as well as the preceding fruit, greatly improve them.
It is astonishing to see their dexterity in rubbing
themselves against the youngest trees in order to shake
them. They will often stand erect and take hold of the
limbs of the trees in order to procure their food in greater abundance.

In the fall of the year, we dry great quantities, and
this is one of those rural occupations which most amply
reward us. Our method is this: we gather the best kind.
The neighbouring women are invited to spend the evening at our house. A basket of apples is given to each
of them, which they peel, quarter, and core. These peelings and cores are put into another basket; and when
the intended quantity is thus done, tea, a good supper,
and the best things we have are served up. Convivial
merriment, cheerfulness, and song never fail to enliven
these evenings; and though our bowls contain neither
the delicate punch of the West Indies nor the rich wines
of Europe, nevertheless our cider affords us that simpler
degree of exhilaration with which we are satisfied. The
quantity I have thus peeled is commonly twenty bushels,
which gives me about three of dried ones.

Next day a great stage is erected, either in our grass
plots or anywhere else where cattle can't come. Strong
crotches are planted in the ground. Poles are horizontally fixed on these, and boards laid close together. For
there are no provident farmers who have not always
great stores of these. When the scaffold is thus erected,
the apples are thinly spread over it. They are soon covered with all the bees and wasps and sucking flies of the
neighbourhood. This accelerates the operation of drying.
Now and then they are turned. At night they are covered with blankets. If it is likely to rain, they are gath-

ered and brought into the house. This is repeated until they are perfectly dried. It is astonishing to what small size they will shrink. Those who have but a small quantity thread them and hang them in the front of their houses. In the same manner, we dry peaches and plums without peeling them, and I know not a delicacy equal to them in the various preparations we make of them. By this means we are enabled to have apple-pies and apple-dumplings almost all the year round.

The method of using them is this: we put a small handful in warm water overnight; next morning they are swelled to their former size; and when cooked either in pies or dumplings, it is difficult to discover by the taste whether they are fresh or not. I think that our farms produce nothing more palatable. My wife's and my supper half of the year consists of apple-pie and milk. The dried peaches and plums, as being more delicate, are kept for holidays, frolics, and such other civil festivals as are common among us. With equal care we dry the skins and cores. They are of excellent use in brewing that species of beer with which every family is constantly supplied, not only for the sake of drinking it, but for that of the bawm, without which our wives could not raise their bread.

The philosopher's stone of an American farmer is to do everything within his own family, to trouble his neighbours by borrowing as little as possible, and to abstain from buying European commodities. He that follows that golden rule and has a good wife is almost sure of succeeding.

Besides apples we dry pumpkins, which are excellent in winter. They are cut into thin slices, peeled, and threaded. Their skins serve also for beer, and admirable pumpkin-pies are made with them. When thus dried, they will keep the whole year. Many people have carried the former manufacture of drying apples to a great degree of perfection in the province of New Jersey. They make use of long ovens built on purpose, and when [the apples are] dried, export them to the West Indies. I have heard many planters say that they received nothing from the continent that was more delicate or better adapted to their climates. For it was transplanting the fruits of our orchards in that state in which they could endure the heat without injury.

In the most plentiful years, we have a method of reducing the quantity of our cider and of making it a liquor far superior. I think it greatly preferable to many sorts of wines which I have drunk at ———. We boil the quantities of two barrels into one, in a fair copper kettle, just as it comes from the press, and, therefore, perfectly sweet. Sometimes I have reduced one barrel and a half into one. This is preserved till the summer, and then affords a liquor which, when mixed with a due proportion of water, affords us an excellent beverage. Strangers have often been deceived and have taken it for some kind of Spanish wine. Other people prefer hauling their hogsheads out of their cellars when it freezes hard. In one night or two the frost will congeal the watery parts. They then draw from whatever remains behind, but this is neither so sweet nor so palatable as the others; it is too potent.

We often make apple-butter, and this is in the winter a most excellent food, particularly where there are many children. For that purpose, the best, the richest of our apples are peeled and boiled; a considerable quantity of sweet cider is mixed with it; and the whole is greatly reduced by evaporation. A due proportion of quinces and orange peels is added. This is afterwards preserved in earthern jars, and in our long winters is a very great delicacy and highly esteemed by some people. It saves sugar and answers in the hands of an economical wife more purposes than I can well describe. Thus our industry has taught us to convert what Nature has given us into such food as is fit for people in our station. Many farmers make excellent cherry and currant wines, but many families object to them on account of the enormous quantity of sugar they require. In some parts of this country, they begin to distil peaches and cider, from which two species of brandy are extracted, fiery and rough at first, but with age very pleasant. The former is the common drink of the people in the southern provinces.

However careful and prudent we are, the use of tea necessarily implies a great consumption of sugar. A northern farmer should never pronounce these two words without trembling, for these two articles must be replaced by something equivalent in order to pay for them, and not many of us have anything to spare.

Our summers grow exceedingly dry, and this is a very alarming circumstance. I have seen these droughts so parching that it was dangerous to light our pipes in the fields. If a spark dropped, it would run along from blade to blade and often reach to our fences. As soon as the snow is melted, the sun begins to be very powerful. Some years we have no spring. Then we often pass in the space of ten days from the severity of frost to the heat of summer. The surface of the ground dries apace. The frost, in quitting the earth, uplifts the surface of the ground and detaches the roots of the grain from the soil to which they adhered. This laceration cannot be repaired but by gentle showers. If these are refused, if it thaws in the day and continues freezing at night, the mischief is irreparable. The grain turns yellow and soon dies, a severe mortification for the American farmer, thus to see crops which have escaped all the severities of the winter entirely perish in the spring.

If you unite the casualties of that season—that is, when the snow does not cover the grain, which perishes by the power of the cold—to the parching droughts of the spring, you will easily see what risks our crops run. The stronger the soil, the better will the grain resist all accidents, in new grounds particularly. The frequency of these dry springs and summers has had a most surprising effect also on our brooks, wells, and springs. Many of the latter have disappeared, and many of the former have been reduced to almost nothing, since so many swamps have been cleared. Hence these brooks which they feed have failed. I could show you in this county the ruins of eleven grist-mills, which twenty years ago had plenty of water but now stand on the dry ground with no other marks of running water about them than the ancient bed of the creek, on the shores of which they had been erected. This effect does not surprise me. Our ancient woods kept the earth moist and damp, and the sun could evaporate none of the waters contained under their shades. Who knows how far these effects may extend? Some of our principal rivers, such as the ——, appear to have powerfully felt the consequence of that cause already, nor are our swamps all cleared yet. Fully one half of them remain in their primeval state.

Nor do the effects of these droughts stop there. They are felt even at a great depth. The first settlers, in digging their wells, only went to what we call the upper springs, those, I mean, which run horizontally, which are obtained at various depths. Almost all these ancient wells, by the droughts of our summer, have failed. I was obliged to have mine taken up and dug until we came to the lower springs, or those which burst upward. They are generally lodged under a stratum of blue clay mixed with gravel. I know nothing more than the simple relation of facts, and to that I confine myself.

As soon as the sun grows warm, we are afflicted with mosquitoes, a species of insect which is very troublesome. Were they as large as they are poisonous, no mortals could inhabit this country. They breed in ponds, lakes, rivers, and swamps. The whole continent is subject to their stings, but among the northern provinces Nova Scotia is the most overspread with them, owing to its many rivers, sea-coasts, and to that surprising height of tide which runs up the Bay of Fundy and at its retreat leaves such extensive shores bare. I should assert a truth should I aver that its present thin population is owing to these insects. Their sting is much more offensive to some persons than to others. Woeful is the appearance of many Europeans I have seen who have been severely stung. Last year a gentleman from Manchester lodged here, and notwithstanding all my care, there happened to be a few of them in his bedroom. Their stings fairly closed his eyes whilst Nature had wrapped them up in sleep. He was blind for above eight hours. Others are totally insensible to their poison. But they are infinitely more troublesome near great lakes and the salt meadows of our maritime counties.

I was once on Lake Champlain, and perceiving a large tree covered with pigeons, I went ashore in order to kill some of them. I had no sooner landed than I found myself in the thickest atmosphere of them that I had ever seen or felt. Their multiplied and aggregate singings formed not a very disagreeable noise; but if it had been ten times more melodious, who could have remained on

that shore in order to have listened? Glad to find some
living flesh that had blood, they covered my face. Far
from being able to shoot, I was obliged to exert all my
faculties in order to defend myself against these enormous swarms of enemies. I dared not open my eyes and
with great difficulty crawled again to my boat, nor did
they quit me until several miles from the shore. Who
could possibly live there? The lands of ancient Eden
could not tempt me to dwell among so many blood-
thirsty insects, which seem to be hatched merely to tease
the rest of the creation. Near the sea-shores they are
fully as terrible, particularly when the wind is not high
enough to drive them away. I think they are of a bigger
size than the inland ones. I can't conceive how the people endure them, for it requires a perpetual exercise to
drive them away, and very often it is no small labour.

So eager are they to fill themselves with blood that I
have sometimes suffered them to alight on my hand and
to suck mine quietly. With very little attention I perceived their bellies replenished with the red liquor until
they would drop down, unable to fly away. I went some
time ago to Mr. ——, who lives near the sea, in order
to procure some clams and oysters. The evening I arrived was calm. The air was impregnated with them. My
horse could not feed, nor could I rest. Towards night
they were succeeded by another brood, which we call
gnats. They are animalculae just big enough to enter into
our pores and there make a lodgement; no sooner entered than they cause a prodigious inflammation and a
desire of scratching. They are almost invisible. I know
nothing in Nature which I can compare them to; they
are the smallest class of the stinging insects. What is it
that heat and moisture will not create? On a hot, sultry
day, I have often stooped down to consider with attention a shallow puddle of water. The variety of beings
which moved on the mud appeared to me infinite. The
whole bottom seemed alive. These maritime counties,
abounding in salt meadows, teem, besides, with a variety of green and blue flies which attack the cattle and
drive them out of their pastures, sometimes in the woods,
at other times in the water, where they plunge up to
their heads.

From this imperfect sketch, you'll easily conceive that

if we enjoy some happiness, we are made to pay for it. Yet I must confess that whilst I was there I observed that the people were not so sensible to their stings as I was. My being a stranger entitled me, it seems, to all their regard. The Indians anoint themselves with bears' grease in order to prevent their punctures, and that is the reason for their being more swarthy than Nature intended them. Mr. —— informed me that a farmer of ——, in order to punish his Negro, had thought proper to tie him naked to a stake in one of his salt meadows. He went home, where he stayed but twenty-three minutes. At his return, he found his Negro prodigiously swelled, in consequence of the repeated stings of millions of mosquitoes which he had received. He brought him back to his house, but all his care could not prevent an inflammatory fever, of which he died. While there I was obliged to make a smoke in my room, and this expedient prevented me from resting. In the cultivated, opened parts of the country, they are not so numerous. The only method made use of in some counties is the smoke, a remedy pretty nearly as bad as the disorder. A large smothered fire is made before the door as soon as the evening comes. I have often seen rings of such fires made and the cows brought into the middle that the people might milk them. You may judge of the situation of these inhabitants. All new settlements are much more exposed to them, and all new settlers have this additional calamity to struggle with. I would not live in any part of Nova Scotia nor on the Island of St. John for a very valuable consideration. I never should have done, were I to recount to you the many inconveniences and sufferings to which the people of these countries are exposed. I have heard that there were in England baronets of Nova Scotia, but as I have never heard of one residing in that province, I conclude that the mosquitoes have driven them off, as they have done so many other persons. At Annapolis Royal, in the Bay of Fundy, there is a small garrison in the establishment of which twelve pounds per annum are given to a soldier in order to keep a constant smoke in the temple of Cloacina.

In most of our swamps we have poisonous vegetables, almost as much to be dreaded as the snakes. In clearing them, we must carefully avoid the mercury and the water-sumach. The first is a small creeping vine resembling ivy which adheres either to the pine, oak, or to the maple. It is so exceedingly poisonous that some people are affected by its effluvia in passing twelve feet to the leeward of it; and if burned, its smoke will cause the same effects at a greater distance still. It swells the people who are liable to receive its baneful impression and often brings running sores and scars. The water-sumach is fully as poisonous. A general swelling, particularly of the legs and face, is the inevitable consequence either of touching it or coming near it, except it is to the windward. I had a Negro who once lost eleven days' work by imprudently having touched one in order to eradicate it.

We are subjected to a trouble and expense to which, I am informed, you are wholly strangers, and that is to salt our cattle regularly once a week. This is in general done from one end of the continent to the other, but on what principle that necessity is founded, none here can tell. From the horses to the sheep, every one must have a handful given them. It seems that all other American wild animals are equally fond of salt. You have heard of licking-places, which have been so long the resort of deer. I am of the opinion that one of the principal causes which brings every year such multitudes of pigeons is not that they visit us on purpose to eat our grains, but only in their progress towards the sea in quest of salt. For during their abode with us, two or three times a week they regularly take their flight towards its shores and as regularly return in twelve hours except they are caught by the inhabitants of these counties. So great is the necessity of salting our cattle that they will all become wild, restless, and incapable of being kept within the bounds of our farms. The gentlest cows will become intractable. They will shake their heads, loll out their tongues, and plainly ask you for salt. They will not stand in the yard, and hardly give any milk; and even that small quantity will yield no butter. These are facts known to thousands. I relate them to you that I may have the pleasure of hearing some of your philosophical reasons on that subject.

When our hogs are fatting up, we must not forget to mix salt with the crude antimony which we frequently give them. My neighbours say that I am very lucky with

my bees and that they never leave me. Would you believe it? The truth of the matter is that I give them fine
salt. You'd greatly wonder to see each of them carrying
away a small grain of it in its proboscis. Often our working horses and cattle refuse to drink and to eat. The
quickest and best remedy is to give them a handful of
salt. This cools them and inspires them with a desire
either to eat or drink. Have you never observed near our
barn-yards logs of twenty or thirty feet long with the
bark peeled? A great number of small cavities are dug
twice as big as one's fist. These are every now and then
replenished with salt, which the big cattle greedily eat.
The young ones and the sheep soon afterwards follow
and with care pick up what has been dropped and spend
whole hours in licking these places. If any salt has been
given them on the ground, their repeated licks will dig
small holes in the earth. I have often given it to them in
this manner, and each would eat at least a peck of the
soil on which I had spilled it. Those farmers who live
near the salt meadows are obliged to turn both their cattle and their horses on their salt grasses in the spring,
which is looked upon as a sovereign remedy for every
disorder.

Nor am I going to complain of this want which you
have not. For were it not for the attractive power of the
salt, what should we do with the dry cattle which we
drive to feed on the mountains every spring? The man
who takes care of them salts them once a week at one
and the same place. By this means he can always bring
them together; and instead of becoming wild, they are
always glad to see him and assemble all around him
whenever he chooses to hold out his hands to them. By
this simple means they are kept there as long as the feed
is good. By the same expedient, each person goes to the
mountains and in the fall gathers them together and easily brings them home. It is [done] only [by] alluring the
belled one with a handful of salt, and the rest will follow
in hopes of having it in their turn. Such, sir, is the simple
mechanism by means of which we keep them healthy.
We conduct them sometimes thirty or forty miles from
home and bring them back.

Thus all countries have their peculiarities, their different customs, and modes of doing perhaps the same thing,

all founded on some hidden cause or locality or climate, or latitude or situation.

Of all the grain which we plant, the Indian corn is attended with the greatest labour, is the most profitable, and the most necessary, but at the same time the most subject to accidents from seasons, insects, birds, and animals. It is so superlative a grain that all that live would cheerfully live on that grain if they could. Necessity hath taught us different methods to protect it and to baffle the combined sagacities of so many enemies.

It is no sooner planted than, if the season proves dry, an infinite number of ants will form societies and establish themselves in the very hills in the midst of which the corn is germinating. There they live on the young, succulent sprouts which want moisture to rise; and they sometimes attack the grain itself. No sooner is it shot above the ground than it becomes exposed to the rapacity of a black worm which cuts its tender stem a little below the surface of the earth. The same worm will sometimes infest our gardens and make a sad havoc. When I plant cabbages, I am obliged to enclose their stems with hickory bark. Its strength and bad taste oblige this worm to desist. The only remedy against the first inconvenience is to stir the hills gently with the hoe. This fills the small cavities the ants have dug and prevents them from being so intent on the destruction of the corn. As for the second, the hills on which the young shoot lies dead must be carefully examined with the finger. The enemy is easily discovered, coiled up near the stem it has fed on, waiting for the coolness of the night to travel on. It is picked up and crushed. This is tedious work, but it must be done. The corn in a little time shoots up again as strong as ever. It has no sooner reached two or three inches above the ground when its greatest enemies, the crows and the blackbirds, come in order to eradicate it by means of their strong bills. Its lobes remain long, entire, and sound. These they dig up as a ready food for their young ones.

With some attention and care, the former are easily kept off. Various are our methods. The first is to make a few images by means of bunches of straw shaped like men and dressed with old clothes. These are fixed in various parts of the field. The other is to hang up several pieces of shingles, painted black on one side and white on the

other, at the end of long threads. The perpetual agitation
in which the winds keep them frighten [the birds]
away. Another method is to hang two bright pewter plates
by means of holes bored in their edges. The rays of the
sun reflected from them as they turn greatly resemble the
flashes of a gun and have the desired effect. Others try to
kill some in the woods and hang them "in terrorem"
about their corn-fields. This is not infallible. It is sometimes among crows as it is among men: the calls of
hunger are stronger than the fear of punishment. But
the most simple and effectual manner to keep them
away from our farms as well as the foxes is to dip a certain number of rags in brimstone, then to fix them on
short sticks cleft at the top, and to plant them on the
ground along the outside fence. They both mistake it for
the smell of powder with which they are well acquainted.
This will prevent the first from alighting and the second
from intruding into our fields and into our poultry-yards.
Thus have I often defeated the superior sagacity of Mr.
Reynard, who is not so well trained as your English ones
yet, as scholars of the same great mistress, are full as
sagacious. In the neighbourhood of towns, rats have been
known to emigrate from them in great numbers and to
go to dig the corn out of the hills; or in the fall of the
year to climb up its stalks and prey on the grain. As this
is done at night by a great number of keen, intelligent
enemies, it is difficult to prevent it because it is impossible to foresee it.

Nature has placed a certain degree of antipathy between some species of animals and birds. Often one lives
on the other; at other times they only attack each other.
The king-bird is the most skilful on the wing of any we
have here. Every spring he declares war against all the
kites, hawks, and crows which pass within the bounds of
his precincts. If they build anywhere on your farm, rest
assured that none of those great tyrants of the air will
fly over it with impunity. Nor is it an unpleasant sight to
behold the contest. Like the Indians, they scream aloud
when they go to the attack. They fly at first with an
apparent trepidation. They err here and there, and then
dart with immense impetuosity and with consummate
skill, always getting to the windward of their enemy, let
it be even the great bald eagle of the Blue Mountains. By

repeatedly falling on him and striking him with their bills and sometimes by attacking him under the wings, they will make the largest bird accelerate its motion, and describe the most beautiful curves in those rapid descents which they compel him to delineate. This amuses me much, on two accounts: first, because they are doing my work; second, because I have an excellent opportunity of viewing the art of flying carried to a great degree of perfection and varied in a multiplicity of appearances. What a pity that I am very often obliged to shoot these little kings of the air! Hunting crows serves only to make them more hungry, nor will they live on grain, but on bees. These precious insects, these daughters of heaven, serve them as food whenever they can catch them.

The blackbird, which you say resembles your starling, visits us every spring in great numbers. They build their nests in our most inaccessible swamps. Their rough notes are delightful enough at a distance. As soon as the corn sprouts, they come to dig it up; nothing but the gun can possibly prevent them. Hanging of their dead companions has no kind of effect. They are birds that show the greatest degree of temerity of any we have. Sometimes we poison corn, which we strew on the ground with the juice of hitch-root. Sometimes, after soaking it, we pass a horsehair through each grain, which we cut about an inch long. These expedients will destroy a few of them, but either by the effect of inspection or by means of some language unknown, like a great many other phenomena, to Man, the rest will become acquainted with the danger, and in two days the survivors will not touch it, but take the utmost pains to eradicate that which lies three inches under the ground. I have often poisoned the very grains I have planted, but in two days it grows as sweet as ever. Thus while our corn is young it requires a great deal of watching. To prevent these depredations, some counties have raised money and given a small bounty of two pence per head. If they are greatly disturbed while they are hatching, they will soon quit that district.

But after all the efforts of our selfishness, are they not the children of the great Creator as well as we? They are entitled to live and to get their food wherever they can get it. We can better afford to lose a little corn than any other grain because it yields above seventy for one.

But Man is a huge monster who devours everything and will suffer nothing to live in peace in his neighbourhood. The easiest, best, and the most philanthropic method is to break up either our summer fallow or our buckwheat ground while our corn is young. They will immediately cease to do us mischief and go to prey on the worms and caterpillars which the plough raises. Their depredations proceeded from hunger, not from premeditated malice. As soon as their young ones are able to fly, they bid us farewell. They retire to some other countries which produce what they want, for as they neither sow nor plant, it is necessary that either Man or Nature should feed them. Towards the autumn, they return in astonishing flocks. If our corn-fields are not then well guarded, they will in a few hours make great havoc. They disappear in about a week.

At this season another animal comes out of our woods and demands of Man his portion. It is the squirrel, of which there are three sorts, the grey, the black, both of the same size, and the little ground one, which harbours under rocks and stones. The two former are the most beautiful inhabitants of our forests. They live in hollow trees which they fill with koka toma nuts, chestnuts, and corn when they can get it. Like man they know the approach of the winter and as wisely know how to prepare against its wants. Some years their numbers are very great. They will travel over our fences with the utmost agility, descend into our fields, cut down an ear perhaps eighteen inches long and heavier than themselves. They will strip it of its husk and, properly balancing it in their mouths, return thus loaded to their trees. For my part, I cannot blame them, but I should blame myself were I peaceably to look on and let them carry all. As we pay no tithes in this country, I think we should be a little more generous than we are to the brute creation. If there are but few, a gun and a dog are sufficient. If they openly declare war in great armies, men collect themselves and go to attack them in their native woods. The county assembles and forms itself into companies to which a captain is appointed. Different districts of woods are assigned them; the rendezvous is agreed on. They march, and that company which kills the most is treated by the rest; thus the day is spent. The meat of these squirrels is an excellent food; they make excellent soup or pies. Their skins are exceedingly tough; they are stronger than eels' skins; we use them to tie our flails with.

Mirth, jollity, coarse jokes, the exhilarating cup, and dancing are always the concomitant circumstances which enliven and accompany this kind of meeting, the only festivals that we simple people are acquainted with in this young country. Religion, which in so many parts of the world affords processions and a variety of other exercises and becomes a source of temporal pleasures to the people, here gives us none. What few it yields are all of the spiritual kind. A few years ago I was invited to one of these parties. At my first entrance into the woods, whilst the affrighted echoes were resounding with the noise of the men and dogs, before I had joined the company, I found a bee-tree, which is my favourite talent. But, behold, it contained also the habitation of a squirrel family. The bees were lodged in one of its principal limbs; the others occupied the body of the tree. For the sake of the former I saved the latter. While I was busy in marking it, I perceived a great number of ants (those busy-bodies) travelling up three deep in a continual succession and returning in the same way. Both these columns were perfectly straight in the ascent as well as in the descent and but a small distance apart. I killed a few which I smelled. I found them all replete with honey. I therefore concluded that these were a set of thieves living on the industrious labours of the others. This intrusion gave me a bad opinion of the vigour and vigilance of the latter. However, as the honey season was not come, I resolved to let them alone and to deliver them from the rapacity of an enemy which they could not repel.

Next day, accompanied by my little boy, I brought a kettle, kindled a fire, boiled some water, and scalded the whole host as it ascended and descended. I did not leave one stirring. The lad asked me a great many questions respecting what I was doing, and the answers I made him afforded me the means of conveying to his mind the first moral ideas I had as yet given him. On my return home I composed a little fable on the subject, which I made him learn by heart. God grant that this trifling incident may serve as the basis of a future moral education.

Thus, sir, do we save our corn. But when it is raised on our lowlands, it is subject to transitory frosts, an accident which I have not mentioned to you yet, but as we can foresee them, it is in our power to avoid the mischief they cause. If in any of our summer months the wind blows north-west two days, on the second night the frost is inevitable. The only means we have to preserve our grain from its bad effects on our low grounds—for it seldom reaches the upland—is to kindle a few fires to the windward as soon as the sun goes down. No sooner [does] that luminary disappear from our sight than the wind ceases. This is the most favourable moment. The smoke will not rise, but, on the contrary, lie on the ground, mixing with the vapours of the evening. The whole will form a body four feet deep which will cover the face of the earth until the power of the sun dissipates it next morning. Whatever is covered with it is perfectly safe. I had once some hops and pole-beans, about twenty feet high. Whatever grew above the body of the smoke was entirely killed; the rest was saved. I had at the same time upwards of three acres of buckwheat which I had sown early for my bees. I lost not a grain. Some of my neighbours have by this simple method saved their tobacco.

These low grounds are exposed, besides, to the ravages of grasshoppers, an intolerable nuisance. While young and deprived of wings, they may be kept off by means of that admirable contrivance which a Negro found out in South Carolina: a few pots filled with brimstone and tar are kindled at nightfall to the windward of the field; the powerful smell of these two ingredients either kills them or drives them away. But when they have wings, they easily avoid it and transport themselves wherever they please. The damage they cause in our hemp grounds as well as in our meadows is inconceivable. They will eat the leaves of the former to the bare stalks and consume the best of our grasses. The only remedy for the latter is to go to mowing as soon as possible. The former devastation is unavoidable. Some years a certain worm, which I cannot describe, insinuates itself into the heart of the corn-stalk while it is young; and if not killed by squeezing the plant, it will eat the embryo of the great stem, which contains the imperceptible rudiments of our future hopes.

Sometimes our rye is attacked by a small animalcula of the worm kind which lodges itself in the stem just below the first joint. There it lives on the sap as it ascends. The ear becomes white and grainless, the perfect symbol of sterility.

I should have never done, were I to recount to you all the inconveniences and accidents which the grains of our fields, the trees of our orchards, as well as those of the woods, are exposed to. If bountiful Nature is kind to us on the one hand, on the other she wills that we shall purchase her kindness not only with sweats and labour but with vigilance and care. These calamities remind us of our precarious situation. The field and meadow-mice come in also for their share, and sometimes take more from Man than he can well spare. The rats are so multiplied that no one can imagine the great quantities of grain they destroy every year. Some farmers, more unfortunate than the others, have lost half of their crops after they were safely lodged in their barns. I'd forgive Nature all the rest if she would rid us of these cunning, devouring thieves which no art can subdue. When the floods rise on our low grounds, the mice quit their burrows and come to our stacks of grain or to our heaps of turnips, which are buried under the earth out of the reach of the frost. There, secured from danger, they find a habitation replenished with all they want. I must not, however, be murmuring and ungrateful. If Nature has formed mice, she has created also the fox and the owl. They both prey on these. Were it not for their kind assistance, [the mice] would drive us out of our farms.

Thus one species of evil is balanced by another; thus the fury of one element is repressed by the power of the other. In the midst of this great, this astonishing equipoise, Man struggles and lives.

III. CUSTOMS

I am glad you approve of my last; I was afraid it might prove tedious. I wanted to have curtailed it, but I knew not what part to lop off lest I should omit some information and repent of my foolish timidity. For the future, I will boldly tell you all and leave the future amendment to yourself.

Within the more limited province of our American wives, there are many operations, many ingenious arts which require knowledge, skill, and dexterity. In that of dyeing, you'd be surprised to see what beautiful colours some families will have in their garments, which commonly are streaked gowns, skirts, and petticoats of the same stuff. This we have borrowed from the Dutch, as well as the art of producing so many colours from the roots and barks of our woods, aided with indigo and alum, the only foreign ingredients we use. I have often, while among the Indians, wished, but in vain, to find out how they dye their porcupine quills with that bright red and yellow which you must remember to have seen on the moccasins I gave you. Nor is the art of their squaws to be despised when you consider it as it is displayed in the embroidery of their belts, shoes, and pouches, knife-cases, etc.

Some families excel in the method of brewing beer with a strange variety of ingredients. Here we commonly make it with pine chips, pine buds, hemlock, fir leaves, roasted corn, dried apple-skins, sassafras roots, and bran. With these, to which we add some hops and a little malt, we compose a sort of beverage which is very pleasant. What most people call health-beer (which is made every spring) would greatly astonish you. I think in the last we made we had not less than seventeen ingredients. The doctors tell us that it is very purgative and necessary, that after the good living and the idleness of the winter it is necessary to prepare ourselves by these simple means for the sweats and the labours of the summer.

It is in the art of our simple cookery that our wives all aim at distinguishing themselves. This wife is famous for one thing, that for the other. She who has not fresh comb-honey, some sweetmeats of her own composing, and smoked beef at tea would be looked upon as very inexpert indeed. Thus these light repasts become on every account the most expensive of any; and as we dine early and work until tea-time, they often are very serious meals at which abundance of biscuits and shortcakes are always eaten. Some people would think it a disgrace to have bread brought on these round tables. Our beef by smoking becomes so compact that we commonly shave it with a plane. The thin, transparent peelings, when curled up on a dish, look not only neat and elegant but very tempting. Thus going to drink tea with each other implies several very agreeable ideas: that of riding sometimes five or six miles; that of chatting much and hearing the news of the county; and that of eating heartily. Considering that our women are never idle but have something to do from one year's end to another, where is the husband that would refuse his wife the pleasure of treating her friends as she has been treated herself?

In the future details which I intend to give you of our modes of living, of our different home manufactures, of the different resources which an industrious family must find within itself, you'll be better able to judge what a useful acquisition a good wife is to an American farmer, and how small is his chance of prosperity if he draws a blank in that lottery! Don't blame us for living well. Upon my word, we richly earn it. Were not we to consume all these articles which our farms produce, were they not converted into wholesome, pleasant food, they would be lost. What should we do with our fruit, our fowls, our eggs? There is no market for these articles but in the neighbourhood of great towns.

Some Europeans would, on reading these candid details, declare and swear that we deserve to be taxed. May those who thoughtlessly and without any real information advance such a doctrine come over and be farmers with us one single year. I will then trust to their feelings. This was your early doctrine, too, until you attentively descended into every detail and saw the immense advances we are obliged to make and the enormity of the price of our labours and the severity of our seasons. You were shocked the first time you saw ditchers and choppers at my table. Like a wise man you soon found that this was but the smallest difficulty which attends our rural operations.

Would you believe that the great electrical discoveries of Mr. Franklin have not only preserved our barns and our houses from the fire of heaven but have even taught our wives to multiply their chickens? The invisible effects of the thunder are powerfully felt in the egg. If, while a hen is hatching, there happens a great storm, not one chicken will appear. (I can express myself but very imperfectly.) To prevent this electrical mischief, our wives, without going through a course of lectures, have been taught to place a piece of iron in the bottom of their hens' nests in such a manner that it touches the ground. By what magic I know not, but all the mischief is prevented, and the eggs bring prosperous chickens. Can the name of that distinguished, useful citizen be mentioned by an American without feeling a double sentiment: that of the pleasure inspired by our calling him our countryman and that of gratitude? Before the erection of his iron conductors, the mischiefs occasioned in Pennsylvania and everywhere else by the thunder annually amounted to a great sum. Now everyone may rest secure. These rods fetch from the clouds (strange to tell) that powerful fire and convey it into the earth alongside the very house which it would have consumed had it accidentally fallen on its roof. Happy Pennsylvania! Thou Queen of Provinces! Among the many useful citizens thou hast already produced, Benjamin Franklin is one of the most eminent of thy sons.

Whilst I was discoursing with you in my last on the many enemies, against the combined instincts of which we had to struggle, I purposely omitted to mention to you several others lest I might appear tedious. Give me leave to resume that subject. You evidently see that I cannot submit to any method. Method appears to me like the symmetry and regularity of a house. Its external appearance is often sacrificed to the internal conveniences.

Our ponds, our lakes, and brooks, with which this country is replenished, abound with enemies which, it is true, touch not our grains, but destroy our fowls. The musquash is the most pernicious on many accounts. Nothing can possibly restrain him. The stoutest and best-made banks cannot resist his instinctive ingenuity. These [animals] undermine and destroy that which has successfully opposed and restrained the fury of the waters. They will pierce them and open a communication for the element in which they swim. They enjoy a double advantage: they can live under water as well as on the earth. The proprietors of the bank-meadows near Philadelphia, and in the county of Salem in West New Jersey, where so much art has been displayed, can well attest the power of their claws. They are the cousin germans of the beavers and greatly resemble them in their instinct, ingenuity in building, and modes of living. But how different is their conduct! The beavers are the philosophers of the animals; the gentlest, the most humble, the most harmless. Yet brutal Man kills them. I was once a witness to the destruction of one of their associated confederacies. I saw many of them shed tears, and I wept also; nor am I ashamed to confess it.

We abound likewise with otters, and they are very mischievous. At least we call by that name everything through which we lose some small part of our property. We have many species of turtles. Some creep through our woods and are harmless. The gold-spotted one is rather an ornament to our ditches. The snapping one is a hideous and very strong animal. Their bills would astonish you as to their size and strength. I have seen them that weighed forty pounds. Whatever goose or duck swims in their waters is soon pulled down and devoured. These [turtles] are good to eat, and as long as we feed on what would feed on us, that seems to be founded on a just retaliation. Traps of various kinds are laid to catch the otters, and their furs are the only reward they yield.

We have another animal which sometimes makes great havoc among our poultry; that is the skunk. It resembles a black-and-white small dog. Its mode of defence is very singular: behind it possesses a bladder containing the most fetid and offensive liquor you can possibly conceive. When pursued either by men or dogs, it scatters it on its enemies. If it touches the eyes, it will cause violent pains. If not, the intolerableness of the smell will turn one's stomach.

We abound with bull-frogs of an enormous size whose deep and sullen voices often startle the unthinking traveller. Common frogs are perfectly harmless. The tree-toads are a species of them; they climb and rest on the limbs of trees. There they live all summer, but on what, I know not. Their notes are not disagreeable. In dry weather, they are perfectly silent, and on the approach of rain they sweetly warble their uncouth notes. We always love to hear them sing because they almost infallibly predict the coming of refreshing showers.

In the summer, our meadows and fields are beautifully illuminated by an immense number of fire-flies, which in the calm of the evening sweetly wander here and there at a small distance from the ground. By their alternate glows of light, they disseminate a kind of universal splendour, which, being always contrasted with the darkness of the night, has a most surprising effect. I have often read by their assistance; that is, I have taken one carefully by the wings and, carrying it along the lines of my book, I have, when thus assisted by these living flambeaux, perused whole pages and then thankfully dismissed these little insect-stars. I am told that a few years ago a Scotch soldier, while he was on duty at ——, fired at the first he saw, thinking that it was the flash of an enemy.

We abound with vultures, eagles, hawks, and kites of many kinds. The best way to preserve our poultry from their rapacity is to plant elders round our fences. This serves them as an excellent shelter where they can run.

I have often told you that the philosophy of an American farmer consisted in doing much with few hands, in manufacturing in his own family whatever he may want. This is true in every possible respect. If he is obliged to purchase many articles, then he works for others and not for himself; he is but a fool and a slave. His profits are so inconsiderable that if they are uselessly expended, there remains nothing of his year's industry.

Our wool, I am afraid, never will be so good as yours; we have no plains. Sheep in our dry summers are so destructive to grass that we can't keep many. I have sixty, and sometimes I think that is a greater number than my farm can support. Our long winters are very prejudicial to them. The snow often renders them blind. We have but one expedient to prevent it, which is to keep some place free from snow where they may see the ground and give them the limbs of pine-trees, the bark of which they peel and eat. Were it not for the wolves, we could turn them out into the woods. It is astonishing how they thrive on wood-feed and how much better their wool becomes. I have often tried the experiment. This feed is certainly stronger and richer than that which our pastures afford.

The best butter in this country is made with the milk of cows that run at large in the woods; it has a more pleasant taste, which a stranger can soon perceive. I intend next fall to send you a firkin that your friends in England may judge whether or not I am right. This is one of the principal advantages which first settlers enjoy. They possess, besides, a certain amplitude of benefits which great cultivated countries have lost. And if they carefully salt their cows at their doors, they are sure that every night they will punctually return home.

The method which is yearly made use of to render the feed of our mountains sweet, tender, and good is to burn them. You must not imagine that by that operation we consume the trees. No, this operation would ruin us all indeed. For in that case they would become barren and useless. In April, the neighbours of each mountain district assemble and, taking the advantage of the wind, set fire to the leaves which lie most contiguous to their fences; and each takes care of his own. Those leaves which fell the preceding fall soon catch. The fire forms itself in a regular line and advances towards the top of the mountains, sometimes with great rapidity. It spreads wherever there are combustibles, etc. This scene viewed at a distance through the trees yields a very pleasing effect in the night. Here the fire, by a sudden puff of wind, is seen to blaze as it advances with great velocity; there, in consequence of some impediment, it takes another turn. Now the rarefied air increases the wind, and the wind urges on that fire which at first caused it. Thus, on a calm day, when employed in burning great heaps of wood in my swamp, I have been surprised at the tempest I have raised and the astonishing agitation of the trees whose limbs have often been torn off and have fallen on the ground. As soon as the operation of burning the mountains is over, which sometimes requires many days, it is surprising to see how amazingly quickly every vegetable will spring up. The surface of the earth is rendered perfectly clear. The heat of this transitory fire and the few ashes it leaves greatly accelerate the growth of every shrub and weeds and plants and grass. This is generally the time I visit them, when I want to get some snake-root, crow's-foot, Solomon's seal, spignet, etc. I can distinguish them as soon as they appear, and that is the best season of the year to procure them.

Our cattle are sent there some time in May. There they feed all the summer, salted regularly, as I told you before. Everywhere springs abound of the purest water, and everywhere a most benign shade. [There are] very few insects, for you know that our mountains are all covered with the most majestic trees. By the assistance of these three blessings, is it a wonder that in the fall they should return home extremely fat? So would our sheep, too, were it not for the danger of the wolves. Some farmers, to render them still fatter, sow several acres of rye on their low grounds, the second week in September, about two bushels to an acre. They are turned into these rye pastures and into our meadows the latter end of October, when they return from the woods. At first this rye grass, as I may call it, purges them; afterwards you cannot imagine what surprising progress they make. The butchers greatly prefer beef thus fatted to those which are constantly kept in the richest of our meadows.

But we have no foreign market. The limits of our trade do not permit us to send our produce where we might find a ready vent for it. Cattle are so cheap that they are hardly worth raising. Three pence per pound is a great price, which is seldom given. This is a very small fraction, more than three of your coppers. Yet I am astonished that the price of labour does not fall. We abound too much in cattle; every other provision is cheap in proportion. Any one can board and lodge himself with the most opulent of our farmers for seven shillings a week; that is, something less than four shillings sterling, yet the wages we are obliged to give are enormous. Many times have I given from five to eight shillings per day to a cradler. It is a problem, however, easily explained; it is a contradiction which nothing but the locality of our situation can possibly resolve.

Those people who live near the sea every spring burn their salt meadows also, that the dead unmowed grass

may make room for the new and leave no impediment
to the scythe. This operation affords likewise a noble
sight. I once saw a body of such meadows consisting of
upwards of three thousand acres [burned] in a few
hours. The whirlwinds of smoke they produce are of an
enormous size and [are] seen at a great distance.

Some of our wives are famous for the raising of turkeys, in which, you know, we abound in the fall of the
year. The great secret consists in procuring the eggs of
the wild sort and then [in crossing] the breed. In
that case, we are always sure of a hardier and heavier
bird. It well repays us for the trouble and care they
have cost. I have often killed them that weighed twenty-
seven pounds. Pray, are they heavier with you? Here
they hate confinement; in the most severe of our freezing nights, they will reach the utmost limbs of our highest trees and there boldly face the north-west wind. Does
their instinct lead them to such lofty roosts to avoid
danger, or because it is not so cold on high as it is
nearer the surface of the earth?

You often used to blame us for not taking better care
of the breed of our dogs. It would be impossible to
amend it. We find that the strength of the climate has
the same effect on them as it has on us. In the course
of a few generations, they become American dogs as
well as we American men. Many of them outrun the fox.
They never fail to attack the wolf with the greatest fury,
nor do they decline encountering the bear. What other
accomplishments could we wish them to possess? We
neither love nor understand small game.

I once saw a remarkable instance of the sagacity of
an Indian dog, which I beg to relate. Mr. D. W., a
distant relation of my wife, lives at the foot of the great
mountains; nay, he is the last settler towards the wilderness. [He] possesses both a good mill and a
very good farm. While I was there, a child about three
years old was missed at ten o'clock in the morning. The
neighbourhood was roused; they all marched with the
afflicted family in quest of him. In vain did they mention his name a thousand times; no other answer was
returned but by the uncouth echoes of those woods; the
search proved vain. I never saw so affecting a scene of
distress. After dinner, they all returned to the woods;

they searched and searched until night came on. The afflicted parents refused to return to the house and spent the night with many of their friends at the foot of a tree, bemoaning the loss of their poor child.

Next day, the search was renewed, but as ineffectually as on the preceding day. Fortunately, about one o'clock, an Indian, followed by his dog, was seen to go by. He was called in; he expressed a great deal of sympathy at the sad adventure; he immediately demanded the child's shoes and stockings, which he made his dog smell; then, taking the house as a center, he described around it a circle of about a quarter of a mile in diameter. Before the circle was completed, the dog barked. This happy sound immediately conveyed to the hearts of the afflicted parents some distant hopes of the recovery of their child. The dog followed the scent and barked again. In about a half hour he returned towards the Indian and guided him to a large log where the child lay, half asleep and half [in a faint]. The Indian tenderly brought him home.

Happily, his parents were prepared for his reception, for they had been full of hopes from the first time the dog uttered the first sounds. They ran to meet the honest Indian; they embraced their child, their newly-found child; they caught the Indian in their arms; nor did his dog go uncaressed and unthanked. I was by all the time and saw this singular scene in all its gradations. They returned to the house; it was full. By means of some light broth, the child recovered, opened his eyes, and began to smile. Alas, one must be a father to participate in all the joys of these parents, to know what they must have felt, and to feel along with them. The Indian had killed a deer, which he gave towards the feast; to it Mr. —— added a calf. Upwards of seventy people were entertained there that evening, that memorable evening, and the whole night.

The story soon ran at a great distance, and from a great distance his neighbours and friends all flocked to rejoice with him. The Indian would accept no kind of reward; all he wanted was the skin of his deer. Mr. ——, with great difficulty, made him accept a fine Lancaster rifle. This honest native's name was Tewenissa. Towards evening, Mr. —— brought his child into the middle of the yard, where everyone was assembled. In a proper talk, he thanked the Indian, acknowledged him as his brother, embraced him and made his child do the same, and earnestly required that his former name of Derick, by which he had hitherto been called, might be forgot and that henceforth he should be known under no other than that of his deliverer, Tewenissa. I had never before assisted at such a scene nor partaken of such a feast; it was a feast for the soul as well as for the stomach. Cider, rum, peach-brandy, all that these good people had was profusely poured out in the most pious and grateful libations on this joyful occasion. The honest Indian all this while seemed embarrassed; [Indians] are not used to such noisy scenes. All he said was: "Brother ——, I have done nothing for you but what you would have done for me. It was my dog that did it all. Since you are all happy, I am happy. Since you are all glad, I am glad."

In travelling through our woods and our swamps, I have often been astonished at the great quantity of grapes which grow in some particular spots. I verily believe that I have grapes enough some years in my south swamp to make a hogshead of wine, but labour is so dear and I am so inexpert that I am discouraged from undertaking any new schemes. All the use I make of it, and perhaps it is all it is good for, [is to make] vinegar, which is exceedingly strong indeed. (A scheme was formed by Captain Carver, author of a book of travels through America, for a settlement on the Missouri, where vines abound and where he was to distil it into brandy to trade with the Indians.)

Some time ago, as I was walking through my woodland, I found a thrifty sassafras tree about three inches in circumference. Close by, there grew a vine twisted round its stem, which appeared to be coeval with its supporter. They seemed to have been the twins of Nature formed at the same time and for each other, a singular circumstance. These spontaneous ideas struck me so much that with infinite care I dug them up and brought them into my garden. Although sassafras will hardly bear transplantation, yet such was my precaution that they both lived, and that very year both bore some small blossoms and fruits. I survey the face of Nature:

the plains of Virginia, the swamps of Carolina. I see nothing there equal to this *lusus naturae*, to this pleasing assemblage. You must recollect the fragrance which the blossoms of our wild vine afford. There is none in the southern countries that equals it. They perpetually exhale the most odoriferous smell. I know two thorn-trees not very far from here which are so entirely covered with these vines that neither thorn-leaves nor branches can be discerned; and each makes a most beautiful arbour. Could they be transplanted or purchased from the owners, I'd be extravagant for once. How often have you and I stopped as we travelled along, to inhale these sweet draughts, as you called them, and to snuff up all the perfume they exhaled! Now to the idea of the young blossoming vine, pray add that of the blossoming sassafras which likewise sends forth the most delicate fragrance. Next conceive them united in their stems, the former entwined through all the limbs of the latter, and tell me whether our coarse wintry climate can yield a fairer symbol of southern vegetation, and whether I was not fortunate in procuring so beautifully combined a production. I never look at it with the same indifference as I do at my other trees. I have given it to my daughter Fanny. This gift still enhances the idea and trebles my pleasure.

Next year I intend to send you some of the sassafras' blossoms properly dried. I think their infusion far superior to the Chinese tea. Alas, had the Chinese exclusively possessed the sassafras, we would think it voluptuous to regale on it; but because it grows wild in our woods, we despise and overlook it, and, like fools, we poison our bodies, lessen our pockets in purchasing those far-fetched Chinese leaves. Yes, with us it is become an epidemic at which your company no doubt smiles. Everyone drinks tea, from the westernmost settlers in western Florida to the northernmost ones in Canada; and I am sure that is a pretty extensive market. The poorer the people the stronger is the tea they drink. Some have told me that it feeds them—a strange food indeed! But such is the infatuation of the age, such is the concatenation of events! It was necessary that our forefathers should discover and till this country in order that their prosperity might serve to enrich a parcel of London merchants who though but citizens in England, yet are nabobs in India; who though mighty fond of liberty at home for themselves and their children, yet do not choose that other people should enjoy these great benefits in their Indian dominions. The idea of merchants becoming sovereigns, lords, and tyrants . . . but a poor American farmer must not say all he thinks.

Our cattle are not subject to so many diseases as yours. I am not learned enough to characterize those to which ours are subject. What we call the Spanish staggers is the most dreadful; it is their plague. Some years ago, a Spanish vessel was cast away on the coast of Carolina. The hides it contained communicated an infection which had been hitherto unknown. Now and then it breaks out in those provinces, but seldom reaches us. I have heard it asserted that they have begun to inoculate their cattle for this disorder, with what success I know not. A few years ago, the proprietors of the great bank meadows of Philadelphia were wont to fetch lean cattle from there in order to fatten them on their rich bottoms, but the severe losses which the northern people upon that road met with in consequence of the infection made them rise in arms and oppose their passage. Trade has been since interrupted. This is long, but, I hope, not tedious.

IV. IMPLEMENTS

Your approbation of my last is an encouragement which I wanted much. Sometimes I despair of finding out anything that may be worth sending over so far. I am obliged to put all my little matters into a sieve; the coarsest and the most useless I throw by, the finest and what I think most valuable I gather together by means of that operation. Upon my word, [this] is almost literal. But alas, my sieve, the sieve of an American farmer, is but a poor criterion of what he should write or not write; but I have no other. Happily, I am so distant from you that I cannot hear your observations. I do not blush, therefore, as if I were present. By your last you demand of me a detail of our implements

of husbandry and of the buildings necessary to constitute a well-established farm. I shall begin with the most
useful.

You have often admired our two-horse waggons. They
are extremely well contrived, and executed with a great
deal of skill; and they answer with ease and dispatch
all the purposes of a farm. A well-built wagon, when
loaded, will turn in a very few feet more than its length,
which is sixteen feet including the length of the tongue.
We have room in what is called their bodies to carry
five barrels of flour. We commonly put in them a ton of
hay and often more. The load is built on shelvings fixed
on their sides. A ladder of 5/6 [*sic*] stands erect in the
front. [The hay is held in place] by means of a boom,
one end of which passes through the ladder, and the
other end [of which] is brought tight down and fastened to a staple in the hindmost axle-tree. Thus the
whole is secured. We can carry twenty-five green oak
rails, two thirds of a cord of wood, three thousand
pounds of dung. In short, there is no operation that
ought to be performed on a farm but what is easily
accomplished with one of these. We can lengthen them
as we please and bring home the body of a tree twenty
or thirty feet long. We commonly carry with them thirty
bushels of wheat; and at sixty pounds to the bushel, this
makes a weight of eighteen hundred pounds, with which
we can go forty miles a day with two horses.

On a Sunday, it becomes the family coach. We then
take off the common, plain sides and fix on it others,
which are handsomely painted. The after-part, on which
either our names or ciphers are delineated, hangs back
suspended by neat chains. If it rains, flat hoops made on
purpose are placed in mortises and a painted cloth is
spread and tied over the whole. Thus equipped, the
master of a family can carry six persons either to church
or to meetings. When the roads are good, we easily travel
seven miles an hour. In order to prevent too great shak-
ings, our seats are suspended on wooden springs, a simple but very useful mechanism. These inventions and
[this] neatness we owe to the original Dutch settlers. I
do not know where an American farmer can possibly
enjoy more dignity as a father or as a citizen than when
he thus carries with him his wife and family all clad in

good, neat homespun clothes, manufactured within his own house, and trots along with a neat pair of fat horses of his own raising. The single-horse Irish car, with wheels not above two feet high, must appear very inferior to our waggons, and yet several people from that country have told me that the whole internal trade of that kingdom is effected with no other carriages. Exclusive of these middle-sized wagons, there are many public ones, driven by six horses, which carry great burthens. In the southern provinces, where the roads are level, they use no other. We generally pay for ours from fifty to sixty dollars. The Dutch build them with timber which has been previously three years under water and then gradually seasoned.

Our next most useful implement is the plough. Of these we have various sorts, according to the soil which we have to till. First, [there is] the large two-handled plough with an English lock and coulter locked in its point. This is drawn by either four or six oxen and serves for rooty, stony land. This is drawn sometimes by two oxen and three horses. The one-handled plough is the most common in all level soils. It is drawn either by two or by three horses abreast; and when the ground is both level and swarded, we commonly put upon these a Dutch lock, by far the best for turning up, and the easiest draft for the horses. A team of four oxen is conducted by a lad. If it consists of two horses and two oxen, the boy rides one of the horses, and another lad drives the oxen. Our two- and three-horse teams are guided by the man who holds the plough. Lines are properly fixed to the horses' bridles on each side and passed around the plough-handle. The ploughman keeps them straight with his left hand while he guides his plough with his right. Three horses abreast are the most expeditious as well as the strongest team we know of for common land. We cross-plough with two horses, commonly one and a half acres a day. We have, besides, a smaller sort, called the corn-plough, with which we till through the furrows, and a harrow proportioned to the distance at which our corn is planted. Our heavy harrows are made sometimes triangular, sometimes square. This last we call the Dutch one. In the rough, stony parts of New England, they use no other team but oxen; and no people on earth understand the management of them better.

They shoe them with admirable skill and neatness. They are coupled with a yoke which plays loose on their necks. It is fastened with a bow which is easily taken off or put on. They draw by the top of their shoulders.

Besides a waggon, most farmers have an oxcart, which is fitter to carry heavy stones and large timbers. With these we convey logs to the sawmills by suspending them under the axle-tree of the cart. A good one, well shod with iron, costs twenty dollars.

The great objects which an American farmer ought to have in view are simplicity of labour and dispatch. The sun, and the great vegetation which it causes, hurry him along. The multiplicity of business which crowds all at the same time is astonishing. This is the principal reason why we can do nothing so neatly as you do in Europe. Could we fallow our wheat-land in the fall, this would greatly relieve us in the summer. We are, therefore, often obliged to keep double-teams in order to accelerate our operations. What I mean by simplicity is the art of doing a great deal with few hands. For that reason, I am extremely fond of ploughing with three horses abreast because it is a powerful team and requires but one person. I have heard many Europeans blame us for many of our operations. Alas, they censured us before they knew anything of our climate, of our seasons, and the scarcity and dearness of labourers. I think, considering our age, the great toils we have undergone, the roughness of some parts of this country, and our original poverty, that we have done the most in the least time of any people on earth. Call it industry or what you will.

The barn, with regard to its situation, size, convenience, and good finishing is an object, in the mind of a farmer, superior even to that of his dwelling. Many don't care much how they are lodged, provided that they have a good barn and barn-yard, and indeed it is the criterion by which I always judge of a farmer's prosperity. On this building he never begrudges his money. The middle-sized ones are commonly fifty by thirty feet; mine is sixty by thirty-five and cost two hundred and twenty dollars. They are either shingled, clapboarded, or boarded on the outside. Therein we lodge all our grain; and within, many operations are performed, such as thresh-

ing, and cleaning of flax and husking the corn, etc.
Therein the horses are stabled and the oxen stall-fed. In
the summer, the women resort to it in order to spin their
wool. The neatness of our boarded floors, the great
draught of air caused by the opened doors, which are
always made wide enough to permit a loaded wagon to
enter, and their breadth afford [the women] an opportunity of spinning long threads, of carding at their ease.
Many farmers have several barracks in their barn-yards
where they put their superfluous hay and straw. Nor
ought the subdivision of these yards to pass unnoticed.
They require great judgement, demand attention and expense. All classes of our cattle, our sheep, our calves
must be placed by themselves, and have in each division
convenient racks and bars in order to communicate easily from one to another.

Next to a good barn, a skilful farmer should have a
good hog-pen. The warmer and more convenient it is,
the easier will these animals fatten and the less grain
will they consume. We generally place a large yard before them, enclosed with posts and rails, where they cast
their dung. Dirty as they appear, yet they love a clean
habitation. You may remember the care with which mine
was erected. Some build them with stones and lime,
others with good framed work, others with dovetailed
logs. The door hangs like a bell, by which means it is
always shut. The floor must be good and tight, for on it
the corn is thrown. There are as many holes as there are
hogs, and on the outside, the great trough is fixed. [The
pens] must be well roofed because the inferior corn is
always placed under it, this being the first grain which is
given them.

Next to this is the hen-house. He that carelessly permits his fowls to roost in the adjacent trees will receive
very little good from them.

The truly economical farmer has always what we call
a shop, that is, a house big enough to contain a loom.
There, in the weaving season, our wives can either weave
themselves, or else inspect the management of the yarn.
There we keep also our seasoned timber, our tools. For
most of us are skilful enough to use them with some
dexterity in mending and making whatever is wanted on
the farm. Were we obliged to run to distant mechanics,

who are half farmers themselves, many days would elapse, and we should always be behind-hand with our work. Some people have their ovens out-of-doors. This I look upon as very inconvenient, but beginners must do as well as they can. They place them so because they dare not erect them adjoining their log-houses, for fear of the fire. Mine is in the chimney of my Negro kitchen. We commonly draw water out of our wells with long sweeps balanced and fixed with an iron bolt in a high forked tree. When the well is deep, it is drawn by means of a pulley and two buckets.

Corn-cribs are indispensable because this grain is pre-served there longer than anywhere else. You well re-member their peculiar structure. Some people are, and all should be, furnished with electrical rods. The best way to place them, in order to save expense, is on a high cedar mast situated between the house and the barn. Its power will attract the lightning sufficiently to save both. Mine is so. I once saw its happy effects and blessed the inventor. My barn was then completely full. I valued it at about seven hundred pounds. What should I have done, had not the good Benjamin Franklin thought of this astonishing invention? Our Negro kitchens are al-ways built adjacent to our dwelling-houses, with a door of communication into the room where we eat in order that we may inspect whatever passes there; and indeed it is the room which is often the most useful, for all housework is done in it.

Our houses are very different from one another. Each builds them agreeable to his taste and abilities. The com-mon length is about forty-five in front, [having] a pas-sage with a room on each side and two smaller ones back and a piazza in front. They are either shingled or boarded and commonly painted.

We are very deficient in gardens, for we have neither taste nor time; and, besides, the labour is too dear. Com-pare for one minute the additional work to which the American farmer must submit over and above what peo-ple of the same class must do in England, admitting that everything else is equal. The very article of fire-wood is an immense addition, although the wood costs noth-ing. One year with another I burn seventy loads, this is, pretty nearly so many cords. Judge of the time and trouble it requires to fell it in the woods, to haul it home either in waggons or sleighs, besides recutting it at the wood-pile fit for the length of each chimney.

Every farmer is obliged to make his own ropes. We must all spin our yarn with simple wheels made on purpose, and lay them out-of-doors by means of simple contrivances. We must likewise weave the collars our horses draw with in little frames made on purpose, though we have leather collars for our holidays. I had almost forgot to mention our smoke-houses; without them we could not live. Each family smokes fully one half their meat, fish, eels; in short, everything we intend to preserve. For, besides the advantage of preservation, it greatly adds to the flavour of our food; it saves it, besides, from the flies. Virginia is the country where they eat the greatest quantity of smoked meat as well as of all other kinds. There they raise their hogs with more facility than we do.

We have another convenience to preserve our roots and vegetables in the winter, which we commonly call a Dutch cellar. It is built at the foot of a rising ground which is dug through, about eighteen feet long and six feet high. It is walled up about seven feet from the ground, then strongly roofed and covered with sods. The door always faces the south. There it never freezes, being under the ground. In these places we keep our apples, our turnips, cabbages, potatoes, and pumpkins. The cellars which are under the houses are appropriated for cider, milk, and butter; meat and various necessaries.

The next building is the bee-house. Some have them elegant; others carelessly leave these insects under the most humble roofs. But as most farmers are not far distant from sawmills where they can always be supplied with boards and scantlings, I think it unpardonable to leave such industrious little beings so poorly housed as some are in this country. Gratitude alone ought to lead them to a better care of those who are at work for them. But Man is a selfish being.

There are but few people who are at any considerable distance from grist-mills; and that is a very great advantage considering the prodigious quantity of flour which we and our cattle consume annually, for we seldom give them any grain but what is previously ground.

I know a miller who has not the command of a very large district who yearly receives fourteen hundred bushels of all kinds of grain, yet his toll is but the twelfth part. Each provident farmer must have, besides all these things, a fanning-mill, by means of which he cleans his grain with very little trouble and even divides the light from the heavy. I have four sets of riddles to mine, each fitted for different sorts of grains. They commonly cost twenty dollars. This is a useful piece of furniture in a barn. He that has them not, often loses a great deal of time for want of wind, or else must submit to the labour of fanning. They are most indispensably useful to a northern farmer in order to enjoy the benefit of conveying his grain on the snow to whatever market he may choose. For when the snow falls, it is necessary to take the opportunity it offers, lest a thaw might come.

The vehicles fit for that season are of two kinds very similar to one another. They are in some respects the same: the first is for the pleasure of the family, the other for heavy labour; the one called sleighs, the other sleds. On these latter I have often carried forty bushels of wheat or the biggest log that can be hauled out of the woods, three feet wide by eighteen long. When the snow is good, these sleds cannot be too heavily loaded. It makes no difference in the draught of the horses because the load slides on large iron bars fastened under the runners. The pleasure-sleigh is accommodated with a box, handsomely painted, and seats which can easily carry six persons as well as a waggon. 'Tis surprising with what ease and volocity we transport ourselves to a great distance. I have often gone at the rate of twelve miles an hour. For winter with us is the season of festivity. When we are going to any considerable distance, we provide ourselves with a globe of pewter which holds two gallons. This is filled with hot, gingered cider and placed at the bottom of the sleigh. It keeps our feet warm, and by now and then swallowing a mouthful, we keep the insides warm also.

Our markets in the winter generally are either some stores built on the edges of great rivers, whence the grain is conveyed in the spring to the capital, or else some great bolting-mills where the proprietor purchases it. In the first place, we must take our chance for the market of the

world; in the second, that chance is fixed by a certain
price then received except we agree to take the current
price of such a month. The advantage of the snow simpli-
fies many other operations. When it does not come, we
severely feel it; the transportation of our grain takes up a
great deal of our time in the spring which should be
employed in ploughing.

Notwithstanding the experience of so many years, yet
it is very extraordinary that almost every winter there are
people drowned in crossing our rivers, either on foot or in
sleighs. Last winter, it was very near being my fate; had
it not been for the assistance of my brother-in-law, I
should have at least lost my two horses. We were going to
——'s, who lives over the river of ——, when in the
middle of it [the horses] broke in and sank to their
heads. Luckily, my sleigh was water-tight, and this gave us
an opportunity of jumping off; and fortunately the ice was
sufficiently strong to bear us within a few feet of the
hole. While I was cutting away the harness, Mr. ——
passed a rope with a slip-noose around the neck of one
of the horses. We pulled as hard as we could and
strangled him. He swelled and immediately rose on the
surface of the water. We then easily slipped him up on
to the ice, and, cutting the ropes, in a few minutes he
came to and got up. The second was saved in the same
manner. As my sleigh was water-tight, it still swam. We
easily hauled it onto the ice, which was perfectly sound,
and, having repaired the mischief, returned back to the
shores as quickly as possible. This place had been an air-
hole lately frozen over. These holes, however dangerous
they may appear, are necessary, for were it not for them,
the ice never would be good, at least in running waters.
The power of the frost compresses the air so much that
it must have a vent somewhere, and by issuing in great
quantities at some particular spots, it often keeps the
water from freezing all winter. When travelling on the
ice, one may go to the very edges; there is no kind of
danger. These openings are more or less extensive.

Nor are the joys and pleasures of the season confined
to the whites alone, as our blacks divide with us the toils
of our farms; they partake also of the mirth and good
cheer of the season. They have their own meetings and
are often indulged with their masters' sleighs and horses.

You may see them at particular places as happy and merry as if they were free-men and freeholders. The sight of their happiness always increases mine, provided it does not degenerate into licentiousness; [and this] is sometimes the case, though we have laws enough to prevent it. But our magistrates, though mostly old, yet are very young in their business. It will take at least one hundred years before our magistracy becomes properly enlightened. Where should the man who daily follows his plough find that spontaneous knowledge which is requisite? Their commissions do not bring along with them the necessary lights and information. These are miracles left to another set of men who by the simple power of the touch receive all they want.

It is in this season particularly that the hospitality of the Americans is most conspicuous. The severity of the climate requires that all our doors should be opened to the frozen traveller, and indeed we shut them not, either by night or by day at any time of the year. The traveller when cold has a right to stop and warm himself at the first house he sees. He freely goes to the fire, which is kept a-burning all night. There he forgets the keenness of the cold; he smokes his pipe; drinks of the cider which is often left on the hearth; and departs in peace. We always sleep in these rooms; at least I do, and have often seen mine full when I was in my bed. On waking I have sometimes spoken to them; at other times it was a silent meeting. The reasons which force these people to travel in these dreadful nights is that they may be able to return home the same day. They are farmers carrying their produce to the market, and their great distance from it obliges them to set out sometimes at twelve o'clock. Far from being uneasy at seeing my house thus filled while my wife and I are abed, I think it, on the contrary, a great compliment when I consider that by thus stopping they convince me that they have thought my house and my fire better than that of my neighbours.

This is, sir, an imperfect sketch of this season, filled with labours as well as the others, but more tempered with pleasures. We then consume the greatest part of what we have earned in the summer, nor can we repine at it. How much happier are we than many other settlers who have no market and can't realize anything on what they raise. Though they might be richer than we are, or living on the best soils, yet they are infinitely poorer; they have not the spirit to enjoy as we have, so that, everything considered, it is all equal. The further from market, generally, the better the land; but it costs a great deal to come to that market. We raise much less; but, then, it costs us but little to convert our produce into money.

I was once at Pa—an, where several families dwelt on the most fruitful soil I have ever seen in my life. The warmest imagination can't conceive anything equal to it. These people raised what they pleased: oats, peas, wheat, corn, with two days' labour in the week. At their doors they had a fair river, on their backs high mountains full of game. Yet with all these advantages, placed as they were on these shores of Eden, they lived as poor as the poorest wretches of Europe who have nothing. Their houses were miserable hovels. Their stalks of grain rotted in their fields. They were almost starved, not for want of victuals but of spirit and activity to cook them. They were almost naked.

This may appear to you a strange problem. This is representing to you two extremes which you cannot reconcile, yet this relation is founded on fact and reason. This people had not nor could they have, situated as they were, any place where they might convey their produce. They could neither transport, sell, nor exchange anything they had, except cattle, so singularly were they placed. This annihilated all the riches of their grounds; rendered all their labours abortive; rendered them careless, slothful, and inactive. This constituted their poverty, though in the midst of the greatest plenty. They could not build for want of nails. They could not clothe themselves for want of materials, which they might easily have procured with their wheat. They were inferior to the Indians. Had they had a market, the scene would have been greatly changed. Neatness, convenience, decency of appearance would have soon banished that singular poverty under which they groaned. I stayed five days with them and could not rejoice enough to think that my farm was so much more advantageously situated. Happily for this country we have but few spots among the many which have been discovered, [from which] the people may

[not] convey what they raise to some markets. But, you'll say, what could induce people to settle on such grounds? The extreme fertility of the soil, necessity, and poverty? This it is, sir, which drives people over the hills and far away.

CHAPTER V

LIBERTY OF WORSHIP

It is astonishing to think how pernicious to the peace of mankind that old maxim has been, that a unity in religious opinions was necessary to establish the unity of law and government, as if law and government could possibly extend to opinions. Yet this has been one of the best established and most respectable maxims of the rulers of the world for many ages, from whence almost all its calamities have proceeded. It is not very long since it has been demonstratively proved that variety, nay, a discord, of religious opinions is the true principle on which the harmony of society is established. As in a concert the inharmonious sounds of some instrument tend to promote the accord of the whole, so in society the perfect freedom of mode of worship preserves that peace, that tranquillity which are the triumphs of some countries.

This above all now in the world presents us with the most extravagant latitude of this kind, and yet no country is so happy in every possible respect. It is true that we everywhere seem to be born for error and illusions. But as truth is so difficult to perceive, and appearance may be modified in so many different ways, what matters it which of these inoffensive ways a citizen follows, provided that he loves his country and is a good

subject? How do we know whether we have faculties fit
to perceive the truth in its unity and in the simplicity of
its precepts? In some countries the people think that it
resides in symbols, hieroglyphics, splendid ornaments.
There pomp chiefly attracts their attention; there ceremonies create respect and promote an artificial venera-
tion. Without being at any pains to investigate anything,
without being permitted to ascend to principles, they
may overlook the essence in the variety of parts, the true
object in the shades and ornaments which encompass it.
There the love of the marvellous and of the extraordinary absorbs every other inquiry; they are satisfied. Here,
on the contrary, every religious institution is simpler,
entirely divested of any exterior pomp; every one reasons
for himself and follows the glimmering of that light which
his imagination furnishes him with. Where is the harm?
Every one is equally happy, nay, infinitely more. That
obstinacy proceeding from compulsion ceases as soon as
that compulsion ceases; and from turbulent sectaries in
Europe they become here peaceable citizens.

'Tis incredible to what a pitch this indulgence is carried; and 'tis equally surprising how beneficial it has
proved—a happy system of policy, the only one
adapted to replenish an empty continent as well as to
tranquillize the old one. Hence these new modes of government, which have greatly relieved mankind; and this
is the light which has rendered the era of the Reformation so remarkable. Like all other human schemes, it was
at first rude, gross, and unpolished. The movements of
its new parts caused a degree of friction which time has
since worn away. Enthusiasm, the child of that era, was
better adapted to navigation and discoveries than the old
superstition. Here it led the first settlers and inspired
them with that courage and constancy which their first
labours required. And if since it has not covered the
earth with sumptuous temples, large monasteries, it has
replenished it with infinite habitations, a numerous people.
It has opened for Man a field of industry which the world
wanted much; and now that the great difficulties are removed, that great principle of action is not so much
wanted, 'tis greatly dimished, and in some parts 'tis no
more.

It has been succeeded by that spirit of toleration, by

that liberal principle which generously allows to others what each wants for himself: a perfect freedom of thought, a latitude of opinion perfectly harmless as to government, which becomes a source of happiness to each individual, to each family, to each district. No other motive, no other system could possibly have replenished the shores of this continent with so many people, and in so short a time. 'Tis true, very opposite motives have led other people to other discoveries. But observe the progress, mark the consequences. They have pulled down, they have destroyed. But have they flourished like these, have they replenished that immense vacuum they caused? No, they barbarously converted fruitful countries into deserts, and a great part of those deserts exhibit to view nothing but the ruins made by the discoverers.

Here not only every community, but every individual worships God as he thinks it most agreeable to Him. Each individual is even allowed, not by virtue of any laws, but by the liberal spirit of the government, to differ from and controvert any of the religious opinions which are here received. This is an amazing indulgence, which, being granted to all, does not in the least disturb the society, but rather serves to unite it even in the most minute of its subdivisions. This is a problem which a great many people in Europe could not comprehend, prejudiced as they are by the ancient manners and customs of the society in which they live.

For instance, a man born of Baptist parents will live and profess the tenets of this sect without ever studying either their propriety or impropriety, and without aiming at any superior refinement. He may for a number of years read and ponder over his Bible and find the precepts of his sects perfectly agreeable to those particular passages on which they are founded when a fit of sickness, perhaps a gloomy mood, a fit of idleness, a sudden volition of the mind will lead him to the study of some particular passages, intended perhaps to confute some particular doctrines advanced by some ministers whom he had accidentally heard. From this new study, he fancies that he has discovered some lights to which his dimmed eyes had hitherto been insensible. This fills him with an idea of perfection to which he immediately wants to direct his steps. Unawed by the decrees of any pontiffs, by inquisitorial timocracy, he boldly follows the new path which he has just found. His conscience, uniting often with his mind, renders the resolution sacred; he cannot deviate; he must begin the new career. Proud of the discovery, he will perhaps promulgate it abroad; he will explain this or that text as he has lately conceived its meaning to be.

He reproaches himself for having so long remained in ignorance, and from that day commences a sort of controversy. But as controversy always implies zeal and ardour, he will feel that zeal and ardour; and the same person who before had been but a passive Christian, following in simplicity and well-meant honesty the precepts he has received in his education, now suddenly enlightened, is surprised at the wonderful change which he, perhaps for want of knowing any other cause, attributes to the particular influence of heaven. This is enough to sanctify his new doctrine and to justify the steps he takes to promulgate it among his neighbours. They are no politicians; a perfect peace prevails throughout their country. What more innocent subject of conversation can they have? The least opposition—and you may be sure he will meet with abundance—proclaims him a separatist, and perhaps a preacher, if he has abilities enough to persuade others to think as he does. Be not afraid of tumult, sedition, and broils; this is only a simple, harmless schism which will rather amuse than convulse society. Here opens that ancient field once so pregnant with the most poisonous weeds, but now in this tolerating age producing only harmless ones. Here is room for the expansion of a variety of passions mixing themselves with this new religious zeal, but these passions have no bad influence. The great and immense room in which they expand themselves prevents them from producing those evil consequences which opposition and contracted limits formerly occasioned. This is the only philosophical remedy that could possibly have been found to stop that rancour, that malevolence which formerly attended this sort of new system, everyone being indulged with the liberty of systematizing, modifying, and promulgating his opinions. These sorts of innovations have lost all merit, merit which consisted principally in the pleasure of opposition, and was swelled by contradiction.

I remember an instance of this kind which happened not long since in the county of ——, in the person of a friend. He had been bred a Presbyterian. For many years he followed bona fide the precepts of this sect and thought, like all the rest of the congregation, that their mode of worship was the purest and the most acceptable to God. Thus he lived on to the age of forty-seven, when he chanced to have a grandson born. His daughter-in-law made some objections to his being baptized. Not that her scruples were founded on any professional abhorrence to this ceremony; but her parents having been Baptists, she derived from them some recollection that they had not undergone that ceremony until the age of adult. She recollected, likewise, that she had never been carried to the baptismal font, nor ever been immersed. She was, besides, secretly flattered with the pleasure of proposing a novelty to a family which was Presbyterian. She therefore pretended scruples of conscience.

The husband, young, inexperienced, and tender, laid before his father these difficulties and affectionately mentioned his wife's religious doubts. The well-meaning man struggled against this innovation, which he thought unchristian, and made use of all the arguments generally mustered in support of infant baptism. She replied, and recollecting some of the ancient rudiments of her education, sternly opposed from Scripture this trifling, useless ceremony which can confer benefit only on those who receive it when of a lawful age and, therefore, capable of knowing the importance of the covenant into which they were entering. Paternal affection overcame religious obstinacy; the old man consented and returned home. Several of the passages his daughter-in-law had quoted returned to his mind; he resolved to study the matter with more carefulness and attention. An inward feeling seems to arise in his breast; imperceptible doubts stagger the validity of his ancient principles. He reads his Bible with redoubled attention; he finds authorities against infant baptism which he had hitherto overlooked; he suddenly awakes to a new set of principles with regard to this religious ceremony; he quits the congregation to which he had hitherto belonged and attaches himself to that of the Baptists, not without entering into many controversies with several of his friends and fellow-Presbyterians.

He thinks that he overcame them, and this essay gives him a taste for controversy, a strange taste for a man who hitherto had been acquainted with nothing but the cultivation of his farm. But he does not stop there; he pursues his new studies with unremitted attention. He reads the Bible, now no longer with that spirit of general confidence he was wont. He finds himself suddenly initiated into a vast field, full of intricate scenes. New doubts, new perplexities arise, which he often communicated to me. The new society in which he had enrolled himself was proud of its conquests. He conforms to all its rules and at last receives the benefits of its immersion in a very cold season of the year, on which he had particularly fixed to enhance his merit. Thus he lived on for two years, a zealous and warm proselyte and the same good man he was before. All the difference I observed in him was that on a Sunday, instead of going east to his former place of worship, he travelled west to the new meeting; and surely no change of religious sentiments could be attended with more trifling circumstances.

But behold the restless state of the human mind and the instability of what we vainly call its principles. In the course of his new studies, he discovers contradictions and absurdities among his new brethren. He remonstrated and argued often on these topics with the elders of the congregation. He entered so deeply into this new controversy that he began to neglect his rural business. The pleasure arising from finding out new lights and communicating them to others is often an irresistible one. He endeavoured to divide the new flock to which he had lately attached himself. The dispute grew warmer, and the opponents, according to custom, more obstinate.

One day he invited the elders and deacons of this society to dine with him, and he pressed me to be of the party. He secretly wanted me as favourable evidence in his behalf; but, alas, I was far from wishing to become a witness in a cause in which I understood nothing. I attended, firmly persuaded to remain in perfect silence, and simply to hear this religious altercation. The fate of this controversy, notwithstanding his good cheer, terminated, as most of this kind always do, in recrimination. Each party always retires as fully convinced of the rectitude of its principles, and often more so than before. The part I was obliged to act was for a while both difficult and disagreeable: each party, full of the irrefragability of its arguments, glowing with conscious rectitude, seemed to address me with peculiar complacency and to demand my approbation. But, unwilling to displease, and indeed incapable of passing a definite sentence, I tried to officiate as a mediator. I reminded them of the nature of the dispute, which, different from those founded on worldly concerns, required a great degree of calmness and serious attention. "You seek to enlighten yourselves. Each of you, good men alike, is come here with a lanthorn in your hands in order to compare your lights. This should be done with that caution and mildness which the nature of the dispute, your age, and your candour require. Great vehemence, improper agitation will only serve either to hide or to extinguish them. Consider me, if you please, as a spectator who came here more from the respect I have for you all than in consequence of any knowledge I have of the different points of doctrine which you are examining."

They listened not to what I said; their zeal got the better even of their common civility; they parted, but no longer as brethren; my utmost efforts were useless. I freely, but in vain, showed them the vanity of all human disputes; attempted to lay before them the necessity of following that standard of rectitude which may be felt and perceived by each individual exclusive of all other forms of tenets. Then I attempted to reunite them, at least in the bonds of their ancient friendship, by means of that communion often practised, by drinking out of the same bowl, by smoking together, that the commixture and evaporation of smokes might become an emblem of the banishing of all rancour and malice. Nothing availed; the new convert separated himself from the new congregation and set up for himself, though there was not any other individual in the country that professed the same sentiments.

Next day he went forth in quest of proselytes. The novelty of his doctrine pleased many who, perhaps indifferent to any particular modes of religion, from remoteness of settlement or from neglect, were glad to have a person coming to their houses in order to rouse them out of that pristine passiveness in which they had so long lived. Encouraged by this new essay, he preached whenever he could find people that would listen to him. He was well received in many settlements which were far removed from any public place of worship. This new revolution in his new religion necessarily introduced a new one in his temporal affairs. He neglected the care of his farm. His Negroes, overlooking their duty, followed their master's example; the labours of the field were no longer prosecuted with the same care and industry. The rest of the family bemoaned in secret the losses which ensued; the master thought them but insignificant trifles when compared to the more spiritual advantages which he was every day gaining.

The first successes of this self-ordained priest were at first confined to single families. He happened to hear of a new settlement where the people, poor and isolated, had remained hitherto without the benefit of any public worship; they were not able to build any meeting [-house] and, much less, to pay the salary of a minister. All, as is customary, practised in their own houses whatever religious duties they had been taught in the countries from whence they had emigrated; many practised none and lived in that indifference which is so common here. Glad to have some part of the Gospel expounded to them, they received the first tidings of his offers with pleasure and invited him to come among them every Sabbath. He received it with peculiar complacency and attended them most faithfully. Never was there any minister so full of zeal and so ambitious to instruct his flock; and in the sequestered situation [in which] they were placed, they could not receive a greater blessing. They soon became the most faithful disciples; and instead of spending their Sundays at home in gloomy silence or unprofitable, untutored meditation, they had the pleasure of meeting together. They were constrained to clean themselves; the young people had an opportunity of seeing each other; and the institution of Sundays, considered in this temporary light only, is of the utmost consequence.

The relations he gave of his successes were astonishing; he attributed them to the peculiar interposition of God's divine providence. The profound ignorance of his new flock made them admire this new apostle, and they thought that he was superior to anything they ever remembered to have heard. All he told them was conceived in oriental expressions and clothed in vehement language. Soon afterwards, he came to pay me a visit. He glowed with conscious approbation; he related to me all his successes throughout their progressive increase. "How providentially does everything happen in this world," did he say; "how wonderfully linked are all the actions of men! What we vulgarly call chance has insensibly led me to the pitch of happiness I enjoy. For, can a man enjoy a greater share than in opening the eyes of benighted people, in carrying the torch of the Gospel in the gloom of the wilderness? What have I been doing these many years, uselessly employed in the servile labour of the field, an unprofitable occupation compared to that to which I now readily dedicate my time and all my abilities? I have already sown a plentiful crop of good seed; my care and vigilance shall not be wanting to bring it to maturity."

"Though these people are so far removed from any established congregation, don't you imagine that the minister of —— yet looks on them as a distant part of his flock, which, to be sure, he has hitherto most shamefully overlooked because they can pay no part of his salary? Like all other priests, he loves to lord it over. The intrusion of a lay-minister will kindle his clerical wrath; he will counteract all your good works as soon as he is informed of your proceedings."

"What if he does? I can confute all his arguments; nay, I can puzzle him in many texts of the Scripture. I fear him not, and by God's grace I will persevere."

"I am afraid of no mischief, but only that he will try to cover you with ridicule. You do not know perhaps as well as I do the effect of black clothes and sacerdotal appearance; and though I am sure he knows as little as anybody, yet I am afraid that the very name of a minister will give him such ascendancy as will rob you of all your young successes."

"I fear him not. Don't you remember the sermon he preached the other day on ——. It was enough to ruin the fame of any minister. Ploughman as I am, I really blushed at it. It was as incoherent, senseless jargon as ever I had heard before. The singularity of the text more than any useful doctrine he could adduce from it was the reason for his expounding on it. I am sure he is as strange a genius as ever ascended the pulpit; he is bold, arrogant. He is sure of his salary, and it is what makes him so different a man; when he depended on the voluntary contributions of the people, he was meek and lowly."

"I never liked him, for my part. 'Tis very true I join with you in thinking that the people have been deceived in their choice. I can see in him two species of men. When in the pulpit, he attempts all the enthusiasm, the rapturous flight of the passionate devotee. He is obscure, hates to touch on morality, always deep in obscure passages. When descended from it, how different! He seems to leave on the cushion those apparent virtues with the few ornaments of that day; none more imperious, more disdainful."

" 'Tis all very true; I know it. An uncle of mine, a man of tender conscience and wanting an explanation of a certain text, went the other day to him for consultation and advice. How did he rebuke him! I am shocked when I think of it: 'Get thee gone, man of ignorance; take care of thy wife and children; mind thy plough and thy scythe.' Why, then," I said, "did the congregation fix his salary? Why did they not leave him like all the rest of his brethren to the good will of the flock? It was done contrary to my advice, I am sure. You see now what the consequence is; old rules should never be altered. The people have a propensity to be always the dupes and the victims of few; the people work and don't think much, but this will teach them better. I will prosecute my plan, however, and by God's grace I am in hopes to bring the people of —— to my way of thinking, which I am sure is the best. What business have they with ordained ministers and salaries and parsonages, etc.?"

For upwards of three years his successes were equal to his utmost wish. The minister of the county did not interfere. The people were poor. They contented themselves with throwing out now and then some few sarcasms, which had no effect. Our apostle was rather proud to suffer some few mortifications for the love of God. His zeal was unabated. He was on the eve of being crowned with the summit of his hopes, that is, of having a place of worship built for him, when a Baptist minister, trav-

elling like many others to review and vivify the scattered
parts of true believers throughout the different colonies,
happened to be taken sick in the vicinage. On inquiring
of the people concerning their religious state, their situation, etc., he was greatly astonished to hear that they
were under the guidance of Mr. ——. The arrogance and
presumption of the attempt shocked him greatly. A self-
ordination, an intrusion in God's service, and, above all,
a mutilated system of obscure doctrines assuming the
title of Reformed Baptist seemed to offer an insult to the
church he belonged to, which he could not bear. Immediately on his recovery, he went to the spot, viewed
with indignation the materials of that meeting [-house]
which was intended to receive the erroneous doctrines of
a man who had no right to promulgate them.

In a little time, he eclipsed by his eloquence the fame
of Mr. —— and soon buried in oblivion the happy beginnings of our new apostle. He made [the people] sign
a paper by which they agreed to receive a lawful Baptist
minister to finish the meeting [-house] they had begun,
whereby they would be made to forget the erroneous
doctrines they had been taught, and receive these pure
ones truly derived from the purity of the Gospel. In short,
he so thoroughly obliterated all my neighbour's good
works that no traces were left of them. He even caused
[the people] to be guilty of ingratitude in persuading
them to despise the many steps and fatigues Mr. ——
had taken for their sake. So powerful is the ascendancy
of the clergy, even in a country where they have so little,
and where by the genius of the people and the locality
of settlements, it is more likely to diminish than to increase. They were so thoroughly reformed that Mr. ——
found himself without a hearer, without a disciple.

I thought this catastrophe a very fortunate one, as it
might perhaps have a tendency to disgust him from these
religious toils and persuade him to stay at home. In the
first rancour inspired by this disappointment, he exclaimed against all ministers as wolves in sheep's clothing, against their inutility, and the poor trifling foundation on which their order was established. He showed
that our Saviour had never ordained any. In short, he
revenged himself, as he thought, very amply for his great
mortification. Thus finished his successes abroad. Fortune

cast him off from her wheel and left him not the least pretension to begin any new attempts. He amply consoled himself by cherishing the idea that he was still in the right. He voluntarily—nay, cheerfully—excluded himself from all religious societies and boasted that he was member of a church which was composed of no one but himself. This extraordinary privilege served him as a rich supplement for all his disappointed views. Thus, shepherd and flock, he still persists in maintaining that they are all wrong but himself.

I observed with pleasure that he seemed entirely to forget his former adventure. He returned to his rural occupations with as much activity as ever. His zeal seemed to cool apace, and that cacoëthes of preaching was almost extinguished, though he loved still to talk of his favourite doctrine, when, all of a sudden, he undertook to convert his family. For that purpose, he began by degrees to expound to them the meaning of several texts, and regularly preached to them every Thursday, not forgetting to invite as many of his neighbours as he thought had any kind of religious awakenings. In his own house his paternal authority and influence were sure of procuring him hearers if not proselytes; and those that came behaved with a degree of attention which proceeded from respect, but which he took to be the consequence of persuasion. His wife was an Episcopalian, strongly attached to her worship. There was a danger lest this new schism should disturb the peace of the family; but as she possessed a great degree of prudence, she said little and condescended to listen to his long discourses with a patience proceeding from the love of peace. Sometimes I attended these religious meetings; but as I am no worshipper of strange gods, and perfectly satisfied with that form to which I have been bred, this new doctrine had no kind of effect on me. The whole of this new system appeared to be composed of many uninteresting parts enveloped in obscurity of diction, frivolousness of matter. You could perceive an eager desire of persuasion, but that is not always sufficient to convey to the heart those powers which can eradicate ancient prejudices, preconceived opinions. The keenest pencil is not adequate to such vague descriptions of an uninteresting subject; and of all subjects, you are sensible that this must be most disgustingly threadbare. I felt myself perfectly indifferent and, considering the value I set on my time, often wished I had invented some excuse to have absented myself.

From the little success which attended his new apostolic endeavours among those over whom he had so much authority, there arose a surprising alteration in his mind. He seemed to lose that tenderness and affability for which he was before so conspicuous; he became gloomy, agitated at night. These symptoms were more alarming to his family than all his new religious systems. I often tried to reason him out of this strange vertigo; it was all in vain. At last I thought that vanity was mixed with and had strongly co-operated in this perversion of his mind.

"What good, pray, do you imagine there can possibly arise in the mind of those who hear you, from these inductions, from these learned interquotations which you have lavished on them with so much profusion? If you delight in preaching, why don't you explain to them some useful moral subject respecting the common duties of life? These elucidations of subjects which it imports everybody to know would strike and enlighten the tender minds of your children with much more efficacy and success. This would be clearing the path which they are to follow, pointing out the probable difficulties which they are to meet in their intercourse with the world. It is the fruit of the tree you should show them, that important fruit, the possession of which is far superior to any other knowledge. These learned discussions of yours have not this tendency; it is the fruit you should hold forth for the inspection of your hearers. What have we ploughmen to do with the occult property of the timber, with the nature of the caterpillars which feed on its leaves? These refinements are very ill-suited to the taste as well as to the understanding of the generality of mankind. When you instruct your Negroes and hired men, do you, pray, waste your time in making dissertations on vegetations and all other occult ways and means by which Nature brings forth the fruits of the earth? No, you content yourself with showing them the theoretical, the useful, the practical, the most advantageous methods of ploughing, harrowing, sowing, dunging, etc. All your lectures on the former philosophical subject would bring you no crop. No harvest would redden in your fields were you in company with your servants to employ your time in these vain and frivolous researches.

"The principal Christian duties are sublime though simple, useful, and absolutely necessary. They are unconnected with any forms; they belong equally to all sects. He that was baptized when young is bound by the same rules of justice, mercy, uprightness as he who was plunged at the age of twenty; you should, therefore, teach and enforce them to your hearers. These are the true points, the essential principles on which the purity, the tranquillity of our lives, and even of society, absolutely depend. A man has no need to be learned, to be religiously wise; the code of these laws is simple and fitted for the meanest understanding, adapted to the lowest conception. From the enforcement of these moral duties, which are the true links of society, a certain, sure, and profitable good will arise; from the former, nothing but cavils, contentions, separations, which, though they disturb not the society we live in, yet do not tend to its improvement as well as to its embellishment so essentially as you might perhaps imagine. Life is spent while we argue; and we remember at last, but sometimes too late, that though we have talked much and read much, yet we have forgotten to act. We are born to labour and not to study. Nature made the soil on which we are and which we till; and to induce us to do this, she surrounded us with wants; but Nature has formed no books. Country farmers, as we are, should, therefore, shun them as the disturbers more than the enlighteners of our minds. Let us peaceably, meekly discharge towards each other those duties which are taught us in the decalogue. Let us with diligence improve this new soil we inhabit; let us, to the best of our power, instruct our children to follow the same simple path; let us teach them by example that sobriety and industry without which they cannot flourish; let us provide for them as our circumstances will permit. This is all we have to do in this world to whatever meeting we may belong; these are the duties of all, and which all must invariably follow if we could wish to be good subjects and good Christians.

"I am, you know, neither preacher nor teacher, yet I am sensible that it requires but very slender abilities to compose sermons to please the ear and to amuse the imagination. But what good would they cause? Some thousands are delivered every year in this province, yet do we see that mankind grows more sober, less contentious? No, because they were intended to promulgate curious but vain theological points which are absolutely unnecessary; because most of our sects think that discourses altogether moral are not popular. Strange perversion! The pulpit of each meeting should be the censor of the neighbourhood and not the promulgator of high controversial lights of which mankind knows nothing, and fit only to amuse idle people in their leisure hours. This is the reason, let me tell you, why so great a part of our inhabitants remain untaught, unacquainted with the primary duties of life. The ministers, instead of clearing up, widening the ancient, useful path pointed out in our Bible, lead their flocks through new and unexplored ways where they are often bewildered and lost; vain theory calculated often to feed the vanity of the teacher more than to instruct the hearers. They should be urged to the practice of moral and, therefore, useful actions. This is all that the Law and the Prophets can teach or require."

"Well, sir, as proof of what you have advanced as a specimen of your ideas, as a sketch of the method you'd pursue were you in the ministry, I should be very glad [if] you'd compose a sermon and let it be delivered to the same company which comes to my house. I am still willing to learn and to improve, though I shall not attempt at present to refute you in many reprehensible points you have advanced. All I have to say to Man in my vindication is that I have no sinister views; I mean well. If Man blames me, God, the searcher of hearts, will, I am sure, forgive me."

I may perhaps surprise you when I tell you that I undertook the task he proposed to me. I saw no impropriety in it, and I flattered myself that the mortification which his vanity might inwardly feel would have a greater effect and a stronger tendency to silence him than all the arguments I could possibly make use of. Not that I thought myself master of greater abilities; but

I depended on the subject I intended to treat, which, being adapted to the comprehension of all, would necessarily become more entertaining and useful.

Agreeable to my promise, I sketched out a few thoughts on that beautiful passage of the Lord's Prayer: "and forgive us our trespasses, etc." I employed neither study nor learning, yet it had the desired effect. Either my performance appeared to him much superior to his own or else the keen and irresistible puncture of truth struck him so deep that he gradually returned to the practice of his former social duties. He preached less often; his former gloom disappeared; he reassumed his former cheerfulness; and although he never would reunite himself to any sect of Christians, he entirely left off teaching and seeking for proselytes. He reacquired the same tranquillity of mind for which he had been so conspicuous. Like a storm which for a while obscures the air and disturbs the atmosphere, when the clouds vanish, the sun shines forth with its wonted lustre.

CHAPTER VI

THE ENGLISH AND THE FRENCH BEFORE THE REVOLUTION

Have you never observed what a happy people these latter [the Canadians] were before their conquest? Notwithstanding the boast of newspapers, no society of men could exhibit greater simplicity, more honesty, happier manners, less litigiousness; nowhere could you perceive more peace and tranquillity. Before the last war, the character of the Canadians was altogether original and singular: they were equally removed from the brutality of a savage and the useless improvements of more polished societies; they were as different from the natives as from their own countrymen; they were extremely temperate, happily ignorant; they possessed a peculiar degree of boldness, activity, and courage which have led them to the remotest parts of the continent. England has found them the best of subjects. If the influence of religion was more visible here than in any other of the English colonies, its influence was salutary; it had here an effect which one would wish to see everywhere else. For what else do we expect to gain by the precepts of religion but less ferocious manners and a more upright conduct? Badly governed as they were, 'tis surprising to observe how prosperous and happy they were. They were in a state of perfect subordination; their government pervaded everything, yet could not change their opinions. They were as free as men ought to be without contest about freedom. They were bold without being tumultuous; they were active without being restless; they were obedient without slavishness; they were truly a new people respectable for their customs, manners, and habits. To this day, the Indians love the name of Canadian; they look upon them to be much more their compatriots than they do the English. Sequestered seven months from the sea by snows and ice, they plunged into the immensity of this continent. Everywhere they lived and associated freely with the natives. Either they more easily imbibed their manners; or else their own were more nearly similar to those of these aborigines; or else they were more punctual in their dealings, less haughty than their neighbours. The struggles of this colony whilst in its infant state are astonishing to read. More than a dozen of times you see the cradle overset, and the infant ready to be devoured by its enemies; and as many times you see it rising superior to the danger.

Had France opened towards it the more philosophic eyes of the year 1776, you'd have seen a nation of Franks rising on Canadian snows, which would have been able to have settled and possessed Acadia, Louisburg, Labrador, the shores of the interior lakes, those huge seas. France overlooked it until it was too late. The very struggle they made during the last war shows what they could have done had they been established on a broader bottom. Now 'tis no longer the same country: the English manners are becoming more and more prevailing; in a few generations they will be no longer Canadians, but a mixed breed like the rest of the English colonies. Their very women were the handsomest on the continent, as is proved by upwards of twenty English officers getting wives at Montreal soon after the conquest. Had they been slaves before, this change would have improved them, but they perhaps were happier than the citizens of Boston, perpetually brawling about liberty without knowing what it was. They were equally secured in the possession of their lands. They loved, though at a distance, the name of a monarch who seldom thought about them. They were united; they were strangers to factions and murmurs and to those evils which disturb society; they were healthy, hardy, subject to no diseases besides old age. Ignorant, they envied not the lot of their more learned, more gaudy neighbours. They ploughed, they fished, they hunted, they discovered new nations. They formed new alliances with the most barbarous nations. They did not spring from felons and banditti; they drew their origin from a purer source and rather improved their breed by the locality of the new climate under which they lived.

Here they multiplied, unknown to France and to Europe, until the demon of politics inspired William Pitt with the idea of continental conquests, exclusive fisheries, exclusive fur trade, a plenum of glory which has so much astonished the world. This very aggrandizement may pave the way to future revolutions. For everything is perpetually revolving; the nearer a state arrives to maturity, the nearer its decline. The very laurel leaves with which William Pitt encircled his sovereign's brow grew on a soil which may produce shoots of a very different nature and may exhibit an instance of colonies more philosophically governed indeed, but not the less ambitious. What did the Canadians possess that could inflame the cupidity of the richest people on earth? What mines did they work that could make them so eager to enjoy them? These hardy people possessed but a few laborious fisheries; they gathered but a few thousand packs of beavers, collected at an expense of fatigues and travels which no European can easily imagine; some wheat, some flour, in which their other provinces abounded; these were all their wealth, which was as limited as their wants. But Massachusetts, New York, Virginia, anxious for dominion, like all other societies, desirous to push their boundaries further, found that the limits of Canada obstructed them. The greatest extent of that colony was supposed by the English to lie towards Labrador and Lake Timiscaming, where no one can live. These colonies clamoured high; they began to talk of the encroachments of their neighbours. (Limitrophe nations are never without such quarrels.) And what were these encroachments, after all, when divested of newspapers' falsehood and misrepresentations?

The hunters and traders of the English colonies happened to meet those of Canada roaming like themselves through these boundless wilds. "How come you here, you rogue of a Frenchman?" "By means of this canoe, which has brought me from Montreal, a few miles of land-carriage excepted; and pray how come you here also, you drunken Englishman?" "By means of my legs, which have enabled me to climb over the mountains of Allegheny, and I have a better right to come here by land than you have to come here by water; and to convince you of it, I'll complain to Major Washington." "You complain, and I, at my return home, I will inform our governor, Mr. Duquesne." Sure enough, each told his story. Secretaries went to writing, from writing others went to arms, to war.

"Pray, Mr. Englishman, don't you raise at home abundance of everything: rice, indigo, tobacco, pitch, tar, etc.? Don't you trade with all the world, the year round? Don't you possess fifteen hundred miles of sea-coasts? We that are deprived of all these advantages, who live under a hard sky and till a hard soil—why would not you give us leave to hunt and to travel about just to keep us out of idleness? For, besides that, we have not much to trade with; we are locked up seven months in the year from any communication with the sea."

"Hunt and welcome towards Labrador, Timiscaming."

"What, in that country! Why, there are neither beasts nor birds, and if we even went that way a little too far, the Roundheads would immediately go to Hudson's Bay and complain there that they have seen Frenchmen in their wild territories."

"That is nothing to me. This river, this soil belongs to our people by virtue of the words of Charles the Second, who says that we may go even to the South Seas, if any such there be."

"To the South Seas? I who am a greater traveller than you have never seen any such. All I can tell you is that if I catch you here next year, we shall see who is the strongest."

"Very well, neighbour."

The ensuing year, sure enough, Major Washington comes and very civilly kills Captain Jumonville, though clad under the sanction of a flag. Each party accuses the other of perfidy; God knows who is to blame. But behold the effects of destiny and one of the freaks of fortune. This very Major Washington, the murderer of

Captain Jumonville, is the idol of the French. From the banks of the Ohio, in a little stockade, behold him there as a major in 1754; and in 1776 behold him again a generalissimo, the friend and the alley of France. O Virtue! O Humanity! And thou, O Justice! Wert thou painted to us as vain chimeras only or as real objects? Individuals may and must be virtuous; great ministers and rulers may commit crimes without reproach or remorse. From the ashes of Jumonville a Frenchman sees, I suppose, with pleasure the shrub of independence growing up, perhaps to a tall tree, perhaps to remain a bush until some more distant period. In that case, a Frenchman could not have died a more useful death for the benefit of this country; his *Manes* are now rewarded by the very hands which dispatched him. Strange concatenation of events! Unfathomable system of things! We know neither causes nor effects, neither beginning nor ending. Success in the conclusion always eclipses the infamy, the perfidy of beginnings.

CHAPTER VII

THE MAN OF SORROWS

Among this infinite variety and combination of evil equally felt by both parties, some, perhaps, I may select more visible, more affecting [and], therefore, more within my reach. What is wanting in the propriety of the following account will be supplied by the truth of the facts it contains. At peculiar times I cannot resist the force of some thrilling vibrations which suddenly invade my soul when I contemplate some great distress on either side. No country can exhibit more affecting ones than these afflicted provinces. Could I have ever thought that a people of cultivators, who knew nothing but their ploughs and the management of their rural economies, should be found to possess, like the more ancient nations of Europe, the embryos of these propensities which now stain our society? Like a great river, the agitated waves of [which] are now devastating those shores which before they gently surrounded and fertilized, great revolutions in government necessarily lead to an alteration in the manners of the people. The rage of civil discord hath advanced among us with an astonishing rapidity. Every opinion is changed; every prejudice is subverted; every ancient principle is annihilated; every mode of organization, which linked us before as men and as citizens, is now altered. New ones are introduced, and who can tell whether we shall be the gainers by the exchange? You know from history the consequence of such wars. In every country it has been a field pregnant with the most poisonous weeds, with recriminations, hatred, rapidly swelling to a higher and higher degree of malice and implacability. How many have I seen which it has converted into beasts of prey, often destroying more from a principle of ferocity than from notions of gain! Too many of these vindictive friends on both sides have stained the cause they have espoused.

But why should I wonder at this political phenomenon? Men are the same in all ages and in all countries. A few prejudices and customs excepted, the same passions lurk in our hearts at all times. When, from whatever motives, the laws are no longer respected; when the mechanism of subordination ceases and all the social bonds are loosened, the same effects will follow. This is now the case with us: the son is armed against the father, the brother against the brother, family against family; the nearer the connexion, the more bitter the resentment, the more violent the rage of opposition. What is it, then, that renders this revolution so remarkable in my eyes? What is it that makes me view some of its scenes with such heart-felt regret? The reason is that before this war, we were a regular, sober, religious people, urged neither by want nor impelled by any very great distress.

Oh, that I had finished my career ere our happiness vanished, or that the time of my existence had been postponed to a future and more tranquil period! In an overgrown society similar effects would not raise within me the same degree of astonishment. There the least subversion either of law or trade or government must cause thousands of people to want bread, and those people are ready for the sake of subsistence to commit all the outrages which the spirit of the times or the will of the leaders may dictate or inspire. However, I must remark here that those scenes which exhibit the greatest degree of severity or cruelty are not the work of every day. Forbid it, that human nature should be so universally debased! Nor do they flow from the reflected policy of the times so much as they do from that private rancour which this sort of war inspires, from that spontaneous resentment and irascibility of individuals upon particular occasions. Men in a state of civil war are no longer the same. They cease to view the former objects through the same medium as before. The most unjust thoughts, the most tyrannical actions, the most perverse measures, which would have covered them before with infamy or would have made them dread the omnipotence of heaven, are no longer called by these ancient names; the sophistry of each party calls them policy, justice, self-defence.

Who can live in the midst of this grand overthrow, who can for so many years be a witness to the pangs of this convulsed society without feeling a compunction which must wrench the heart of every good citizen, without wishing to describe some remarkable scenes, if it were only to sympathize with the unfortunate mourners?

Our rulers are very sensible of the impolicy and inexpediency of these severe deeds, but their authority and influence can hardly reach everywhere. I have heard many of them say: "If we are finally victorious, cruelty tarnishes the glory of our achievements; if conquered, we would shudder at the precedent we have given and dread the hour of retaliation." The experience of all revolutions, the uncertainty of all human events must strangely teach them that necessary caution. Alas, let the attempts be ever so wrong or ever so commendable; let war be ever so just or so unjust; the world places its applause only in the success of the enterprise. Success alone is the reward which in the eyes of men glitters and shines; 'tis the symbol of true merit. This is a melancholy proof of the strange fatality which seems to preside over all the actions of men. But I do not pretend to hold this great scale even; I am no politician. I leave with submissive humility the issue of this dispute in the hands of Him who holds the balance of the universe. This problem will be solved like so many others by the strongest. Yet I well know that in great as well as in small undertakings, nothing is acquired by too precipitate ardour, which, instead of hastening, often leads into incoherent measures. There is in all schemes a necessary development of effects, a chain of steps which gradually shows maturity at a distance. Too great a velocity of action, running too fast towards fruition without waiting for the accomplishing moment, may lead into erroneous paths. A bold confidence may be the source of arduous deeds, yet it cannot command the event. No one can bring success from the wheel of fortune before it has undergone a certain number of revolutions.

The situation of these people who live on our frontiers is truly deplorable. No imagination can conceive, no tongue can describe their calamities and their dangers. The echoes of their woods repeat no longer the blows of the axe, the crash of the falling trees, the cheerful songs of the ploughman. These happy sounds are changed into mournful accents, deep exclaims; howling of poor orphan children just escaped from the flames, of desolate widows bemoaning the fate of murdered or captivated husbands. Human society presents here nothing but tears and groans, and every species of calamity; the most innocent of our blood is daily shed. Some districts, more unfortunate still than the rest, are exposed to the fury of Indian excursions, as well as to the mischief of parties that are sent to protect them. So slender, so impermanent a protection only serves to increase their misfortunes. Their houses become little citadels, often defended and attacked, and, when taken, exhibit the most hideous scenes of blood and conflagrations. These cruel flames are reaching nearer and nearer; nothing can prevent or extinguish them—no, not even the blood that is shed within their walls. Judge then what ferment, what state of irascibility the minds of people thus situated must be in throughout all these last-settled countries!

Some time ago the beautiful settlement of ——, upwards of a hundred years old, was utterly destroyed. It presented to the eyes a collection of all that the industry of the inhabitants and the fertility of soil could exhibit [which was] most pleasing, most enchanting. Their lands were terminated by the shores of a beautiful river; their houses were all elegantly built; their barns were the most spacious of any in that part of the country; the least wealthy inhabitant raised at least a thousand bushels of wheat a year. Their possessions were terminated by the steep ascent of a great chain of mountains, beyond which no improvements ever can extend. From their bosoms enemies came and laid everything waste. Many sober, industrious people were killed, and all they had was destroyed.

Some parties of militia, which had been employed in protecting the contiguous settlements, on their return home were informed that some white people and Indians had, on their way to ——, lodged at a certain man's house, which was described to them. This discovery suddenly inflamed them with the most violent resentment and rage. Full of the most vindictive sentiment, they hastened thither. The man of the house was in his meadows making hay. They instantly surrounded him, and in the most opprobrious language upbraided him with the crime laid to his charge. He solemnly denied it. A strong altercation ensued. Some of the party were resolved to bayonet him instantly, as their friends had been bayoneted before. Their passions were too highly inflamed; they could not hear him with patience or give him an opportunity of justifying himself; they believed him guilty. Their unanimous wish seemed to be that he should confess the crime, a wish founded probably on some remains of ancient justice. He still denied it and appealed to heaven for the truth of his assertions. They disbelieved him, and in the madness of their rage they resolved to hang him by the toes and the thumbs, a punishment which, singular as it may appear, yet has been frequently made use of by the wretches of both parties.

Whilst in this painful suspension, he attested his innocence with all the energy he was master of. By this time his wife, who had been informed of the tragical scene, came from her house, with tears gushing in streams and with a countenance of terror. In the most supplicating posture, she implored their mercy, but they rejected her request. They accused her of having participated also in her husband's abominable crime. She repeated her entreaties, and at last prevailed on them to relieve her husband. They took him down after a suspension of six minutes, which will appear a long interval to whoever considers it anatomically. The bitter cries of the poor woman, the solemn asseverations of her husband seemed for a few moments to lull the violence of their rage, as in a violent gale of wind Nature admits of some kind intermission which enables the seaman to bring his vessel to. But all of a sudden one of the company arose, more vindictive than the rest. He painted to them their conflagrated houses and barns, the murder of their relations and friends. The sudden recollection of these dreadful images wrought them up to a pitch of fury fiercer than before. Conscious as they were that he was the person who had harboured the destroyers of their country, they resolved finally to hang him by the neck.

Hard was this poor man's fate. He had been already suspended in a most excruciating situation for not having confessed what was required of him. Had he confessed the crime laid to his charge, he must have been hung according to the principle of self-preservation which filled the breasts of these people. What was he then to do? Behold here innocence pregnant with as much danger as guilt itself, a situation which is very common and is a characteristic of these times. You may be punished to-morrow for thoughts and sentiments for which you were highly commended the preceding day, and alternately. On hearing of his doom, he flung himself at the feet of the first man. He solemnly appealed to God, the searcher of hearts, for the truth of his assertions. He frankly owned that he was attached to the king's cause from ancient respect and by the force of custom; that he had no idea of any other government, but that at the same time he had never forcibly opposed the measures of the country; that his opinions had never gone beyond his house; that in peace and silence he had submitted to the will of heaven without ever intending to take part with either side; that he detested from the bottom of his heart this mode of war which desolated and ruined so many harmless and passive inhabitants who had committed no other crime than that of living on the frontiers. He earnestly begged and entreated them that they would give him an opportunity of proving his innocence: "Will none of you hear me with patience? I am no stranger, no unknown person; you well know that I am a home-staying man, laborious and peaceable. Would you destroy me on a hearsay? For the sake of that God which knows and sees and judges all men, permit me to have a judicial hearing."

The passive character of this man, though otherwise perfectly inoffensive, had long before been the cause of his having been suspected. Their hearts were hardened and their minds prepossessed; they refused his request and justified the sentence of death they had passed. They, however, promised him his life if he would confess who were those traitors that came to his house, and who guided them through the woods to ――――. With a louder voice than usual, the poor culprit denied his having the least knowledge whatever of these persons; but seeing that it was all in vain, he peaceably submitted to his fate and gave himself up to those who were preparing the fatal cord. It was soon tied round the limb of a tree, to which they hanged him.

As this execution was not the action of cool, deliberate justice, but the effects of mad revenge, it is no wonder that in the hurry of their operation they forgot to tie his arms and to cover his face. The struggles he made as soon as he was suspended; the agitations of his hands, instinctively trying to relieve him; the contortions of the face necessarily attending such a state presented a most dreadful spectacle, which in common executions are hid from the public's eyes. But so irresistible is the power of self-preservation, so high was their resentment, so great their consciousness of his being guilty that these dreadful images conveyed neither horror nor thoughts of mercy to the minds of these incensed people. Whilst they were thus feeding their passions, and whilst unmoved they stood gazing on their departing enemy, Nature was hastening his final dissolution, as evidently appeared by the trembling nerves, the quivering appearance of the limbs, the extension of the tongue. The shades of patibulary death began to spread on his face; the hands, no longer trying to relieve the body, hung loose on each side.

Fortunately at this instant some remains of humanity sprung up in the breasts of a few. They solicited that he might be taken down. It was agreed and done. The next threw cold water on him; and to the surprise of some and the mortification of others, he showed some signs of life. He gradually recovered. The first dawn of his returning reason showed what were the objects which had engrossed his last thoughts. He most tenderly inquired for his wife. Poor woman! At a small distance she lay stretched on the ground, happily relieved from feeling the horrid pangs with which the preceding scene must have harrowed up her soul, by having fainted as soon as she saw the fatal cord fixed round her husband's neck. The second part of his attention was attracted by the sight of his children, who were crowded at the door of his house in astonishment, terror, and affright. His breast heaved high, and the sobs it contained could hardly find utterance. He shed no tears, for their source had almost been dried up along with those of life. Gracious God, hast Thou then intended that Man should bear so much evil, that Thou hast given him a heart capable of resisting such powerful sensations without breaking in twain?

Again he was commanded to confess the crime he was accused of, and again he solemnly denied it. They then consulted together, and, callous to the different impressions occasioned by so complicated a distress, unwilling to acquit him, though incapable of convicting him, they concluded him guilty and swore that he should die. Some in mercy repented that they had taken him down. Whilst they were employed in fixing on this last resolution, the poor unfortunate man was leaning against a tree. His wife, who had been brought back to life by the same means that had been used with him, sat near him on a log, her head reclined and hid in her hands, her hair dishevelled and loose. On hearing his second final doom, he tenderly and pathetically reproached them with making him pass through every stage of death so slowly when malefactors have but one moment to suffer. "Why, then, won't you confess that you have harboured our enemies? We have full and sufficient proofs." "Why should I confess in the sight of God that which is not true? I am an innocent man. Aren't you afraid of God and His vengeance?" "God and His vengeance have overtaken you for harbouring the incendiaries of our country." "I have nothing but words to make use of. I repeat it again for the last time: I am innocent of the accusation." "What say you, men, guilty or not guilty?" "Guilty he is and deserving of death." "Must I, then, die a second time? Had you left me hanging, now I should be no more. Oh, God, must I be hanged again? Thou knowest my innocence; lend, oh, lend me a miracle to prove it."

He shed a flood of tears; and looking once more toward his children and wife, who remained stupid and motionless, he approached those who were preparing to hang him.

"Stop a while," said the first man; "'tis the will of these people that you should die and suffer that death which all the enemies of their country so justly deserve. Prepare yourself, therefore; you have ten minutes to make your peace with God." "If I must die, then God's will be done." And kneeling down close by his wife, who kneeled also, he pronounced the following prayer, the sentiments of which are faithfully transcribed, though, through want of memory, clothed in words somewhat different from the original ones: "Gracious God, in this hour of tribulation and of mind and bodily distress, I ask Thee forgiveness for the sins I have committed. Grant me that grace by which I may be enabled to support my fainting spirits, and to quit this world with the confidence of a Christian. Despise not the sighs of my heart, which, though sometimes unmindful of Thee in its worldly hours, yet has never been guilty of any gross impiety. The patience with which I have borne my preceding trials, my innocence, my resignation, and Thy divine goodness make me hope that Thou wilt receive me into Thy kingdom. Thou, O Lord, knowest without the assistance of words the sincerity of my sentiments; to Thee I appeal for the manifestation of my innocence, which unjust men want to rob me of. Receive the repentance of a minute as an atonement for years of sin; Thy incomprehensible mercy and justice, unknown to Man, can do it. Endow me with all the benefits of our Redeemer's cross, the great Pattern of all those who, like Him, untimely perish by the hands of violence. Allowed but ten minutes to live, I seize my last to recommend to Thy paternal goodness my wife and children. Wilt Thou, O Master of Nature, condescend to be the protector of widows, the father of orphans? This is, Thou knowest, the strongest chain which binds me to the earth and makes the sacrifice of this day so bitter. As Thou hast promised pardon to all men, provided that they also pardon their enemies, I here before Thee cheerfully pardon all my persecutors and those by whose hands I am now going to be deprived of life. I pray that the future

proofs of my innocence may call them to early repentance ere they appear before Thy awful tribunal. Forgive
me my sins as I forgive the world, and now I go to Thee,
the boundless fountain, the great ocean of all created
things. Death is but the gateway towards Thee. O Lord,
have mercy on me and receive my soul."

"You have prayed so well and so generously forgiven
us that we must think at last that you are not so guilty as
the majority of us had imagined. We will do you no
further injury for the present, but it is our duty to send
you to ——, where, according to law, you may have a
fair trial; and there let the law of the land hang you
and welcome, if it is found that you deserve it. For my
part, I'll wash my hands of you as soon as I have delivered you into safe custody. I wish we had not gone on
so precipitately. What say you men?" "Aye, aye, let him
go, but mark our words and see if the judges do not
completely do what we have done."

With a feeble voice, he thanked them and begged a
few minutes to speak to his wife, who with a kind of
stupid insensibility and an unmoved countenance had
heard her husband's last sentence and even joined him
in prayer. I have no words to describe her joy, for her
joy was a mixture of frenzy, of fear, of laughter, of
strange expressions. The transition had been too sudden;
her nerves, rigidly strained by the preceding scene, were
too soon relaxed on hearing the joyful news; it very
nearly cost her the loss of her reason. They embraced
each other with a tender and melancholy cheerfulness.
She ran towards the house whilst he called his children.
Poor little souls! They came as quickly as their different
strengths permitted them. "What has been the matter,
Father? We have been crying for you and Mother." "Kiss
me, my dear little ones, your daddy thought he would
see you no more, but God's Providence has spoken to
the heart of these people." They all partook of this new
and extraordinary banquet in proportion to their ages
and understandings. This was a scene which Humanity
herself would with peculiar complacence have delineated
in all the pleasing hues of her celestial colours. It was
indeed so powerfully energetic that it melted all the
spectators into a sudden sensation of regret and tenderness, so singularly variable are the passions of men. The

most dreadful and afflicting spectacle which the spirit of civil discord could possibly devise was metamorphosed into the most pleasing one which a good man could possibly wish to behold.

O Virtue, thou, then, really existest! Thou, best gift of heaven, thou then secretly residest in the hearts of all men, always ready to repair every mischief and to dignify every action when not repelled by the force of superior vice or passion. [If] I had the pencil of true energy, of strong expression, I would dip it into their best colours; I would discard those which my scanty palette contains.

After a few hours' rest, they carried him to ———, where some time afterwards he had an impartial trial and was acquitted. No government, no set of men can ever make him amends for the injury he has received. Who can remunerate him for all his sufferings, for his patience, for his resignation? He lives, a singular instance of what the fury of civil wars can exhibit on this extensive stage of human affairs. How many other instances, if not similar, at least as tragical, might be recorded from both sides of the medal! Alas, poor man, I pity thee. I call thee "poor man" though not acquainted with thy circumstances. I would be meant to conceive by that expression all that sympathy and compassion have of [the] most exquisitely tender and expressive. What a subject for a painter who delights to represent mournful events! What a field for a judge and a master of the passions! A man leaning against a tree, hardly recovered from the agonies of death, still visible in the livid hue and altered lineaments of his face, still weak and trembling, his mind agitated with the most tumultuous thoughts, racked by the most anxious suspense, hearing his third and final doom. At a little distance, his wife, sitting on a log, almost deprived of her reason. At a more considerable distance, his house, with all his children crowded at the door, restrained by amazement and fear from following their mother, each exhibiting strong expressions of curiosity and terror, agreeable to their different ages. I can conceive the peculiar nature of all these colourings, but where would the painter find the originals of these faces who, unmoved, could behold the different scenes of this awful drama?

CHAPTER VIII

ON THE SUSQUEHANNA;
THE WYOMING MASSACRE

When an European arrives in this country he is surprised to see the extent and neatness of our towns, he views our various improvements and that multitude of settlements which adorn our extended shores with admiration, he hardly can persuade himself that he has crossed the Great Atlantic, that he is in a country scarcely 150 years old. He observes in many places the richesses of Europa, the taste and elegance of many of its capitals; these are the fruits of long and successful trade, of national industry and universal prosperity. He observes farms tilled with as much care and knowledge as those of his native lands; this first examination however gives him but a superficial idea of the state of our agriculture. Along the sea shore and in the neighbourhood of our cities the soil is enriched by the manures it affords, by the mud of rivers, with those salt grasses everywhere to be found; these produce a fertility which he did not expect. This is not however the natural state of our fields in the Northern provinces. The fecundity of the earth is greatly diminished; you may in those of Jersey, New York, Connecticut, etc. already perceive a great vegetative decay. The rich coat which was composed of old decayed leaves and other particles preserved for

ages by the existence of timber and sheltered from the
devouring impulse of the sun by the shades it produced,
is long since exhausted and gone. This it was which enriched the first settlers and procured them such abundant
crops. All the art of Man can never repair this. . . .

In order to obtain more uniformly fertile soils, deeper
loams, inexhaustible farms, which hitherto have wanted no
manure, you must recede from the sea, you must ascend
nearer the sources and springheads of those immense
rivers everywhere traversing the great continent, you
must visit the shores of Kennebeck up to its falls, those of
Connecticut everywhere abounding with the richest land
of Nature, you must visit the Mohawk, the Susquehanna,
as well as those innumerable streams on which Ceres and
Pomona have fixed their pleasing abode. . . . Bountiful
Nature seems purposely to have given this soil a degree
of fertility proportioned to its distance from navigable
rivers, in order, no doubt, that men tho' so far removed
from markets might afford in their extreme plenty the
means and expense of an unavoidable transportation.
Whoever has penetrated in any of the interior parts of
this boundless continent has been struck with this observation. The history of the New England settlements on the
east branch of the river Susquehanna is a most convincing
proof of what I have advanced as the following details will
sufficiently demonstrate.

I acknowledge that the history of this new and singular
settlement exhibits to our view nothing very remarkable.
Yet, methinks an European must take a pleasure in seeing
so great a tract of wilderness, imperceptibly smile in following a branch of humanity shooting up all round and
replenishing in the course of a few years those beautiful
shores hitherto savage and wild and entirely uncultivated
save for some scattered spots, the ancient habitation of few
extinguished tribes. . . .

The long dispute between the provinces of Connecticut
and Pennsylvania concerning the property of the lands
lying on both branches of the river Susquehanna, a tempting soil, the petty wars they carried on in support of their
mutual claims are objects too extensive, too antecedent,
and perhaps to you would appear too uninteresting. The
part which I want to select for your amusement is a geographical account of this country, a description of its

soil, a general idea of this noble river which by its immense ramifications extends its course through so vast a region. . . .

If on the map you follow the river Susquehanna, you will soon come to the great forks which divide it into two branches. In your passage to this remarkable spot you will not fail to observe many fair rivers which fall and mingle their waters with those of this parent stream. One of those branches issuing out of the lakes Caniadarage [Caniaderago] and Otsege, is commonly called the East one; the other formed by a thousand brooks descending from the Allegany (Chestnut, Nittany, Panther, Bald Eagle ridges) is known by that of the West. About 40 miles up the former, from Shamoctin [or Shamokin] (the name of the forks) begins the claim of the New England people which they carry upwards of 90 miles to the bounds of Wissack [Wysox] and Wiolucing [Wyalusing] in the 42 degree of latitude which is their boundary line at home with the Massachusetts. The right by which Connecticut claims a tract of land so uncontiguous and distant proceeds from the ambiguous words of their charter which grants them a continuation of territory even to the South Sea. Little did the grantors know of the geography of this country. Necessarily inclosed as Connecticut is by Rhodes island on the east, Massachusetts on the north and New York on the west, it cannot emerge from its present bounds but by conquest, Indian purchases or voluntary emigration without any claim of jurisdiction. About 20 years ago, some of their missionaries went to preach the Gospel among the tribes which inhabited those beautiful shores. 'Tis said that some even went so far as Tiogo [Tioga], Sisucing, Anaquaga [Ouaquaga] further up the river. As they had long complained of their confinement at home, and as their national characteristics lead them to aggrandisement and new schemes, some people in Connecticut by means of those missionaries set about negotiating a considerable purchase from the natives of more than 90 miles in length on the east branch, beginning somewhere at Wapwalippen [Wapwallopen] 40 miles above the forks, thence to the 42 degree of latitude, and in width extending within the before described limits as to include the west branch and up the Allegany ridge. The whole property of this immense tract was conveyed by a solemn bargain

properly ratified. This important affair transacted by bold
adventurers without even the countenance of their government greatly alarmed the proprietaries of Pennsylvania
who by their last authentic purchase had set their line of
frontiers at a great rock 4 miles above Shohactin [She-
hocking] on the Delaware river, very near the same latitude. . . . This proceeding of the New England people
was therefore look'd upon as a breach of that law by the
people of Pennsylvania. A considerable paper [*sic*] was
carried on by the two provinces, which convinced none of
the parties concerned. . . .

Several families at last went to begin this famous settlement. They crossed the North River and by the way of the
county of Orange crossed the Menisink [Minisink] mountains, passed over Delaware and entered the Pennsylvanian
territories in a N.N.W. course. Others taking advantage of
the high waters went up Delaware to Kechecton [Cochec-
ton] and Shohactin which is the forks of Delaware, thence
followed its west branch 12 miles up to the great landing
place, thence proceeding by lands to the Indian town of
Anaquaga on the river Susquehanna, thence down the river
Wyomen [Wyoming], the center of their purchase. In the
progress of this relation you will permit me to describe
these two extraordinary routes more minutely in order to
make you acquainted as much as I can with the locality of
this country physically so different from Europe.

Most of these first adventurers sat themselves down on
the first and most convenient spots they could find, fatigued
by so long a journey; for the partition had been hitherto
but simply ideal, a more accurate one was needless until
the number of inhabitants should increase. Immense were
the difficulties which these people had to encounter: roads
to explore for the passage of their waggons, temporary
bridges to erect, women and children to transport, provisions to carry, cattle, sheep, horses to lead through an immense tract of wilderness; when arrived, they had some
sort of houses to erect, grain to plant and to sow, fodder
for the insuing winter, provisions to secure by the chase
or by fishing whilst their first crop was ripening. These and
many more were the Herculean labors and difficulties they
had to encounter with and to overcome, but the vivid
hopes of greater prosperity, the near prospect of future
ease and comfort, the advantages of so fine, so pleasant a

situation, the very aspect of the new soil they were come to inhabit made them joyfully overlook those obstacles as well as the severe trial of want and penury to which they first exposed themselves. . . .

In my first excursion thither, I followed exactly the path which these people had made, and which I mean to describe reserving the account of the other route by Shohactin when I return. Please to follow me on the map and to cast your eyes on the western frontiers of the province of New York; you will observe few spots of arable grounds interspersed on the shores of the river Delaware running in the middle of narrow valleys formed by the junction of the Kaatskill, Shawagunck [Shawangunk] and Menissink Mountains, for on this side everything is mountainous. These disunited chains meet afterwards and run through the provinces of Pennsylvania under various names. No contrast in this country can be greater and afford a more pleasing idea when on the summit of the Menisink heights, you contemplate below fruitful farms, smiling fields, noble orchards, spacious houses and barns, the substantial habitation of wealthy people settled these 120 years on those happy bottoms. Everything around is smooth, smiling and calculated for the use of Man, whilst the surrounding mountains which incompass them on every side, present nothing but huge masses of rocks and marbles, hideous ridges on which nothing hardly grows. Here and there some spots are covered with a thin stratum of exhausted soil. One would imagine that by some superior art, by some anterior miracle, the ancient vegetative mould has been washed away to form those romantic plats below. Near the spot where you first descend from the mountains the Mahacamack [Mahacomacker] empties itself into the Delaware, and the point of its confluence is the end of that line which beginning on the North divides the provinces of New York and New Jersey. On the shores of the former as well as on those of the latter are to be seen the most excellent farms, excellent houses; but these are soon terminated by the perpendicular foot of those mountains which entirely overspread this part of the province and forever prevent its aggrandisement on that side. In the midst of these desolate ridges runs the river Delaware. Indulged by Nature like the Susquehanna, the Hudson and many other rivers, it winds through all those obstacles which obsequiously open and leave a free passage to its stream,—a stream navigable for rafts and canoes both in the spring and fall when it is swelled by the melting of the snows or when the autumnal rains, which with us always precede the setting of winter, have raised it above the level of the rocks and shallows with which its bed abounds.

Three miles below, where the Mahakamack empties itself into Delaware, I crossed that river which is about ½ mile wide, and in the space of two miles inhabited principally by people who keep saw mills. I entered the great wilderness. It is an immense piny forest consisting of hemlock, some spruce growing on an even soil composed of short ridges and valleys. The soil was a compound of red sand and a species of red loam greatly resembling clay; with good husbandry it bears excellent wheat as I observed in the first two miles I traversed after I had crossed the river. Every here and there, another sort of soil seem'd intermixed, presenting itself in separate and distinct hillocks seemingly higher than any other. The soil of these was blacker and it was covered with scrubby mountain oak, witch hazel, and dog wood. Most part of the underwood was wild laurels, which by their low size and the extreme ramifications of their crooked limbs are the greatest and the most unsurmountable impediment a traveller can meet with. I have often gone a mile or two out of the path either to pursue a partridge or a wild turkey, and I declare that I was most part of the time obliged to creep on the ground or to open to myself a passage with the utmost difficulty; when the first snows are fell, and by their weight depress their limbs still nearer the ground, you may then safely pronounce such tracts absolutely impassable.

After having travelled about 27 miles, I met with pleasure and surprise a little settlement of 3 houses on Shoholy [Shohola] creek, on the west side of a considerable ridge. There a few acres of low and fertile lands spread on its shores had invited 3 families to settle themselves; nor was there room for any greater number, the shores of this creek as well as the neighbouring territory offering no soil on which man can live and flourish. This creek is formed by several springs issuing from the great swamp about 25 miles off, and running N.E. into Delaware. At its confluence I am informed that there are two excellent saw mills, for even here in this secluded melancholy part of the country every advantage which Nature presents is immediately improved. You'd think by the ingenuity displayed on the saw mills erected on these rough shores that the country had been settled these 1000 years.

'Tis a feast for an unexperienced traveller to see the sun shine on some open'd grounds, to view clear'd fields. You seem to be relieved from that secret uneasiness and involuntary apprehension which is always felt in the woods by persons that are not used to them. 'Tis as it were a new element more pregnant with danger than the cleared fields and visible atmosphere to which we are accustom'd. In the latter the sight alone is sufficient to guard us from any unforeseen danger, in the former hearing has the pre-eminency, 'tis through that channel we receive every necessary idea, and I must confess ingeniously that at first I was alarmed at every distant sound and could not find myself at ease until I was either informed or I had guessed what it would be. The drumming of partridges, for instance, heard at a distance greatly resembles the discharge of cannon; the roaring of distant falls produces likewise a singular effect strangely modified either by the wind or the situation in which you stand. I with pleasure, rested all night under the hospitable roof of these people. They had a considerable orchard, some few pitch trees at their door, their cattle seem'd small but fat and hearty, feeding at large through these forests and returning regularly every night to their pens. They abounded likewise in hogs which equally free and uncontrolled in their range as the other, by their instinctive ingenuity know where to find a variety of ground nuts and roots on which they live. Far happier in these respects those people were than farmers who live in a thick settled country. These must provide artificial pastures for their cattle and necessary grains and milk for their hogs. Here on the contrary Nature provided them, without any trouble to the master, with their daily food. This however appeared to me an awful situation for so few people surrounded on each side with the most gloomy forests. They seem'd pleased with it and spoke of it with great predilection. They were all hunters and very skillful ones as I saw by the great plenty of deer's meat that hung in their house. The few acres of land they cultivated were extremely fertile and produced them with little labour 32

bushels of wheat, 55 bushels of corn pr. acre; they also
abounded in flax. When sick they had learnt of the Indians
how to find in their woods the remedies they wanted. One
of the neighbours' wives was a weaver, and you must know
that it is a trade which few women are strangers to. Necessity had taught my landlord's wife to cut and make clothes.
With their leather they made their shoes after the Indian
or rather the Canadian fashion; they seem'd to want for
nothing and to be happy.

Next day I proceeded on my journey through much the
same ground extremely well watered as I saw by the many
springs I found as I went along. Upon a due examination
of this tract of land, so far as I have traversed it, it appears all susceptible of being one day cultivated, and I
make no doubt that, was this part of the continent in
China, not a inch of it would be wasted; rye, buck wheat
and Indian corn would thrive, I believe, admirably well.
My landlord at Shoholy shew'd me a piece of ground on
which he had corn the preceding year which was before
covered with nothing but wild laurel, and which he cleared
with the utmost difficulty. In about 10 or 12 miles I came
to another little settlement, more awful still than that
which I had left, for it was composed of one single family,
it was called Blooming Grove, tho' I must confess that I
saw nothing here very tempting or blooming. It was situated on a creek which runs into the Wallenpaupack river
at a considerable distance, but this creek appears to be
nothing more than the huge bed of a torrent which when
the snows melt in the spring serves to convey into the
Delaware an amazing body of waters from the little lakes
and spring heads descending from the mountains to the
Northward. Everywhere along its shore I saw almost with
a fright immense trees lodged sometimes across its stream,
at other times deep ponds it had dug by carrying away all
the earth, at other places single rocks left naked bare, as
having resisted the fury of the waters, at other places immense heaps of gravel and sand, over which you might
pass dry footed in the summer.

By a fortunate bend in this river and by means of few
button wood trees which Nature had planted on these
banks, the low lands inclosed within it have escaped being
tore away by the impetuosity of this torrent, and on this
isolated spot which did not contain above of 22 acres,

dwelt the family above mentioned, seemingly happy and unconcerned at their hermit situation; situation much inferior to that of the inhabitants of Shoholy, in case of fire, sickness or enemy. The husband and his wife, 6 children, the oldest of which were grown up and help'd their father, composed this little community which answers to them every social purpose. That round of labour and perpetual industry which fills the measure of their time supplies the place of every deficiency. They seem'd to have no wants, their victuals were as good and wholesome as those I had seen in more opulent neighbourhoods. The father read every night prayers to his little flock, and on Sundays, which they attentively marked down, he expounded to them some text of the Scripture, and this was all the religious duty they had performed in many years. Pray, what would your opulent civilized neighbours think of this regimen, thus to live and toil alone in the woods without the assistance of one mechanic, without the comfort of a clergyman and the assistance of a physician? I conversed with this people until 12 o'clock at night, and was greatly pleased with the account they gave me of their resources, that is, the means they possess of supplying all their wants, which you may be sure were but simple. This man was like all inhabitants of forests a very expert hunter, I saw him with a Lancaster rifle kill a bird at 300 yards distance which I measured myself. He had brought in, the day before I arrived there, a bear which he overtook by chase; had not I heard of such a feat before, I could hardly have believed him.

Next day I left Blooming Grove, and pursuing the path of the New England settlers, I crossed at about 12 miles distance the Wallenpaupack a considerable river raising, as I am told, out of a considerable lake of the same name and running into the Delaware. The way was far from pleasant, I discovered some few swamps on each side of the road but extremely cold and of a shallow soil. These produced nothing but alder, water birch, otherwise candle wood, few pines the limbs of which were hung with very long moss, a most dreary appearance evidently shewing the sterility of the soil on which they grew. The rest of the woods seems to be but a continuation of the same piny tract accompanied with wild laurel. Near the river I saw some small tracts of maple and ash which grew on a rich soil and joined its shores. The water being shallow, I forded it and entered with pleasure on a leveller ground. The pines were more straight and lofty, some of whom which were oversat [*i.e.*, overturned] measured 51 feet without limbs; could there be found any navigable rivers here, what beautiful masts and spars could be conveyed to Philadelphia.

From thence ascending a considerable ridge extremely well timbered with a mixture of pitch pine, oak of various kinds and some chestnuts, I descended into a valley or low grounds extremely wet and disagreeable, and in 16 miles reached the great swamp of which I had so often heard. Tho' it was late, yet I was obliged to proceed on in order to enjoy the benefits of lodging in a log house built midway by the New England people for the accommodation of benighted or weary travellers. The great quantity of roots and of trees oversat across our path were very troublesome and obliged us to go round them in quest of passage, an operation which was often attended on horseback with many difficulties. I arrived at last at this solitary house, which bad as it was, yet afforded us sufficient shelter to call forth some emotion of gratitude towards those who had erected it. There seem'd to be about ½ acre of land cleared around it, probably from the materials with which it had been built as well as from the fuel that had been cut by successive travellers: it was a Karavansera, an Estalagen if you please, and tho' we found no polite landlord to hand us in and cook our victuals, yet it had many advantages of which I stood in need. A good appetite made me eat cheerfully the smoked venison and the piece of bear I had procured at Blooming Grove. Grass grew all round for my horse, some pieces of wood ready cut presented themselves to kindle the fire, and the fatigues of the day purchased a most excellent night's rest, tho' a little disturbed towards break of day by a company of wolfs that saluted us as they passed by to go a hunting. This swamp is one of the largest of the kind in the Northern Provinces, it lies as you may see; between the great ridges near Delaware and those more westerly ones which seem to inclose and regularly to follow the Susquehanna stream in all its windings. It is precisely 12 miles across in this place, it takes its raise a vast way to the N., towards the endless mountains near the heads of Massape creek, and in vari-

ous breadths reaches down into Pennsylvania or rather
into the cultivated parts of it, where the Tobyhannah and
many other creeks issue out of it to form the stream which
falls into the Delaware at East Town [Easton]. It is said
to contain about 6000 acres of lands; few small ridges
cross it, it is not subject to any great inundations having
but the lake of Wapenpanpack [Wallenpaupack?] in it and
giving raise to many streams by which it is disencumbered
of its waters.

When the age, the wealth, the population of this country will be arrived to such a pitch as to be able to clear
this immense tract; what a sumptuous, what a magnificent
sight will it afford! The soil appears to be as good as that
of our Northern meadows, for it bears the same sort of
trees, such as swamp or pin oak, maple, white and black
ash, willow, alder, etc. . . . Here imagination may easily
foresee the immense agricole richesses which this great
country and this spot in particular contain. I never travell
anywhere without feeding in this manner on those contemplative images.

Next day I set out early and observed the same trees
throughout until I entirely quitted it. Here the waters take
another course and instead of that eastern declivity of the
earth which leads the waters into Delaware, they all run
west in quest of the river Susquehanna. The first of these
which I perceived was the Lackawack, and seven miles
from the edge of the great swamp I fell in with the embryo
of a settlement composed of 7 families happily settled on
the bank of that creek. They had been induced to pitch
their tents here, allured like all other first founders of districts by the singular fertility of its shores commonly called
with us low lands, that is lands which seem to have been
form'd by the water as you may see by the perfectly
levell'd stratums of which they are composed, and by the
recess of those waters into their present bed. Anxious to
finish my journey, I staid here but a little while and proceeded through a fine country, if I may judge by the
timber, to the banks of the Susquehanna at a place known
by the name of Wiomen—32 miles.

I am arrived at last on the shores of this fair river issuing from the two lakes I have mentioned before, bending
itself in an amazing number of curvatures to gather in its
course a greater number of creeks and rivulets and to im-

part mankind a greater degree of benefits. Few rivers in this part of the world exhibit so great a display of the richest and fertilest land the most sanguine wish of man can possibly covet and desire. . . . The eye stops with pleasure from considering attentively the level plains which it can easily pervade, to view the next rocky points covered with the finest pines, affording springs of the most excellent waters, producing brooks where mills are erected to turn grain into meal and the neighbouring logs into boards. The plains contained between those cliffs are of different dimensions, some 1000, some 250 acres, they are formed of sand and loam in pretty equal quantities, they are perfectly levell'd, not but that the different rivulets from the high grounds have declivity enough without spreading over the land. In their furrows I have carefully follow'd some of these stratums; they appear of an equal thickness and reach, of the same depth and colour to where the upland begins to rise. Here the soil changes all at once from a sandy loam into a more strong and compact sort of ground, these beautiful plats or plains produce in the greatest abundance all sorts of grains fit for the use of Man. The first settlers found them covered with a sort of wild grass peculiar to these low lands, commonly called *Blue Bent,* so extremely high that its tops reach'd a man's shoulders on horseback. When this grass is cut early it makes an excellent fodder, but maturity gives it too great a degree of coarseness. There are to be seen few trees on these plains, and those are the Wild Cherry of an immense size as to their bulk and ramifications, the Sweet Butter Nut equally bulky but more extended in their limbs, and the Button Wood surpassing them all in height and the dimensions of its trunk. I saw at Shamoctin now Northumberland a canoe excavated out of one of those, which carried seven tons. Judge of the depth and fertility of a soil which produces such exuberant instances of vegetation. They abound besides with the White Snake Root, the Senecca Root, the Nindzin, vulgarly called by the chinese name of Ginseng, a most valuable plant too much neglected because too common: the Penny Royal, Liverwort, Water Cresses abound in their brooks.

Nearer the river another tier of low lands present themselves to your view, less elevated than the first and covered every spring with the annual flood which raises the river sometimes 10 feet. Nothing can be conceived more fruitful and more pleasant than these inferior grounds. They contain the strongest vegetative powers which Nature can give, they are separated from the upper ones by natural ditches, by winding canals of about 40 feet wide, which often render them perfect islands; over these the inhabitants had already thrown little bridges. These are the fields where they sow and cultivate their spring grains: Corn, Oats, Hemp, Flax, Pease, Barley, etc. These are yearly enriched by the strong healthy slime deposited by the floods, which come down and pass away so gently as to do very little damage. These contain no timber, but they are covered with a quantity of weeds which grow to an enormous size. I have seen whole acres of nettles from which I hardly could defend my face, the Hog Weed, the bitter weed, the Red Root, the Anekin greatly resembling the angelica, the Calamus and lastly the wild angelica upwards of 12 feet (it is as strong and as odoriferous as those cultivated in our gardens), the Brook Lime, the Winter Savoury, etc. One of the most common and the most remarkable plants that grow in those luxuriant soils is the Wild Cucumber; 'tis the bane of the farmer, no precaution whatever can possibly extirpate them, for an immense quantity of seed is annually left on those inferior shores by the swelling of the river. . . . I have often observed them crowning with peculiar verdure the summit of Cherry trees upwards of 80 high, yet its seeds are exceedingly small. The same exuberancy is remarkable in the plants and grains which the farmer sows on them; they are obliged to tame the ground, as they call it, by previously sowing 3½ bushels of hemp seed on an acre, in order that this rank weed may exhaust some of the too great fertility of this soil and prevent by its compact shade the growth of any other, yet I have seen it shoot to the height of seven feet; nothing will grow to any degree of maturity without this operation. I have seen 78 bushels of sound corn gathered out of an acre, 97 bushels of oats from 1½ bushel sowing, that is from ¾ acre, 1370 pounds of clean hemp out of 1½ acre. The only labour they are obliged to perform is to find proper means to keep the weeds down and to watch their growth.

This fine river contains likewise a great number of islands which seem to be a soil more recently made. Nothing can exceed their fertility and the richness of their soil. Most of them are higher than the grounds last described, tho' they are subject also to annual Spring inundations. They are covered with maple and ash; and those which are already cleared yield the best timothy and other grasses.

The high grounds, from whence their brooks and rivulets descend, yield them the best of stone and timber, all kinds of oaks, tulip trees, chestnut, hickory, Keske Toma. In those woods I have seen plenty of wild grapes of various sorts, strawberries, wild rasberries, small filberts, hurtle berries, slaws of white thorn as big as our cherries, the spignet, the golden rod, the unicorn, solomon's seal, the white snake root, etc. These ridges of timbered lands have been much injured by repeated fires kindled by the Indians in order to frighten and to inclose their game. These fires have greatly exhausted the surface of these grounds and prevented the growth of the young shoots and small timber. This devastating calamity to which hunters are insensible, tho' the utmost affliction to farmers, is now pretty much kept out, and it is inconceivable in how few years the soil will recover its pristine strength and fertility. At present they cultivate no parts of these ridges, tho' their soil is good; this will not be the case until the great numbers of people settled on the river and the subdivisions of their farms of low lands oblige future generations to move back. 'Tis very natural for the first settlers to choose the best lands and the easiest to till, the boldness of their undertakings, and their great fatigues well deserve the most ample rewards. The labour and difficulty however of breaking up the low lands at first is very considerable; it is an operation which must be performed with 3 and sometimes with 4 yokes of oxen, but when once this is effectually done, 2 horses will plough 1½ acres a day very easily.

This fine river is at a medium between 70 and 80 rods wide, interspersed at every little distance with pleasing islands, points of low lands, some of which seem to be detached from the main. That pleasing variegated mixture of high, low, and still lower grounds, that alternate vicissitude of extensive plains and high promontories view'd at every angle as you either ascend the river, the prodigious number of houses rearing up, fields cultivating, that great extent of industry open'd to a bold indefatigable enterprising people afforded me a spectacle which I cannot well describe. . . .

Spring and Fall that river is navigable for boats of 12 tons, managed with 7 hands, 6 with poles and 1 at the helm. Their general market at present is at Middle Town in Pennsylvania where they begin to carry abundance of white pine boards, logs of white cherry, walnut etc., wheat and hemp. In the month of May they catch plenty of shads, an extraordinary sort of fish which penetrates yearly up to the spring heads of all the great rivers of the middle continent; their instinct leads them at such a distance from the sea in order to deposit their spawn out of the reach of their enemy. I have seen trouts as large as bass, 17 inches long, a little below the falls of Wiomen, where numbers are daily catched. The waters of this river are about 10 feet deep along the low lands and have a mighty gentle current, but where the heads of mountains put up towards the river it is always shallow and in the summer sometimes dry.

It was not until the fourth year that I visited them, and I was highly entertained at every thing I saw. Their modes of living and behaving towards one another when they had no government greatly surprised me, but I cannot possibly describe to you that variety of means, that medley of chances and accidents by which every one tried to lay the foundation of his future fortune. The sum of exertion exhibited on these shores astonished me much; not a single person idle, those who were fatigued with labour recreated themselves by fishing. Most of these were poor people who had very little more property left than the bare means of transporting themselves there with their stock; and who that could live with tolerable ease and middling plenty would run so great a risk and expose themselves to so many inconveniencies and difficulties? They had already erected a good number of saw mills with which the settlement was supplied with all the boards and scantling they wanted, nay, they had already begun to float them down the river in rafts very ingeniously fasten'd together, on the top of which they always placed a great many black walnut logs commonly 14 feet long, and 18 inch. wide; these were delivered to the upper Pennsylvania settlements for a dollar a piece. Even sea coal is found here, for strange to tell, bountiful Nature has placed an amazing bed of this precious mineral under almost all their high low lands which are not above 12 feet from the surface of the water. The coals appear all along those banks within 4 feet of the surface. Their method of getting it is to haul their boat alongside and tumble the coals into it; it is said to be of an excellent quality and is daily used by their blacksmiths. Here are reunited all the advantages which can render men happy and rich. Most of their mills are built at a small distance from the mouths of the creeks on which they stand and navigable for boats to their very gates. No situation in every respect can be conceived more advantageous for the emolument of human nature; here they enjoy a climate peculiarly healthy, excellent spring water, the most fertile lands in the world, on their high ground every species of timber, wild turkeys in great flocks, partridges, deers, bears, mouse deer, etc., fish in their river all the year round, every convenience for mills on the river at proper distances, the best of white pine, sea coals, spring and fall, a debouche by water to exchange their exuberancy for what they want. What a pity that this and other branches and ramifications of this immense river, all possessing on their shores low lands proportioned to the size of their streams cannot be permanently settled and be made to unite the advantage of peace, political tranquillity with every other which nature offers them with the most liberal hand. Here a man, to live well is not obliged to work ½ of his time, the rest he can dedicate to some trade or to fishing and fowling. It is here that human nature undebased by servile tenures, horrid dependence, a multiplicity of unrelieved wants as it is in Europa reacquires its former and ancient dignity,—now lost all over the world except with us. May future revolutions never destroy so noble, so useful a prerogative. The equal partition of the lands, the ignorance in which we happily are of that accursed feudal system which ruins everything in Europa promises us a new set of prejudices and manners which I hope will establish here a degree of happiness to the human race far superior to what is enjoyed by any civilised nation on the globe. The first spot the New England people settled on was by the Indians called Wiomen, an extensive plain surrounded like all the rest with gentle ridges.

The warm patriots of N. E. gave it the name of Wilkes-bury [Wilkes-Barre] in honor of the then potent, popular Lord Mayor of London. Strange it may appear to you that the great stream of applause he enjoy'd with you should have caused his name to be given to a little town founded on the shores of Susquehanna 400 miles from the sea; but such is the spirit of the inhabitants of this country, such is the circulation and the effect produced by our newspapers, that their contents are read, studied even under the new built log house and often serve to alleviate the labour of the fields where they are perused whilst the people rest.

not ignorant of Europe

Lest you might think me unfaithful and careless and omitting to give you every information which this country affords, and also to satisfy my own curiosity, I cheerfully embraced the opportunity of 2 Indians and a white man going to Warrior's Run on the west branch [of the Susquehanna], a stream of which I had long heard wonders, for as it is much larger than the east, so are the plats of low lands it contains. These people were going to Bald Eagle's Nest, [a] hundred miles higher up. I was confident that once at Warrior's Run I should find some boats going to Shamoctin from whence at any time I might get opportunities to reascend the river to Wilkesbury. We sat out at 12 o'clock from Lackawane or Kingtown [Kingston], a village just settled almost opposite to the former on the west shore. We soon entered the woods, proposing to reach that night a hunting cabin which the Indians knew of. About midway we met with many ridges but of an easy ascent, full of excellent timber, each of them divided by large valleys of excellent lands, but fitter for pasture and the scythe than the plough. The ridges appeared to be of a stony soil such as I had seen in New England and the New Hampshire grants, the bottoms were not properly swamps, yet they were somewhat wet; each had a little brook winding through the middle. A northern farmer could not, in the most romantic effort of his imagination, conceive or wish to possess any land better adapted to grazing and every where contiguous to the uplands on each side where their habitations might be erected. But here hunger began to teach us the folly of not bringing provisions with us and depending too much on what we might kill, for we saw nothing and the sun was not above an hour high. The 2 Indians desired us to follow a particular course which would shortly lead us to the hut, while they would make an excursion and try to procure some game. My guide and I, we cheerfully proceeded on until the sun disappeared, and yet saw nothing of our expected habitation. On the contrary we were all at once suddenly stopt by a huge pine swamp which had been partly consumed by some accidental fire; immense trees burnt at the roots were oversat, one over the other in an infinite variety of directions, some hung half way down, supported by the limbs of those which still stood erect. Others had fallen flat to the ground and had raised an immense circumference of earth which adhered to their roots. In short, there was no penetrating through such a black scene of confusion; it was a perfect chaos. Besides, as the Indians had not mentioned this swamp, we concluded that we had missed our way and that we were lost for that night; a very disagreeable conclusion. Amidst the different feelings which this situation awakened in me, hunger was the superior one and silenced all the rest. To accomplish our misfortune it began to rain, we could not kindle a fire, everything was so wet, finally we were obliged to stand against one of the largest trees we could find in order to save us from the greatest violence of the shower. It had the desired effect, but as soon as the wind abated, the drops falling from the top of this lofty tree upwards of 70 feet high greatly annoyed us, their weight was astonishing. In that posture we slept or rather dozed on with our guns along side of us, we learnedly recapitulated the error which we supposed we had committed and sincerely promised that whenever day light should appear, we would cautiously go back and turn more to the west at a certain little brook we knew of. Towards 3 o'clock we were roused out of our sleep or rather slumbers by the yell of about 20 wolfs which I thought but at a little distance. My blood ran cold, my companion cheer'd my spirits in telling me that there was no danger, that on the contrary the smell of man always kept them off; this yell was intended to alarm the rest and put them on their guard. "Give me your moccasins," said he, "which with mine will effectually guard us." He accordingly hung them on bushes at about 2 rods from us. "This," he said, "being strongly impregnated with our smell is a sufficient rampart against the violence of these animals; this is the only charm the Indians make use of to repell their attacks." Thus protected they lie down and sleep unconcerned as we do in our houses. It was done, they still repeated their howlings but after some time they went away. Light returned at last. We went back, exactly follow'd our preceding resolutions, amended our course when we came to the brook, and soon ascended to the top of a fine chestnut ridge which the Indians had described. I fired a gun, conscious that we could not be far from the hut: to our great joy it was answer'd and accompanied with a war whoop or yell which alarmed the dull silent echoes of these woods. Soon after we saw M——n himself coming towards us, he laugh'd heartily at our adventure and soon conducted us to the little transitory habitation we had missed the evening before. I heartily ate of several partridges that were ready cooked for us, drank of the water of the brook and proceeded on. We were then about 25 miles from Lackawane or Kingtown. During the remainder of our journey to Warrior's Run, being 18 miles, I saw nothing but an immense champaign tract full of the largest white oak and hickory. We were then, as the Indians told me, near the heads of Chikisquaque [Chillisquaque] creek. Here we might have travelled with chars or coaches for there was no kind of underwood, neither did I see either stones or roots.

Warrior's Run is a beautiful little river emptying itself into the west branch. It had been in some measure entirely settled by the Pennsylvanians some years before. I never saw a greater display of plenty in my life than these people possessed; they had every kind of grain that they chose to sow, excellent cattle, great number of swine in the woods, venison and fish for catching. They were mostly Germans, their houses were neat and at a good distance from the river. I saw no negroes and I believe there was not one in the whole settlement. Every door led to the Temple of Hospitality in the true sense of that word. I saw at last the great river [Susquehanna], as they call it; it is twice as large and as deep as the other, and prodigious are the tracts of low lands it exhibits on its shores. I heard the people here talk of still higher branches of the same river, more distant sources equally rich, and equally navigable either for bateaux or canoes. They told me of a young settlement just begun at Bald Eagle's Nest, upwards of 100 miles higher up. They told me twenty other wonders of the famed shores of this river up to its spring head, between the great Buffalo swamp and the Allegany ridge. 'Tis very surprising to observe the boldness, the undiffidence with which these new settlers scatter themselves here and there in the bosom of such an extensive country without even a previous path to direct their steps and without being in any number sufficient either to protect or assist one another. I have often met with these isolated families in my travels, and 'tis inconceivable how soon they will lose their European prejudices and embibe those of the natives. Their children born and educated at such a distance from schools and opportunities of improvement become a new breed of people neither Europeans nor yet Natives. These are not in general the best people of this country. Here I spent seven days and at last embark'd in a canoe for Shamoctin and in the way stopt awhile to view another Pennsylvanian settlement, on the west shores of this river, called Buffalo Valley. It lies about 12 miles from the forks, the land appeared equally fertile and advantageous to the settlers, but as I did not go up their river [Buffalo Creek], I shall say nothing more, being unwilling to repeat hearsays. Soon after, we past by the mouth of Chikisquaque creek which is very considerable and on which I saw the appearance of settlements. In short, I hardly saw any creek and low lands where there were not families, some just arrived, others settled at different periods.

Shamoctin, now Northumberland, is a Pennsylvania settlement intended to be the county town. It consisted of 40 houses inclosed with palisades from river to river. Here the soil is extremely poor and sandy, nothing but pines grew where the town now stands, and all the ad acent country consists of nothing but pine; but yet it bids fair to become one of the most considerable inland towns in this country. . . . I staid here 3 days, happy in the acquaintance and friendship of Mr. Plunket, surveyor of this county. I returned to Wilksbury or Wiomen in a New England boat which was returning from Middle Town in Pennsylvania, nor am I sorry that I undertook this small journey. . . .

Every spring the roads were full of families travelling [from "the Northern Provinces"] towards this new land of Canaan; this formed a strange heterogeneous reunion of people unsupported by their metropolis, therefore considered as intruders on the Pennsylvanian territories, tilling, fishing, hunting, trafficking with one another without law or government, without any kind of social bond to unite them all. This assemblage was composed of a strange variety of sects and nations, all equally filled with that pride which sudden ease and consequences necessarily inspires. . . .

At last some demagogues appeared, for hitherto they had been all equal. A few men arrived from Connecticut of more property and knowledge, some of the original patentees who came to enjoy and realize the benefits of so much art and so much intrigue. Their claims gave them an immediate consequence, but this new era did not abate their land contentions. Families daily arrived that either could not find the lots they had bought, or else found them occupied by others; happily the country was boundless. Thus they went on for a while, they tilled their fertile lands, they easily supported themselves, they even began to enjoy some little exuberancy with which they supplied the wants of the newcomers, they even began to trade with the Pennsylvanians, their rivals and enemies;—but trade knows no enemy,—the very Indians from the upper towns resorted here and began to exchange their venison and skins for flour and other articles. They brought with them and reared a multitude of children, the blessing of a healthy climate, the consequence of an easy subsistence. But as they grew more populous they felt that they grew likewise more potent, at last they had the boldness to think of dispossessing by arms the Pennsylvanians who were settled on the west branch. This singular step awaked the attention of that mild province. These were immediately supported and protected, they saw with indignation these aspiring people now become their neighbours traversing the whole breadth of the province of New York to come and occupy their lands believing with the ancient credulity of New England men that the charter words of Charles the 2d could possibly give them an indefeasible right to this great dominion. After having in vain remonstrated this matter to the assembly of Connecticut, they at last opposed

them and even attacked them in their new settlements.
Some blood was shed on these occasions; for where are
the societies of men that are not tinged with this precious
liquid? Several families were ruined on both sides, some
men were carried prisoners to Philadelphia, nothing material was done.

At this period the province of Pennsylvania ordered it
to be laid out into a new county by the name of Northumberland. Soon after the New England people made an
incursion to Warrior's Run, but they did not succeed.
Open war was declared on both sides, on both sides shocking retaliations took place. The year after, 1773, the government of Connecticut publicly espoused their cause and
ordered it to be laid out into a new county by the name of
Westmoreland, in allusion to their great western claim.
. . . About this time this grand quarrel was referred to
the King and his council, which like all other great tribunals are so incumbered with the load of business that they
must necessarily act slow; this grand process required
years ere all the pleadings, documents and papers could be
examined, and final judgment given. . . .

The opinions of the people grew more and more divided
about the issue of this grand dispute. . . . The names of
Yankees and Pennamites were invented and became two
words of reproach not only among the two rival provinces
but even among themselves. . . .

During this interval the grand landed contest remained
undecided. They flattered themselves with the happy consequences which so strong a possession seem'd to give
them. They began to count upwards of 1250 families scattered in the embryo of 16 townships, and all this was the
work of 8 years. . . . But mankind carries in their bosoms the rudiments of their own misfortunes and unhap-
piness, place them where you will. . . .

After having returned through the same path I followed,
I thought proper to revisit them 2 years after,* and to
satisfy my curiosity went by the way of Delaware and
Anaquaga. Please to follow me attentively that you may
acquire a sufficient knowledge of the western frontiers of

* According to Crèvecoeur his second journey, the account of which
begins here, was made just before the Revolution, probably in 1776.

New York as well as some idea of the eastern dominions of that part of Pennsylvania.

A little above the place where I crossed the Delaware, I embarked in a canoe in which with great labour I ascended to a place called Kechiecton [Cochecton?] where the mountains do not approach quite so near to the shores of the river. There lived about 60 families scattered within the distance of about 20 miles. This spot is computed to be 62 [miles] from the Mahakamack. They live by the cultivation of a few acres of grounds which is very fertile but sometimes subject to great inundations, by floating masts, logs to Philadelphia, by sawing boards at the many saw mills which they have erected on every convenient brook; (these shores abound with excellent pines) this is a laborious way of earning subsistence which requires a peculiar degree of judgment, skill and precaution. I have often been amazed to see the boldness and dexterity with which they guide those huge drafts through all the rapids of this river.

The shores on both sides all the way from Mahakamack are exceedingly asperous and rocky. The mountains which entirely overspread this part of the country both on the Pennsylvania and New York sides do not gradually descend towards the river, but seem purposely excavated for the intended channel. Bold rough projecting points in various forms and shapes present to the eyes nothing but a series of promontories frightful to behold. Yet as this river is navigable spring and fall it is become settled at every little distance, and without that easy communication no human foot could ever have trod or cultivated these lands,—an astonishing contrast when compared with the smiling ones of the Susquehanna. No traces of habitation can possibly be expected where everything seems so barren, yet there are a good number scattered at a great distance one from another, placed in some little bays formed by the winding of the river. A few acres of arable land have been discovered, 'tis seized with avidity without the trouble of surveys and deeds, for it seems to belong to the great common of Nature, a log house is reared and a family established. At other places where convenient brooks are, they have erected saw mills with immense labour, and with singular ingenuity convert the neighbouring pines into the finest boards; I have seen many upwards of 3 feet wide and 18 feet long.

At this recital, you'd imagine that this country is extremely limited and as fully settled as it is in China; yet it is far from being the case. The facility of navigation, the ease with which few acres are cultivated, the great field opened for hunting habituates this people to a desultory life, and in a few years they seem to be neither Europeans as we observe them in our flourishing settlements nor yet natives. This mode of life which sometimes implies a great share of laziness produces a sort of indolence, indifference, which is the consequence of limited industry. The great range which their cattle and hogs enjoy in those woods affords them milk and meat on the most easy terms. Few bushels of grain easily raised from the little fertile spot they inhabit, dried venison and fish maintain them sufficiently. Clothing is sometimes deficient, tho' many of them have sheep, however by barter they find means to supply themselves with the most necessary articles. In short, they appear to me to live comfortably and happy tho' situated in the midst of this piny forest and on the verge of a rough stream navigable only twice a year. I have purposely stopped to converse with some of them. I found that they originally had been very poor and had been drove from their ancient abodes by the necessary severity of the laws and that they thought themselves very happy in their asylum where they had found safety, tranquillity and independence.

Such is in general the state of this river until you come to Shohactin the forks of Delaware. There the river spreads itself into two arms, one called the Pawpacton [Pepacton] or East branch, the other the West or Fish Kill. As you ascend up the East part, the shores gradually grow less asperous, the mountains recede from the river and recrossing it at unequal distances leave as on the Susquehanna small but beautiful spots for cultivation and improvement. It is but lately that this part of the province of New York has been inhabited and in some measure tilled. I am informed that no roads have as yet been found out; none therefore can remove here but the most indigent sort of people who can transport what little they have on the back of horses. . . .

At Shohactin there lived 5 families enjoying about 25 acres of land each, which is all this point affords, the rest is all pine and unfit for the plough. They were likewise hunters, a resource to which the back inhabitants are obliged to have recourse and which becomes a peculiar talent to which their children are always brought up, for the Americans know how to wield the gun and the ax better than any other people on earth. From Shohactin I proceeded 12 miles up the west branch abounding with excellent pines. 4 miles up I observed a large rock on which the characters 42 had been ingraved; I was informed that this was the latitude at which the last purchase of Pennsylvania from the Indians had been fixed. 8 miles higher up we came to the general landing of a carrying place which in 16 miles leads to the Susquehanna at the town of Anaquaga. The lands between those 2 rivers were not so bad as I expected, there was a mixture of pine tracts and good arable grounds without any considerable hills.

Anaquaga is a considerable Indian town inhabited by the Seneccas. It consists of 50 odd houses, some built after the ancient Indian manner, and the rest of good hew'd logs properly dove-tailed at each end; they afford neat and warm habitations. The low lands on which it is built, like all the others, are excellent, and I saw with pleasure great deal of industry in the cultivation of their little fields. Corn, beans, potatoes, pumpkins, squashes appeared extremely flourishing. Many Indians had cows and horses tho' they seldom plough'd with them; they were greatly civilized and received me with their usual hospitality. My old friend M——n who had gone with me to the west branch was there and expressed great pleasure at seeing me. I brought him [a] few presents for which he was very thankful. Next day I became acquainted with the minister of the town who was of the sect of the Moravians, and I enjoyed great satisfaction in his conversation; he had resided there several years, and tho' he had never been able to make of them entire converts, yet he had in a great measure abated their ancient ferocity to their prisoners, and in general soften'd their manners. Their wandering life is not fit to receive the benefits of our religion which requires a more sedentary life; they forget in the woods the precepts they have learnt, and often return as ignorant as ever. Their women who are most constantly at home appeared on the contrary tractable, docile; they attended prayers in their chapel with great modesty and attention. I was greatly surprised when I was at Anaquaga to see several white people from different parts of Pennsylvania who had purposely come there to put themselves in the hands and under the care of some Indians who were famous for the medical knowledge. Several were cured while I was there; a woman in particular who had a running ulcer in her breast for 5 years before appeared perfectly well cured and the ancient wound entirely healed. You'd be astonished to see with what care and caution they hide from the Europeans their method. I procured the receipt by which the white woman was cured by making one of their principal squaws drunk; the good I have done with it will, I hope, compensate the method I made use of to procure it. The smallpox,—the plague of these people,—had done great ravages in some of the upper towns. With the greatest joy, I persuaded my old friend M——n and his family to submit to be inoculated; it consisted of 11. . . .

Here I spent a week conversing with the oldest and wisest people of the village, lodging sometimes with one and sometimes with the other. I was greatly edified at the knowledge and sagacity they displayed in the answers they made to my many questions. I should grow too diffuse was I to enter into further details, I must therefore quit this subject and go down to Wiomen again to contemplate the increase of this famous settlement. I embarked with 3 Indians who were going to exchange some furs for flour, and in 2 days safely landed on the spot where I had arrived 2 years before.

I observed with pleasure that a better conducted plan of industry prevailed throughout, that many of the pristine temporary huts and humble log houses were converted into neater and more substantial habitations. I saw everywhere the strong marks of growing wealth and population; it was really extremely pleasing to navigate up and down this river and to contemplate the numerous settlements and buildings erected at different distances from these shores. Some had pitched their dwellings close by the high timbered ground in order to see at one cast of their eyes the most valuable part of their possessions in an uninterrupted level to the very water edge, others on account of some brooks, winding canals, had built in contrary direction almost close to the highest low land shores and view'd their settlements in a different disposition. Nothing could be more pleasing than to see the embryo of future hospitality, politeness, and wealth disseminated in a prodigious manner of shapes and situations all along these banks. As I went to Wiolucing I observed several parts of this river which were mountainous for many miles, but these spots all were replenished with excellent pine timber. This little town is the last the Indians gave up, and by a singular chain of circumstances, which never happens among these people, the whole property of this tract, being upwards of 500 acres, devolved on one cunning old fellow, Job Jelaware by name, who had learnt of the Europeans the use of money, and craftily purchased the shares of all the rest. He sold the whole property, while I was there, to a stout Pennsylvania farmer for £2500 of that currency; and a better bargain I never saw. Here the soil has a greater mixture of clay than any other spot, therefore richer pastures; I have seen nowhere larger cows and oxen. There are still standing many good Indian houses. Was I a farmer here, with pleasure I would pitch my tent, for Nature in her most indulgent hours could not form a richer assemblage of all that man wants; here have I seen her dissolving into the kindest volupty. I observed likewise several apple trees bearing a peculiar sort of apples which make a very durable cider and is known in Pennsylvania by the name of Indian apple; it is thought that these are native of this country. Some part of these grounds are covered with the small dutch white clover and it is very remarkable that if you clear any spot of ground ever so far from the sea or any European settlement, this grass will start up of itself; whence can its seed proceed from?

Soon after my return from this last excursion began the great contest between the Mother Country and this [the Revolution]. It spread among the lower class like an epidemy of the mind which reach'd far and near, as you well know. It soon swallow'd up every inferior contest, silenced every other dispute, and presented the people of Susquehanna with the pleasing hopes of their own never being decided by Great Britain. These solitary farmers, like all the rest of the inhabitants of this country, rapidly launch'd forth into all the intricate mazes of this grand quarrel, as their inclinations, prepossessions, and prejudices led them. A fatal era which has since disseminated among them the most horrid poison, which has torn them with intestine divisions, and has brought on that languor, that internal weakness, that suspension of industry, and the total destruction of their noble beginning.

Many, however, there were who still wished for peace; who still respected the name of Englishman; and cherished the idea of ancient connection. These were principally settled in the upper towns; the inhabitants of the lower ones were strongly prepossessed with the modern opinions. These latter ill-brooked that anyone who had come to settle under their patronage should prove their antagonists and, knowing themselves to be the strongest party, were guilty of many persecutions—a horrid policy. Every order was destroyed; the new harmony and good understanding which began to prevail among them were destroyed. Some of the inhabitants of the upper towns fell victims to this new zeal; gaols were erected on these peaceful shores where many sticklers for the old government were confined. But I am not going to lead you through the disgusting details of these scenes with which your papers have been filled, for it would be but a repetition of what has been done from one end of the continent to the other. This new ebullition of the mind was everywhere like one and the same cause, and therefore everywhere produced the same effects.

Many of those who found themselves stripped of their property took refuge among the Indians. Where else could they go? Many others, tired of that perpetual tumult in which the whole settlement was involved, voluntarily took the same course; and I am told that great numbers from the extended frontiers of the middle provinces have taken the same steps—some reduced to despair, some fearing the incursions with which they were threatened. What a strange idea this joining with the savages seems to convey to the imagination, this uniting with a people which Nature had distinguished by so many national marks! Yet this is what the Europeans have often done through choice and inclination, whereas we never hear of any Indians becoming civilized Europeans. This uncommon emigration, however, has thrown among them a greater number of whites than ever has been known before. This will ere long give rise to a new set of people, but will not produce a new species, so strong is the power of Indian education. Thus war, tyranny, religion, mix nations with nations; dispeople one part of the earth to cause a new one to be inhabited.

It will be worthy of observation to see whether those who are now with the Indians will ever return and submit themselves to the yoke of European society; or whether they will carefully cherish their knowledge and industry and gather themselves on some fertile spot in the interior parts of the continent; or whether that easy, desultory life so peculiar to the Indians will attract their attention and destroy their ancient inclinations. I rather think that the latter will preponderate, for you cannot possibly conceive the singular charm, the indescribable propensity which Europeans are apt to conceive and imbibe in a very short time for this vagrant life, a life which we civilized people are apt to represent to ourselves as the most ignoble, the most irksome of any. Upon a nearer inspection, 'tis far from being so disgusting. Innumerable instances might be produced of the effect which it has had, not only on poor illiterate people, but on soldiers and other persons bred to the luxuries and ease of a European life. Remember the strong instance of the people taken at Oswego during the last war, who, though permitted to return home, chose to remain and become Indians. The daughters of these frontier people will necessarily marry with the young men of the nation in which they have taken refuge, they have now no other choice. At a certain age, Nature points out the necessity of union; she cares very little about the colour. By the same reason and in consequence of the same cause, the young Europeans will unite themselves to the squaws. 'Tis very probable, therefore, that fishing, hunting, and a little planting will become their principal occupations. The children that will spring from these new alliances will thoroughly imbibe the manners of the village and perhaps speak no other language. You know what the power of education is: the Janizaries, though born of Frank parents, were by its impulse rendered the most enthusiastic enemies of the Christian name.

Some time after the departure of these people a few Indians came down under the sanction of a flag to demand their effects, representing that they had been so much disturbed in their huntings that they were not able to maintain so many of them; that, had they their cows and horses, they would give them land enough to raise their own bread. But instead of complying with this just request, in the hour of the utmost infatuation they seized these ambassadors, whipped them, and sent them away. Ignorant as we suppose them to be, yet this treatment inflamed them to most bitter revenge and awakened those unguided passions which are so dreadful among this haughty people. Notwithstanding this high insult, the nation sent a second and more numerous embassy than the first. Colonel Dyer, a member of Congress for the province of Connecticut, expostulated with them by letter and pointed out the injustice and impolicy of their proceedings, but in vain. Though they should have been astonished at a step so new and extraordinary as this second embassy, yet they attempted to seize them. Two only were apprehended and confined; the rest made their escape.

A short time before this, the Congress had ordered a body of four hundred men to be raised in order to cover more effectually the frontiers of this long-extended settlement. The people readily enlisted, and this regiment was soon completed. But what was their surprise and alarm when it was ordered to join General Washington's headquarters! They then, but too late, began to emerge from that state of blindness in which they seemed to have been plunged. They began to fear lest their ill-judged conduct should bring down at last the vengeance of a much larger body of assailants than they could well repel. The absence of this regiment, composed of the flower of their youth, not only left them very much exposed but even seemed to invite the enemy. As they had foreseen it, it hastened the long-premeditated storm which had been gathering. The Europeans who had taken refuge among the natives united with them in the same scheme which had been anteriorly proposed, and set on foot by the commandant of Niagara; they were, therefore, joined by several English officers and soldiers. The whole body of these assailants seemed animated with the most vindictive passions, a sacrifice to which many innocent families as well as guilty ones were doomed to fall. As no bard has as yet appeared to sing in plaintive strains: "Mourn, Susquehanna! Mourn thy hapless sons, thy defenceless farmers slaughtered on thy shores!" shall I be excused in following my feelings and in finishing the short account of their final catastrophe as my untutored but honest impulse directs?

Oh Man, Thou has made the happy earth thy hell,
Filled it with cursing cries and deep exclaims;
If thou delight to view thy heinous deeds,
Behold this pattern of thy butcheries.

The assailants formed a body of about eight hundred men, who received their arms from Niagara; the whites under the conduct of Colonel Butler, the Indians under that of Brant. After a fatiguing march, they all met at some of the upper towns of the Susquehanna; and while they were refreshing themselves and providing canoes and every other necessary implement, parties were sent out in different parts [of the country]. Some penetrated to the west branch and did infinite mischief; it was easy to surprise defenceless, isolated families, who fell an easy prey to their enemies. Others approached the New England settlements, where the ravages they committed were not less dreadful. Many families were locked up in their houses and consumed with all their furniture. Dreadful scenes were transacted which I know not how to retrace. This was, however, but the prelude of the grand drama. A few weeks afterwards, the whole settlement was alarmed with the news of the main body coming down the river. Many immediately embarked and retired into the more interior parts of Pennsylvania; the rest immediately retired with their wives and children into the stockade they had erected there some time before.

Meanwhile, the enemy landed at Lackawanna or Kingston, the very place where the stockade was erected. Orders were immediately issued by their commanders for the rest of the militia to resort to them. Some of the most contiguous readily obeyed; distance prevented others. Colonel Butler, seeing they had abandoned their dwellings, proposed to them to surrender and quit the country in a limited time. It was refused by the New England people, who resolved to march out and meet them in the open fields. Their number consisted of five hundred and eighty-two. They found the enemy advantageously situated, but much weaker in numbers, as they thought, than had been reported. This encouraged them; they boldly advanced, and the Indians as sagaciously retreated. Thus they were led on to the fatal spot where all at once they found themselves surrounded. Here some of the New England leaders abandoned them to their evil destiny. Surprised as they were at this bad omen, they still kept their ground and vigorously defended themselves until the Indians, sure of their prey, worked up by the appearance of success to that degree of frenzy which they call courage, dropped their guns and rushed on them with the tomahawk and the spear. The cruel treatment they expected to receive from the wrathful Indians and offended countrymen animated them for a while. They received this first onset with the most undaunted courage; but, the enemy falling upon them with a redoubled fury and on all sides, they broke and immediately looked for safety in flight.

Part of them plunged themselves into the river with the hopes of reaching across, and on this element a new scene was exhibited not less terrible than that which had preceded it. The enemy, flushed with the intoxication of success and victory, pursued them with the most astonishing celerity, and, being naked, had very great advantage over a people encumbered with clothes. This, united with their superiority in the art of swimming, enabled them to overtake most of these unfortunate fugitives, who perished in the river pierced with the lances of the Indians. Thirty-three were so happy as to reach the opposite shores, and for a long time afterwards the carcasses of their companions, become offensive, floated and infested the banks of the Susquehanna as low as Shamokin. The other party, who had taken their flight towards their forts, were all either taken or killed. It is said that those who were then made prisoners were tied to small trees and burnt the evening of the same day.

The body of the aged people, the women and children who were enclosed in the stockade, distinctly could hear and see this dreadful onset, the last scene of which had been transacted close to the very gates. What a situation these unfortunate people were in! Each wife, each father, each mother could easily distinguish each husband and son as they fell. But in so great, so universal a calamity, when each expected to meet the same fate, perhaps they did not feel so keenly for the deplorable end of their friends and relations. Of what powerful materials must the human heart be composed, which could hold together at so awful a crisis! This bloody scene was no sooner over than a new one arose of a very similar nature. They had scarcely finished scalping the numerous victims which lay on the ground when these fierce conquerors demanded the immediate entrance to the fort. It was submissively granted. Above a hundred of them, decorated with all the dreadful ornaments of plumes and colour of war, with fierce and animated eyes, presented themselves and rushed with impetuosity into the middle of the area, armed with tomahawks made of brass with an edge of steel. Tears relieved some; involuntary cries disburdened the oppression of others; a general shriek among the women was immediately heard all around.

What a spectacle this would have exhibited to the eyes of humanity: hundreds of women and children, now widows and orphans, in the most humble attitude, with pale, dejected countenances, sitting on the few bundles they had brought with them, keeping their little unconscious children as close to them as possible, hiding by a mechanical instinct the babies of their breasts; numbers of aged fathers oppressed with the unutterable sorrow; all pale, all trembling, and sinking under the deepest consternation were looking towards the door—that door through which so many of their friends had just passed, alas, never more to return! Every one at this awful moment measured his future punishment by the degree of revenge which he supposed to animate the breast of his enemy. The self-accusing consciences of some painted to them each approaching minute as replete with the most terrible fate. Many there were who, recollecting how in the hour of oppression they had insulted their countrymen and the natives, bitterly wept with remorse; others were animated with the fiercest rage. What a scene an eminent painter might have copied from that striking exhibition if it had been a place where a painter could have calmly sat with the palette in his hands! How easily he might have gathered the strongest expressions of sorrow, consternation, despondency, and despair by taking from each countenance some strong feature of affright, of terror, and dismay as it appeared delineated on each face. In how many different modes these passions must have painted themselves according as each individual's temper, ardent or phlegmatic habit, hurried or retarded the circulation of the blood, lengthened or contracted the muscles of his physiognomy.

But now a scene of unexpected humanity ensues, which I hasten to describe, because it must be pleasing to peruse and must greatly astonish you, acquainted as you are with the motives of revenge which filled the breasts of these people, as well as with their modes of carrying on war. The preceding part of this narration seems necessarily leading to the horrors of the utmost retaliation. Happily these fierce people, satisfied with the death of those who had opposed them in arms, treated the defenceless ones, the women and children, with a degree of humanity almost hitherto unparalleled.

In the meanwhile the loud and repeated war-shouts began to be re-echoed from all parts; the flames of conflagrated houses and barns soon announced to the other little towns the certainty of their country's defeat; these were the first marks of the enemies' triumph. A general devastation ensued, but not such as we read of in the Old Testament, where we find men, women, children, and cattle equally devoted to the same blind rage. All the stock, horses, sheep, etc., that could be gathered in the space of a week were driven to the Indian towns by a party which was detached on purpose. The other little stockades, hearing of the surrender of their capital, opened their gates and submitted to the conquerors They were all immediately ordered to paint their faces with red, this being the symbol established then, which was to preserve peace and tranquillity while the two parties were mingled together.

Thus perished in one fatal day most of the buildings, improvements, mills, bridges, etc., which had been erected there with so much cost and industry. Thus were dissolved the foundations of a settlement begun at such a distance from the metropolis, disputed by a potent province, the beginning of which had been stained with blood shed in their primitive altercations. Thus the ill-judged policy of these ignorant people and the general calamities of the times overtook them and extirpated them even out of that wilderness which they had come twelve years before to

possess and embellish. Thus the grand contest entered into
by these colonies with the mother country has spread
everywhere, even from the sea-shores to the last cottages
of the frontiers. This most diffusive calamity, on this fatal
spot in particular, has despoiled of their goods, chattels,
and lands, upwards of forty-five hundred souls, among
whom not a third part was ever guilty of any national
crime. Yet they suffered every extent of punishment as if
they had participated in the political iniquity which was
attributed to the leaders of this unfortunate settlement.
This is always the greatest misfortune attending war. What
had poor industrious women done? What crime had their
numerous and innocent children committed?

> Where are heaven's holiness and mercy fled?
> Laughs heaven at once at virtue and at Man?
> If not, why that discouraged, this destroyed?

Many accused the king with having offered a reward for
the scalps of poor inoffensive farmers. Many were seized
with violent fevers, attended with the most frantic rage,
and died like maniacs; others sat in gloomy silence and
ended their unhappy days seemingly in a state of insensibility; various were the ultimate ends of some of these
people.

Towards the evening of the second day, a few Indians
found some spirituous liquor in the fort. The inhabitants,
dreading the consequence of inebriation, repaired to
Brant, who removed every appearance of danger. After
this, every one was permitted to go and look for the
mangled carcass of his relation and to cover it with earth.
I can easily imagine or conceive the feelings of a soldier
burying the bodies of his companions, but neither my
imagination nor my heart permits me to think of the
peculiar anguish and keen feelings which must have seized
that of a father, that of a mother avidly seeking among the
crowd of slain for the disfigured corpse of a beloved son,
the throbbing anguish of a wife—I cannot proceed.

Yet was it not astonishing to see these fierce conquerors, besmeared with the blood of these farmers,
loaded with their scalps hardly cold, still swelled with the
indignation, pride, and cruelty with which victory always
inspires them, abstain from the least insult and permit

some rays of humanity to enlighten so dreadful, so dreary a day?

The complete destruction of these extended settlements was now the next achievement which remained to be done in order to finish their rude triumph, but it could not be the work of a few days. Houses, barns, mills, grain, everything combustible to conflagrate; cattle, horses, and stock of every kind to gather; this work demanded a considerable time. The collective industry of twelve years could not well be supposed, in so great an extent, to require in its destruction less than twelve days. During that interval, both parties were mixed together, and neither blows nor insults tarnished the duration of this period; a perfect suspension of animosities took place. The scattered inhabitants, who came to take the benefit of the Painter Proclamation, all equally shared in the protection it imparted. Some of the Indians looked for those families which were known to have abhorred the preceding tyranny. They found the fathers and mothers, but the young men were killed; they bestowed on them many favours. The horrors of war were suspended to give these unhappy people full leisure to retire.

Some embarked in boats and, leaving all they had behind them, went down the river towards Northumberland, Paxtung, Sunbury, etc., to seek shelter among the inhabitants of Pennsylvania; others, and by far the greatest number, were obliged to venture once more on foot through the great wilderness which separated them from the inhabited part of the province of New York. They received the most positive assurances that they would meet with no further injuries, provided they kept themselves painted in this long traject. This was the very forest they had traversed with so much difficulty a few years before, but how different their circumstances! 'Tis true they were then poor, but they were rich in hopes; they were elated with the near approach of prosperity and ease. Now that all-cheering, that animating sentiment was gone. They had nothing to carry with them but the dreadful recollection of having lost their all, their friends, and their helpmates. These protecting hands were cold, were motionless, which had so long toiled to earn them bread and procure them comfort. No more will they either hold the plough or handle the axe for their wives and children, who, destitute and forlorn, must fly, they hardly know where, to live on the charity of friends. Thus on every side could you see aged parents, wives, and a multitude of unhappy victims of the times preparing themselves as well as they could to begin this long journey, almost unprovided with any kind of provisions.

While the faithful hand is retracing these mournful events in all the various shades of their progressive increase, the humane heart cannot help shedding tears of the most philanthropic compassion over the burning ruins, the scattered parts of a society once so flourishing, now half-extinct, now scattered, now afflicted by the most pungent sorrow with which the hand of heaven could chastise them.

For a considerable time the roads through the settled country were full of these unhappy fugitives, each company slowly returning towards those counties from which they had formerly emigrated. Some others, still more unfortunate than others, were wholly left alone with their children, obliged to carry through that long and fatiguing march the infants of their breasts, now no longer replenished as before with an exuberant milk. Some of them were reduced to the cruel necessity of loading the ablest of them with the little food they were permitted to carry. Many of these young victims were seen bareheaded, barefooted, shedding tears at every step, oppressed with fatigues too great for their tender age to bear; afflicted with every species of misery, with hunger, with bleeding feet, every now and then surrounding their mother, as exhausted as themselves. "Mammy, where are we going? Where is Father? Why don't we go home?" "Poor innocents, don't you know that the king's Indians have killed him and have burnt our house and all we had? Your uncle Simon will perhaps give us some bread."

Hundreds were seen in this deplorable condition, yet thinking themselves happy that they had safely passed through the great wilderness, the dangers of which had so much increased the misfortunes of their situation. Here you might see a poor starved horse, as weak and emaciated as themselves, given them perhaps by the enemy as a last boon. The poor beast was loaded with a scanty feather-bed serving as a saddle which was fastened on him with withes and bark. On it sat a wretched mother with a child at her breast, another on her lap, and two more placed behind her, all broiling in the sun, accompanied in this pilgrimage of tribulation by the rest of the family creeping slowly along, leading at a great distance behind a heifer once wild and frolicsome but now tamed by want and hunger; a cow, perhaps, with hollow flanks and projecting ribs closed the train; these were the scanty remains of greater opulence. Such was the mournful procession, which for a number of weeks announced to the country through which they passed the sad disaster which had befallen them. The generous farmers sent their waggons to collect as many as they could find and convey them to the neighbouring county, where the same kindness was repeated. Such was their situation, while the carcasses of their friends were left behind to feed the wolves of that wilderness on which they had so long toiled, and which they had come to improve.

CHAPTER IX

HISTORY OF MRS. B.
AN EPITOME OF ALL THE MISFORTUNES
WHICH CAN POSSIBLY OVERTAKE
A NEW SETTLER, AS RELATED BY HERSELF

I was born at ——, a very ancient and opulent settlement. My father was the minister of the town; he reared me with the greatest tenderness and care. At seventeen I married. My husband possessed a farm of one hundred and twenty-six acres, but, afraid lest he should not have the means of providing as amply as he wished for children that were not born, [contrary to my advice] he sold it and removed to the county of ——, where he purchased a track of four hundred acres. But even in this first step toward the amelioration of our fortune, we met with a severe disappointment which has proved the type of that adversity which we were destined to meet with in the course of our career. My husband was honest and unsuspicious and soon found that he had been cruelly deceived by a villain who pretended that the farm he had sold us was free from any encumbrances. We were obliged to pay upward of four hundred and twenty-nine dollars, besides an immense deal of trouble for fees, lawyers, and clerks. However, by means of great industry, sobriety, hard labour, and perseverance, we retrieved ourselves in a few years. I had then become the mother of eight children, six sons and two daughters. Soon afterwards, the asperity of the climate, the roughness of the land, discouraged my husband. He heard of the Number 2 scheme and purchase on the shores of the Susquehanna. Captivated with the pleasing report which was everywhere propagated, avidly comparing the fertility of those new grounds with the inferior quality of his own, he early became an adventurer in the scheme, which at that time occupied every mind and was the subject of general conversation. Soon afterwards, we sold all we had and removed to Wyoming, as it was then called. We were almost the first who emigrated there. Unspeakable were the fatigues, the hardships we sustained from want of roads, of bridges, from storms of rain and wind, and a thousand other accidents which no tongue can describe, but we were all healthy and felt inwardly happy. Born as I was at ———, you may be sure that I knew nothing of so great, so hideous a wilderness as we had to traverse; I was a stranger to its intricacies and infinite difficulties. For nothing is so easy as to travel on a map: our fingers smoothly glide over brooks and torrents and mountains. But actually to traverse a track of one hundred miles, accompanied with eight children, with cattle, horses, oxen, sheep, etc.—this is to meet with a thousand unforeseen difficulties.

We arrived at last on that spot so long talked of, and so long promised, on which we were sure to meet plenty, ease, and happiness. The aspect pleased me much. I never could admire enough these extensive plats of admirable grounds which by their grass, the weeds they produced, seemed to be the seat of fertility itself. I contemplated with peculiar satisfaction the fair, the placid stream with pebbly bottom, running along these delightful banks. This afforded me a very great contrast when I recollected the stormy ocean near which I had been bred. There we found a few scattered families, poor but as happy as we were. We laboured under the same difficulties, and had been impelled by the same motives. We had to think of bread for present subsistence, but that was not to be had. My sons and my husband were obliged to dedicate part of their time to hunting and fishing, else we must have starved. We had a shed to erect, fodder to provide in due time, for the preservation of the stock we had brought along with us. There were the honest cows, which, even through the wilderness, had given us milk; there were four oxen, which had brought our baggage and the younger children; there was the faithful mare which I had ridden; and there was a score of sheep —they were all part of our household, without the assistance of which we could not subsist. Judge of the fatigues we met with, of the anxiety and earnestness with which we applied ourselves to provide future subsistence for so many mouths. Ah, what a summer that was! And what was worse, I became a mother soon after my arrival. I was the first who added to the population of this country a child, which on that account I called Susquehanna B. A piece of round bark ingeniously fixed by my husband served him for a cradle, and had it not been for this cruel war, he might have lived to have been an opulent farmer, though rocked in so simple a machine.

Three years afterwards, we were involved in a quarrel with the people of Pennsylvania. My husband, though a most peaceable man, fell a victim to these disputes and was carried away prisoner to Philadelphia. We lost all our horses and cows, for in these petty wars these movables are always driven off. I was ready to starve, and ashamed to become troublesome to my neighbours. I placed five of my oldest children with the best of them; they began to be able to earn their bread. The oldest was already married and settled thirty miles higher up, and myself with the second and youngest intended to return to the county of ——, whence we had emigrated. It was then the beginning of winter; the earth was covered with a foot of snow. I was provided but with a single blanket. This snow, which I dreaded so much, proved my kindest support; it kept me warm at night; we must have perished had it not been for the timely assistance it procured me. I was six days in traversing the long tract which divides Wyoming from the first settlements of ——. My sufferings and the patience with which I bore them would be but trifling objects; I therefore pass them over, though the different images of those calamitous stages are as present to my mind as they were the day I got out of the wilderness.

The following summer, my husband procured his freedom. He returned to Wyoming, then called Wilkes-Barre. There he found everything in ruins. He went to see his children. He heard that I was returned to ―― in order to procure horses, without which we could do nothing. After many regrets and many weary steps, he rejoined me. Soon afterwards, we plucked up a new stock of courage, bought two horses, and returned to our ruined settlement; and a joyful day it was, though we had not a mouthful of bread then. I found my children all healthy and hearty; this was a sufficient feast for a mother. We soon procured plenty of provisions among the neighbours who, less unfortunate than we, began to enjoy a great abundance of everything. We toiled and soon recovered our ancient losses, but the ancient contentions with Pennsylvanians kept us all in suspense and uncertainty. But this was not all; the New England men of the town where we lived were forever at variance with one another about the boundaries, the divisions of the town. We had no government but what the people chose to follow from day to day, just as passion or caprice dictated. We had, however, everything in plenty; and we looked on these transitory disturbances as evils which would soon cease.

This, however, did not happen so soon as we expected. We loved peace and, [owing] to the strong desire of acquiring it, we resolved to remove to Wyalusing, sixty miles up the river; to abandon the labour of three years and to submit ourselves once more to the toils of first settlement. My husband made there a considerable purchase. We thought ourselves far happier as soon as we arrived there. We found the inhabitants satisfied with their lands, with their lots. They spent their time in useful labours and sought to disturb nobody. They were mostly Yorkers, Jersey men, and Pennsylvania High Germans. There lived old G――e, a crafty Indian who had acquired a love of riches and property, contrary to the general disposition of these people. He had successfully bought several Indian rights and was possessed of upwards of five hundred acres of excellent lands, with many houses. He was kind and hospitable. Here we soon lived in affluence. The beautiful grass of this country, the uninterrupted repose we enjoyed, made us soon forget our pristine calamities. We thought that we were to be happy for the rest of our days. My husband owned land enough to provide for all children; we wished for no more. Two of them were then married and settled a few miles below, towards Wysox. It was a little paradise; not a wrangle or dispute ever tarnished our tranquillity in the space of three years or more.

Congress affairs came, and behold us once more involved in calamities more distressing than any we had as yet met with! What we had hitherto suffered was a sting of bees; we have received the wounds since which came from much more malevolent beings. The great national dispute caused great divisions in the opinions of the people. My two oldest sons unfortunately joined in the most popular one. There was a disunited family, the worst of all evils; this proved a sad heart-breaking to my poor husband and me. The respect many people paid him made him, after a time, interpose in these new disputes, with which we poor back-settlers had nothing to do. The people of these upper towns were settled principally by people called Tories. A secret war was declared against us all by the more populous below. Parties were frequently sent up to apprehend people of this denomination and oblige them to retract their pernicious principles. These operations were never performed without a good deal of plundering under various pretences, sometimes as fines for non-appearance, at other times for the fees of those who were sent up.

This occasioned a new and unforeseen distress among us all. Many banished themselves and voluntarily abandoned their possessions. The flight of several families intimidated those which remained. They retired also, some one way, some the other. Some young districts just settled were thus depopulated. I think, to the best of my remembrance, that there was not one family left at Standing Stone. They were all frightened; they took wings. Our old Indian sold all his possessions and retired among his countrymen. Happy man, he knew where to find peace! Although we call them wild, we, more civilized, did not know where to go. Would to God we had followed him as he often persuaded us! I would have gone to the extremities of the earth to avoid the broils in the midst of which we lived, and which daily increased.

We were left almost alone; my sons were compelled to enlist in this new sort of warfare. A mother's representation, a father's command, had no kind of effect on their hearts. They had in some measure imbibed a good deal of the spirit of the times and thought themselves justifiable in what they did; they were deaf to our remonstrances. The militia-laws, as contrived by the New England people, were extremely severe. There was no middle course to take; one was obliged either to quit the settlement or else to obey. For, as they considered themselves as the founders and legislators, they unhappily thought likewise that they were possessed of the right of establishing their [beliefs] concerning this great dispute as the general one of the whole settlement. My husband and I often trembled at the recollection of all these strange deeds. We foresaw nothing very distinctly, and yet we could sometimes perceive that it might have a longer trail and heavier consequences than most people were aware of.

One day my oldest son brought us by way of present some of the furniture of one of the plundered families. I kicked it out-of-doors. I would not so much as look at it; I was afraid it would bring us bad luck, of which we had already a sufficient portion. Many at last resisted. Several parties of Indians began to appear, and in one of these encounters my third son was taken. I forgot his principles; I forgave him his past conduct; I shed tears over the unfortunate child, though disobedient. Soon afterwards, I heard he was at Ockwackon; and since, I have been informed of his being at Niagara, on his way to Quebec. Judge of my feelings—but I am almost grown callous! What a hard destiny for that poor fellow! Now often in my dreams have I followed him through the great tract he had to cross to arrive where he is, traversing the great Ontario, descending the huge rapids of the upper Saint Lawrence. How I have trembled for his life, lest the great tumbling waters, by the least mismanagement of the steersman, should submerge him and all the crew! I have followed him as far as Montreal, emerging from his slavery, and obtaining leave to work with some honest tranquil farmer. Happy shall I be if this part of his fate may reclaim him and bring him back to my arms an honest man like his father. Dear boy, how many tears hast thou cost thy poor aged mother!

The cruel necessity of the times obliged us at last to quit our favourite habitation; the good opinion they had hitherto entertained of my husband no longer served him as a protection. We bade, without knowing it, an eternal adieu to our house, to those fertile fields which were ploughed with so much ease and which yielded us such plentiful crops. Thus by the fatality of the times were cut off the reasonable hopes we had conceived of living tolerably easy in our old age and providing amply for each of our children. What a sacrifice we made! We had already lost above one half of our stock and many other movables.

With the remains, we embarked and returned to Wilkes-Barre, where we met with but little kindness. They seemed to think us of a suspicious character. As if it mattered much what a couple of old people thought! There we cultivated some little grounds, but, alas, they were not our own! We lived but scantily, and in vain regretted the affluence we had left behind us, an affluence we only enjoyed three years in twenty-nine of hard toils, disappointments, and sufferings. As a woman, I made no scruple to speak my mind with my usual freedom and candour. I was condemned by some; by others I was accused of speaking my husband's sentiments, and they began to insult him accordingly. He bemoaned and bemoaned in vain his hard fate. We regretted that ever we should have abandoned Wyalusing. We often thought that it would be better to have remained exposed to every incursion than to the daily mortification of receiving unmerited abuse. I could, methinks, harden myself to the dangers, to the noise, to the perturbations of war; but contumely unmerited—contumely, to an honest mind, is daggers to one's soul. You have no doubt heard of the treatment some Indians of Ockwackon met with. It was blindness itself. Some few well-disposed men saw it in that light, but none dared speak. Alas, how often we lamented our fate! How often we wished us away! But we were now old, now worn down with accumulated fatigues. Our ancient spirits, vigour, and courage were no more. Three of our boys had left us; they were married happily with people who lived higher up.

I shall not tire your patience with repeating what is so well known, our great disaster. The destruction of that great settlement, the death of many hundreds of people, are circumstances with which everyone is ac-

quainted. No sooner were we informed of the arrival of
the enemy than I hastened with my family to the stockade which had been erected at Kingston, on the opposite side of the river. In getting into the boat, I fell and,
unhappily, broke my thigh. Full of the most acute pains,
I was carried into the fort and there laid on straw broiling in the sun—my husband and myself, my daughter,
and three young boys. Judge of our consternation and
affright! We heard the howling of the Indians, the fire of
the musketry, the shrieks of the wounded and dying. I
heard and felt more on that day than I thought it
possible for a woman to hear, to feel, and to bear.
Heaven's arrows were launched against us in all manner
of directions, and yet I lived, lived to tell of all this great
chain of calamities. Sometimes I am astonished at it. Oh,
my God, how thankful was I that my two sons lived at
Mahapeny Exeter; they were beyond the reach of the
militia commander. This single reflection alleviated all the
rest. My poor daughter's husband never returned. She
fainted away by my side. But in so great, so general a
calamity, when I thought as I did then that my two sons
might be in the fray, how could I feel for a son-in-law?

H—e, the Indian whom I had known before, was among
the number of those who entered our fort—an awful
remembrance. He singled out my husband, with whom he
shook hands with all the signs of ancient friendship. He
immediately asked for our boys; we informed him where
they were; he seemed to rejoice. Soon afterwards we were
informed that we must all paint ourselves red and that
we must depart from the settlement in five days. Towards
the close of the evening, H—e returned again and took
my husband along with him. It proved to him a strange
evening, and replete with the strongest impressions of
joy and sorrow. In travelling towards the Indian's tent,
he was obliged to pass through the field of battle, where
he involuntarily was obliged to view the mangled carcasses of many of his best friends and acquaintances. He
was ready to faint with anguish and a multitude of ideas
which then crowded on his mind. As soon as he arrived
at the tent, H—e presented him with his two sons
painted red, which prevented him from knowing them so
readily as he otherwise would. They tenderly embraced
each other and shed abundance of tears; they were the

tears produced by joy alone. Their joy was mixed with strange ingredients which you can easily comprehend. My sons, as well as my husband, had seen many of their friends lying on the ground. They foresaw the approaching ruin of all their property and the total destruction of their country. I scarcely can tell of all these things yet without feeling my heart ready to break and my eyes full of tears. "Honest brother," said H——e to my husband, "your house at Wyalusing is not burnt. Nothing shall be destroyed of what you have. If you incline to remain, which I wish you would, observe to keep all your family painted red and wear something of that colour when you go to the fields. If you prefer going away, take as many of your things as you can, and may Kitchy Manitou be favorable to you wherever you go."

In a few days we procured a canoe and prepared ourselves to go down to Shamokin, towards Pennsylvania. I would not have remained here among all my departed acquaintances for the most valuable consideration. House, cattle, property—none of these things appeared now to me of any value. I had lost what I never could regain: the peace of my mind. I cared very little where I went; I was now a poor, helpless, infirm old woman. We soon arrived at Shamokin; but as the settlement is small, we crossed over the river to Northumberland, where we met with all the kindness and hospitality we possibly could expect. But Heaven had not done yet with its frowns. Gracious God, what had we done that we were doomed to meet with so many species of evil? While I was confined to my bed, my husband and one of my sons took the smallpox and died. They died without my being able to see them for the last time. Judge of my situation: to have escaped the fury of such an enemy and thus to die among strangers, unpitied and perhaps unattended! What a singular fate, what peculiar hardships, was I born to bear! I had not had the dreadful disorder myself, and they would not let me come near them. Thus was I left destitute, desolate, a cripple deprived of any settlement, my husband and one of my sons dead.

O Britain! Little do thy rich inhabitants know of the toils to which we are subjected, and of the sufferings thy mandates have caused. I recommended myself to God and earnestly prayed that He would take me from a

world in which I had found so little comfort. Still I had
friends and relations, but they were at a great distance.
How, in my condition, should I be able to reach them?
But after all I had lost, what was it in this world that
could give me any concern? I got up, and in company
with my surviving son and my daughter and her infant,
we ventured through what they call the lower road, which
leads into the cultivated parts of Pennsylvania. We had
two horses, which had been given us by H—e. However, they were so poor and emaciated that I was
obliged often to alight in order to ease them. I scrambled
along on my crutches as well as I could, and in these
various essays travelled upwards of twenty miles. We had
hardly arrived among the inhabitants when my poor
daughter was seized with the distemper which had carried off her father. My hard fortune obliged me to leave
her one hundred and twenty miles behind me in the
hands of strangers who promised to take good care of
her. I took the charge of her infant, nine months old,
and with a heart that could not break, I proceeded on
my journey until overtaken by a prodigious shower
of rain. I stopped at your son's door; he received us
with kindness and humanity. My son had left his wife at
—— and had purposely come so far in order to see me
safe among my friends. Though I had not then reached
them yet, as I found myself among Christians, I insisted
on his going back and dismissed him; his own family
wanted his presence. But, alas, the measure of my sorrows was not yet filled. The grandchild I had brought with
me had suckled his mother too long. He caught the infection and died in my arms and communicated to me
the same disorder. I dreaded it not, for I wished to die
and have done with so many adverse accidents.

Yet I survived and am almost blind, fitter to descend
among those shades which already encompass me than
to remain any longer among the living, to which I am
become an object of useless pity. My daughter happily
recovered and has since rejoined me, but her infant is
dead. She has taken a log-house in the neighbourhood
of my friends, where we are removed. The industry of
my daughter and of my three youngest children, with
the extreme kindness of my relations, enable us to live
with decency and comfort. Such has been the singular

fate, the long peregrination, the total ruin of a family once possessed of three good estates, born and bred of decent parents, endowed with good education; now half destroyed and now reduced to own not a single foot of land.

CHAPTER X

THE FRONTIER WOMAN

I met accidentally not long since an ancient acquaintance of mine, who from the beginning of this war has been a principal actor in these bloody scenes which are seldom attended with any dangers to the aggressor, for everything is done in the night and by surprise.

"I am afraid," he told me, "that I shall not be permitted to die in peace whenever my hour comes. Even now I never lie down or smoke a pipe alone but a thousand frightful images occur to my mind. Yet when I did those things, I felt no more concerned than if I had been girdling so many useless trees." These are his very words. "At times I feel involuntary remorse which oppresses me with melancholy and sorrow. My heart, oh, my heart!" (putting his hand on it). "Sometimes it beats as if it would palpitate its last, and I cannot tell for what.

"I am well in health. The strength of those ancient infatuations is now vanished which enabled me to commit those ravages. I dread going to my bed, that bed where I used before to enjoy such an uninterrupted sleep. I feel a mixture of horror and repentance, but what is it good for? What good does it avail those poor people whom we have destroyed? What recompense can I make to the fugitive survivors? By what astonishing power does

Blood

it come to pass that Man can so thoroughly imbibe the instinct and adopt the ferocity of the tiger, and yet be so indifferent in his faculties and organs? The tiger sheds no blood but when impelled to it by the stings of hunger; had Nature taught him to eat grass, he would not be the tiger. But Man, who eats no man, yet kills Man and takes a singular pleasure in shedding his blood.

"The voices of the many infants I have seen perishing in the wilderness, the curses and imprecations of the desolated fathers, the groans of the afflicted mothers whom I have beheld reduced to a variety of the most distressed circumstance—these are some of the retrospects which distract me. Ah, that young woman! Because she tried to escape from the Indians whose prisoner she was! That she had never been born! I never should have committed the horrid deed! One single humane action I once did, impelled by—I cannot assign the cause; and this is the only balm which I try to bring to my wounded heart.

"In an excursion which we made to ——, our party consisted of twenty-three: five white people and eighteen Indians of the very worst class. We came close to the woods of the settlement about sundown, but perceived nobody in the fields. We concluded that the people had retired to their houses, of which we counted nine. We divided ourselves in as many companies, so that every house was to be entered at once at the signal of a gun.

"God forbid that I should tell you the history of that attack, where there was so much innocent blood shed. I entered that which had fallen to my lot, and the first object I perceived was a woman of a comely aspect, neat and clean. She was suckling two children, whilst at the same time she was rocking the third in a cradle. At the sight of me who was painted and dressed like an Indian, she suddenly arose and came towards the door: 'I know your errand,' she said. 'Begin with these little innocents that they may not languish and die with hunger when I am gone. Dispatch me as you have dispatched my poor aged father and my husband last April. I am tired of life.'

"So saying, with her right hand she boldly pulled the handkerchief from her breast, whilst she still held her two infants with her left, and presented it to me bare.

I was armed with my tomahawk and was going to strike when a sudden and irresistible impulse prevented me. 'Good woman, why should I kill you?' I told her. 'If your husband and father are already dead, you have suffered enough. God help you.' 'Strike,' she said, 'and don't be faint-hearted. You are only mocking God and me. The rest of your gang will soon be here; this will only serve to prolong my misery. Hark! Hark! The butchers! The villains! Hark to the shrieks of my poor cousin Susy in the next house! Gracious God, why hast Thou thus abandoned me?' She wept bitterly. Motionless, I stood like a statue, my hand uplifted still, my eyes irresistibly fixed on her. My heart swelled; I wept also; I had not shed tears in many years before. 'No, good woman,' said I, 'not a hair of your head shall be touched. Are these three children yours?' 'Two only belong to me,' she answered; 'the mother of the third was killed last April as she was defending her husband who was sick on his bed. The cries of the poor baby who was left alone in its cradle, while its father and mother lay bleeding close by, made me go to its assistance. The neighbours buried them, as soon as they returned from the woods where they had hid themselves, and I have suckled it ever since.' 'And you have suckled it ever since! Live, honest woman, live! Would to God you were at ——, free from any further danger! Let my generosity now serve as a reward for your humanity in making this poor forlorn orphan share the milk of your breast with your own children.' The rest of our people soon rushed into the house with what little plunder they had collected. It cost me a great deal of patience and struggle before I could make them consent that this poor woman should live. Her husband had been a rebel, and no rebel's wife should be spared. Her situation during the barbarous debate was terrible; her fortitude abandoned her. She was seized with the most violent fits, but the dreadful sight which she exhibited as she lay convulsed on the ground, with the shrieks of her children, enabled me to melt my companions into some little transitory humanity.

"What shall I do to get rest, and to restore my mind to its pristine serenity? We had orders for laying everything waste. Read a copy of them and see whether I can be justified before God." I read it. I paused a long while, and casting my eyes towards heaven, that heaven where incomprehensible justice and mercy reside, I returned the paper to him. Thus ended our conversation.

Nor are these all the mischiefs caused by these devastations. Their effect is felt at a great distance, even where the danger is not so imminent, like a great storm on the ocean, which not only convulses it and causes a great number of shipwrecks wherever its greatest violence bursts, but agitates the air so powerfully that it becomes dangerous to the mariners even at a great distance. The various accounts of these incursions have spread a general alarm far and near. The report of these dreadful transactions is even frequently magnified in the various relations of them which circulate through the country. It has set every family a-trembling; it has impressed every mind with the most terrific ideas. Consequently, rural improvements are neglected; the former cheerfulness and confidence are gone. The gloomy, treacherous silence of the neighbouring woods prevents the husbandman from approaching them; everywhere we dread the fire of an invisible enemy from behind each tree. What mode of resistance, what means of security, can be devised in so extensive a country? Who can guard every solitary house? He who has been toiling all day to earn subsistence for his family wants rest at night.

I have often persuaded many to retire into the more interior parts of the country—so much easier is it to give advice than to follow it. Most of them are not able; others are attached to the soil, to their houses. Where shall we go, how shall we fare after leaving all our grain, all our cattle behind us? Some I have seen who, conscious of the integrity of their conduct, had flattered themselves with some marks of predilection; they seemed to comfort themselves with that idea. Poor souls! The same treacherous thoughts have often come into my head. They do not consider the spirit with which this species of war is conducted, and that we are all devoted [to it]. In consequence of this strange infatuation, I have lost several relations and friends, one in particular who was possessed of an ample fortune, literate, industrious, humane, and hospitable to a great degree. He was shot through the body as he was fearlessly riding home. As he fell, they scalped him and clove his head, and left him in that situation to become a most shocking spectacle to his poor wife. Unfortunate woman! Neither reason nor religion have since been able to convey her the least consolation.

What astonishing scenes of barbarity, distress, and woe will not the rage of war exhibit on this extended stage of human affairs! Pardon my repetitions: these people were so far situated from the theatre of war, so unconcerned with its cause, and in general guiltless, that it is astonishing to see them daily fall as if loaded with every degree of iniquity. But iniquity is not the cause of the calamities we suffer in this world. Neither our insignificance, our lakes, our rivers, our mountains, can afford us the least shelter. Our new enemies penetrate everywhere and hardly leave any traces of the flourishing settlements they are hired to destroy. Had a proper moderation, so useful and so necessary even in the most just wars, been prevalent, it would have saved from ruins a great many innocent families. If clemency was banished from the more immediate seat of war, one would have retraced it with pleasure on the extremities. Some part of the whole would have been saved from the general havoc. One would with admiration have observed the benignity of the chastising hand; and, to the praise of its humanity, some thousands of innocent families would have been overshadowed in peaceful neglect, wrapt up in that cloudy recess in which they were situated.

If I have dwelled so long on these inferior calamities and passed over those of the more opulent, more populous parts of the country, now in ruins, it is because in the latter it is unavoidable. The possessors of rich settlements have friends, connexions, and a variety of resources which in some measure alleviate their calamities. But those whom I have been speaking of, we who till the skirts of this great continent, once ruined, are ruined indeed, and therefore become objects much more deserving your compassion and pity.

CHAPTER XI

THE AMERICAN BELISARIUS

Journals, memoirs, elaborate essays, shall not fail hereafter to commemorate the heroes who have made their
appearance on this new American stage, to the end that
Europe may either lavishly praise or severely censure
their virtues and their faults. It requires the inquisitive
eye of an unnoticed individual mixing in crowds to find
out and select for private amusement more obscure,
though not less pathetic, scenes. Scenes of sorrow and
affliction are equally moving to the bowels of humanity.
Find them where you will, there is a strange but peculiar
sort of pleasure in contemplating them; it is a mournful
feast for some particular souls.

A pile of ruins is always striking, but when the object
of contemplation is too extensive, our divided and
wearied faculties receive impressions proportionably
feeble; we possess but a certain quantity of tears and
compassion. But when the scale is diminished, when we
descend from the destruction of an extensive government or nation to that of several individuals, to that of
a once opulent, happy, virtuous family, there we pause,
for it is more analogous to our own situation. We can
better comprehend the woes, the distresses of a father,
mother, and children immersed in the deepest calamities

imagination can conceive, than if we had observed the overthrow of kings and great rulers.

After a violent storm of north-west wind, I never see even a single oak overset, once majestic and lofty, without feeling some regret at the accident. I observe the knotty roots wrenched from the ground, the broken limbs, the scattered leaves. I revolve in my mind the amazing elemental force which must have occasioned so great an overthrow. I observe the humble bushes which grew under its shade. They felt the impression of the same storm, but in a proportion so much the less, as was that of their bulk when compared to that of the oak. I acknowledge that were I to observe a whole mountain thus divested of its trees by the impulse of the same gale, I should feel a superior degree of astonishment; but, at the same time, my observations could not be so minute nor so particular. It is not, therefore, those great and general calamities to the description of which my pencil is equal; it is the individual object as it lies lowly prostrate which I wish to describe. I can encompass it; I can view it in all situations; and the limited impressions admit within my mind a possibility of retracing them. Reserve this, therefore, for the hours, for the moments, of your greatest philanthropy. The enormity may shock you. Here we are more used to it; and having so many objects to feel for, one is able to feel so much the less for each.

The horror, the shocking details of the following tragedy, 'tis true, show mankind in the worst light possible. But what can you expect when law, government, mortality, are become silent and inefficacious? When men are artfully brought into a chaos, in order, as they are taught to believe, that they may be raised from their former confined line to a much preferable state of existence? To make use of a modern simile: the action of ploughing seems to be laborious and dirty; numberless worms, insects, and wise republics of ants are destroyed by the operation. Yet these scenes of unknown disasters, of unnoticed murders and ruins, happily tend to produce a rich harvest in the succeeding season.

In the township of —— lived S. K., the son of a Dutch father and of an English mother. These mixtures are very frequent in this country. From his youth he loved and delighted in hunting, and the skill he acquired confirmed his taste for that manly diversion. In one of the long excursions which he took in the mountains of —— (which he had never before explored), mixing the amusements of the chase with those of more useful contemplation, and viewing the grounds as an expert husbandman, he found among the wilds several beautiful vales formed by Nature in her most indulgent hours when, weary with the creation of the surrounding cliffs and precipices, she condescended to exhibit something on which Man might live and flourish—a singular contrast which you never fail to meet with in the mountains of America: the more rocky, barren, and asperous are the surrounding ridges, the richer and more fertile are the intervales and valleys which divide them. Struck with the singular beauty and luxuriance of one of these spots, he returned home, and soon after patented it. I think it contained about one thousand acres.

With cheerfulness he quitted the paternal estate he enjoyed, and prepared to begin the world anew in the bosom of this huge wilderness, where there was not even a path to guide him. He had a road to make, some temporary bridges to make, overset trees to remove, a house to raise, swamps to convert into meadows and to fit for the scythe, upland fields to clear for the plough— such were the labours he had to undertake, such were the difficulties he had to overcome. He surmounted every obstacle; he was young, healthy, vigorous, and strong-handed. In a few years this part of the wilderness assumed a new face and wore a smiling aspect. The most abundant crops of grass, of fruit, and grain soon succeeded to the moss, to the acorn, to the wild berry, and to all the different fruits, natives of that soil. Soon after these first successful essays, the fame of his happy beginning drew abundance of inferior people to that neighbourhood. It was made a county, and in a short time grew populous, principally with poor people, whom some part of this barren soil could not render much richer. But the love of independence, that strong attachment to wives and children which is so powerful and natural, will people the tops of cliffs and make them even prefer such settlements to the servitude of attendance, to the confinement of manufactories, or to the occupation of more menial labours.

There were in the neighbourhood two valuable pieces of land, less considerable indeed, but in point of fertility as good as his own. S. K. purchased them both and invited his two brothers-in-law to remove there; generously making them an offer of the land, of his teams, and every other necessary assistance; requiring only to be paid the advanced capital whenever they should be enabled; giving up all pretensions to interest or any other compensation. This handsome overture did not pass unaccepted. They removed to the new patrimony which they had thus easily purchased, and in this sequestered situation became to S. K. two valuable neighbours and friends. Their prosperity, which was his work, raised no jealousy in him. They all grew rich very fast. The virgin earth abundantly repaid them for their labours and advances, and they soon were enabled to return the borrowed capital which they had so industriously improved. This part of the scene is truly pleasing, pastoral, and edifying: three brothers, the founders of three opulent families, the creators of three valuable plantations, the promoters of the succeeding settlements that took place around them. The most plentiful crops, the fattest cattle, the greatest number of hogs and horses, raised loose in this wilderness, yearly accumulated their wealth, swelled their opulence; and rendered them the most conspicuous families in this corner of the world. A perfect union prevailed not only from the ties of blood, but cemented by those of the strongest gratitude.

Among the great number of families which had taken up their residence in that vicinage, it was not to be expected that they could all equally thrive. Prosperity is not the lot of every man; so many casualties occur that often prevent it. Some of them were placed, besides, on the most ungrateful soil, from which they could barely draw a subsistence. The industry of Man, the resources of a family, are never tried in this cold country, never put to the proof, until they have undergone the severity of a long winter. The rigours of this season generally require among this class of people every exertion of industry, as well as every fortunate circumstance that can possibly happen. A cow, perhaps, a few sheep, a couple of poor horses, must be housed, must be fed through the inclement season; and you know that it is from the labour of the summer, from collected grasses and fodder, this must proceed. If the least accident through droughts, sickness, carelessness or want of activity happens, a general calamity ensues. The death of any one of these precious animals oversets the well-being of the family. Milk is wanting for the children; wood must be hauled; the fleeces of sheep cannot be dispensed with. What providence can replace these great deficiencies?

Happily S. K. lived in the neighbourhood. His extreme munificence and generosity had hitherto, like a gem, been buried, for he had never before lived in a country where the needy and the calamitous were so numerous. In their extreme indigence, in all their unexpected disasters, they repair to this princely farmer. He opens to them his granary; he lends them hay; he assists them in whatever they want; he cheers them with good counsel; he becomes a father to the poor of this wilderness. They promise him payment; he never demands it. The fame of his goodness reaches far and near. Every winter his house becomes an Egyptian granary where each finds a supply proportioned to his wants. Figure to yourself a rich and opulent planter situated in an admirable vale, surrounded by a variety of distressed inhabitants, giving and lending, in the midst of a severe winter, cloaks, wool, shoes, etc., to a great number of unfortunate families; relieving a mother who has not perhaps wherewithal to clothe her new-born infant; sending timely succour, medicines, victuals to a valetudinarian exhausted with fatigues and labours; giving a milch cow to a desolated father who has just lost his in a quagmire as she went to graze the wild herbage for want of hay at home; giving employment; directing the labours and essays of these grateful but ignorant people towards a more prosperous industry. Such is the faithful picture of this man's conduct, for a series of years, to those around him. At home he was hospitable and kind, an indulgent father, a tender husband, a good master. This, one would imagine, was an object on which the good genius of America would have constantly smiled.

Upon an extraordinary demand of wheat from abroad, the dealers in this commodity would often come to his house and solicit from him the purchase of his abundant crops. "I have no wheat," said he, "for the rich; my harvest is for the poor. What would the inhabitants of these mountains do were I to divest myself of what superfluous grain I have?" "Consider, sir, you will receive your money in a lump, and God knows when you are to expect it from these needy people, whose indolence you rather encourage by your extreme bounty." "Some do pay me very punctually. The rest wish and try to do it, but they find it impossible; and pray, must they starve because they raise less grain than I do?" Would to God I were acquainted with the sequel of this humane conversation! I would recapitulate every phrase; I would dwell on every syllable. If Mercy herself could by the direction of the Supreme Being assume a visible appearance, such are the words which this celestial Being would probably utter for the example, for the edification of mankind. 'Tis really a necessary relief and a great comfort to find in human society some such beings, lest in the crowd, which through experience we find so different, we should wholly lose sight of that beautiful original and of those heavenly dispositions with which the heart of Man was once adorned.

One day as he was riding through his fields, he saw a poor man carrying a bushel of wheat on his back. "Where now, neighbour?"

"To mill, sir."

"Pray, how long since you are become a beast of burthen?"

"Since I had the misfortune of losing my jade."

"Have you neither spirit nor activity enough to catch one of my wild horses?"

"I dare not without your leave."

"Hark ye, friend, the first time I see you in that servile employment whilst I have so many useless ones about my farm, you shall receive from me a severe reprimand." The honest countryman took the hint, borrowed a little salt and a halter, and soon after appeared mounted on a spirited mare, which carried him where he wanted to go and performed for him his necessary services at home.

In the fall of the year it was his usual custom to invite his neighbours in, helping him to hunt and to gather together the numerous heads of swine which were bred in his woods that he might fat them with corn which he raised in the summer. He made it a rule to treat them handsomely and to send them home each with a good hog as a reward for their trouble and attendance. In harvest and haying he neither hired nor sent for any man but, trusting to the gratitude of the neighbourhood, always found his company of reapers and hay-makers more numerous than he wanted. It was truly a patriarchal harvest gathered for the benefit of his little world. Yet, notwithstanding his generosity, this man grew richer every crop; every agricultural scheme succeeded. What he gave did not appear to diminish his stores; it seemed but a mite, and immediately to be replaced by the hand of Providence. I have known Quakers in Pennsylvania who gave annually the tenth part of their income, and that was very great; but this man never counted, calculated, nor compared. The wants of the year, the calamities of his neighbourhood, were the measure by which he proportioned his bounty. The luxuriance of his meadows surpassed all belief; I have heard many people say, since his misfortunes, that they have often cut and cured three tons and a half per acre. The produce of his grain was in proportion; the blessings of heaven prospered his labours and showered fertility over all his lands. Equally vigilant and industrious, he spared neither activity nor perseverance to accomplish his schemes of agriculture. Thus he lived for a great number of years, the father of the poor and the example of this part of the world. He aimed at no popular promotion, for he was a stranger to pride and arrogance. A simple commission as a militia-captain was all that distinguished him from his equals.

Unfortunate times came at last. What opinion he embraced in the beginning remains unknown. His brothers-in-law had long envied his great popularity, of which, however, he had never made the least abuse. They began to ridicule his generosity, and, from a contempt of his manner of living, they secretly passed to extreme hatred; but hitherto they had taken care to conceal their rancour and resentment. At the dawn of this new revolution, they blazed forth. Fanned by the general impunity of the times, they, in an underhanded manner, endeavoured to represent him as inimical. They prevailed upon the leaders to deprive him of his commission (though fifty-six

years of age), and even made him submit to the duties of a simple militiaman. They harassed his son by all the means which false zeal and uncontrollable power—[all] too unhappily—suggested to them. In short, they made themselves so obnoxious as to expose them to every contumely devised by the rage of party and the madness of the times.

As he was a great lover of peace and repose, he obeyed their commands and went forth, as well as his son, whenever ordered. This unexpected compliance became a severe mortification and an insupportable disappointment to his enemies. They became, therefore, more openly outrageous. They began by causing his son to be deprived of a favourite rifle, a rifle that had constantly and successfully contributed to his father's youthful amusements. This outrage the old gentleman could not patiently endure. He seized on the house of the officer who had committed this act of violence. A great dispute ensued, in consequence of which he was cast (into prison) and severely fined. Innumerable other insults were offered to the youth, who, young, bold, and courageous, preferred at last a voluntary exile to so much insult and vexation. He joined the king's troops. This was what had been foreseen, and [was] a part of that plan which had been previously concerted by his brothers-in-law and his other enemies. Thus these people, from the wild fury of the times, contrived the means of S. K.'s destruction, which was to ensure them the possession of his fine estate. This elopement with the doubtful confirmed the preceding suspicions, realized the conjectures of his enemies. Among the more irascible, the torch now blazed with redoubled heat. His life was immediately demanded by the fanatical, and his estate secured by the detestable devisers of his ruin.

What a situation for an honest, generous man! Despised, shunned, hated, calumniated, and reviled in the midst of a county of which he was the founder, in the midst of a people the poorest of which he had so often assisted and relieved; pursued and overtaken by his brothers-in-law, whom he had raised from indigence! Gracious God, why permit so many virtues to be blasted in their greatest refulgency? Why permit the radiance of so many heavenly attributes to be eclipsed by men who

impiously affix to their new, fictitious zeal the sacred
name of liberty on purpose to blind the unwary, whilst,
ignorant of Thee, they worship no deity but self-interest,
and to that idol sacrilegiously sacrifice so many virtues?
If it is to reward him with never-fading happiness, condescend to manifest some faint ray of Thy design proportioned to the weakness of the comprehension of us, frail
mortals and fellow-sufferers, that we may not despair,
nor impious men may arraign Thy eternal justice. Yes, it
is virtue Thou meanest to reward and to crown. The
struggle, the contest, the ignominy to which it is now exposed, the greater disasters which will soon terminate
this scene, have some distant affinity with the suffering
of Thy Son, the Moral Legislator, the Pattern of Mankind.

S. K. bore his misfortunes with a manly constancy.
However, the absence of his son impaired his industry
and almost put an entire stop to his designs of improvement. He saw but neglected his farm, his fields, his pastures, and his meadows; the ruinous and deplorable
state in which the country was involved. His house,
once the mansion of hospitality and kindness, was entered now but by secret emissaries, enemies, committee-
men, etc. The few friends he had left dared not visit
him, for they, too, were struggling with their difficulties;
they dared not expose themselves to a declaration of
their sentiments by soothing his oppressed mind and
comforting him in his adversity. He was taken ill. Nevertheless, militia duty was demanded and required of him.
He was fined forty pounds for every fortnight he had
been absent. He recovered and resolved either to cease to
be or else to exist with more ease. He went towards
New York, but the guards and other obstacles he met
with prevented him from accomplishing his design. He
returned, but ere he reached his house, he heard the
melancholy tidings that it had been plundered and that
there was a general order for the militia to hunt him
through the woods. For a great number of days he had
to escape their pursuit from hill to hill, from rocks to
rocks, often wanting bread, and uncertain where to hide
himself. By means of the mediation of some friends, he
was at last permitted to return home and remain there on
bail. A dejected, melancholy wife, a desolated house, a

half-ruined farm, a scarcity of everything, struck him to the heart at his first coming; but his sorrow and affliction were all passive. These impressions, however, soon wore away; he insensibly grew more reconciled to his situation. His advanced age, his late sickness, his fatigues, had wearied him down; and his mind, partaking of the debility of his body, did no longer view these disagreeable images in the same keenness of light.

This happened in the fall. The following winter, some poor people repaired to his house for relief and supplies as usual. "Alas, my friends, committees and rulers have made such a havoc here that I have no longer the means to relieve you. A little hay, perhaps, I may spare, for they have stolen all my horses. Pray, were not you one of those who hunted me whilst I was wild?"

"Yes, sir, I was unfortunately one of them, but I was compelled. I was driven to do it. You know as well as I the severity with which we poor militiamen are treated: exorbitant and arbitrary fines, corporal punishments. Every kind of terror is held out to us. What could I do?"

"I know it, and am far from blaming you, though I greatly lament and pity your situation. Pray, have you been paid for your services against me?"

"No, sir."

"How many days have you been out?"

"Two."

"What! Two days in the woods and you have received no wages? Have neither committees nor captains ever settled that matter yet?"

"No, sir, our services are gratis, and we must, besides, find our victuals, our blankets, and the very ammunition we expend—we must pay for it."

"I hate, and always did, to see poor men employed for nothing. Take two loads of hay for your two days' work. Will that satisfy you?"

"You were always a good man. God loves you yet, though some men are dreadfully set against you."

"Do tell me, would you really have killed me as you were ordered, if you had met me in the woods?" Here the poor man, hiding his face with his hat, shed tears and made no other answer.

The patience, the resignation with which he seemed now to bear his fate, greatly alarmed his enemies. They reproached themselves with the facility with which they suffered him to return and to procure bail; new devices were, therefore, made use of to push him to a final extremity. His determination of thus remaining at home, quiet and inoffensive, might abate that popular rage and malice which were the foundations of their hopes. The keen edge of popular clamour might become blunted; there was a possibility of their being frustrated in their most favourite expectations. They therefore secretly propagated a report that he had harboured Indians on their way to New York. No sooner said than believed. Imprisonment, hanging, were denounced against him by the voice of the public. This new clamour was principally encouraged by his brothers-in-law, the one now become a magistrate and the other a captain of the militia.

Finding himself surrounded with new perils, without one friend either to advise or to comfort him; threatened with his final doom; accused of that which, though they could not prove, he could only deny; knowing of no power he could appeal to, either for justice or relief; seeing none but prejudiced enemies in his accusers, judges, and neighbours, he at last determined to join the Indians who were nearest to him, not so much with the design of inciting them to blood and slaughter as [of finding] a place of refuge and repose. This was what his enemies expected. His house, his farm—all were seized, even the scanty remains of what had escaped their former avidity and plunder. All was sold, and the house and farm were rented to a variety of tenants until laws should be made to sell the lands.

> Such a house broke!
> So noble a master fallen! All gone! And not
> One friend to take his fortune by the arm,
> And go along with him.

It has been said since, that this famed farm has ceased this year to bear as plentifully as usual; that the meadows have brought but little hay; that the grain has been scanty and poor. This is at least the tradition of the neighbourhood. It may be that these inconsiderate tenants neither plough nor cultivate it as it was formerly; that the meadows, late-fed and ill-fenced, have no time to bear a crop;

and that in the short space of their lease they refuse the necessary manures and usual care, without which the best land produces nothing.

His wife, alas, has been hitherto overlooked and unnoticed, though you may be sure she has not been passive through these affecting scenes! In all these various calamities which have befallen her family, she has borne the part of a tender mother, an affectionate wife. Judge of her situation at this particular and critical moment! The repeated shocks which she has sustained within these three years have impaired the tone of her nerves—you know the delicacy of the female frame. Though her cheerfulness was gone, the gleamings of hope, the presence of her husband, still supported her. This sudden and unexpected blow completed the horrid catastrophe. Soon after his elopement, when the armed men came to seize him, she fainted, and though she has since recovered the use of her limbs, her reason has never returned but in a few lucid intervals. She is now confined to a small room, her servants sold and gone; she is reduced to penury; she is become a poor tenant of that very house which in the better days of her husband's prosperous industry had glowed with the cheerful beams of benevolence. She is now an object of pity without exciting any. When her reason returns, it is only to hear herself and family reviled. "You yourselves have driven my son, my husband away," is all she can say. Could tears, could wishes, could prayers relieve her, I'd shed a flood, I'd form a thousand, I'd proffer the most ardent ones to heaven. But who can stem the tide of Fate? It is the arbiter of kings and subjects; in spite of every impediment, it will rise to its preordained height. She lives, happily unknown to herself, an example of the last degree of desolation which can overtake a once-prosperous family, the object of raillery to those who are witnesses of her delirium. It would have been a miracle indeed had her senses remained unimpaired amidst the jars, the shocks of so many perturbations. A Stoic himself would have required the spirt of Zeno to have withstood, placid and composed, the convulsions of so great a ruin.

One stroke of fortune is still wanting. S. K., in his flight, met with a party of Indians coming towards ——, which they intended to destroy. He accompanied them, never ceasing to beg of them that they would shed no blood and spare the lives of poor innocent farmers. The deaths of three or four, to which he was witness, shocked his humane soul. He quitted them and returned once more towards home, choosing rather to meet his final doom in his own country than be any longer a witness to the further mischiefs meditated by these incensed people. On his return, he was soon informed of the deplorable state to which his wife was reduced and of the destruction of his property. He balanced what to do, as if amidst so much evil there was still a possibility of choice. Sad, however, was the alternative: whether to venture and deliver himself up at all hazards, and thus end the suspense; or whether to live a vagrant, a fugitive, in these woods and mountains, with the paths and intricate ways of which he was so well acquainted. But whence was he to procure subsistence? It could not be by the chase. Was he, then, to turn plunderer? Weary of life, he at last found means to inform the rulers of his return and repentance; but he received no other answer than what was soon afterwards delivered by the mouths of the dogs and by the noise of the militia which was ordered out to search the woods for him. He luckily escaped their pursuit, but hunger, his greatest enemy, at last overtook him. He ventured towards a cabin, the tenants of which he had often relieved in their adversity. They gave him some bread and advised him to fly. Soon afterwards, by means of the indiscretion of a child, this mystery of generosity and gratitude was revealed. The aged couple were severely whipped, being too poor to be fined. For a long time he skulked from tree to tree, from rock to rock; now hid on the tops of cliffs, seeing his pursuers below him; now creeping through the impervious ways of marshes and swamps, the receptacle of bears less cruel than his enemies.

Ye angels of peace, ye genii of placid benevolence, ye invisible beings who are appointed to preside over the good, the unjustly persecuted, is there no invisible aegis in the high armouries of heaven? Gently cause one to descend in order to shield this mortal man, your image, from the imminent danger he is in, from the arrows of malice, from the muskets of his ancient friends and dependents—all aimed towards him. Whichsoever way he steers, he has to dread the smell of dogs, now become his enemies. Where can he go to escape and live? But if he lives, what life will it be? The goaded mind incessantly represents to itself and compares the ancient days of ease, felicity, tranquillity, and wealth with the present hours of hunger, persecution, and general hatred; once the master and proprietor of a good house, now reduced to the shelter of the woods and rocks; once surrounded with servants and friends, now isolated and alone, afraid of the very animal which used to be his companion in the chase. Such, however, was the fate of this man for a long time, until, abandoning himself to despair, overpowered by the excess of fatigues, debility, and hunger, he suffered himself to be taken. He was conducted to gaol, where he expected he should not long languish. Mercy was now become useless to him. What good could it procure him, now that his wife was delirious, his son gone, and all his property destroyed? His only remaining felicity was the remembrance of his ancient humane deeds, which like a sweet ethereal dew must cast a mist over the horrors of his confinement and imperceptibly prepare him to appear in that world which blesses the good, the merciful, without measure, and has no bitterness for such tenants.

The day of trial soon came, and to his great surprise, as well as to the astonishment of all, he was released on bail and permitted to go to work for his daily bread. Like Belisarius of old, he is returned to live in that small part of his own house which is allotted him for his habitation, there to behold once more the extensive havoc which surrounds him, and to contemplate in gloomy despair the overthrow of his wife's reason and the reunion of all the physical evil that could possibly befall him, without resources and without hope.

Yet he lives; yet he bears it without murmuring. Life seems still to be precious to him; 'tis a gift he has no thought of parting with. Strange! What is it good for when thus embittered, when thus accompanied with so much acrimony, such irretrievable accidents? 'Tis a perpetual state of agony. Better part with it in a heavy, final groan and trust to Nature for the consequence than to drag so ponderous a chain. How much happier the felon, the murderer, who at one fortunate blow ends the remembrance of his life and his crimes, and is delivered from chains, putrid holes, and all the other wants of Nature!

Compare now the fate of this man with that of his more fortunate persecutors. I appeal to the enlightened tribunals of Europe, to the casuistical doctors of the colleges of science, to the divan, to the synods, to the presbyteries, and to all bodies and conventions of men reunited to judge of the various cases which the combined malice of men exhibit on the stage of the world, as well as of the various preventives and punishments designed to check malice and evil deeds. I appeal to the American tribunals on that day when the mist of these times shall be dissipated. I ask them all on what principles can this man be punished? What has he done that can deserve so much severity? The graft, by the virulence of these times, is made to poison the parent stock; the vine is made to corrode the tutelar elm which has so long supported its entwined limbs and branches. 'Tis the jealousy, the avarice, the secret thirst of plunder, sanctified under new and deceiving names, which have found means to vilify this generous citizen and have set the aspic tongues reviling this innocent man. Can it be? Can this be the reflected work of three years? Yes, it is. But for their demoniacal fury he might have remained at home passive and inoffensive. The produce of his fertile farm might have served to support the cause. But this was not sufficient to satisfy the rage, the malice of an ignorant, prejudiced public.

Are ye not afraid, ye modern rulers, to attract the wrath of heaven, the vindictive fires of its eternal justice in thus trampling under, in thus disregarding the most essential laws of humanity, in thus neglecting the most indispensable ones contained in that code which ought to reign supreme, exclusive of all parties, factions, and revolutions? Is not the deplorable state into which this man and all his family are reduced more than sufficient to atone for the popular offences he is supposed to have been guilty of? Must poverty, languor, and disease terminate in want, penury, and ignominy a life hitherto pursued on the most generous principles, a life which, contrary to the tenor of yours, has been so useful, so edifying?

But I am not pleading his cause; I am no biographer. I give way to an exuberance of thoughts which involuntarily crowd on my mind, unknown to all the world but its Ruler

and yourself. I don't presume that this man was match-
less, devoid of vices and faults. Like all other men, his
cup was no doubt mixed with those ingredients which
enter into the beverage of mortals. It is not the minutiae
of his life into which I want to descend. This unfortunate
epoch is *that* alone which I want to select and to describe as a proof of his hard destiny, and as one of the
characteristics of the times in which we live. Yet I am
persuaded that there are several members in Congress
and in every province who, moved into compassion at
this relation, would shed tears over the ashes of this
ruin; but these men at a great distance direct the revolution of the new orb. It is the inferior satellites who
crush, who dispel, and make such a havoc in the
paths which it is to follow.

Yet his enemies exult, triumph, and rule. They bear
sway, are applauded, gather every harvest, and receive
every incense which the world can give, whilst he be-
moans his fate, and is obliged to support himself and his
wife. His enemies, now become his masters, were, before
these times, mostly poor, obscure, and unnoticed; great
psalm-singers, zealous religionists who would not have
cracked a nut on the Sabbath—no, not for any worldly
consideration. They were meek, lowly Christians, always
referring every accident to God's divine providence and
peculiar appointment; humble in their deportment, composed in their carriage, prudent in their outward actions,
careful of uttering offensive words; men of plausible
countenances, sleek-haired, but possessed at the same time
of great duplicity of heart; sly in their common social
intercourse, callous—pushing, with an affected charitable
language, from their doors the poor, the orphan, the
widow.

I have known some of these country saints to tena-
ciously detain in gaol some debtors for twelve pounds,
which S. K., unknown to everybody, would privately
cause to be paid. These are the people who before these
times were ostentatiously devout, laboriously exact in
their morning prayers, reading, expoundings, etc. These
are the men who now in the obscure parts of this country
have assumed the iron sceptre and from religious
hypocrites are become political tyrants. That affected
meekness, that delusive softness of manners, are now

gone; they are discarded as useless. They were formerly the high road to popularity, applause, and public respect, but this new zeal for their new cause must not, like the ancient one, moulder under the ashes and be afraid of sunshine and of air. It must burn, it must conflagrate; the more violent the flames, the thicker the smoke, the more meritorious. Whilst the unaffected good man, the sincere Christian, who proved his principles by his actions more than by his vain words and his disputations, is reprobated, shunned, despised, and punished, the secret liar, the hidden fornicator, the nocturnal drunkard, the stranger to charity and benevolence, are uplifted on modern wings, and obtain the applause of the world which should be the reward of merit, of benefits conferred, of useful actions done.

Surely this points out the absolute necessity of future rewards and punishments. Were not I convinced of it, I would not suffer the rebukes, the taunts, the daily infamy, to which I have conscientiously exposed myself. I'd turn Manichaean like so many others. I'd worship the demon of the times, trample on every law, break every duty, neglect every bond, overlook every obligation to which no punishment was annexed. I'd set myself calumniating my rich neighbours. I'd call all passive, inoffensive men by the name of inimical. I'd plunder or detain the entrusted deposits. I'd trade on public moneys, though contrary to my oath. Oath! Chaff for good Whigs, and only fit to bind a few conscientious Royalists! I'd build my new fortune on the depreciation of the money. I'd inform against every man who would make any difference betwixt it and silver, whilst I, secure from any discovery or suspicion by my good name, would privately exchange ten for one. I'd pocket the fines of poor militiamen, extracted from their heart's blood. I'd become obdurate, merciless, and unjust. I'd grow rich, *fas vel nefas*. I'd send others a-fighting, whilst I stayed at home to trade and to rule. I'd become a clamorous American, a modern Whig, and offer every night incense to the god Arimanes.

CHAPTER XII

LANDSCAPES

The following "American Landscapes" are not beneath your attention, though they are the works of neither Salvator Rosa nor Claude Lorrain. They are sketches which, like Chinese paintings, admit draperies and ornaments.

I leave to artists the harmony of shades and brilliance of perspective arrangements. 'Tis not the pompous, the captious, the popular, the ostensible, the brilliant part of these American affairs I want to portray; this is the province of the historiographer, biographer, etc. My simple wish is to show you the vulgar thread of that canvas, once so rude and neglected, the work of low and ignorant artists, but now transmuted into a wide, extended surface on which new and deceiving perspectives are represented. 'Tis now surrounded with a superb frame; 'tis now covered with tinsel colours hiding the coarse ligaments and texture beneath. My simple wish is to present you with some of the primary elements and original component parts in their native appearances ere they were artfully gathered, united, new-modelled and polished by our modern legislators. 'Tis not the soaring eagle, rivalling the clouds in height and swiftness, I mean to show you; 'tis only the insignificant egg from which it is hatched.

My pencil wants not to sketch the august bird arrayed
with majestic feathers; 'tis only the nest in which it was
hatched, composed of sticks and twigs cemented with dirt,
lined with clay, whence has sprung this new master of
the sky.

Such, you know, has always been the turn of my
thoughts. 'Tis not in general so much the perspective I
admire as the knowledge of this secret from which the
deception arises; 'tis not so much the sceneries which
attract my attention as the hidden methods by which
they are held suspended, shifted, and alternately presented to my view. Ambition, we well know, an exorbitant
love of power and thirst of riches, a certain impatience
of government, by some people called liberty—all these
motives, clad under the garb of patriotism and even of
constitutional reason, have been the secret but true
foundation of this, as well as of many other revolutions.
But what art, what insidious measures, what deep-laid
policy, what masses of intricate, captious delusions were
not necessary to persuade a people happy beyond any on
earth, in the zenith of political felicity, receiving from
Nature every benefit she could confer, enjoying from
government every advantage it could confer, that they
were miserable, oppressed, and aggrieved, that slavery
and tyranny would rush upon them from the very sources
which before had conveyed them so many blessings. Behold, then, a new source of revolution, a new class of
calamity never before experienced. That excess of misrule
should rouse a generous people is very natural to conceive; that the avarice of individuals, the cupidity of the
republics, the ambition of princes, should kindle and promote wars—we are well acquainted with these veteran
causes. Ambition, hypocrisy, enthusiasm, are continually
travelling from one end of the earth to the other. But this
American manœuvre is altogether without a precedent;
history affords us no parallel. Feeble, emaciated colonies,
ill-governed, cost as much as they are worth. They are the
offspring of tyranny; they are excrescences that perhaps
may add to the weight, but not to the vigour of the
body politic. Those, on the contrary, which, linked by
freedom, are supported and upheld by the most rational
bonds—those rush towards manhood. They rapidly acquire the strength of nations; and regardless of every

consideration, forgetting the pride, the honour, the
safety of ancient connections, they seize the club as they
advance; they threaten. A new and unheard-of impunity,
grafted on parental indulgence, grows and expands and
settles into pertinacity and arrogance. Is this, then, the
state of human nature? Is this the source of things?
Premature event! Fatal disposition! My astonishment is
boundless when I recollect in a short retrospect the beginning and progressive increase of this unnatural revolt.
At present I would choose to consider it as a characteristic anecdote in the annals of mankind; but at the same
time, the object is so large that I cannot enclose it
within the reach of my horizontal vision. 'Tis necessary,
for the sake of more explicit details, to view it at different
periods, in its beginnings and successive degrees of advancement. These were not an enslaved people whose
senses and organs were at the command of a haughty
prince. No, these were an immense number of tribes collected together and living on an extensive coast of fourteen hundred miles, who, from their childhood, were bred
to censure with the utmost impunity the conduct of their
governors and other rulers. Yet these men have insensibly been led through the most flowery path to
enter a long career of sorrow and affliction, at the end
of which a phantom is exhibited which seems to recede
as fast as they advance. No European can possibly conceive the secret ways, the great combination of poisons
and subtle sophisms which have from one end of the
continent to the other allured the minds, removed every
ancient prejudice, and, in short, prepared the way for the
exhibition of this astonishing revolution. From rest-
lessness, from diffidence, from that jealous state in which
free men always live, to pass in the course of four years
to the implicitness of belief, to passive obedience, is indeed a melancholy proof that if slavery is often extended
and cherished by kings, the people, in the hour of infatuation, will sometimes become the artificers of their
own misfortunes.

I am now tired of the company of generals, rulers,
imperial delegates, modern governors. My predilected
province at present is more humble but perhaps not less
interesting. I choose now to converse with those vulgar
hands to whom the drudgery of ploughing and scattering

the good seed has been committed, seed from which that great harvest is to spring forth, ripening fast for the sole use of the great state reapers. It is not every lung, 'tis not every breast which can bear long unaffected the subtle, the penetrating air of Tenerife's top, or the exalted crater of Mount Vesuvius. But in my descent I find crevices, as well as a variety of new plants, which afford me some amusement as I proceed downwards. But what if these obscure scenes are scenes without purpose and exhibit characters without meaning? Great will be my guilt indeed. However, it will be a guilt proceeding from ignorance only and want of proper discernment. Some of these, however, must appear to you very striking and strongly marked. They are the genuine copies of originals such as have presented themselves to my view. If the thoughts are not always clad in the garb of the original words, the reason is that I have attached myself much more to the sentiment, the impression of which forcibly strikes and remains, than to the phraseology and uncouth dialect, to which I am in a great measure a stranger. The faithfulness of representation, the authenticity of facts, the truth of anecdote, as well as that of the circumstances, which pervade the whole, seem to constitute, however, a sort of merit which I shall one day claim at your hands. These are committed to the bosom of friendship, there to remain until you have made them worthy a witness.

AN AMERICAN PERSPECTIVE DIVIDED INTO SIX LANDSCAPES

The several transactions herein represented and comprised in the following scenes begin at seven o'clock in the morning and end at one on the same day. The subject is so diffused throughout that but a very imperfect idea can be given by way of abstract. Each part must help to elucidate the other. The hypocrisy, slyness, cupidity, inhumanity, and abuse of power in these petty country despots are evident and manifest. But to be of genuine American produce, they should be viewed clad under these modish garbs in which they appear, or else they might be taken for that of some other country.

First Landscape: A Deacon's House. Sabbath Morn.

The Deacon unites to the sacred functions of elder those of chairman, colonel, and commissioner for selling Tory estates.

BEATUS, deacon, etc.
ELTHA, his wife.
RUTH, his daughter.
ELIPHALET, his son.
PHILIP REARMAN, the squire.
TOM, the Negro.

DEACON: Do, wife, let the family know that it is time to go to morning prayers. Somehow we have overslept ourselves. The sun is quite high.

ELTHA: Come, come, girls; boys, your daddy says 'tis now time to pray.

(They all enter the room.)

DEACON: Gracious God, Thou knowest our infirmities. But where is Anthony? I don't see him here.

ELTHA: As to that, the poor lad deserves to be excused. He was all night a-Tory-hunting and did not get home till 'most break of day.

DEACON: Well, well, if so be, let him lie, but 'tis but a poor action indeed that doesn't bring along with it its own rewards. Any one of you know what luck they have had?

ELIPHALET: I have heard him say that he has not had such fun this great while. He likes the light-horse service wonderfully. They have caught old Stubb, who is as deaf as a wall. They challenged him as he was riding by, and as he made no answer, they fired and killed his horse.

DEACON: What have they done with the old wretch?

ELIPHALET: They pricked his stubborn flesh pretty well, as he lay on the ground, with their bayonets, and then sent him in irons to the fort.

DEACON: That was well done. These youngsters will really make fine soldiers.

ELIPHALET: Next they went to Adam Mill's house, huzzaing all the way. They caught him in his bed by the side of his old wife. They seized all his papers, which were chiefly Continental sheets. They stripped him; then tarred and feathered him till he looked nearly like an owl; and clapped him upon an old jade; and then led him to the Cross-Keys tavern, where they had abundance of diversion. For the honest lads began to gather, and they all hooted and shouted at him till their sides merely ached, as they said. Then they turned him off. They put up his clothes at raffle for the fees and drank merrily on it. The other writings and the money are in the hands of Sergeant Broad-Alley.

DEACON: Why, as to the money, they should have divided it among the company. That is the intention of Congress, I am sure. It looked, however, desperate well to see them so moderate.

ELIPHALET: As they passed by What's-his-name's house, they killed his dog, which kept a-barking; then fired through the doors and windows a fine round volley; and they say that the old Tory and his family were almost scared to death. They say that he went into his cellar and got one of the Negroes to hide him in a hogshead.

DEACON: Come, come, we shall hear the rest by and by. Let us proceed in our prayers and return God thanks that He has given us strength to overcome our internal enemies. (*Here he fetches a deep sigh, and with a quivering voice, he goes on.*) Gracious God, pour Thy blessings on Thy favourite people. Make their chosen race to increase and prosper by the influence of Thy heavenly showers——

ELTHA: Without interrupting you, my dear, I see somebody a-coming this way.

DEACON: Do then sweep the hearth and spread the bed, while the rest of us do proceed—and enable us to find out and punish those traitors to our cause——

(*Somebody knocks.*)

Come in—who put on the appearance of Whigs and thereby deceive the vigilance of our committees. Ah, ah,

Squire, is it you? I did not perceive you before. Come, children, you may retire into the kitchen; the Squire and I have somewhat to talk about. Be ye reading in the meanwhile that excellent chapter I just began.

(*Exeunt omnes, except Eltha.*)

DEACON (*with his left hand on his left knee, his right uplifted, his head hanging downwards*): Well, Squire, it is but talking of some people, as the saying is, and you are sure to see them shortly. My wife and I were a-saying, before you came, how glad I was that you had somehow settled matters with the committee. I sent for you last night to shake hands with you on't. (*He shakes hands with the squire.*) It really does my heart good to see you so fat and hearty—and pray, how have you fared through all your trials? It was not my fault, you may depend on it. I hope you have nothing in your heart against me.

SQUIRE REARMAN: Fared? Sir, hard enough, I can tell you. Your putrid gaols, your cruel turnkeys, your barbarous guards, forever insulting, teasing the prisoners— all these render a man's fate ten times harder. I fared so well that I was very near starving.

DEACON: Why! How could that happen? I am sure to the best of my memory I never gave such orders.

SQUIRE REARMAN: You know, I suppose, that they took me just after my family had been inoculated; and, under pretence of danger, they would suffer no provisions to come to me. In vain I offered to purchase some of their own. "Suck your paws as your brother bears do," was all the answer I received.

DEACON: Why, that is as true as the Devil is in London. I never did give such orders as those. I wonder what should make them act in that manner.

SQUIRE REARMAN: What orders they had, I know not. What was wanting in explicitness was supplied and most amply dictated by the fruitful spirit of the times. And really, how can it be otherwise? You have made no provision for the support of those whom you confine. If their friends and relations live at a great distance, great must their distress be until they can be relieved. If they have no friends or connexions, they must depend on the charity of the neighbourhood, and that is pretty cold nowadays, you know, Mr. Chairman. Even those that have any humanity left are obliged to send provisions in a private manner, or else they run the risk of incurring the hatred of the mob, a terrible evil. What, then, must become of poor prisoners thus situated? They can expect nothing from law; it extends its benefits but to the favourers of the new cause. Common mercy is departed.

DEACON: 'Tis hard, I confess. I never knew it was so bad. I am glad truly that you have made shift to overcome this severe trial. I hope you will forget it all and live with us all, as formerly.

REARMAN: The horror one meets within those walls, the misery and despair which awaits your victims there, the horrid scenes I have seen there—all these have made impressions on my mind which I never, never can forget. Oh, that poor young man who died raving, distracted in the midst of us, who begged, but in vain, to be removed where he might enjoy fresh air; who died at last the most cruel death! How can I ever forget him? Every night I see, I hear him still as soon as I close my eyes. Had we had the same fever, we must all have perished in the same manner.

DEACON: Well, well, as to that and other things, they are unavoidable. The necessary struggles are great and mighty. The billows of the sea in a mighty tempest often shake and tear the resisting shores. I want to know how you came off so well, and by what means you have been able to return home.

REARMAN: By the assistance and protection of ———. I found in him a spark of humanity. So much misery, so great a punishment inflicted for mere suspicions shocked him. He became my security, and I stay at home as his prisoner. This is what none of the committee would have ever done for me.

DEACON: That was really fortunate. But how did you escape from ——— prison? By what means did you find your way home again?

REARMAN: These are mysteries which I can never disclose. Suffice it for you that I have given proper bail and am enabled to remain with my family, from which I have been so long torn. Surely you don't wish it otherwise. The many moments of anxious suspense I have experienced seem to entitle me now to some degree of repose. Although I left all sick with the smallpox, yet from the instant of my confinement I never could be permitted even to hear the least tidings of their health, although but nine miles distant. Confinement, hard fare, obscurity—all these things, it seems, were not enough.

DEACON: That is really fortunate. I hope you will become deserving of it; but if you will follow my counsel, you will no longer hold —— security. Give it up. Take my word, Squire; you shall be no longer molested.

REARMAN: I, give up all my protection! No, sir, on the contrary, I shall repair to his house as soon as the time expires, when I make no doubt to re-obtain a further indulgence to stay at home and cultivate my farm. Have not the committee a field extensive enough to act in without trying to extend it? Thousands obey or rather dread your laws; suffer a poor individual to be scratched out of your list.

I willingly forgive you and the rest of your brethren for what is past, but, at the same time, shall take care how I renounce the favour of a man who, though a stranger to me, yet from motives of the purest generosity has thus relieved me. What else could or should I have done in the few days I lurked at home after my escape from ——? How often was my house surrounded? It seems to me that these people instinctively smelled me, as hounds do smell their game. How often false friends, hypocrites, sly emissaries, came to my wife under pretence of congratulating her! A less vigilant man than I would have a second time fallen a victim to their fury. Yet I had the courage to hold my ground. I had the dexterity to escape. I could not bear the thoughts of being torn from my family a second time, and leaving them to suffer the stings of that poverty, adversity, and exile which necessarily awaited them. This is what has made me rise superior to the strongest impulses of the human heart; for you know, I suppose, sir, that Tories are men as well as yourself.

DEACON: 'Tis hard, I must needs confess. I am glad to see that you have nothing in your heart against me in particular. I am, you know, but the voice of the people; 'tis they that govern us. The strongest motives force us to follow, nay, to indulge, their native inclinations. —— has really nothing to do with the internal management of our county. This interfering of his in your case, I perceive, begins to displease some of our principal people. I do not know how we shall manage this point. 'Tis of more consequence than you think, for you still have friends.

REARMAN: I hope I have, but I am very sure not one of that name is on the committee. Give me leave to tell you that the majority of them have been guided all along by their blind passions much more than by any settled plan of conduct. How have they used —— and ——? Yes, I'll be bold to say that there was not in their proceedings the least show of humanity or even reason. And what amends have they met with since? Nothing but exorbitant fines, the most unjust assessments. No, sir, expect not that I ever shall pay the committees so great a compliment at the expense of my safety. If this merciful step of —— is unpopular, let the matter be settled with him. Surely you don't mean to make me answerable for it.

ELTHA: No, no, my husband has no such thoughts. But you do know how it would make you popular; it would show that you throw yourself into the arms of the country. Our folks would then begin to look on you with better eyes. You do know so well, as my husband and I do, how clever it would look. This affair may take another turn, for what we know; 'tis hard to tell how it may turn out. The chairman, to be sure, has got power, but he can't always do as he pleases. I'd have you, good sir, take notice of that. My husband is too good, and were he to follow my advice, some people would not have to reproach him, as they do, with tenderness of heart. He is so teased that he has no peace in his life.

REARMAN: This has been the bait held to me, as well as to many others, from the beginning; I have caught at it many times and have always been duped. Surely you'll allow me that degree of caution which deception naturally inspires. When first the Association was launched forth, how earnestly did you press me to sign it! It was to be the great bond of union, which was to unite us all. It was to serve to the weak and unpopular "as a shield against the strong"; this was your expression. Yet, how has it turned out? In all contributions to raise soldiers, in the raising of taxes, in the assessment of teams, forage, etc., I and many others have always been oppressed in the most partial, shocking manner. What is become of your fair promises? It was nothing but delusion. I have signed to please you; I have paid; I have borne everything without a visible murmur. Yet nothing can satisfy your people; nothing can assuage that rancour which they possess but utter extirpation, banishment, and confiscation. This is now the reward for my passive sufferings, for that long train of oppression and contumely to which, you well know, I have been subjected these three years.

Collected within the bounds of my farms, I have resigned every principle of action into your hands. I have submitted myself to the guidance of fate and hoped for better days. Yet what has my patience, my retirement, my voluntary absence from society, deserved? Nothing but contempt, injurious language, and repeated oppression. I have been cruelly confined; put in irons, without hearing, without the least show of reason. I have heard of no evidences deposing against me; and at this very minute I know not what reasons you have had to tear me from my family at the most critical juncture, when my wife and nine children had just received the poison of the smallpox.

DEACON: Why, as to that and all you have said, I could not help it. The good of the cause required it, and the captain that took you has said in my presence many times that he had orders from the government; and, you know, it behooves not inferiors to meddle or interfere with the conduct of their superiors. What is done over the river, you know, cannot be undone on this side.

ELTHA: Why, though I am but a woman, as you may say, yet I can see things pretty plain and from my wheel cast my eyes all over the county. Though I say it to such a squire, my wheel, to tell you the truth, puts me in mind of our affair. I can't help sometimes wondering how wonderfully the affairs of our county are turned. There is a great difference, Squire, between managing the law as you used to—and passing judgement and pronouncing sentences and sitting on the bench—and the present times. Now is the prophet's turn. Methinks I can see all these things in John's Revelations as plain as I can see my distaff. And, to tell you a plain truth—for I am a plain woman—I have often heard the neighbours say—aye, even those who live within sight of the smoke of your chimney—as how formerly nobody ever went to places of public meetings first and last so punctually as you. There was nothing done up and down the county, not even a road laid out, not a poor bastard put out, but you were at the head and tail on't, as the saying is. Now, Squire, your keeping yourself at home and washing your hands of all public concerns is an evident demonstration that you dislike them. It does not show well; it does not signify.

DEACON: So I have heard and, indeed, myself observed, to tell you the plain truth, that you grew as scarce as gold. Everybody talked; everybody remarked it; and you know that our people are afraid. They are jealous, and there is no knowing sometimes where their suspicions arise from.

REARMAN: This never could be the cause of my misfortunes. Many have been taken up and confined for being at all your public meetings and sometimes prudently showing their dissent to a great many things which they did not think altogether proper.

DEACON: 'Tis hard, I confess, but these are mere trifles compared to the good of the cause, a cause which doesn't carry on so much for our sakes as for those of our posterity. 'Tis a bleeding cause, as our minister says of it; therefore sufferings must come from it. This great land of Canaan cannot be purged of its ancient idolators without abundance of trouble. Now, the Jews had a much better chance because the Canaanites did not speak the same language. We must guess and sift and find out; no wonder if we make mistakes sometimes. However, I am glad you have weathered it. I hope you will now become one of us and help to defend this country where you were born. What man must that be who turns against the house of his father and tries to burn these fields which have nourished him so long! A malediction overtake him, I say!

ELTHA: So say I. They don't deserve to live except it may be in Guinea with the other slaves of that country.

DEACON: Come, come. Let us forgive and forget. Next time the militia marches, take up your musket and follow us; that will be the best proof you can give.

REARMAN: I, take up my musket! Not I! Let those who shine, who rule, who grow rich, who meet every encouragement, go and fight. For my part, I am not mad enough to help those who these three years have cut me off from the benefits of society.

DEACON: That won't do either! But to-day is Lord's day. God forbid that I should suffer any wrathful word to defile the sanctity of the day. You must abide by the consequences; that is all I can say. Pray, do you know what is become of your fellow-prisoner, F. M.? I mean him that escaped with you.

REARMAN: He is returned home, sir, I suppose, unless he has been hunted and pursued. For, poor man, he can't endure so much as I can; he has not such a set of nerves. I do not know what fear and despair may induce him to do, but he has told me many times that he wished for nothing more than to remain at home with his family. Have you heard of him lately?

ELTHA: Heard of him! Why, don't you know? Come, come, don't plead ignorance; you know it as well as we do ourselves. Why, he is gone to the enemy. He had it always in his heart; it is an old darling scheme of his.

REARMAN: You astonish me. He, *gone,* of all men! Well, then, he must have met with some new persecution; he must have fallen a second time into the hands of his enemies. He wanted to apply to the Council of Safety, and I believe did do it. Poor man! What he suffered in gaol, I believe, would induce him to run the risk of his life rather than endure confinement again. He must have been forced to it by some new dangers or insults. His age, besides, did not admit of a very active life. His heart now will break in twain to be separated a second time from his wife and children, to whom he is so attached. Oh, could I but repeat what I have heard him say whilst we were both confined! A worthier man never did exist. Though in an obscure station, very few men in the country are there that deserve so much the respect of all. You know him well, sir; is not it so?

DEACON: No matter for what he was, the question is what he is now. However, 'tis all over with him, and I am sorry.

ELTHA: Sorry! Why, my dear, where did you learn to throw sorrow away in this manner? Keep your sorrow for our poor soldiers that die fighting for us; keep it for the hundreds of our prisoners whom they are wilfully starving in New York. For my part, I have no notion at all to be sorry for any such thing as F. M.'s elopement. He has now confirmed the opinion we had all along entertained of him. He ever was a worshipper of kings. Let him go now and worship his favourite idol, "over the seas and far away," as the song says. For what care we? What he leaves behind him is now become an acceptable offering to his much-injured country.

REARMAN: Thus it is with thousands whom your barbarous treatment daily converts into enemies. You follow a strange policy, I must confess, but you are not sure of victory yet.

DEACON: Every man to his lot. 'Tis all pre-ordained, as the Scripture says. Yours, sir, has appeared hitherto much happier; but take care how you behave yourself. The arms of the committee can overtake you yet.

REARMAN: As a scalded cat dreads the fire, so will I remember the state of probation through which I have passed. I propose to remain at home, wholly passive as before, and to wait for my fate with resignation and fortitude. Your servant, sir.

DEACON: Yours, sir. Remember me to all at home.

REARMAN: Ah, sir, this compliment puts me in mind of our old time of peace and concord. 'Tis now out of fashion to remember one another but in the hour of wrath and vengeance. Farewell.

(Exit Rearman.)

DEACON: Well, my dear, we have been so long conversing with that proud squire that it is almost time to go to meeting. Come, try what haste you can make; get us breakfast as quick as you can.

ELTHA: I had a little jaunt to propose to you, to which I could wish you would agree. You won't refuse me, I hope. Do, my dear, come. Shall we go?

DEACON: Well, what is it? Where is it that you want to go?

ELTHA: I long, as much as I did for anything in my life, to go to F. M.'s. I do not know how it is, but I have been dreaming of it all night, and I cannot banish the thoughts from my head. What is it that impels me? I cannot tell. We should not refuse obedience to these impulses. Who knows but they come from above?

DEACON: Oh, fie, fie, wife. This won't do, I am sure. To-day is Lord's day, you know. Who is to set the Psalms and accompany the minister and read the newspaper at the meeting-house door? It will cause, besides, a prodigious misedification. What will the people, the neighbours, think?

ELTHA: Think! Why, don't they know very well that you have so given up your time to the good of the cause that you have scarce leisure to eat or rest, and that as a chairman, as a colonel, as a commissioner for selling Tory estates, you do not know which way to turn yourself? They will charitably imagine that some particular business belonging to either of these commissions has necessarily called you away. Don't you remember last night there was a talk, just as we were singing our evening Psalms, that some of these pestilential people had risen in the mountains because, forsooth, you had fastened to the ground a half dozen of them the day before. The people, I am sure, will readily excuse you. Somebody will kindly take your place at meeting, and those who for so many years have known you to be so constant an attendant won't begin to censure you at this time.

DEACON: Why, what is it that urges you so strongly? What do you want to do there? To-morrow, you know, the committee is going to seize all. If you are so inclined, you must come along with us.

ELTHA: To-morrow won't do so well. There will be abundance of people. I could wish to see beforehand the good furniture, their bedding, their plentiful cellar, the well-stored granary. I want to see how the woman looks with all her little Tory bastards about her. Do, my dear, do now; I cannot resist it. Who knows—and I am sure you do not know yourself—but these roguish people will sequester something and rob the state of some part of its lawful inheritance? And you are sensible that they have always been the very worst sort of people among us.

DEACON: Well, well, wife, this last reason seems to carry along with it some degree of plausibility. Do you, then, mention it in that light to the family. I will retire to my Bible while you are getting ready.

ELTHA: I will, Colonel. You may be sure we may, besides, sanctify the day and talk, as we go and come, of something about God; and though there will be nobody by that we can edify, thereby the whole good will be unto us.

(*Exit Deacon.*)

ELTHA: Ruth, Ruthy, do, my child, tell Tom to come to me. Be quick, be speedy. Do you hear?

RUTH: Yes, Mammy. Tom is here at the door, brushing the snow from his feet.

ELTHA: Tom, get ready your master's mare and my old jade. We are not going to meeting to-day as he proposed. Some private intelligence he has received obliges him to go another way. Now, Tom, let us see how quick you can do that. Will you have a dram of whisky this morning?

TOM: Tanke you, Missy. Wisky is good these cold weather for Negro. Me go, Missy; me have the horses by and by. Massa want me along?

ELTHA: No, Tom, you must stay at home and help the girls to cook and pray.

RUTH: What is that, Mammy, I have heard say—not go to meeting to-day? Why, Mammy, what shall we do? We shall know nothing, neither about the chapter or the Psalms, for, thanks to these plaguy Tories, we cannot go either, as all our other horses have been out all night after them.

ELTHA: Make yourselves easy, children; the Lord will forgive us all for once. What we are now doing is for the good of His own chosen cause. 'Tis serving Him to serve His worthy representatives, the Congress. In the meanwhile, that you may not spend your time without gathering a blessing, read the second of Jeremiah and twenty pages of the journal of the Reverend George Whitefield's life. This will be edifying, I am sure, and do you pretty near as much good as though you had gone to meeting.

RUTH: No, not quite, Mammy, I am sure. Why then should all the young fellows and all the young girls attend there so constantly every Sabbath?

ELTHA: It must be so to-day, however. You know I never hinder you from going any other time, but to-day your father has particular reasons. Do you hear me?

RUTH: We shall do as you bid us. But before you go, see, Mammy, that you leave us a good dinner. Some of the young people, perhaps, may come to join in our devotions.

ELTHA: You know that your father and I have never had any objection to these religious meetings; it promotes a holy sympathy, edification, and proper awakenings. See that you keep good decorum; and if anybody knocks, mind that they find you with your Bibles in your hands.

RUTH: We shall do so, Mammy. I hope you'll come back before it is dark. We are afraid, you know, since the militia are gone down below.

ELTHA: Go then, quick; call the Colonel and tell him that I am ready.

Second Landscape: On the Road.

On horseback proceeding towards F. M.'s house.

BEATUS, deacon.
ELTHA, his wife.
SPLASH, militia-lieutenant.

ELTHA: 'Tis really plaguy lucky that this fellow's cowardice has at last driven him off. I wish his good mate, the squire, had done the same. But at home he will be, and I am really afraid that his stubbornness will enable him to weather it. 'Tis best these rich fellows should go, for they won't fight, and by decamping they leave plaguy good fleeces behind. We want them all, and many more, to raise the credit of our money and to help us to carry on the war.

DEACON: There you are right, wife; all these quondam gentry are our bitterest enemies, though they dare not declare it. For that purpose, I have set the committee of the county upon ways and means to make them scamper or do worse. I have communicated my plan to the governor and his council, who mightily approve of it. Did I ever show you, wife, the public thanks I received the other day from——?

ELTHA: Public thanks? As God is my judge, I never have heard a single syllable on it. So much humility, Colonel, is not always good, even to your wife. Really, I don't understand it. Keep secret from your wife, the flesh of your bones, the ribs of your sides, your second self! Why, I am amazed! You know that I have given you many good hints on the pillow which have proved desperate good and serviceable.

DEACON: Hush, hush; speak lower. Look round before you express yourself so freely. When we thus converse together, let us watch and mistrust even the wind that blows.

ELTHA: No, no, my dear. None but God hears us from above, and I make no doubt with great complacency. When will that day come that we shall all enter His new Jerusalem and be as one of His chosen nations, decked in the robes of His Institution, ready to rebuild His temple and make the mounts of His new Zion resound with His praises?

DEACON: God is good; God is great; His mercy is immense. If we serve Him faithfully, I am sure, He tells my heart, that He will reward us with the spoil of our enemies. But, stop, stop. Here comes Lieutenant Splash! Not a word more of this. What news, Lieutenant?

SPLASH: Nothing very material at present, honourable Colonel, only they say that our folks are a-killing the redcoats by thousands down below. We will hang these Britanneers, see if we don't. Oh, I forgot to tell you that we were like to catch F. M., that great scoundrel. We shot at him a half-dozen times, but, as God is my judge, the Devil saved him that we might hang him awhile hence. But if we missed him, we surely hit in the head ———, the great thief.

DEACON: What? Have you killed him? Have you really shot him down?

SPLASH: Aye, aye, have I. Well, Colonel, if it were not your honour that asked me the question—well, to be sure, not killed him! And why not? As dead as a doornail. But what a pity that the fellow had been once a lieutenant in our service and a good Whig! I am really sorry that he has thus brought a disgrace on the name.

DEACON: A Whig, did you say? That wants confirmation, I am sure; 'tis very improbable. Now you mention it, I recollect that he never was what you have called him. It is my opinion that [had] he been a Whig, this never could have happened. Why, do you think that if he had been sincerely one of us, God's divine providence would have thus abandoned him? Believe me, Lieutenant Splash, he was a Tory in his heart. I know it as I do know a great many other things, and I charge you to give him that name wherever you mention him. Besides, let me tell you that you may bring yourself into bad bread by doing otherwise. He was a Tory in his heart, I tell you—that I am sure of—and the committee have agreed to punish the first man who shall call him otherwise.

SPLASH: Well, Colonel, you'll excuse me. No man but what may fail. I am but an ignorant countryman, that is to be sure. You know better in all things; all the country knows it. I am quite sensible of my error. It would indeed reflect a great, very great blemish on our cause. Let the Tories bear all the iniquity, for they deserve it richly.

DEACON: I know you mean well and, therefore, I excuse you. Which way now?

SPLASH: To meeting, honoured sir. Any command there?

DEACON: No, tell the people that I shall be there for the afternoon service.

SPLASH: I shall not fail. Farewell, sir.

DEACON: Farewell, Lieutenant.

Third Landscape: At a Tavern.

BEATUS, deacon.
ELTHA, his wife.
POTTER, landlord.

ELTHA, THE CHAIRWOMAN: Well, Landlord, how goes it on to-day? I haven't seen you, no, not I, since my husband tried some Tories in your back-room. Have you got any of that good spiritual you used to have?

LANDLORD: Why, as to that, Mrs. Chairman, if I may be so bold, I must tell you that since the people are become a lump of clay in the hands of our masters, the juices of the community are become exhausted. And now to talk in conscience, who can afford to sell for ten shillings what one is obliged to give twenty shillings for?

CHAIRWOMAN: Aye, aye, that is true in some respects,

but in others we may say that it is all for the good of
the cause. Every one must contribute something. How
should we carry on the war? My good husband—he gives
all his time towards it; others give their labour; others
some money; others their teams; we must all help. I hope
you don't flinch and draw back.

LANDLORD: As to that and many other things, that is
more than true; 'tis evident to the greatest demonstration. But Mrs. Chairman should consider that I spend
the best part of my time in doing militia-duty; that I
pay heavy taxes—thirty-seven good honest pounds do I
now disburse towards Congress instead of fourteen towards the King; that my Negro and team is forever
more a-going. Is not that enough, besides losing so much
on tavern amounts? But though I have taken my sign
down, you are welcome to any little remnant I have.

CHAIRWOMAN: Well, let us taste then. What do you
[think], Colonel, my dear?

DEACON: Why, a little in reason will do no harm,
this cold morning.

LANDLORD: Here, Mrs. Chairman. I could give no
better to his honour, General Washington, if he was to
pass by.

CHAIRWOMAN: It is the true juice of the cane. Oh,
how sweet it smells! Old stores, are they not? Or else
you must deal with the enemy, I am sure. Now tell me
where you got this.

LANDLORD: Deal with the enemy? Aye, aye, that's to
be sure; and so we do, but after a strange sort of fashion.
Our friends to the eastwards have taken some of their
ships, and I have given the Bostonians thirty dollars a
gallon for this. Now you understand me.

CHAIRMAN-DEACON: 'Tis really excellent. What must
I give you for this dram?

LANDLORD: Give? Why, nothing. I told you that I
kept tavern no longer. You are welcome. Besides, to-
day is Lord's day, and God forbid that I should defile it
with filthy lucre; you are welcome, as I told you before.

DEACON: I am really glad to see you taking such good
ways; I have been told as how you used to be a pretty
tight churchman. I hope these times will make a good
Christian of you, and teach you to worship as we do

since your churches are shut up and your priests have abandoned you all.

LANDLORD: Why, sir, I always professed myself a Christian and hope I am so still. There is nothing in names that I know of.

DEACON: At times this may do very well, but now we are the favourite Christians, the defenders of liberty; and if we succeed, you may be sure we shall take care of ourselves. The reapers should enjoy the benefits of harvest, as the saying is. Hard times for poor Tories and churchmen, I must confess; well may they call themselves the militant folks every way. But 'tis the fortune of war; they must grin and bear it. They must become pliable, humour the times, and submit.

LANDLORD: And so we must, and so we should, and so we do to the best of our power. But it takes time, honourable Colonel, to part with the old stuff and put on new garments. For my part, I always mean well and do the best I can.

DEACON: As people shake off the dust from their feet before they go into meeting, so must you and yours part with their old attachments and prejudices, or else they cannot enter into the new Jerusalem, that new temple of liberty so wonderfully reared in so short a time. Take my word for it; bid farewell to your kings, bishops, and monarchy. But if you still long after the last, you must look toward heaven for the fifth which is there manifested. Though my thoughts are thus, what you have seen concerning monarchy in this world should estrange you from the other.

LANDLORD: Why, sir, if I might be so bold as to speak my own mind unto you who knows a great deal more than such poor folks as I do, and as to what concerns kings, bishops, and monarchy, is it not under them that we have grown rich and fat? Is it not by their good contrivance that we have become so numerous, that we have so many cleared fields and mowing-grounds and a fine market for what we raise? What! Would you, Mr. Chairman, impute it as a crime because some people do still revere and respect that form of government from which so much good has arisen and dared at least respect these new inventions, the usefulness and advantages of which we have never experienced yet? It may be all for the better, and I am sure, for my part, I hope so. But who can tell how the coat will wear, though the cloth may look well?

DEACON: That is all very well said, honest landlord, but yet we must make a good Whig of you and an honest man—do you hear? And we must be sure of your conversion.

LANDLORD: A Whig, sir? I don't understand that word.

DEACON: Why, have you lived so long and do not know yet what a Whig is? 'Tis a lover of Congress and committees, a lover of his country.

LANDLORD: And so I do. But why should I wish that our navigable rivers should be converted into a great number of brooks on which our canoes could not swim?

DEACON: Navigable rivers? Brooks? What is the meaning of all this? You shall love the country such as we shall make it for you. Well, to be sure, you Toryfied gentry shall cut and carve for yourselves no such thing. Mourn and bow down; your hope is cut off; you trust in a spider-web. You lean upon an old house, but it is falling. You hold it fast in your heart, we know; but it shall not endure, for it is passing away; the Scriptures condemn you. Well, to be sure, let me hear one word more about your brooks and your rivers!

LANDLORD: Mr. Chairman, to be sure, understands the threads of these things better than we poor folks, who have nothing to do with the affairs of the county. For my part, I work and sweat and obey, and I hope the honourable committee will find no fault with us little ones, who are but herrings in the school.

DEACON: That is well put in for a plaster, but I know full well where the sore lies; the canker is now at your heart. Many and repeated complaints have been made unto me, for all you can say, about your keeping a Tory house. I have always made believe as though it could not be.

LANDLORD: You have done me justice, good sir; my house was public then. How should I know what sentiments those entertain who resort to it?

DEACON: That is well enough, to be sure, but take care that the people don't talk too much about you. I am their organ, but I am led by their desires; I must please them at any rate. That is between us. Well, landlord, what do you charge for your pint of good spirituals?

LANDLORD: Not a farthing, honourable Colonel. I am no longer a tavern-keeper, as I told you before; you are heartily welcome.

ELTHA: Now, landlord, mind what my husband has told you; 'tis to him you must look, and 'tis him you must please. It will all go well with you if you mind your steps.

LANDLORD: I shall so, Mrs. Chairman.

(*Exeunt.*)

Fourth Landscape: At the Tavern.

IWAN, a foreigner.
ECCLESTONE, an American gentleman.
LANDLORD.
AARON BLUE-SKIN, a new-made squire.
COLONEL TEMPLEMAN.
THREE QUAKERS (tied).
CAPTAIN SHOREDITCH, with a black beard, bushy head, stockings half-way down his legs, and a naked cutlass in his hands.
SIX ARMED MILITIAMEN, with linsey-woolsey blankets, one end tied over their left shoulders, the other end under their right arms.

While the deacon and his wife proceed on their journey, the scene continues at the tavern.

ECCLESTONE: I am right glad the fellow and his doxy are gone. Were there ever seen such scenes of low absurdity and tyranny exercised in so unaccountable a manner over a people who pretended to be so jealous once of their liberties? They have consigned them over to Congress without the acknowledgment even of a peppercorn.

IWAN: Pooh, these are the very people that are the soonest caught. Only speak to them in their style; make a great fuss about property; talk about encroachments, privileges, etc.; they'll well take you to be their zealous friends and follow you anywhere and everywhere. 'Tis really enough to disgust one of the world and its dependencies to see and trace the conduct of this fellow throughout the meanderings of his pride, ignorance, vanity, consummate hypocrisy. He is a perfect epitome of the times.

ECCLESTONE: I, who am an American, am as sensible as you. This delegation of power ad infinitum from the imperial Congress to these low-lived rulers is intolerable in proportion to the distance of the sovereign and to the antecedent passions and ignorance of these country chaps. What a devoted people we are that we should be thus suspended between poverty, neglect, and contempt if we go to New York, and fines, imprisonment, and exile if we stay!

IWAN: 'Tis a shocking circumstance, I acknowledge; but, alas, there is nothing new in all this! Read [in] history, my friend, that the same low, dirty chains lead mankind through all the variations of fate, through all the changes of fortune. We are victims of these two singular powers. What can we do but submit with cheerfulness and resignation? Talking about it only serves to make matters worse.

ECCLESTONE: 'Tis cursed hard to see, for instance, this fellow, his wife, and the junta dispose of all the social happiness of a county; commit the greatest barbarities, accumulate injustice on injustice, with impunity trample on every law; yet go and worship with an easy conscience. What must that same conscience be? It must be a false guide.

IWAN: Was not it so before these times? Did they not use to juggle and cheat mankind before, in all their dealings and arbitrations? They are the same men raised only five or six feet above the surface of the earth. Their consciences are only modes of thinking, and they have contracted the horrid bias long ago.

ECCLESTONE: I can't endure their slavish rule. I can't bow and prostrate myself before such wretches who have perverted every idea of right and wrong.

IWAN: But you must do it. Go home, then, and read Seneca, Isocrates; learn to fortify yourself by reason, and run not in despair like a fool; learn to bear the insolence of men. Societies, like individuals, have their periods of sickness. Bear this as you would a fever or a cold.

ECCLESTONE: How long will this last? This is the question. When the accounts of this mighty revolution arrive in Europe, nothing will appear there but the splendid effects. The insignificant cause will be overlooked; the low arts, this progressive succession of infatuations, which have pervaded the whole continent, will be unknown. The brave, the warlike Americans will be blazoned out as the examples of the world, as the veteran sons of the most rational liberty. Whereas we know how it is: how this country has been trepanned and insensibly led from one error to another, conducted by the glare of false-deceiving meteors.

IWAN: Small causes have generally the most extensive effects; 'tis so all the world over. When you read the resolves of some mighty councils, the edicts of potent kings, you see but the ostensible side of the medal. Could you pervade the little, insignificant cabals of their cabinets, the combination of female influence, the jars of parties, you'd observe the same train; you'd see that it is by the distance, the dense medium through which we little folks contemplate the actions of the great, that we are deceived. We have naturally such respect for grandeur that we are fools enough to think that they are made of other clay. Go learn of our grave-diggers whether there is any difference between the bones of a general and those of the common soldier that used to tremble at the least of his nods.

ECCLESTONE: That is all very true; that is commonplace talking. But does it not appear to you somewhat strange that there should be no analogy between causes and their effects, and that the chain which links both ends should be invisible to the keenest observer?

IWAN: Not in the least. What connexion or similitude, pray, do you find between the acorn and the lofty oak? The few causes which rule the world are derived from the Great One; and if we are so incapable of comprehending anything about it, why should we have the presumption to think that we can follow these threads, these sublime ramifications which pervade both the moral and the physical world?

ECCLESTONE: I have read with attention of the revolutions of Sweden, of Portugal, of Switzerland, and Holland, and they seem to me to be founded on plain, palpable, distinguished causes. The people were horribly tyrannized; the yoke was too heavy; they agreed to shake it off. The idea is simple.

IWAN: Why is not it the same here? At least they tell you so; and if everybody believes them, it answers the same purpose.

ECCLESTONE: The people can never believe what they have never felt. I am very sure 'tis not the weight nor the galling of the yoke which has hurried them on in this sorrowful career. 'Tis a multitude of motives adapted to the locality of provinces, which they have artfully reunited into one grand motive. The whole has been gilded by deception, and now forms a singular phantom, to which it is sacrilegious not to pay proper adoration.

IWAN: You are mistaken in the first part of your assertion. The ancient revolutions you have been mentioning had their origin, perhaps, in the same causes: the ambition of a few. But the distance of time, the tinsel of language, the care which the historian has taken to bring on the scene nothing but what is great, conspicuous, and grand, have left the rest behind. Look at the reformation of Russia, for instance. To what cause does it owe the rapid improvements it has made of late, and the conspicuous figure it now exhibits on the stage of the world? Why, to about two grains of poison.

ECCLESTONE: Two grains of poison! I don't understand you. What connexion can you find and trace between two grains of poison and the vast schemes of your immortal czar?

IWAN: You must remember that his sister, Sophia, who was much more advanced in age than himself, in order to rule alone, thought it political and expedient to give him a dose of poison, which the strength of his constitution enabled him to overcome. Now, an addition of two grains would certainly have dispatched him; and I will have you calculate how many millions to one but that St. Nicholas the Primate and the boyards would still have been the wretched masters of a wretched people. There is myself, for instance. Could you believe the original cause which led me here, you would hardly believe me.

ECCLESTONE: Did not you come to this country on purpose? Was it not a premeditated plan agreed on by your parents and friends?

IWAN: Not a bit. 'Twas a horseshoe nail which sent me to England and thence to America.

ECCLESTONE: Surely you must think me as credulous as a New England man to tell me with a serious face that a horseshoe nail drove you to this country.

IWAN: I am serious, and have too much respect for you to advance anything but what I can prove.

ECCLESTONE: Do, then, let us hear this curious anecdote. It is, I believe, the first shoe-nail since man learnt the art of fabricating them which has the magical power to send a man from the polar regions across the Atlantic to this new-found land.

IWAN: After my academical studies were finished, I served an apprenticeship with a merchant at Saratov, whose son resided at Archangel—for which place I was destined also. Going one day to see the marriage of a friend, my horse, which had been shod purposely the day before, was severely pricked by a nail. This accident obliged me to hire a hackney one, which proved so bad that I got a very dangerous fall. This determined my father to send me to the bath of Olonets, where I met by mere accident a maternal uncle who had resided in England, to which country he soon after returned and took me along with him. You know the nature of commercial connexions: in consequence of new views and schemes, he sent me here, where I have lived ever since the most perfect itinerant life. Had I time, I could convince you that from the single circumstance all the shades and variations of my life afterwards flowed with as uninterrupted a connexion as the thread of a ball after you have unravelled the intricate beginnings.

ECCLESTONE: 'Tis really melancholy to see what puppets we are that can't distinguish even the wires that move us on.

IWAN: 'Tis so, and who knows whether we would move at all could we see to what purpose we are moving? Fate leads the willing, drags the backward on.

ECCLESTONE: Must I, then, see my native country conquered by low, illiterate, little tyrants? Must I see the dearest bonds of society torn asunder? All our hopes, our views, our peace, all we had been bred to look on as sacred and useful—must I look upon all these things as indifferent, and passively bear every contumely, suffer every insult, repress the swellings of the big heart, swallow the bitter cup to the last drop, see our famed constitution levelled with the dust, observe the new and imperfect embryo rising out of its dissolved, disunited parts? Must I without either a sigh or a groan, but with a passiveness derived from fatality, worship the pretended saints, veteran Puritans, hair-brained fellows of the East? In the South, bend the knee to the little Negro lordlings, to haughty, imperious planters who wish to revenge themselves on their native country for the ancient banishment of their forefathers? Must we obey, without repining, their hard rule and overlook all the deceit and disappointment it contains? No, I cannot do it. Let me bleed out of every pore what blood I have, and expire with the pleasing consciousness of having done what I could to prevent it. God grants us no blessing without purchase: health by temperance, harvest by severe labours, riches by industry. Shall not the peace, the glory of the land, be repurchased by blows, by struggles, by a well-supported contest?

IWAN: These are laudable sentiments; this is the enthusiasm without which even a peer is unworthy of the name of citizen, and with which the meanest plebeian can become superior to kings. But you can do no more than what you are permitted by your situation and abilities. Who knows but it is irrevocable? In that case, you must submit with prudence and not expose yourself in vain; or else you must quit it.

ECCLESTONE: Quit it! That I shall if this event happen. I will go and hide the shame of being born an Englishman on Terra Australis, in Patagonia, in the most unknown part of the world. Great Britain shall lose the awful name. I shall ever after look upon it as a country lost to the vices of extreme riches, and pray to heaven that some great national misfortune may befall her and reinstate her in all former virtue and energy.

IWAN: The Master of the World alone knows how the event will be. I am not a politician—and a foreigner besides. But surely some sort of order, if it is the fruit of fear and coercion, will be better than committee rule, the most detestable of any.

ECCLESTONE: I do not know how it is, but if these

people succeed, I shall certainly think that this world was made for knaves, hypocrites, and fools.

IWAN: What this world was made for, I am sure I cannot tell. There is rather a degree of impiety in wishing to investigate so sublime a scheme. But in our obscure gropings and strange wanderings, it really appears as if it was even so. For they are the greatest majority, and the greatest number surely should have the greater right in a system where everything depends on force. This is infallibly the case except where the wisdom of the few has set itself in opposition and become superior.

ECCLESTONE: Sad reflections! Terrific thoughts, big with every bitterness! Poor consolation! Oh, my native country, why did not I die and quit the scene ere our ancient, refulgent sun was eclipsed by these accursed evaporations? To aim at a greater share of political felicity, to make the world believe we were slaves, to make us exchange the silken cords of our ancient government for the rattling chains of our timocracy, is perhaps the most monstrous instance of perfidy, ingratitude, and successful hypocrisy that ever was exhibited in the world before.

IWAN: This is all very true, but if Providence really interferes in the little quarrels of the ants, which are perpetually busy in rearing and pulling down some part of the mole-hill, who knows but this revolution might have been necessary in order to check the prodigious career of prosperity enjoyed by England? Redden not with anger, but hear me patiently. Who knows but if she had enjoyed the peaceable possession of this country thirty years longer, undisturbed, but what she might have had power enough to have ruled the world and to have collected within her extended arms all its commerce, all its riches, and the influence they bring along with them? The next thing to power, you know, is the inclination to abuse it. Who knows but that the mischiefs that might have ensued would have been far greater, far more extensive, than those you now experience? Could we with our mole-eyes foresee these distant consequences, trace these subsequent dependencies, we might then talk more respectfully of the wisdom of these links of which we now so bitterly complain.

ECCLESTONE: That is all very well said, but why

should everything be so constituted as to be founded on evil, rise from evil? Poor choice! Sad situation! And so we must think ourselves happy to undergo but seven years' calamity instead of twenty! Why one? Why any? Is not the common chance of diseases, hurricanes, and other natural misfortunes sufficient to keep mankind in remembrance of their dependence, mortality, and of the precarious tenure of their leases?

LANDLORD (*hastily coming into the room*): Hush! Hush! For God's sake, gentlemen! Let not a word more escape your lips. Be as if you were just come in, weary and tired. Put on your dirty boots, and be as if you knew nothing of me. Here comes N. S. Esq. He is the very inquisitor of these parts; he is a merciless committee-man. The sight of him always makes me shudder. 'Tis said that Mercy and Truth turned their heads from him at the time of his nativity and never looked at him since.

AARON BLUE-SKIN (*enters with a wild, irascible countenance*): Landlord, have you got anything that an exhausted, fatigued man may recruit himself with, this chilly, cold morning?

LANDLORD: Why, great and good sir, you know that the law has taken my sign down. I don't shut my doors against my friends and acquaintances, but I keep tavern no more. The new law which limits the prices of everything has put it out of my power to entertain folks as I used to.

AARON BLUE-SKIN: That is very wrong, my word for it; and I say so. What is more, this is a pure, good stand for the business. I believe you are stiff and stubborn, yet you won't submit as the rest do. The committee, I believe, must take you in hand; they are pure people to bring obstinacy and malice quite low. If they do, depend on't, they will make you as pliant as a glove. I believe you know pretty roundly what they can do. Well, on my word! Taken your sign down to spite your best customers, who were Whigs! Well, really this is defying a power which no one else dares to do within the precincts of the county.

LANDLORD: What can, what should, what must I do, great and good sir? I wish you'd tell me. If the honourable committee will supply me with a sufficient stock at my price, I shall then entertain them on the old footing. But, good sir, good sir, let not that ruffle you. Whenever your honour goes by and is pleased to stop, you shall always be welcome to such as I have for my own family.

AARON BLUE-SKIN: Who are those two strangers eating there? Surely some part of the public is still welcome to your board.

LANDLORD: As to these two gentlemen, they just came in and merely forced themselves upon me. They said as how they were weary and would go no further without refreshment. I have given them such as I have, and they allow me so much by the hour for the benefit of my fireside; and you know this severe season a tight room and a good fire are more valuable than the best of victuals.

AARON BLUE-SKIN: Well, that is really a very impudent way of evading the law and defeating its meaning. What power must legislators have to bind such a set of infamous rascals as we have up and down the country! Charge for the use of his fire, I suppose, as much as the entertainment amounts to! Well, really, this is something new, to be sure! The first time I attend the house, I will produce an amendment such as will never want amendment again. I profess, never fear, Mr. Landlord, we shall keep you in our eyes all the time, and by frustrating your sagacity shall defeat that of your fellows.

LANDLORD: Could the laws be founded but on common justice they would not need of any amendments. But who can afford to lose two thirds on the retail of everything, and have the house full, besides?

AARON BLUE-SKIN: Come, come, sir! I am piping hot from the committee. No sarcasm, no biting reflections, if you please! Not the most distant reflection, to be sure, will allow you to set your poor, pitiful judgement in competition with that of our whole legislative body. Take care that I don't handle you; if I lay my hands on you, it shall be tightly. I promise you that we sent last night thirty-four of your brethren to be fastened to the ground who had not said a fourth part so much; but in consideration of the burley [sic] I am willing as a neighbour, besides, to pass over—but have a care next time! Your name stinks, you know.

LANDLORD: Good sir, I meant no harm; but when I

am a-speaking, I can't tell where nor when to stop. My tongue is so used to its ancient declivity it will run off itself, as it were. But you know me very well. Every man has his enemies. God help us!

AARON BLUE-SKIN: God help you, pretty fellows! Indeed it is we whom God will and does help every day in enabling us to vanquish our cruel enemies. When our triumph is complete, when these soldiers of Pharaoh have left our land, which they have polluted, you shall see what you shall see: what an orderly set of people we shall make of you all. Look at the Jersey; thanks to their laws and their worthy governor, the very primrose of the continent, they have brought the people to fear and reverence the laws. 'Tis really admirable. I just now voted that for the future no law should pass without a good wedge clapped at the end on't; that whenever any of your qualmish people and your evasive folks make their appearance, some of us may be ready to drive it on and fasten the rascals. In the Jersey aforesaid, they never pass a law without enacting that he, they, or she that shall find fault with the same shall pay a good stout fine or be imprisoned. That is the matter we want. (*He yawns. He strokes and rubs his eyes.*) God forgive me, these plaguy Tories have made us intrude on the Sabbath. I do not know how it happened.

LANDLORD: What! Are you but just come from the committee, Squire Aaron?

AARON BLUE-SKIN: Not a half-hour ago did we break up.

LANDLORD: Who are they that have been so severely handled?

AARON BLUE-SKIN: Why, there are Squire —— and Major ——, quondam major, I mean; and there is farmer ——, that proud, rich old miser; and there is friend Hezekiah, the simple but wealthy Quaker. God knows who the rest were; our clerk may tell. Oh, how it pleases me to bring the pride of these quondam gentry down! This is fulfilling the Bible to a tittle; this is lowering the high and rewarding the low; this is humbling the proud; this is exalting the Christian, the meek man. He, she, or they that fulfil thus the word of God shall be blessed; that is, shall prosper in this world and the next.

(*He drinks.*) Here is, God bless the Congress and damn the popish king. Who says *amen* to it?

TWO STRANGERS: As we belong not to your congregation, we owe you, therefore, no response.

AARON BLUE-SKIN: What? Responses? Congregations? Why, you talk like suspected persons. I presume you are Tories travelling towards New York.

TWO STRANGERS: We travel where we want to go. The road is opened, and we know of no difficulty that can stop us. Whenever we meet with guards, if required, we produce our authority, which no man dare call in question.

AARON BLUE-SKIN: This is the sauciest speech I have heard this great while. I vow, if it were not that the committee is gone to meeting, I'd have you seized and sent to gaol *ipso facto,* as the old law used to say. You travel where you please! Well, to be sure, you do not know, I suppose, before whom you are a-speaking; and that I am the very soul and quintessence of a committee-man; and that we are the appointed guardians, the watch-towers of this county, the collective wisdom of the four precincts; and that it is our bounden duty to see and to observe from our high stations everything that passes.

TWO STRANGERS: This all may be, and much more which your modesty prevents you explaining. We are afraid of no man or of no set of men, and as we, by our principles, wish well to all mankind, we have a stock of confidence which nothing can alter. Authority is a commodity which is become so common that it is become less valuable than heretofore. There are so many givers of passes and pretenders to power and control that we are extremely cautious of adulterating our general pass by the addition of new and unknown names.

AARON BLUE-SKIN: You travel thus under authority, gentlemen?

TWO STRANGERS: That's what we do.

AARON BLUE-SKIN: That is another affair. I presume your authority is from the army?

TWO STRANGERS: Yes, sir. Is not it superior to that of committees?

AARON BLUE-SKIN: Sometimes we may allow it; but in the administration of our own county, we know no superior but God.

Two Strangers: That may be as you say, but as we are not inhabitants of your county we think ourselves not at all amenable to your jurisdiction, as long as we offend nobody, but travel on peaceably.

Aaron Blue-Skin: You are right, gentlemen. By your speech I should take you to be lawyers travelling to headquarters, I suppose?

Two Strangers: Yes, sir, we have heard so much of the Continental army that we want to go and take a view of these noble defenders of American liberty.

Aaron Blue-Skin: Do tell General Washington that we are preparing ourselves to send him a fine parcel of volunteers, stout lads that turn out for the good of the cause.

Ecclestone: What bounty do you give them in this part of the country?

Aaron Blue-Skin: Bounty! Oh, for shame! The government would be extremely wrong to give them any; it would be putting an affront upon us. But our people, who are naturally generous, club together and make them a purse of about eleven hundred dollars.

Ecclestone: Eleven hundred dollars! Very pretty volunteers, indeed. I hope they are better than those who are a-coming from the eastward; they are old Negro boys, lads of all size, etc——

Aaron Blue-Skin: Why, gentlemen, as to that, our stock of young men begins to grow very scarce with us. These lads in a year or two will be grown up; they will be much more pliable and fitter for the great school of arms.

Two Strangers: That may be, but where are the men to do their duty whilst they are growing up?

Aaron Blue-Skin: Enough of them to the southward. 'Tis said that Governor Casewell is a-coming with a powerful number, who bring with them a nation of rice-cakes ready made. Landlord, what have I to pay?

Landlord: Nothing, good Squire, as I told you before.

Aaron Blue-Skin: Why, that is really clever. If the good creature is absolutely so cheap, God bless the law and the law-makers for it. Let us have another tumbler.

Landlord: Here it is, Squire.

AARON BLUE-SKIN: Come, honest Tom, won't you pledge me?

LANDLORD: No, sir, you'll excuse me, I presume to pledge none but my equals; I know what respect I owe to a worshipful committee-man.

AARON BLUE-SKIN: Why, as to that, you were a-saying, to be sure, who dares say nay. We committee-men, we can do a great deal; think a great deal; write a great deal; and order abundance of things. But, Tom, never mind it for this time. We are neighbours still. Plague on my head! It contains so many things that it's almost ready to burst; it sadly aches. I believe I shall not go to meeting to-day. Can't you lend us a bed for an hour or two?

LANDLORD: A bed! Nay, two at your service and welcome! But how comes it that you good Christians have so much intruded on the Lord's day? Why did not you finish your business betimes?

AARON BLUE-SKIN: Haven't I told you already that the Tories' affairs are so large and so manifold. Transactions of these gentry are to be examined into so that it takes abundance of time.

LANDLORD: Generally you don't trouble your head much about evidences. It seems to me that this short method of yours requires but a short time.

AARON BLUE-SKIN: That is very true, Tom. We lump it sometimes pretty expeditiously. But then there was waiting for the honourable chairman; and there was eating supper and smoking a pipe or two and drinking a little whisky toddy and reading the newspapers and examining Governor Johnstone's fine speech—why, all these take abundance of time.

LANDLORD: That is very true.

AARON BLUE-SKIN: And there was hunting of some of the Tories who were lurking in the neighbourhood and were asleep. And there was treating our light-horsemen with a dram apiece, to be sure, for they are really quite smart fellows. They understand surrounding a man's house quite charmingly well and pulling and hauling the Tories out of their beds as well and better than any folks in the world.

LANDLORD: But, pray, in the midst of all your fes-

tivity, what did your sober, serious deacon say and do—
he that begins his Sabbath Saturday sundown?

AARON BLUE-SKIN: He was the very merriest of us
all, but the poor man was caught one of the very first;
his head is so weak. He quitted his chair early in the
session; he took a good nap and went home four hours
ago. I hope God in His mercy will forgive us all, but
upon thinking on it, I must go home. What would folks
say to find me abed here? They would swear that I
have got drunk here. That won't do either. Farewell,
Tom.

IWAN: This is a curious fellow, admirably well-fitted
for the time. No wonder he stands so high in the estimation of the people. Profligate yet apparently religious,
conceited and stubborn, he can do mischief with all the
placidity of a good man and carefully avoid the ostensible parts of the sinner.

ECCLESTONE: These people have a much easier task to
fulfil than what you imagine. Let them but act as their
passions guide them; it is only calling the effects of their
brutality the good of the cause and pleading in excuse
an order of Congress. 'Tis all well, and the suffering
world must remain passive and silent.

IWAN: Have these people no idea of reverses? Are
they so confident as to think it impossible the scale may
turn? For my part, were I in their place I would shudder at the thought and tremble for the hour of retaliation.

ECCLESTONE: They trust, from the highest to the
lowest, to the chapter of events and seem to have shut
their eyes to their soundest policy. They read Montes-
quieu; better for that man never to have written. You
see that he has expended twenty years of his life to very
little purpose. The Bible, the *Spirit of the Laws,* Seneca's
Morals, are excellent things to furnish us with theoretical
pleasures and serve to a few as spiritual food. 'Tis too
refined for the common herd of mankind.

(*Whilst Aaron was getting his horse, who should drop
in but Colonel Templeman!*)

COLONEL: Where now, Squire? I thought you abed
and asleep this good while.

AARON BLUE-SKIN: For the matter of that, I want it

enough, but you must know that when I left the committee this morning, I had to go round by —— house, you know, as it was agreed on; and I had to go and give a peep at ——; and hearing, on my way home, Landlord Potter had taken his sign down, I had a mind to talk to him a little on the subject, and he has sufficiently convinced me for this time. Aren't you coming in? Do alight, Colonel. There are two strangers there; I know not what to make of them. You'd better step in and hear them speak. We may pick up something and teach them good breeding.

COLONEL: With all my heart. Is there anything to drink?

SQUIRE: Oh, yes, though the stubborn dog won't sell. But he will give us as much as we want, and that is so much gained from the enemy. (*They walk in.*)

COLONEL: Why, Landlord, early at it! I see your business, like a clock, goes on Sundays and holy days.

LANDLORD: Truly, sir, I follow no business. But people can't leave off yet calling here, and as long as I have anything to eat or drink the honourable committee, above all, are welcome.

COLONEL: Well, this will make but poor business at this rate, but am in hope you'll put up your sign again.

LANDLORD: Not I, Colonel. As long as the new law will take away the means of subsistence by my old sign, I will put up some other and live by some new calling.

COLONEL: Law should be respected. There never was a law but what galled at first. You must obey with cheerfulness and seek in perfect obedience that resignation which sweetens everything. Before the chapter of the kings was out, we had nothing but will. Now that delegate reigns, we have nothing but law.

LANDLORD: True, sir, but if these laws are the will of a few it comes to the same thing, does it not?

COLONEL: No, no! 'Tis the will of a few, it is true, but these few are chosen by ourselves, and their will deserves the respect and attachment of all.

LANDLORD: How can I respect people with whom I am not acquainted? They say that they are a parcel of lawyers and merchants who are removed to Yorktown. They say that they do just as they please without consulting the people.

COLONEL: That is a palpable mistake. They often speak to you through their crises and their resolves.

LANDLORD: That is true. They now and then address us, whom they call the "good people of America," and no set of beings ever deserved so great a name; but it is only to tell us what they want and to oblige us to furnish it; and they sometimes cause us to be informed of their will by means of the pulpit.

COLONEL: Well, but as you never go to our meetings, you never hear anything about it; is it not so?

LANDLORD: My neighbours tell me on't. That is the same thing, but that is not all. We have so many more masters than we used to have. There is the high and mighty Congress, and there is our governor, and our senators, and our assemblymen, and there is our captain of light-horse. God bless him, he never comes here but upon good and lawful errands. And there is you, sir, our worthy colonel; and there are the honourable committee. And there are, let me see, one, two, three, four, five commissaries who want nothing but our horses, gain, hay, etc., and from whom we never can get any recompense. There is the sergeant of the gate and there is the good squire here present; and there is—I can't tell them all. Why, upon my word, put at the end of it the respect we owe to each single law and you'll find that we poor people have abundance to do in order to please them all and live.

COLONEL: Aye, aye, such refractory folks as you are, such a stubborn set, really want bringing down. The time is come when it shall be in our power to make good subjects of you all. I know where the shoe pinches you——

LANDLORD: That is what you may, and it never pinched nor galled before. Is it a wonder we should shrink a little and wink and blink?

COLONEL: You did not know what government was before. We will make a united, strong people of you by and by. A little while longer, and the job will be done.

(*Somebody knocks.*)

LANDLORD: Walk in.

(*Enters Captain Shoreditch heading a party of six militiamen surrounding three Quakers.*)

COLONEL: Aye, aye, what is this? More pigeons caught?

CAPTAIN SHOREDITCH: Why, honourable sir, I cannot make these men turn out in the militia. Some will come down to us sometimes, but they will neither handle a musket nor touch our victuals. These prisoners pretend to claim some exemption from you. They say that they were at your house last night; that you sent them to me with a message to abate somewhat of their fines and to let them alone for the present.

COLONEL (*rubbing his head*): I just remember something about it. I am so pestered with this sort of people that I often say or do anything to get rid of them. I am quite sick and tired of these pretended conscientious non-fighting mortals. I have reasoned with them and, for the soul of me, I cannot find in the whole Bible any passages whereon they can build so preposterous a doctrine.

QUAKERS: Our principles are not new; they are those of a large, numerous society to which they have adhered in the hottest time of persecution. Our forefathers have witnessed them with their lives. Thou should'st consider that these rights, founded on the purest motives of conscience, deserve some respect. The legislature of Great Britain has showed thee an example in our exemption from swearing, etc.

(*Soldiers scoffingly deride them. They snatch their hats off, saying: "Rude boors, don't you know that you are speaking to our honourable colonel?"*)

COLONEL: Pray, gentlemen, do you makest a point of conscience to remain covered before everybody?

QUAKERS: We make it no point of conscience; it is a custom among our society. Does it offend thee that we should speak to thee covered? Does it add to thy power and honour to see us thus abused by thy soldiers?

COLONEL: I don't care three farthings about it. If you are so attached to your broad-brims, put them on, and welcome! (*The Quakers put on their hats.*) But, Captain, tell me in a few words what is the upshot of this people's case. I have quite forgot what I told them last night.

CAPTAIN: Why, honourable sir, they won't train or appear among us when they are ordered.

COLONEL: Does not the law fine them?

CAPTAIN: Yes, sir, but this seems not to satisfy the people. They insist on their bearing arms.

QUAKERS: This very captain of thine who has led us before thee has taken almost everything we had for fines and other penalties. No later than last week he took from our Friend James an ox worth seventy pounds, as thy money goes, for a fine of ten pounds; yet nothing is returned. Can't we appease thy people without so much plunder? It gives them an example of rapine.

COLONEL: That is not the case. The people must be indulged. There is, let me see, besides the fees: trouble, time, advertisements, serving, lawyering, and what not. So the law demands. The rest goes to encourage and support our people. If you'll lie every night by the sides of your wives in whole skins, why, you must expect to pay for it.

QUAKERS: Then the Lord have mercy on us if neither law, law-makers, nor rulers of hundreds can protect us, but rather give us up to persecution.

COLONEL: Why, don't you know, good people, that you are devoted first and foremost? The law rates you all at ten pounds a year, rich and poor. This, as you may say, for not wearing a button in your hat; and then, let me see, I forget what, besides, for not drafting, not training. Why, we were computing it the other day in the assembly that we shall raise in this state as much as will pay the salaries of our governors and judges, or pretty near the mark.

QUAKERS: Are, then, the spoils of an inoffensive sect to feed some parts of thy new rulers? Dost thou, then, mean to establish and support thy new government on wilful, premeditated tyranny and oppression?

COLONEL: Tyranny? Oh, no, we don't give it such a name, by any means. Oppression of such a people as ye are is no oppression; 'tis an act of justice done to the rest of the community, which you will not help to defend.

QUAKERS: Thou wilt never flourish. Follow the example of thy once mother country: encourage every denomination; they are all useful in their way. And keep them all by gentle means under the benign shadow of a just and upright government. Then the world will think indeed that thou art descended from its famed loins.

COLONEL: As to that, we shall do as we please. Now we have got the power, God forbid we should take pattern after its arbitrary rule. The nation of which we are descended is an old rotten stock full of [dead] and decayed limbs; the white worm is at its roots. Flagitiousness, peculation, venality, are arrived there at their utmost pitch. My friends, 'tis an old machine, rusty and extremely out of repair. It takes so much grease to keep it a-going that it requires all the substance of the people. Ours, on the contrary, is brighter, simpler; 'tis new and vigorous.

QUAKERS: We Friends have nothing to do with the powers of the world. We submit for conscience' sake to the rulers of the land, but at the same time should wish that rule were rational, impartial, and mild.

COLONEL: Pooh, pooh, you'll fare here as well as anywhere else. Look at your birthplace and cradle, Pennsylvania. Even there you are an oppressed people and like to lose entirely your ground. How thankful are the good Presbyterians of that country for all the pains your old patron, William Penn, took, the good old soul that he was! We are really the chosen people; we reap the benefits of the Canaanites' labours!

QUAKERS: Canst thou really imagine a glorious conquest to despoil a harmless set of inhabitants of their lawful inheritance? If the Jews had a title to the possessions of the Gentiles, that title was given them by God, who is Master of all. Which of the two dost thee imagine will be recorded by future historians in the most conspicuous manner: our great founder, William Penn, who displayed so much knowledge and ability for the good of mankind, who reared on justice and mercy so beautiful a fabric, who introduced into Pennsylvania every distressed European and constituted him his brother, or those who impiously have defaced this noble monument?

COLONEL: It is even so. The conquered seldom attract the attention of the world; the conquerors are the people who are talked of. Success is an emanation of the shrine of fortune; 'tis all that the world looks at. Haven't you seen a medal which they say our people are striking there?

QUAKERS: No, we know nothing of these new things. What dost thou mean by medal?

COLONEL: Why, 'tis a round piece, something like a dollar, on which some of our people are represented with rods in their hands driving Friend Pemberton and others away. They seem to be loaded with bundles and followed by their wives and children.

QUAKERS: And where dost thou imagine this poor people must go who have showed to the world such patterns of toleration, who have made that country to flourish as a rose?

COLONEL: To Otaheite, to Patagonia, anywhere they please. I fancy they will unite with the Scotch of the Carolinas and the Mertgayees [?] of Virginia; and a pretty company it will be.

QUAKERS: Would'st thou think proper to discharge us?

COLONEL: Discharge you? Why, to be sure. Will you first and foremost take up your muskets and go to fight the redcoats down below? That is the question.

QUAKERS: Thou know'st well our answer. Why would'st thou then ask a needless question?

COLONEL: Well, then, you broad-brims, you must abide by the consequences.

QUAKERS: We will, most cheerfully. We are not men of blood nor of resistance; we obey this community. When all men must turn fighters, then the plough must stand still; then famine must come. Art thou not afraid of it?

COLONEL: Not I; as long as there is bread in the land, I'll get my share on't. The rest must share for themselves, but they say that the southern colonies abound with grain.

QUAKERS: How shall we fetch it from there, now that our horses and waggons are pressed?

COLONEL: Well, then, eat potatoes. That is good enough for those who stay at home.

QUAKERS: We were brought before thee to obtain and to hear the words of justice. Thou art a ruler, a commander. Who shall administer it unto us, if not thou?

COLONEL: If you want justice, go to our supreme and

inferior courts; there it is retailed. My duty, as well as my inclination, is to make you all fight.

QUAKERS: Thy new laws excuse us.

COLONEL: It does not. Besides, it was a palpable mistake in those that framed it. I know better, and that very clause shall be repealed next session. I am lawmaker in my own regiment. If you profess yourselves such passive folks, obey them.

QUAKERS: And is that all the redress we can obtain of thee? God will help us in our distresses if our sins have not rendered us unworthy of His protection. But if thou art determined to sacrifice us all, wilt thou kindly [spare] our wives and children, those innocent creatures who have not yet shared in the guilt of their fathers?

COLONEL: Your wives and children shall be bound out to our people. They are able to work, and after they have lost the sight and the remembrance of their fathers' damnable principles, they then will become worthy to become members of our society.

CAPTAIN: What is to be done with these people, noble Colonel?

COLONEL: Let them even go home. I am sick at the sight of their broad-brims and immovable countenances. You, Quakers, go home for this time, and hold forth in my praise or dispraise as you will. If as pernicious a spirit moved me now as often moves you, I'd send you to the ground. Take care next time! Quakers in the midst of a civil war, and yet pretend to their rights of peace! A most laughable thing, indeed! You may go to the moon and be Quakers there with all my heart, provided God places none else there; and call it New Pennsylvania if you please. There you may have some chance, but here among the other warlike sects of the land—for shame! Get you gone! A few years more, and you'll be sponged away. Quakers truly! When our cruel enemies are at our door! I shall presently lose my temper.

(Exeunt Quakers.)

CAPTAIN: I wish, Colonel, you'd give me your final orders. These folks are really a dangerous example to the rest. "Why should [not] one fight as well as the other?" says one. "Why should that society be exempt from militia-duty?" says the other. "When our independency is established, they will be ready enough to come in for their share of the harvest," says the other.

COLONEL: I'll tell you what: when you hear any of these Toryfied gentry say the least word disrespectful anyways of our cause, or averse to do their duty, without any ceremony knock them down with the butt of your gun—do you hear? And then send them away to the gaol. That's my orders.

CAPTAIN: I shall so, noble Colonel; I'll make short work of them, I'll warrant. Your servant, Colonel.

(Exit Captain.)

COLONEL: I really ask your pardon, gentlemen. Men in my station have really so much plague with Tom, Dick, and Harry that I am sometimes beside myself.— Boy, hand me a coal of fire; this plaguy pipe—. By your dress, I presume you belong to the army.

STRANGERS: No, sir, we are going to view it. 'Tis said that it contains more officers than soldiers.

COLONEL: Aye, aye, you surprise me. What is become of our soldiers then? I am sure the newspapers don't give an account of many killed.

STRANGERS: Why, you know how it is; soldiers perish very fast. Some are returned home, some deserted, and a good many [were] cut off last campaign.

COLONEL: And how do you know?

STRANGERS: Why, sir, we were at the battle of Brandywine, where we saw a good many fall. We met even General Washington in the utmost distress of mind, praying to heaven for some friendly ball to put an end to his pains. Night, however, saved them.

COLONEL: Why, this is not the account we have had of it. However, there are men enough in the country. Liberty can't be purchased too dearly. New recruits, I suppose, will be wanted.

STRANGERS: They are sending them from the East as fast as they can.

COLONEL: Do they? Indeed these people are always ablest. They began the revolution and it is on their vigour and strength we must ultimately depend.

STRANGERS: Why should you pay them so great a compliment at the expense of your own state?

COLONEL: We are a smart people too, that is sure, but

we have unfortunately so many disaffected persons; and [so are] some of our principal families. We are not so knotty and united as they are there.

STRANGERS: As to that, Colonel, it is a misfortune under which every state labours, and I cannot conceive how you'll remedy this great evil.

COLONEL: As to that, we are much divided in our opinions. Some there are who are for crushing, banishing everything that is not consonant. I and many more are for palliating, for consolidating our new society by all the means in our power. War and other accidents have weakened us already sufficiently. Why should we [be] severe forever? These maxims, however, I am sorry to say, prevail among a minority only.

TWO STRANGERS: A pity 'tis. Your new laws and governments would become more respectable at home and abroad, and the character of non-persecution would procure friends and well-wishers. What a pity that so noble an enterprise should be contaminated with so much mischief and evil!

COLONEL: That is true. I have often shed tears over it and blushed within myself that the foundation of American liberty should have been laid in oppression and injustice. Yet zealous as I am, I must needs confess it. God forgive us, what can men do in which they don't mix some strong native poison?

TWO STRANGERS: Had the first legislators and movers of this American scheme thought as you seem to do, America would have triumphed before now. Their justice and humanity in the support of their own cause compared to the cruelty, injustice, arrogance, and flagitiousness of the E. Am. [sic] which in the same manner we lament.

COLONEL: Things cannot be helped at present. I am in hopes the contest won't be long now. Surely the people of England will get tired of feeding and paying soldiers and officers who do nothing. Our connexions with Europe are such, and such is the nature of our cause, that all nations wish us well. The opening of this grand mart or the alternative of shutting it for the sole use of the selfish English—this consideration alone, united with our successes, make me confident that Providence sees our progress with complacency.

IWAN: This is grounding hopes on too presumptuous a foundation. Both parties have been very much to blame, as all the judicious part of the world knows. For my part, I am so much the humble servant of events that I am determined to wait the issue and live if possible like Atticus, shaking hands with both parties.

ECCLESTONE: That is impossible, at least to a native. I easily can conceive that the feelings of a foreigner cannot be so keen.

IWAN: I beg pardon; if you mistrust my zeal, I am sure you don't mistrust my probity.

COLONEL: Come, come, you are both honest men and see the same object with different eyes. Let us wait with patience the grand issue; 'tis not your wishings or my wishing that will turn the scale. Whenever you return this way again, I should be glad you'd call at my house; your talk is sober and clever.

TWO STRANGERS: We shall so, Colonel. Farewell to you.

COLONEL: The same to you.

(*Exeunt strangers.*)

COLONEL: Landlord, who do you think they are?

LANDLORD: Upon my word, I do not know. They seem to be clever gentlemen. They never were here before that I know of.

Fifth Landscape: Francis Marston's House.

BEATUS, deacon.
ELTHA, his wife.
MRS. AURELIA MARSTON.
FAMILY OF CHILDREN.
NERO, the Negro of the house.
PETER MARSTON, a young lad.
MAJOR POPINO.

COLONEL [Deacon]: Oho, I say, my lad, is your mother at home?

YOUNG MARSTON: Where should she be, now that our poor father is shot and murdered by your orders? What do you [want] more, for God's sake?

ELTHA: Come, come. Lads must not spruce up quite so high neither. Well, really, Mr. Lad, do you know who we are? Is your mother at home or is she not?

NERO (*just come up with an alarmed countenance*): Yes, yes Massa; Missy at home and all the little family. Missy been crying all night. 'Tenant 'Plash stop here last night and told her as how Massa, poor Massa, was shot, and that he himself had cracked his brains after he fell down and just quivered him a little with leaves. Missy is sickly and I, too. Massa, what your hona please to have?

CHAIRMAN: Come, come; leave off crying. Go in and inform your mistress that my wife and I are come to bring her good tidings.

(*In comes Mrs. Marston with a chlid in her arms, four daughters, and the lad.*)

MRS. MARSTON: What can the colonel demand of me on this day? Do you mean to rob me of that rest which the oxen and the beasts of burthen enjoy this day?

COLONEL: Madam, I am like Eliphaz, the Temanite, Job's friend. We are come, on the contrary, to commune with you and assuage your pains. Even my wife wanted to share with me the pleasure of bringing you the glad tidings. Your husband has escaped the pursuit of our people below, and is safe arrived in New York.

MRS. MARSTON: God be praised! But is it true, sir? Perhaps you mean to increase still more my woes and feed on the object which a desolated family presents you. 'Tis duty, it seems, to spread misfortunes far and wide. But can it be your inclination to glut yourself on the objects, individuals, on which they happen to fall? Since you were talking of Job's friend, what Zophar says is that the triumph of the wicked is but short and the joy of the hypocrite but for a moment. Do you really come on purpose, and is it really so, that my husband is safe?

COLONEL: You know, madam, that I never swear. What proofs then must I give you? My word of old has been and is to this day proof enough.

ELTHA: It shows really bad to be received with so much diffidence, and to see suspicions, fears, and terror spread over all those faces.

MRS. MARSTON: We are so used to being treated as

enemies, to be cut off from every share of compassion and feelings.

COLONEL: Enemies, madam? To be sure the law does not mean that we should show you much mercy; that I will allow.

MRS. MARSTON: Poor unhappy man! How many are they who have longed for his blood that they might glut themselves on his property!

COLONEL: Now you are talking of property puts it into my mind to suppose that you know that to-morrow the board of commissioners is going to sell all you have, [it] being forfeited to the use of the state by the elopement of your husband.

MRS. MARSTON: Sell all I have! How should I fish out of your political abyss such a thought as this? Must I, then, and my children, starve or go a-begging?

COLONEL: Aye, aye, and to that and a great many other things the law says it, and the law must be obeyed.

MRS. MARSTON: I am not deceived. I expected the very worst that could possibly befall me, and I am ready to submit to my fate. Let us, Mr. Chairman, [hear] the whole of it. Would you not please to sit down, you and your wife? Or have I already lost all right and title to what this house contains? (*The chairman takes a chair and reads in the Bible.*)

MRS. CHAIRMAN: As to that, it is but precarious, indeed. However, you hide nothing. You may look at it all until to-morrow, three to six p.m. Upon the whole, I am glad to see you so well prepared. We must try to do something for you and your little ones. I cannot endure to see good substantial farmers' wives and children, that always lived on the fat of the land, turned out to starve and to grin. Let us see some of your best things, and I will give you my advice about saving them, and other little bargains which I mean to make for your good alone.

COLONEL (*pulling off his spectacles from his nose*): Oh! Fie, fie, woman! Remember, above all things, this day. No worldly thought, I pray.

MRS. CHAIRMAN: Oh, my dear, there is no danger. I only meant to save something useful and clever from the general inventory. Surely I mean no harm. God knows my heart.

COLONEL: Well, well, if it be your real intention; it

whitewashes often the worst of actions, as our minister says. Talk a little lower among yourselves while I finish digesting this excellent chapter.

(*In comes Nero, the Negro, with a billet of wood.*)

MRS. CHAIRMAN: Well, Nero, won't you come and live with my son, Anthony? They say you are a good fellow, only a little Toryfied, like most of your colour.

NERO: No, Missy, me stay and help Massa children. What do here without Nero, you been by, take all meat, all bread, all clothes?

MRS. CHAIRMAN: That's nothing. You must be sold, too, and if you'll live with my son, you shall have Saturday to yourself to plant tobacco and make brooms and trays.

NERO: No, Missy, me never live with a white man who shot my master here at the door by the sleigh.

CHAIRWOMAN: You are a liar, you black dog, and I'll soon make [you] sing a new song.

MRS. MARSTON: Excuse me, ma'am, your son most certainly was one of those who hunted my husband and at last fired at him twice by the sleigh while he had this very infant in his arms. This it is which obliged him at last to quit his own house. Can you reasonably expect that a slave of some sensibility, as a great many are, could live with his master's intentional murderer?

CHAIRWOMAN: Ma'am, you are too high. You must come down; your pride must have a downfall. Lower your top-gallants, as the saying is. That fellow must be sold. In that case, what is it to you who buys him?

MRS. MARSTON: Oppression rather inflates me; misfortunes animate me. How else should I bear their weight? What precaution have I need to take? You have insulted and treated my husband worse than a slave these six months. You have hired myrmidons to hunt him, to kill him if possible; if not, to threaten setting fire to his house that he might fly to save it; and that, by flying, his extensive estate might become a sweet offering to the rulers of this county. Now you are going to strip me and his children of all we possessed, and pray, what can you do more?

CHAIRWOMAN: You have forgot, I suppose, the kind proposition I have been hinting to you just now. You should at least acknowledge favours when certain folks mean to confer them.

CHAIRMAN: Come, come, no pride, I desire. Let it be all done in lowliness and meekness.

CHAIRWOMAN: That is true, my dear; we all know it. But can common flesh bear such ingratitude?

MRS. MARSTON: The amount of your favours I do not well understand. Do you mean to compound with me, do you mean to tamper with your law, or do you really mean and wish that mercy should silence tyranny for a while?

ELTHA: What signify so many questions? The thing you know is this and nothing more: your husband has been inimically inclined from the beginning. He may plead his oath of office, but the just demands of his country are far superior. They bind us at the day of our nativity; all others are more recent, less ancient, and far less respectable. His fate has not overtaken him for nothing. Remember, good ma'am, if you please, the right of the conquerors. How did the Jews behave to the Canaanites? Do you think that they offered them gowns and linen and some gammons in mere compassion? No, not they; they took all because the law commanded it.

MRS. MARSTON: I understand you, I believe. If you want to feast your eyes on what I have, if any part of my furniture or clothing attracts your attention, I suppose that you have but to speak, or perhaps to will, and the things are yours.

CHAIRWOMAN: Why, to be sure, to speak within the compass of possibilities, you are right, for you know well that my husband has got the power.

MRS. MARSTON: Aye, aye, that ineffable word, power. I know full well all its extensive meaning. 'Tis like the New England drams; they have no kind of effect except they produce intoxication. If you'll please to follow me, I will endeavour to satisfy not only your curiosity but what ever other passion may come uppermost. You are sure of this, that impunity awaits you both in this world as well as in the next, in this as wife of a chairman, in the next as that of a deacon.

MRS. MARSTON'S DAUGHTERS (crying): What, Mammy, are we going to lose all our gowns and shifts and petticoats that we have spun ourselves and dyed, according to your rule, with so much care? Must we lose all we have?

CHAIRWOMAN: And why not, pray? The sin of Adam overtook all his descendants, and so must the sin of the squire, your father. We won't leave you in your naturalibus, don't be afraid.

MRS. MARSTON: Come, dear children, I wish you'd withdraw. We must all submit, and your tears and reflections behind me quite disarm me of my fortitude. Go into the other room till I call you.

(*Exeunt children.*)

CHAIRWOMAN: Pretty good advice, truly; and in answer to what you were saying before, although you mean to joke, yet I'd have you know that there is a good deal of truth in it. Do let us see that sweet teapot that I have heard so much of.

MRS. MARSTON: Here it is, madam. 'Tis remarkable for nothing but for being made in England with crowns of Charles the Second, as you see, artfully soldered together. My grandfather brought it from Britain, that renowned native land, which you so fervently curse and hate.

CHAIRWOMAN: Upon honor 'tis a sweet thing. Pity it should go out of the family; but your family is, as it were, divided and annihilated. What will you do with it? However, I'll take it away to save it from the inventory.

MRS. MARSTON: Do! So be it with yourself, but put yourself in my situation and feel for me.

ELTHA: My daughter Judith was a-mentioning the other day—poor child, she had no bad thoughts in so doing—a very handsome purple gown, a large cloak, and a new-fashioned bonnet. Pray, where are they?

MRS. MARSTON: Did not your daughter Judith think then of my daughter Julia? To tell the truth, I have nothing fashionable. I and my daughter wear nothing but what is solid, decent, and substantial, becoming the condition of independent American farmers. (*Here, sighing involuntarily, and restraining the tears from gushing out of her eyes, she empties several large chests of drawers.*)

ELTHA: Extravagant indeed! What, so much of everything! You must have been a costly wife. It has been flood with you, and the ebb should take place and let out some of your long-accumulated stores.

MRS. MARSTON: 'Tis the fruit of my industry and that of my daughters. My husband gave us every fourth cheese, every third firkin of butter, and all the honey of our stores, and a few calves. With these well-earned perquisites, I decently clad the family with Sunday clothes. The rest we spin, we dye, we weave ourselves in this house. Can you find any great harm?

ELTHA: This is really a beautiful quilt. These shoes with the buckles, I believe, will suit my daughter's foot admirably well. She is about being married; these things will come in good time.

MRS. MARSTON: Would you as a mother encourage her to wear the spoil of fraud and tyranny? Would she enter the pale of matrimony decked with the plunder of the desolated family, of the banished husband, the oppressed wife, the orphan children? An't you afraid that she would entail a curse, though latent, in that very womb which [is] to bear her and her husband the source of future joys? Would you [not] be afraid that some evil destiny would attend children born under such fatal omens?

ELTHA: This is all a matter of simple opinion, as I may say. I take it to be rather a matter of triumph; the daughters of Israel were never ashamed to wear the golden bracelets which their youth brought from the field.

MRS. MARSTON: Excellent doctrine, madam. The Old Testament affords you abundance of such proofs, but if you have a mind to be merciful, open the New.

ELTHA: Pshaw, woman, that is no excuse. Both are conjoined together and give us one set of laws and precepts. The latter is well enough for you bigoted church people.

MRS. MARSTON: Then take, ravish, and plunder. Glut yourself, but I beg you'll carry your insults no further.

ELTHA: Well, then, put up together these things which I have set apart. Let your wench wrap them up together that I may carry them home. A proper compensation, a certain degree of indulgence, you may expect if I have any influence over my husband.

MRS. MARSTON: Any way you please. But what do you

think the pious man will do, he who is now sanctifying the day in the next room by reading the Bible?

ELTHA: As to that, he has a certain rule which he reconciles with his conscience and the duty he owes his country. I am but a woman; this is not the first time that such cases have come before him.

MRS. MARSTON: Excellent evasion! Admirable sophistry!

(*Colonel re-enters the room, sanctified and demure.*)

ELTHA: Well, Colonel, my dear, are you ready to go? I have viewed what I thought most proper to be removed out of the sight of the other commissaries lest they should imagine that so much wealth was ill-got.

COLONEL: Wife, if you mean well, I am satisfied. I will suffer no transaction anyways fraudulent. Our bleeding country wants everything that can strengthen it and relieve it from the burdens under which it labours. I am but the executor of laws, and they must be obeyed.

MRS. MARSTON: I am sure, sir, you don't execute them for nothing. You pay yourself well for your trouble, I know it; and it is this which inflames your patriotic zeal to so high a pitch. Remember that the world was created round to convince us that therein nothing is stable and permanent. The time may come when you could have wished to have felt for the misfortunes of others, but your heart is callous. How you can reconcile the profession of so much religion with the execution of so many evil deeds, I know not.

COLONEL: I shall not enter with you into any such disquisition. Where the crime lies, the lawful revenge should take place. Your husband from the beginning has been a supporter of the oppressive acts of Parliament, that venal body which wants freedom at home and loves to spread tyranny abroad. They have not to deal with the inhabitants of Bengal, I promise you. Mr. Marston has been, in short, exceedingly inimical and a bad man in the true sense of the word.

MRS. MARSTON: You have so subverted the course and order of things that no one knows what is a bad man in your new political sense; but in spite of modern definition the true meaning of that word stands yet on its old foundation. A bad man is he, sir, who tears up the bowels of his native country; who subverts its best laws; who makes tyranny, informing, injustice, oppression of every kind, the cause of God; who arrests people without cause; imprisons them for whole months and seasons without hearing or inquiries; and leaves them to languish under the accumulated weight of want, despair, and disease. A bad man, sir, is he who, when he had it in his power to prevent it, suffered an innocent young man to perish in a suffocating gaol, panting for breath, burnt and scorched by the most excessive fever; and yet would not release him. A bad man is he who sternly denied the most earnest solicitations of an unfortunate aged couple, imploring on their knees that their child might be removed. Such deeds you must remember. What cause can you serve when you support it by such systems?

COLONEL: Madam, madam, you go too fast. Hoity-toity! Neither general nor private reflections! I see that you are pointing them to me. My hands were tied by the committee; I could not help it.

MRS. MARSTON: Well, well, sir, the horrid deed is committed; the innocent young man removed out of your clutches. God, I hope, will reward him.

COLONEL: And so He will your husband, whom I have so long indulged. I might a year ago have thrown him into gaol; the breath of my lips was sufficient. Yet I suffered him to remain; I overlooked his night visitors, his correspondents. I am obliged to let the law descend on his head. And now he has joined our cruel enemies, he is civilly dead, and when overtaken, hard will be his fate; no mitigation can be introduced.

MRS. MARSTON: No man ever behaved with more prudence, but it was that very prudent conduct of his which shocked you and yours. You never ceased laying snares for him, swelling the public report till he was put on the list, sent to gaol. While there you never brought him to trial. All the messages you sent him were that if he had a mind to disprove himself guilty, he had nothing to do but to take up his musket and go into the field. Did you want that he should attempt impossibilities to redeem himself and betray his conscience? Did you really expect that a man of his age, a magistrate, a person once respectable to all and respected even by you, whom he has often indulged, should herd with your soldiers and fare as they do? The fate he has met with is the supreme wish of his heart; I can prove it.

COLONEL: No irascibility, I pray. He is gone; he has pronounced sentence on himself; and fate cannot redeem him.

MRS. MARSTON: What could he do less than what he has done? A clay-fabricated animal would have done the same. He has sacrificed his repose to that of his family. He broke his fleet-prison and came here with the view of imploring a trial, and that he might remain either on security or otherwise peaceably on his farm. But, no, that would not have answered the excellent purposes.

COLONEL: As his wife, you are necessarily prepossessed. You do not see things in the same impartial light which men in my station do view it. Bitter as the pill is, you must swallow it. What can I do? I cannot dry up all the tears which perfidy to our cause will make people shed. This is but the beginning of their sorrow, but so great is their attachment to the English government that to it they will sacrifice everything in the world.

MRS. MARSTON: Irony, deceit, and mock-hypocritical show of mercy are your distinguishing characteristics, and that is the reason that you have been placed at the helm of this county. Permit me once more to recapitulate to you some of his proceedings. Compare them with yours. It shall not be recrimination nor a claim of justice; 'tis but a simple satisfaction which I cannot, and I hope you won't, refuse me.

COLONEL: It will be vain, madam. If we intended to have heard any preaching to-day, we might have gone to town and heard that of our worthy minister.

MRS. MARSTON: I preach not. I simply repeat facts, the recollection of which is too much for the frailty and common nerves of a woman to bear.

CHAIRWOMAN: You know, it seems, full well my husband's good nature and patience, and you mean to abuse them. We merely came to inform you as how your husband was safely arrived. We meant it as a comfort, and behold, here is the return! Like a Tory who, bred and nourished by the milk of this country, yet aims at stabbing it and plunging the dagger in its breast! But, ma'am, lest you might hurt your longing, pray go on.

MRS. MARSTON: Everything is strangely perverted;

black is become white, and white is become black. Blush thou, O Justice, O thou fair Truth; fly; quit this terrestrial abode; go beyond the reach of these pervert rulers; we are no longer worthy of you! Yes, my husband as well as a great many more have been driven to seek shelter far, very far from their homes and families. Last April, poor man, he was hurried to gaol after having been seized from my side at twelve o'clock at night. With all the aggravated insults that brutal militia could invent, through dirt and mire and darkness he was hurried to gaol, where he was kept three months. I was not permitted to see him, nor could he be [informed] during all this time of the state of his children. Next he was fastened to another man as unfortunate as himself and thus sent on foot to N. W. on a hot sultry day, without the least compassion save what he met with along the road from people who, remembering his better days and his former hospitality, secretly shed tears over his hard fate and relieved him with meat and drink. Not being able to reach the destined place of embarkation, he and his mate begged each a horse, which was granted. With what derision they were both uplifted from behind, thus obliged to ride chained! Your wild, your profligate guard soon afterwards fired a gun and frightened the horses, which brought to the ground the two unfortunate objects, thus abandoned to popular fury. In the fall, my husband broke his arm, and the other [suffered] several terrible contusions. Next they were married in a waggon to N. W., and from thence carried by water to their fleet-prison. There he was for three months longer without hope of ever regaining his liberty. He made his escape and returned here. He applied to J. W., who promised protection and a final release. He took some steps to effect these good purposes. You heard of it—I know precisely when—and to defeat these benevolent purposes and prevent him from sharing the fate of his companion, Squire Rearman, who had somehow slipped through your fingers, you sent at different times a party of men headed by your son Anthony. He, after lurking about the house a considerable time, spied my husband at last, leaning over his sleigh with his child in his hand. They fired two rifles at him and missed him. This atrocious deed made him imagine that the offer of protection he had received from J. W. was but delusive and calculated to lead him on. "If J. W. proves a traitor, a bad man," said he, "after all his humane actions, I have nothing more to do than to leave you. When I am gone, they will swear that I am gone from choice. God hears me and bears witness that I'd rather stay with you here than go to New York where I cannot subsist and do anything." These are his words. He marched through the woods. Next night his oppressed heart would not give him the means of proceeding any further. He returned, determined to wait his fate. Unfortunately, some of your gang perceived him. They sent word that if he did not quit in three hours, the whole should be in flames. He roused himself up once more and with streaming eyes and a bleeding heart he bade me farewell. Yet this is the man you proclaim a traitor. He would have been a traitor to himself had he stayed any longer. 'Tis for my sake and that of his children, 'tis to preserve these buildings and what they contain, that he quitted. Can you in the face of that pure sun, can you say he went away out of choice?

COLONEL: This all may be as you have represented it, though some parts about my son Anthony I will never believe. But what can I do? Had I shown him any favours, the people, whose confidence I possess, might immediately have suspected me; perhaps they might, for want of encouragement, become more languid in their opposition. All, all depend on their brawny arms. Better for one man, nay, twenty, to suffer innocently than to hold forth such a mercy as might be attended with such dangerous circumstances.

MRS. MARSTON: Aye, aye, popularity is the word. 'Tis the God to whom you must sacrifice the dictates of your conscience, the peace of your lives, and your future felicity.

CHAIRWOMAN: Come, come, Mrs. Marston, learn to bear and to suffer. Leave off fine reasoning. The more oxen fret in the yoke, the more they gall themselves. Tell me, when you are turned out of this house, what hopes have you got? Where will you go?

MRS. MARSTON: On what motives have you built your curiosity, pray? I propose to build myself a little loghouse at the foot of the Great Snake Rock close by Beaver Pond, which, they say, is king's land.

ELTHA: King's land, ma'am! Why, you make me laugh in spite of my melancholy. Don't you know, poor soul, that we know of no king in America and that all king's lands, as you call them, are seized for the benefit of our Congress?

MRS. MARSTON: Well, well, ma'am, we shall not dispute about the proprietor's name. I meant to erect a little cottage on some such lands as nobody claims and then to send out two of my daughters a-spinning. As for my son, he vows he will never let his mother want bread. Thus our industry and the kindness of people will, I hope, enable us to go through the rigorous season.

ELTHA: Your son, ma'am, must go into the militia and perhaps into the Continental service; there you are deceived. 'Tis the least he can do to atone for his father's deficiency. Nor can you depend so much on the assistance of your friends; you mean Tories, I suppose. You may expose them by that, and the committee will have a particular eye to these things.

MRS. MARSTON: Would you make it a crime for these people to relieve me in my distresses, me, who have for so many years been so kind and so serviceable to them all? This is the very quintessence of poison. Can this be the genuine spirit of your cause? My son, sir, shall not go into the Continental service. God, I hope, will give me no more to bear than what I can. Help me, help me, Thou protector of widows and orphans! (*Somebody knocks.*)

COLONEL: Walk in, whoever you are.

(*Enter Major Popino.*)

COLONEL: How does the Major do to-day?

MAJOR: Quite cheerly, and I give you thanks. The Colonel upon private business here?

COLONEL: No, by no means. To-day, you know, is not a day for business except it is that of mercy and consolation, and that is really our errand here.

MAJOR: Why, what is the news here?

COLONEL: Nothing worth mentioning, only that Francis Marston is gone to New York. All his effects are to be sold to-morrow, and we came here to prepare his wife lest the shock should be too great.

MAJOR: Ah, oh, Colonel, that is like your work—always more kind than need be to this sort of cattle. Your neighbours won't thank you for this thrown-away humanity, I am sure, for they are well known up and down among us. Let them die the death, I say—and so say many more.

COLONEL (*whispers into the major's ears*): I meant principally to see [how] effects stood here. I see everything is well replenished—'tis a good prize. Won't you be here to-morrow?

MAJOR: By all means. Why, this is a very fine farm: hogs, cattle, and horses in great abundance.

COLONEL: Yes, I have just been a-visiting the granaries, chambers, and cellars—all full. Fine harvest to carry on the war—my heart merely exults. I want, Major, to purchase to-morrow that large rick of hay, counting maybe forty tons. Won't you bid for me, and I give a hint to you here that I want it for the service, and for the service it will be at last. But they will be sure to triple my advance. These hard times we must turn a penny. The hay will be wanted at the fish kill before the spring.

MAJOR: That's what I will, Colonel. I have been viewing the young fellow leading a fine stallion to the well. I want very much such a war-horse when we train the militia. Could not you help me to the bargain?

COLONEL: Why, I do not know. The young man claims him as his property. I am at a loss what to do on the occasion.

MAJOR: Why, you must find a couple of the neighbours who will swear that they heard somebody say that they heard F. Marston say that he gave so much for the horse, which in fact I believe is very much so. Then it will be proved to be the father's property and then it will be sold.

COLONEL: Well, well, I'll tell you better. First, the horse must be out of the way to-morrow, and we will indulge you with him at private sale in the evening.

MAJOR: Thanks, thanks, noble Colonel. I shall ever acknowledge this as a great and worthy favour indeed. We that bear the brunt of the battle should have some rewards for it. The Congress prodigiously overlooks the merits of the militia; neither tents nor hospitals through the bushes. My lads, that's all we have. We therefore should take care of ourselves at home. And who is better entitled to the spoils of the Tories than we who have the trouble to hunt them, to clap them in gaol, and so forth?

COLONEL: You are very right, Major; you speak like unto a man of experience. Did you see anywhere in your travels the great blaze the other night which made us all gaze?

MAJOR: Yes, yes, that's what I did, and with all my heart, too. Why, haven't you heard yet? Why, our folks down below say that New York is all in ashes, and that Howe was like to be Burgoyned.

COLONEL: Well, never was a day since the creation crowded with such important events. God is with us; God is with us all; God will abide by us, I believe.

MAJOR: We are in a fair way, that is to be sure. What will the dogs do in New York now it is levelled? They say as how our people have caught this lucky moment on a windy night and set it on fire.

COLONEL: Hush, hush, Major, there you are wrong. We should never inquire by what means God's divine providence orders things for our good. Suffice it for us that it is done. Let us be thankful. 'Tis the angel, not our own prowess, that accomplishes all these great things.

MAJOR: That's well observed, Colonel. As a deacon of a church and a proficient in religion, I see that you take things in their proper light; you view every event as good Christians ought to do. I am now of your mind and must haste or else I shall be too late at meeting. I am in hopes to reach there before the sermon begins, and we shall have a fine text, and the minister will handle it well. There is not, you know, such an enemy to Tories, no, not again in fifty miles. How he makes them fly! How he sets them out! And they hate him in abundance for it. Farewell.

COLONEL: God with you, Major. Hope yours are all hearty?

MAJOR: Thank you, Colonel; we are all triumphing, happy, and impatient for the last day.

COLONEL: Wife, wife (*speaking loud*); wife, wife, where have you been all this time?

ELTHA: Why, Mrs. Marston and I have been visiting up and down and making little bargains which I hope you'll confirm. Upon my word, 'tis a well-replenished house and kept perfectly clean.

COLONEL: 'Tis high time to go. Who knows but we may reach yet for afternoon sermon? Well, Mrs. Marston, farewell. Take things as patiently as you can. We will try to indulge you all we can to-morrow. Don't distress yourself too much.

MRS. MARSTON: Come what will, I shall have on my side God, my innocence, my little children, and, I hope, some bread. Take, take the rest away and then you'll be satisfied. (*Exeunt.*)

MRS. MARSTON: As a county canting, religious hypocrite I had always known thee; now as Congress delegate, and in that service dost thou use thy former qualifications.

Sixth Landscape: On the Road, Returning from Francis Marston's House.

BEATUS, deacon.
ELTHA, his wife.
MARTHA, wife to B. Corwin, hanged by Lord Sterling; otherwise the woman in despair.

ELTHA: Well, Colonel, my dear, did not I tell you that we should sanctify the day, gather a blessing as we went, and do good to the cause and to ourselves? What could heaven do more in its most gracious hour? You see that a wife is very often a useful and necessary companion. You see, Colonel, we have relieved Mrs. Marston from that load of anxiety she laid under concerning the pretended death of her husband. We have merely squared her from hiding anything. We have heard the good news of Major Popino, that good man, and here is a bundle containing several very valuable things for which our daughter Dorothy shan't be sorry. The wisest counsellor could not have done more. What say you, my dear?

COLONEL: Well, what consideration have you promised this woman?

ELTHA: Oh, I have bought nothing, as you may say, to be sure. I would not so far trespass on your authority.

I promised that you'll let [her] have some provisions and her bed and her children's clothes. We must not be so tight either. After all, I did not engage to work miracles. I have discharged my conscience. I have left the matter wholly in your hands. Oh, that's true. There are the other commissioners. Maybe they won't like anything should go.

COLONEL: Strange, strange woman, you buy and you don't buy. Why, you should be more careful, and the woman must have some consideration, to be sure. How I shall settle the matter with my mates, I know not. They must have their share or else we shall discord. Another time you must stay at home. But if you meant to oblige the woman, you are really commendable. But hush, hush. One hardly dares speak of these things even through the woods. Who is that there a-coming?

ELTHA: 'Tis a poor woman with a bundle on her back. Hark, she cries, methinks.

COLONEL: Yes, she does. Let us haste and see. What is the matter, good woman? What are you doing here all alone?

MARTHA: I, a good woman! For God's sake, don't call me a good woman! Call me a wretch, a miserable object, if you please—all, all you can think that is unfortunate, and you shall be welcome.

COLONEL: Well, tell us what is the matter. I am [afraid] that the fear of God is gone from before your eyes and that the evil spirit overshadows you.

MARTHA: Evil spirit? Aye, truly the evil spirit of these accursed times has overshadowed me; there you are right. It has encompassed me all round. The malice and power of our great ones have overtaken me. They pursue me still. I know not where to go nor what to do.

COLONEL: Do, pray, let us hear what this great matter is. Are you insulted, are you abused? There is the precinct; there is the county; there are the united committees of the county. You must apply to them; they replace all other authorities.

MARTHA: Committee! That name conveys to my brains the most horrid smell; 'tis the most offensive sensation I can receive. 'Tis from them I have received all my distresses and misfortunes, and God in heaven is silent. He lets them hang the innocent, persecute the poor, the widows, the naked orphans.

ELTHA: Good woman, you should know before whom you speak: this is the chairman of the committee.

MARTHA: This the man of the chair! 'Tis you, then, who have done me all this mischief; 'tis you who have reduced me into despair and reduced me into affliction and poverty lower than ere was a poor living soul reduced. Gracious God, why dost Thou suffer these rulers to plunder the widows and their children and call their rags their country's inheritance—a miserable one, which, to feed and pamper a few, leaves hundreds desolate, a prey to death and despair? And you are the chairman! Do me justice, then—but, alas, they say you are deaf and blind to remonstrances.

COLONEL: What would the woman be at? Why accuse me thus? I know you not, neither the beginning nor the ending of your story. You are mad.

MARTHA: Does not the sight of me make you recollect some late transactions? Is there nothing in you that vibrates and palpitates as in other men? Is everything tight and rigid? Do you fear neither God nor His judgements? How do you expect mercy at His hands when you show none to no one for His sake?

COLONEL: If you won't declare who you are, what it is that afflicts you, so that I may know how to relieve you, I'll get a party to carry you to gaol before night. Depend on it.

MARTHA: Do so and complete the horrid tragedy. The tears I have shed have dried the milk of my breasts, and my poor baby, by still suckling the dregs, fed a while on the dregs of sorrow. He is now dead, and I was going to look for somebody to bury his emaciated carcass now lying on my straw bed. That is my business, if you must know. The sweet angel will call on you one of these nights and wrench your heart with bitterness and repentance.

ELTHA: The woman is surely mad, my dear. Why, she is not worth minding. We shall lose here much more precious time. Do let us haste.

MARTHA: Aye, ma'am, that's spoken like yourself. Mingle religion with obduracy of heart, softness of speech with that unfeeling disposition which fits you so well for a chairman's wife. Despise the poor; reject the complaints of the oppressed; crush those whom your husband oversets; and our gazettes shall resound with your praise. Mad woman! Yes, I am mad to see ingratitude and hypocrisy on horse-back, virtue and honesty low in the dirt.

ELTHA: If it was not Sabbath, I'll warrant I'd take you up myself and bring you still lower.

MARTHA: Well, then I'll defy you, for I am reduced to live alone in a wretched hut with three naked and almost famished children. The fourth lies dead among them. I am past your vengeance, great as you be.

COLONEL: Come, wife, let her alone; she is not worth minding.

MARTHA: That is true, Colonel. I am not worth minding, for what I would ask is mercy and justice, and you have none of that commodity for me.

COLONEL: You haven't told me yet who it was that has reduced you so low. I really feel for you, and if I can help it, I will relieve you if possible. My head is so perplexed with business that I am apt to overlook.

MARTHA: Forget me, and welcome. I expect nothing at your hands whatever you may say. I'll bury my child and return to feed on despair until death delivers me. Then I'll rejoin my poor unfortunate husband, whom your great generals have brutally hanged, and I shall be able to do then without that heifer and three ewes which you have ravished from me.

COLONEL: I can't help these things, honest woman. Your random talk does not offend me. You are really so low that your tongue's end does not reach me.

MARTHA: That is true. What are the shafts of a poor desolate widow? They are blunted by weakness. How can you say that you know nothing of me? Does not the name of that cow and ewe I have mentioned bring to you some distant recollection?

COLONEL: I am tired. Good-bye, stubborn woman.

MARTHA: Do stop. I will tell you all.

COLONEL: Well, then, let us hear you out. What have you to say?

ELTHA: Ah, no, I am quite weary. The better one is to these people, the worse they are. These Tories are just like the Negroes; give them an inch, they will take an ell. I begin to know who she is.

MARTHA: Do you really? With what emphasis of hatred you pronounce that word *Tory*. What [have] they done? Alas, they have neither conspired nor plotted; they have neither banished nor hanged anyone. They are suffering the worst of punishments for the sake of a country which never will thank them, but they act from principles —hard is their fate.

COLONEL: Pooh! Pray thee, leave off conscience, principles, etc. These people have none but those of the worst sort, and harder will be still their fate. Come, what have you to say?

MARTHA: How came you to strip me of all I had after my husband was hanged? How came you to release those effects one day and to have them reseized on the third? On what principles can you take from me and my children our bread and subsistence?

COLONEL: Because you are looked on as an enemy.

MARTHA: Even as an enemy, you have no right to starve innocent children. How great a deceiver you have been! Formerly so meek, so religious, so humble; now wild, fiery, and a tyrant.

COLONEL: In consideration of your situation, I will have your cattle restored. Go to work, and cease to behave in this frantic manner. I cannot help the sufferings of every one.

MARTHA: Great God, give me strength and patience to wait with resignation for that day when the restoration of government shall restore to us some degree of peace and security.

COLONEL: That day is far off, good woman. Go home and take care of your children, and leave off your political wishes.

(*Exeunt.*)

1. One copper plate representing two men on horse-back, chained together; a firing gun; and the two men falling.

2. A plate representing Capt. Shoreditch with a bushy head, six militiamen with linsey-woolsey blankets tied from the right shoulder to the left arm, and three Quakers at a tavern door with a post and no sign.

3. The woman in despair leaning on a tree, the chairman and his wife on horseback talking with her.

4. A stallion rushing from the woods and covering the mare on which Eltha rides; she stoops on the neck; her husband whips the horse, but in vain.

Index

FOR THE BEST IN PAPERBACKS, LOOK FOR THE

In every corner of the world, on every subject under the sun, Penguin represents quality and variety—the very best in publishing today.

For complete information about books available from Penguin—including Pelicans, Puffins, Peregrines, and Penguin Classics—and how to order them, write to us at the appropriate address below. Please note that for copyright reasons the selection of books varies from country to country.

In the United Kingdom: For a complete list of books available from Penguin in the U.K., please write to *Dept E.P., Penguin Books Ltd, Harmondsworth, Middlesex, UB7 0DA*.

In the United States: For a complete list of books available from Penguin in the U.S., please write to *Consumer Sales, Penguin USA, P.O. Box 999—Dept. 17109, Bergenfield, New Jersey 07621-0120*. VISA and MasterCard holders call 1-800-253-6476 to order all Penguin titles.

In Canada: For a complete list of books available from Penguin in Canada, please write to *Penguin Books Canada Ltd, 10 Alcorn Avenue, Suite 300, Toronto, Ontario, Canada M4V 3B2*.

In Australia: For a complete list of books available from Penguin in Australia, please write to the *Marketing Department, Penguin Books Ltd, P.O. Box 257, Ringwood, Victoria 3134*.

In New Zealand: For a complete list of books available from Penguin in New Zealand, please write to the *Marketing Department, Penguin Books (NZ) Ltd, Private Bag, Takapuna, Auckland 9*.

In India: For a complete list of books available from Penguin, please write to *Penguin Overseas Ltd, 706 Eros Apartments, 56 Nehru Place, New Delhi, 110019*.

In Holland: For a complete list of books available from Penguin in Holland, please write to *Penguin Books Nederland B.V., Postbus 195, NL-1380AD Weesp, Netherlands*.

In Germany: For a complete list of books available from Penguin, please write to *Penguin Books Ltd, Friedrichstrasse 10-12, D-6000 Frankfurt Main I, Federal Republic of Germany*.

In Spain: For a complete list of books available from Penguin in Spain, please write to *Longman, Penguin España, Calle San Nicolas 15, E-28013 Madrid, Spain*.

In Japan: For a complete list of books available from Penguin in Japan, please write to *Longman Penguin Japan Co Ltd, Yamaguchi Building, 2-12-9 Kanda Jimbocho, Chiyoda-Ku, Tokyo 101, Japan*.

FOR THE BEST LITERATURE, LOOK FOR THE

□ **A SPORT OF NATURE**
Nadine Gordimer

Hillela, Nadine Gordimer's "sport of nature," is seductive and intuitively gifted at life. Casting herself adrift from her family at seventeen, she lives among political exiles on an East African beach, marries a black revolutionary, and ultimately plays a heroic role in the overthrow of apartheid.

354 pages   ISBN: 0-14-008470-3

□ **THE COUNTERLIFE**
Philip Roth

By far Philip Roth's most radical work of fiction, *The Counterlife* is a book of conflicting perspectives and points of view about people living out dreams of renewal and escape. Illuminating these lives is the skeptical, enveloping intelligence of the novelist Nathan Zuckerman, who calculates the price and examines the results of his characters' struggles for a change of personal fortune.

372 pages   ISBN: 0-14-009769-4

□ **THE MONKEY'S WRENCH**
Primo Levi

Through the mesmerizing tales told by two characters—one, a construction worker/philosopher who has built towers and bridges in India and Alaska; the other, a writer/chemist, rigger of words and molecules—Primo Levi celebrates the joys of work and the art of storytelling.

174 pages   ISBN: 0-14-010357-0

□ **IRONWEED**
William Kennedy

"Riding up the winding road of Saint Agnes Cemetery in the back of the rattling old truck, Francis Phelan became aware that the dead, even more than the living, settled down in neighborhoods." So begins William Kennedy's Pulitzer-Prize winning novel about an ex-ballplayer, part-time gravedigger, and full-time drunk, whose return to the haunts of his youth arouses the ghosts of his past and present.   *228 pages   ISBN: 0-14-007020-6 $6.95*

□ **THE COMEDIANS**
Graham Greene

Set in Haiti under Duvalier's dictatorship, *The Comedians* is a story about the committed and the uncommitted. Actors with no control over their destiny, they play their parts in the foreground; experience love affairs rather than love; have enthusiasms but not faith; and if they die, they die like Mr. Jones, by accident.

288 pages   ISBN: 0-14-002766-1

FOR THE BEST LITERATURE, LOOK FOR THE

☐ **HERZOG**
Saul Bellow

Winner of the National Book Award, *Herzog* is the imaginative and critically acclaimed story of Moses Herzog: joker, moaner, cuckhold, charmer, and truly an Everyman for our time.

                    342 pages   *ISBN: 0-14-007270-5*

☐ **FOOLS OF FORTUNE**
William Trevor

The deeply affecting story of two cousins—one English, one Irish—brought together and then torn apart by the tide of Anglo-Irish hatred, *Fools of Fortune* presents a profound symbol of the tragic entanglements of England and Ireland in this century.   *240 pages*   *ISBN: 0-14-006982-8*

☐ **THE SONGLINES**
Bruce Chatwin

Venturing into the desolate land of Outback Australia—along timeless paths, and among fortune hunters, redneck Australians, racist policemen, and mysterious Aboriginal holy men—Bruce Chatwin discovers a wondrous vision of man's place in the world.   *296 pages*   *ISBN: 0-14-009429-6*

☐ **THE GUIDE: A NOVEL**
R. K. Narayan

Raju was once India's most corrupt tourist guide; now, after a peasant mistakes him for a holy man, he gradually begins to play the part. His succeeds so well that God himself intervenes to put Raju's new holiness to the test.

                    220 pages   *ISBN: 0-14-009657-4*

You can find all these books at your local bookstore, or use this handy coupon for ordering:

Penguin Books By Mail
Dept. BA Box 999
Bergenfield, NJ 07621-0999

Please send me the above title(s). I am enclosing _____
(please add sales tax if appropriate and $1.50 to cover postage and handling). Send check or money order—no CODs. Please allow four weeks for shipping. We cannot ship to post office boxes or addresses outside the USA. *Prices subject to change without notice.*

Ms./Mrs./Mr. _____

Address _____

City/State _____ Zip _____

FOR THE BEST LITERATURE, LOOK FOR THE

☐ **THE LAST SONG OF MANUEL SENDERO**
Ariel Dorfman

In an unnamed country, in a time that might be now, the son of Manuel Sendero refuses to be born, beginning a revolution where generations of the future wait for a world without victims or oppressors.

464 pages   ISBN: 0-14-008896-2

☐ **THE BOOK OF LAUGHTER AND FORGETTING**
Milan Kundera

In this collection of stories and sketches, Kundera addresses themes including sex and love, poetry and music, sadness and the power of laughter. "*The Book of Laughter and Forgetting* calls itself a novel," writes John Leonard of *The New York Times*, "although it is part fairly tale, part literary criticism, part political tract, part musicology, part autobiography. It can call itself whatever it wants to, because the whole is genius."

240 pages   ISBN: 0-14-009693-0

☐ **TIRRA LIRRA BY THE RIVER**
Jessica Anderson

Winner of the Miles Franklin Award, Australia's most prestigious literary prize, *Tirra Lirra by the River* is the story of a woman's seventy-year search for the place where she truly belongs. Nora Porteous's series of escapes takes her from a small Australia town to the suburbs of Sydney to London, where she seems finally to become the woman she always wanted to be.

142 pages   ISBN: 0-14-006945-3

☐ **LOVE UNKNOWN**
A. N. Wilson

In their sweetly wild youth, Monica, Belinda, and Richeldis shared a bachelor-girl flat and became friends for life. Now, twenty years later, A. N. Wilson charts the intersecting lives of the three women through the perilous waters of love, marriage, and adultery in this wry and moving modern comedy of manners.

202 pages   ISBN: 0-14-010190-X

☐ **THE WELL**
Elizabeth Jolley

Against the stark beauty of the Australian farmlands, Elizabeth Jolley portrays an eccentric, affectionate relationship between the two women—Hester, a lonely spinster, and Katherine, a young orphan. Their pleasant, satisfyingly simple life is nearly perfect until a dark stranger invades their world in a most horrifying way.

176 pages   ISBN: 0-14-008901-2

FOR THE BEST IN HISTORY, LOOK FOR THE

□ **THE FACE OF BATTLE**
John Keegan

In this study of three battles from three different centuries, John Keegan examines war from the fronts—conveying its reality for the participants at the "point of maximum danger."

    366 pages   ISBN: 0-14-004897-9

□ **VIETNAM: A HISTORY**
Stanley Karnow

Stanley Karnow's monumental narrative—the first complete account of the Vietnam War—puts events and decisions of the day into sharp, clear focus. "This is history writing at its best."—*Chicago Sun-Times*

    752 pages   ISBN: 0-14-007324-8

□ **MIRACLE AT MIDWAY**
Gordon W. Prange
with Donald M. Goldstein and Katherine V. Dillon

The best-selling sequel to *At Dawn We Slept* recounts the battles at Midway Island—events which marked the beginning of the end of the war in the Pacific.

    470 pages   ISBN: 0-14-006814-7

□ **THE MASK OF COMMAND**
John Keegan

This provocative view of leadership examines the meaning of military heroism through four prototypes from history—Alexander the Great, Wellington, Grant, and Hitler—and proposes a fifth type of "post-heroic" leader for the nuclear age.   *368 pages   ISBN: 0-14-011406-8*

□ **THE SECOND OLDEST PROFESSION**
Spies and Spying in the Twentieth Century
Phillip Knightley

In this fascinating history and critique of espionage, Phillip Knightley explores the actions and missions of such noted spies as Mata Hari and Kim Philby, and organizations such as the CIA and the KGB.   *ISBN: 0-14-010655-3*

□ **THE STORY OF ENGLISH**
Robert McCrum, William Cran, and Robert MacNeil

"Rarely has the English language been scanned so brightly and broadly in a single volume," writes the *San Francisco Chronicle* about this journey across time and space that explores the evolution of English from Anglo-Saxon Britain to Reagan's America.   *384 pages   ISBN: 0-14-009435-0*

FOR THE BEST IN HISTORY, LOOK FOR THE

☐ **THE WORLD SINCE 1945**
   T. E. Vadney

This magnificent survey of recent global history charts all the major developments since the end of World War II, including the Cold War, Vietnam, the Middle East wars, NATO, the emergence of sovereign African states, and the Warsaw Pact. *570 pages   ISBN: 0-14-022723-7*

☐ **THE ECONOMIC CONSEQUENCES OF THE PEACE**
   John Maynard Keynes
   Introduction by Robert Lekachman

First published in 1920, Keynes's brilliant book about the cost of the "Carthaginian" peace imposed on Germany after World War I stands today as one of the great economic and political works of our time.
   336 pages   ISBN: 0-14-011380-0

☐ **A SHORT HISTORY OF AFRICA**
   Sixth Edition
   Roland Oliver and J. D. Fage

While the centers of European culture alternately flourished and decayed, empires in Africa rose, ruled, resisted, and succumbed. In this classic work, the authors have drawn on the whole range of literature about Africa, taking its study a step forward. *304 pages   ISBN: 0-14-022759-8*

☐ **RUSSIA**
   Broken Idols, Solemn Dreams
   David K. Shipler

A national best-seller, this involving personal narrative by the former Moscow bureau chief of *The New York Times* crystallizes what is truly Russian behind the facade of stereotypes and official government rhetoric.
   404 pages   ISBN: 0-14-007408-2

You can find all these books at your local bookstore, or use this handy coupon for ordering: **Penguin Books By Mail**
Dept. BA Box 999
Bergenfield, NJ 07621-0999
Please send me the above title(s). I am enclosing _____
(please add sales tax if appropriate and $1.50 to cover postage and handling). Send check or money order—no CODs. Please allow four weeks for shipping. We cannot ship to post office boxes or addresses outside the USA. *Prices subject to change without notice.*

Ms./Mrs./Mr. _____

Address _____

City/State _____ Zip _____

FOR THE BEST IN HISTORY, LOOK FOR THE

☐ **MOVE YOUR SHADOW**
  South Africa, Black & White
  Joseph Lelyveld

Drawing on his two tours as a correspondent for *The New York Times*, Lelyveld offers a vivid portrait of a troubled country and its people, illuminating the history, society, and feelings that created and maintain apartheid.

402 pages   ISBN: 0-14-009326-5

☐ **THE PELICAN HISTORY OF THE WORLD**
  Revised Edition
  J. M. Roberts

This comprehensive and informative survey of the growth of the modern world analyzes the major forces of our history and emphasizes both their physical and psychological effects.

1056 pages   ISBN: 0-14-022785-7